THE *South Asia* PAPERS

Stephen Philip Cohen is the author, co-author or editor of over fourteen books, mostly on South Asian security issues, including *Shooting for a Century, The India-Pakistan Conundrum* and *The Future of Pakistan*. He has also written books on India, Pakistan, nuclear proliferation, disaster management and the application of technology to the prevention or amelioration of terrorism.

In early 2008, Cohen was a visiting professor at the Lee Kuan Yew School of Public Policy in Singapore, where he taught a course on the politics of man-made and natural disasters. He also taught in Japan at Keio University, and in India at Andhra University. He has consulted for numerous foundations and government agencies, and was a member of the policy planning staff at the Department of State from 1985 to 1987. He was a visiting scholar at the Ford Foundation in New Delhi from 1992 to 1993.

Praise for the works of Stephen P. Cohen

Shooting for a Century

"*Shooting for a Century's* timing is shrewd and it makes its appearance at a time when the US is changing the way it looks at the world."—*Mint*

"Dr Cohen has succinctly summed up the history of the conflict since 1947 ... and has attempted to offer solutions that address the major outstanding issues." —*Dawn*

India: Emerging Power

"Cohen's mastery of India, India's security and military strategy, and the dramatic changes which have taken place in India since Independence are well and clearly presented." —Ambassador Thomas R. Pickering, former under secretary of state for political affairs and U.S. ambassador to India

"A powerful tour d'horizon of modern India's strategic past and a valuable reflection on its prospects in the international system."—*The Hindu*

"A timely, comprehensive, well-grounded study of India as a rising power and its implications for the U.S. ... Cohen's perceptive, insightful and balanced account of emergent India will be essential reading for U.S. foreign policymakers, scholars and informed citizens."—*Choice*

"Stephen Cohen's *India: Emerging Power* is an objective, lucid and incisive analysis of India's emerging role in the global village."—*Dawn*

The Idea of Pakistan

"Cohen is the United States' leading analyst of South Asia, and this authoritative work of broad scope and meticulous research will surely become required reading on Pakistan."—*Foreign Affairs*

"A lucid, penetrating and brilliantly constructed book on the state and nation of Pakistan. Cohen, an old South Asia hand, brings to the fore all his knowledge and expertise of one of America's most important allies in the war against terror."—A Choice Outstanding Academic Title

***Arming Without Aiming: India's Military Modernization* (with Sunil Dasgupta)**

"Cohen's unmatched four decades' experience, studying and writing on security issues gives this book an exceptional degree of feel for the ground."—*Economic and Political Weekly*

"This cautionary tale will be required reading for all those concerned about Indian defense policy and military modernization."—Ashley Tellis, Carnegie Endowment for International Peace

THE *South Asia* PAPERS

A Critical Anthology of Writings

by Stephen Philip Cohen

HarperCollins *Publishers* India

First published in 2016 by
The Brookings Institution Press, Washington, DC, USA

First published in India in 2016 by
HarperCollins *Publishers* India

Building 10, Tower A, 4th Floor, DLF Cyber City, Phase II,
Gurugram Haryana – 122002, India
www.harpercollins.co.in

P-ISBN: 978-93-5264-019-5
E-ISBN: 978-93-5264-020-1

2 4 6 8 10 9 7 5 3 1

Typeset in Adobe Caslon

Composition by Westchester Publishing Services

Printed and bound at
MicroPrints India, New Delhi

Contents

Preface

The sixteen essays, chapters, and speeches in this book are drawn from more than 150 published pieces, excluding fifteen books. Several of them were, I think, important and original contributions to the fields of military history and military sociology, as well as useful contributions to the policy debates of their time. All are "critical" in that they are about important issues and policies, often neglected both by South Asian scholars and the Washington policy community. (In 1998 I became the only first full-time South Asian specialist at a Washington think tank.)

This book also reflects a career shift from an early interest in the Raj's military history and "Hindoostan"—basically, as a historian—to hard-core security issues, such as the role of armies and nuclear proliferation. A recent essay, not included here, examines South Asia as a regional entity and brought me back to my early interests.[1]

Republishing these articles and chapters gives me a chance to reflect on how accurate my analyses were. I have made a few revisions in the text and footnotes, many of which are seamless and some more obvious. An epilogue brings several chapters and issues up to date.

Working in British archives, and interviewing a number of British, Indian, and Pakistani officials in London, I was early on steeped in the Raj's strategic literature. The chapters in this book traverse the identity of this area from the now quaint Hindoostan to contemporary South Asia.[2] This interest is mirrored by the book cover (of the American edition), a photo of an encounter between a British officer, his Indian crew, and an American tank with an elephant in Burma near India's northeast during World War II. My interest in disaster management is not represented here, but I hope to republish one study.[3]

Over the years I have learned that it is difficult to balance the stance of a scholar and that of an advocate. As for the latter, George Schultz once told a group of us on his staff, "Get me a policy," and as for the former, I recall the words of a former Indian army chief (General Sunith Francis Rodrigues) about "the arrogance of ignorance."

There were frustrations as well as rewards in moving through academically uncharted territory on a geographical region not often regarded as important by most American policymakers. The rewards have been to see South Asia figure larger in the American imagination, and to see many of my own students contribute to our understanding of India's hopeful and Pakistan's perilous futures. The frustrations come from the knowledge that the two states, so different yet so similar in their origins, cannot reconcile their differences and are unlikely to do so soon, and that American policymakers are still confounded as they grapple with these states and the region.

Chapter 1, "Approaching India's Military and Security Policy, with a Detour through Disaster Studies," describes the research puzzle that influenced my interests and career. How did military power and its supporting institutions (especially the army) shape relations within the region and within the constituent states? It also discusses the context in which many chapters were written.

Chapters 2, 3, and 4 look at ancient, modern, and recent history and ask how past social, technological, and bureaucratic structures influenced contemporary affairs. Plunging into the historical record, I sought perspectives and propositions relevant to the present.[4] In "Rulers and Priests: A Study of Cultural Control" from 1964 (chapter 2), I wrote, "To search for the sources of contemporary Indian defense policy, we should turn to Clausewitz, Sandhurst, and Dehra Dun; to search for the sources of attitudes toward defense policy held by traditionalist Hindu elements in India (which, it can be argued, are becoming increasingly powerful as democratization makes an impact on Indian society), we can more readily look to the Mahabharata and the *Arthashastra*." My general point was that the role of the warrior/soldier is critically important in shaping politics and society. In a new democratic India, the rise of regional power centers and the rediscovery of some of its great non-Brahmin figures, such as B. R.

Ambedkar, the scheduled caste (or "untouchable," now termed Dalit) leader who wrote India's Constitution, is leading to new approaches to Indian strategy and military organization, analogous to parallel events in the United States. Some of the best new scholars are represented in the above-cited Oxford collection.

As I note in "Issue, Role, and Personality: The Kitchener–Curzon Dispute" from 1968 (chapter 3), the Raj could support both military dominance and militarism, but Pakistan inherited the military-dominant side of the Raj, while India inherited the civilian-dominant pattern. This was fixed in place by Nehru and Sardar Patel after the British departed. I have jokingly referred to it as civilian oppression of the armed forces, but this extraordinary level of civilian supremacy over the armed forces certainly sets India apart from many other states, especially among former colonies.

As a student, I was puzzled by Subhas Chandra Bose's continuing popularity and wanted to understand his appeal in India. I learned that it had its own tradition of authoritarianism, notably Bose's melding of fascism and communism, one of the subjects of chapter 4, "Subhas Chandra Bose and the Indian National Army" (1963).

It is surprising that the first serious work on ethnicity in the military, after *The Indian Army* (1970), was not published until 2015, in the form of Steven Wilkinson's important study.[5] Chapter 5, "The Untouchable Soldier: Caste, Politics, and the Indian Army" (1969), was the first and perhaps remains the only study of how the British, and then the Indian government, dealt with social distances between high and low castes. An irony of recent Indian historiography is that the so-called Subaltern studies school ignores the subaltern—that is, military history—and some find the notion of "martial races" a better subject for ridicule than analysis. Chapter 6, "The Military in Indira Gandhi's India" (1976), further explores the authoritarian tradition in India, specifically the year and a half of Indira Gandhi's Emergency. While I am assured by many that this cannot happen again, the issue is discussed further in the epilogue.

Chapter 7, "Toward a Great State in Asia?" (1980), compares China, India, and Japan along several dimensions and, when published, laid the intellectual groundwork for two books on India as an emerging or rising power. I later turned to the obverse problem, state breaking, and chapter 8, "The State Is Dead: Long Live the Armed Ethnic Group" (1992), argues that the new identity pole for unhappy young people will no longer be communism, but ethnicity and religion. Chapter 9, "Solving Proliferation Problems in a Regional Context" (1989), argues for a *regional* approach to containing nuclear proliferation in South Asia.

It was famously said by Charles Tilly that armies make states, and states make wars, but in Pakistan's case it is also the case that armies can break nations.[6] Two chapters focus on contemporary Pakistan. Chapter 10, "State Building in Pakistan" (1986), offers a comprehensive approach to the state, while chapter 11, "The Jihadist Threat to Pakistan" (2003), looks at the rise of extremist Islamic groups with and without the aid of the state itself.

Studying India and Pakistan from the early 1960s, I realized that each was the other's obsession. Chapter 12, "India and Pakistan: The Armed Forces" (2004), develops the theory of a paired minority conflict, while chapter 13, "Kashmir: The Roads Ahead" (1995), discusses, and is an example of, futile efforts to resolve the Kashmir issue.

Most of my recent writings that deal with policy came after a tour on the State Department's Policy Planning Staff in 1985–87. Chapter 14, "The Reagan Administration and India: Right for the Right Reasons?" (1988), reflects that experience, while chapter 16 disagrees with received opinion at the time and discusses "How a Botched U.S. Alliance Fed Pakistan's Crisis" (2011).

Acknowledgments

Four institutions were central to my career. The University of Chicago offered a classic education grounded in philosophy, the social sciences, and humanities, plus the guidance of Robert E. Osgood and Hans J. Morgenthau. At the University of Wisconsin, I was ably advised by Henry Hart, whose work on water and rivers was pioneering. The University of Illinois–Urbana provided me with an academic base for thirty-five years and the freedom to cofound the Program in Arms Control, Disarmament, and International Security, and the opportunity to meet several fine friends and colleagues, notably Edward J. Kolodziej and Marvin G. Weinbaum. The Brookings Institution hired me for one year, which has stretched to eighteen. Mike Armacost, Richard Haass, Martin Indyk, and Strobe Talbott facilitated my transformation from a full-time professor with policy interests to a think-tank scholar with one foot in academia.

Above all there were innumerable South Asian officers, scholars, journalists, and officials. None was as remarkable as the late P.R. Chari, a coauthor, tactful critic, institution builder, and close friend. It is hard to imagine India without him.

Thanking students is always a pleasurable duty, as I learn much from them. Several worked on this book; interns included Shruti Jagirdar and two University of Chicago students, Walker King and Maayan Malter, and at the last minute Dr. Sunil Dasgupta, a former student, coauthor, and one of five research assistants who made my eighteen years at Brookings so useful. The others were Professor Dinshaw Mistry, Dr. Tanvi Madan, Dhruva Jaishankar, and Constantino Xavier.

This book is dedicated to the memory of my parents, Bess and Saul Cohen; to my brother, Howard; my wife, Roberta; and our children (Edward, Jeffrey, Peter, Benjamin, Tamara, and Susan). The latter tolerated an often-absent father. I hope that our collective journey was worth it to them, their wonderful spouses (Caren, Kim, Andrea, Nadja, Matt, and Brent) and our grandchildren—Finn, Fritz, Louden, Lucas, Miles, Nora, Posey, Sebastian, and Wren.

2008

ONE

Approaching India's Military and Security Policy, with a Detour through Disaster Studies

From the 1930s onward, India was known for two things: poverty and the charismatic politician-saint Mahatma Gandhi. Through Gandhi's influence, the practice of nonviolence became understood globally as a legitimate and effective political strategy. Gandhi, of course, would have said that it was more than a strategy—that ends must be equated with means, and that a violent strategy of political liberation was incompatible with true freedom. Martin Luther King Jr. was (via Gandhi's writings) one of his greatest students. As a civil rights activist in the United States, I understood how important nonviolence was to the movement's success and in preserving American values and democratic practices. The pattern was repeated in South Africa by Nelson Mandela, and in a host of other states, as well, with varying degrees of success.

This paper does not deal with Gandhi's influence on the American civil rights movement—a subject that deserves its own essay—but with American academic interest in how the India of Mahatma Gandhi and Jawaharlal Nehru managed the use of force, both domestically and abroad. It begins with my own research puzzle. I was the first American, and perhaps the first scholar, to explore these issues. But the narrative also moves down two other tracks: one the study of Indian military history, which was forced on me by circumstances, the other a study of India's foreign and security policy, which evolved naturally from my interest in the armed forces' internal role. All three are tightly connected: contemporary affairs are the growing roots of history, and the links between domestic politics and foreign policy are especially strong in non-Western states, although it took me several years and the guidance of many friends to understand what now seems obvious. My work on India took a detour in 1977 when I wrote a book on the political and organizational response to a mass disaster, the Andhra Cyclone. This is a field where there has been very little, if any, American interest, but it is worth discussing because India's future will include more and more such events.

The Puzzle

The worst words from the mouth of a potential student advisee are: "Professor, what should I study?" Privately, I would think of suggesting going into real estate or getting an M.B.A., but my response usually is: "What is your 'puzzle'? What issue or problem really motivates you; what keeps you up at night?" Only that level of intensity will get a graduate student over the hump of prelims, advanced training, and field research in a difficult country, and keep them motivated when the writing just does not seem to be coming along, when money is running out, and when advisers cannot help.

My first puzzle can be simply stated: How do states manage their armed forces, rather than being managed by them? More broadly, how is the use of deadly force contained in such a way that it is directed toward real enemies and not toward the goal of obtaining power within the state? In brief, force may sometimes be necessary, and the state must be prepared to use it, but how do we prevent those who wield power in the name of the state from using it for their personal advantage, and derailing normal politics?

Trying to solve this puzzle was what led me to India and Pakistan, the perfect comparative pair. They had started off with exactly the same army, they shared a South Asian culture, their political leaders came out of the same background, and they even shared a struggle against the British in the creation of an independent India. Yet by the early 1960s it was evident that Pakistan had become a praetorian state and India's democracy was thriving under Nehru's leadership. Why did they diverge? Was it Nehru's personality, some aspect of the army itself, or were outside forces an influence here? Further, are there any lessons for other "emerging," "developing," or "non-Western" states in the Indian experience?

Later there was a second puzzle. How did a poor state manage its international politics? How did it remain more or less neutral or nonaligned? I had been U.S. trained in arms control and the logic of nuclear deterrence. Why did India reject nuclear weapons at a moment when they seemed to be the weapon of choice for the superpowers and China, which exploded its first nuclear device in 1964?

Preparation

It was perhaps naive to propose these questions. They were not only unasked in the South Asian context by scholars; they were also frowned on by the Indian government. This made preparation both interesting and difficult. It was interesting because a burgeoning literature on civil military relations in non-Western states could be applied to India. Most of it dealt with two themes: the "man on horseback," or how the military came to power in a large number of new states, and how the military could assist in the developmental process.[1] No one had asked these questions of India, although the first was relevant to Pakistan, then still governed by the Pakistani army in the person of Field Marshal Ayub Khan.

For my generation, it was assumed that any serious research on India would involve language training and a background in Indian culture and society, thus courses in Hindi (continued at the missionary language school in Landour), Indian philosophy (taught by the great A. L. Basham on a visiting professorship at Wisconsin, which led to my first published article—see chapter 2), and extensive reading in Indian society and culture, guided by Joseph Elder and Henry C. Hart. As for research, I was on my own. There were no experts in the United States on Indian civil–military relations and few on Indian foreign policy. Improvisation followed: I met and worked with Morris Janowitz of the University of Chicago, who had written the first book on the military of non-Western states, and later had contact with Samuel Huntington, author of the majestic and still-relevant *The Soldier and the State*.[2]

The Accidental Historian

My research visa application, submitted through the American Institute of Indian Studies (AIIS) was delayed for well over a year.[3] Still waiting for a visa, I explored the few American sources. The Ames Library at the University of Minnesota was a treasure trove. It contained a good collection of Indian army caste handbooks and many key documents, but there was no faculty member there with expertise in Indian military affairs. I made the best of a bad situation by going to London to work in the India Office Archives, the Public Records office, the British Museum, and even the library of the Ministry of Defense, which allowed me to survey its unclassified material (with no barrier to the classified section, a situation that was rectified after the Profumo scandals).

I became, in effect, a historian. Having been trained in both international relations and comparative politics, I understood how armies face outward and inward. Now I was to see how their roots extended into the past. Self-taught, I learned something of the historian's trade, and that historians usually did not have puzzles, only time periods.[4] My focus became learning how the British Indian army fit into British imperial strategies (see chapter 3), the relationship between the caste system and military recruitment, the attitude of Indian politicians in the interwar period to the army, and the Indianization of the army's officer corps. All of these themes became chapters in my dissertation and eventually in my first book. Also valuable were materials I uncovered on the role of the princely states' armies, and how they were incorporated into the British Indian army. One lesson from my political science background was that the control of legitimate force was the mark of a state, and a state could be defined by the extent that it could impose its will, by force, on a particular geographic region. This was a critical factor in the partition of the Indian army by the British. Once the Indian National Congress had agreed to the army's partition, the emergence of a sovereign Pakistan was inevitable. When the competence of the Pakistani state proved questionable, the army itself assumed command and displaced the politicians, with American approval.

Other than the retired officers working on regimental histories, there were no scholars interested in the army's role in India. However, I did take the opportunity to interview many high-ranking British (and Indian) officers of the British Indian army who had retired to the London area.

Thus, I had long and fruitful sessions with two former commanders of the Pakistan army (Generals Douglas Gracey and Frank Messervy), several Indian King's Commissioned Officers who settled in the United Kingdom, and, above all, Field Marshal Sir Claude Auchinleck, who told me that the greatest failure of his life was his inability to prevent the partition of the old British Indian army. "The Auk" understood the need to establish a Pakistan, but giving it its own army would only invite war between the two successor states. He was correct.

This was both new and interesting, and it did much to help me unravel elements of my central puzzle: What in the British tradition was passed on to India and Pakistan, and what was not? I also met and learned from the great British Indian civil servant Philip Mason, who had been British India's defense secretary during World War II. Mason was later to write one of the definitive histories of the Indian army, but at that time he was engaged in creating the new Institute of Race Relations.[5] Mason was especially helpful on the wartime period and the role of the Indian National Army (INA) (see chapter 4), the breakaway army sponsored by Germany and Japan that eventually mounted an attack on India from Burma. The INA represented a crack in the unity of the old Indian army. It was interesting to explore the conditions under which it was formed, and even more interesting to learn from Mason and others how Nehru ensured that the INA would not find an independent role in free India.

Of the scholars in London, Hugh Tinker and Peter Lyon shared their own understanding of how the British had trained an army in India that performed very well militarily, but took two different paths after partition. They were helpful but sometimes baffled by my interest in a country, and a problem, that was so distant from usual American obsessions regarding India, which were the spread of communism, the Soviet hand in India, and population control.[6]

1963–65: In India

With a visa finally in hand in November 1963, my wife and I departed London for New Delhi. Many of my academic peers had made the passage to India by sea. In preparation a copy of Murray's *Handbook for Travelers to India, Pakistan, and Ceylon* was purchased. Murray's handbook has a chapter on not only how to behave on board but one on what to do in the passage through the Suez Canal. This obviously did not interest us as our generation was the first to fly to India.

Nor was the chapter on what to buy in preparation for the trip of much use: I went to one of the "tropical" outfitters, where they still sold solar topis, but the prices and the ridiculousness of it all led me to walk out empty-handed. If I was going to go to India, it would be on my own terms, as an American and a veteran of civil rights marches and sit-ins. My research tools were high-tech, and I splurged on a tiny Olympus portable typewriter, later learning how to repair it and wind on Indian ribbons when the originals wore out.

During this first trip to India—1963–65—my family and I lived with a scheduled caste Indian member of parliament, which piqued my interest in caste and the Indian army (see chapter 5, "The Untouchable Soldier"). I was already alert because of an interest in racial integration in the American military, and I used whatever references to African Americans in the U.S. military I could find. That essay was written in the pre-Dalit years, but the Dalits were already on the horizon, partially in the person of my own landlord, B. P. Maurya, one of the most assertive of the neo-Buddhist ex-scheduled caste politicians. He scorned the Indian National Congress's untouchable leaders, such as Jagjivan Ram, but later joined Congress himself—after developing secret ties to Indira Gandhi. One of the opportunity costs of my growing interest in strategic matters was that I never returned to the subject of the role of caste and class in the Indian military after completing *The Indian Army*.

The Sapru House Maelstrom

After arriving in Delhi, we stayed briefly at the newly opened India International Centre, but we left because it was more than my AIIS stipend allowed, eventually finding housing in the brand-new Defense Colony. A spare bathroom became an office, and I was, at last, in business as a research scholar in the country I had studied for three years. When the summer came, we retreated to Landour, where we took courses at the Landour Language School, then run by various Christian missions, and struggled with a goose quill so we could write Devanagari properly.[7]

The unofficial Delhi headquarters for foreign scholars working on foreign policy and related issues was Sapru House, then India's premier (that is, only) center for the study of international relations. Sapru House at the time housed both the Indian Council of World Affairs and the School of International Studies (SIS). Later, the Institute of Defense Studies and Analyses (IDSA) moved in, further livening up the scene. Sadly, when SIS left to form one component of the new Jawaharlal Nehru University (JNU), the library was divided. Later the council itself fell on hard times.

At Sapru House I made my first and best connections with Indian scholars and retired diplomats. Sisir Gupta, not much older than me, was a mentor and friend who taught me much about how India really worked. He had just completed a book on alliances and foreign policy and was then writing a classic book on Kashmir.[8] Gupta was an Indian patriot, but he understood and wrote how India had damaged its own case in Kashmir. No one else in Sapru House had the slightest interest in my research, but I was a rare American and thus the object of much good-natured kidding about the Vietnam War, race relations in America, aid to Pakistan, and other egregious U.S. policies.

Michael Brecher, the Canadian author of a magisterial biography of Nehru, was working on a book based on extensive interviews with V. K. Krishna Menon and was a frequent visitor to Sapru House.[9] Brecher's works on Nehru and Menon were essential for understanding how Indians approached the use of force and therefore the role of the military. Brecher later turned away from India, not least because of irritation over Indian policy toward the Middle East, and became one of the world experts on examining how states in general make and implement their foreign policies. Like many scholars, Brecher found that studying India toughened you up. By comparison, the rest of the world was easy.

Through Brecher I met and came to know Menon, then in sullen retirement because of his role in the 1962 India-China war, a fiasco, but still playing with his model airplanes and tanks, the only useful products of the defense production empire. Menon posed as an intellectual, mostly by keeping copies of books open and scattered around his bungalow, and his most notable quality was his vanity. He could afford this: an ailing Nehru was still prime minister, and Menon was allowed to stay on in his official bungalow. While there are Indians who implausibly later argued that Nehru was pro-nuclear (at best he wanted to keep open the nuclear option), Menon was clearly scornful and told me, "Bhabha's notes," after the politician K. C. Pant gave a speech on whether or not India should go nuclear in response to the Chinese test.

One scholar, a Canadian like Brecher, shared my interest in the Indian military. He was Lorne Kavic, the author of the first comprehensive study of Indian defense policy.[10] Kavic and I met on several occasions, once when we were interviewing the same retired Indian official. A former diplomat, Kavic's interests were slightly different from mine, but he did offer useful suggestions, and the book he ultimately published was of great value in outlining India's major strategic and defense concerns.

It was the journalists, rather than academics, who were of practical help, who understood my interest in the role of the armed forces in politics in India and Pakistan, and who shared my belief that this was a legitimate and important subject to write about. Selig Harrison, then writing his own pathbreaking book on India's future,[11] put me in contact with Romesh Thapar, the founder-editor of *Seminar*. Romesh and Raj Thapar, his wife, shared their thoughts and put me in contact with others, including General B. M. Kaul and friends (mostly retired) from the Indian army. The Thapars came from distinguished Punjabi families, and their relatives included a former army chief. I should note here that my visa was for a study of the role of the military in the *British* period, and I did my best to confine my work to pre-Independence developments. When General Kaul started to show me classified material from the 1962 war (in the hope that a favorable biography might result), I politely declined, as my first work in India was on the historical aspects of the army. I was able to establish contact with the Indian armed services, and the Ministry of Defense arranged several visits to cantonments and regimental training centers and gave me access to its own library, which was a treasure trove (and now off-limits to outsiders). Armies are conservative bureaucracies, and the infantry is the most conservative branch of them all, so visiting a Gurkha regimental training center, or the Rajputana Rifles (or, more recently, the Madras Regiment's Centre in Wellington, housed in a structure built in 1857 for British troops), was pure Raj, a form of time travel. The library of the United Services Institution of India (USI) became a second home, where Colonel Pyaralal, the secretary, was my guide. Fittingly, the library of the new USI building is named after him.

Meeting with Romesh Thapar and working in the USI opened up opportunities for publishing. Romesh commissioned several articles, at least one of which appeared under a pseudonym, as it was part of the 1964 debate over the Indian nuclear program, a subject that was off-limits as far as my visa was concerned.[12] I argued that India had to think of the development of tactical nuclear weapons as well as strategic ones, as the threat from China across the Himalayas could be met with smaller devices. It was a silly argument, reflecting my own American strategic training. I find it chilling to see echoes of that argument in the ongoing debate over whether or not a "tactical nuclear war" can be fought between India and Pakistan. Publishing short articles and book reviews in the USI *Journal* was also very rewarding, and I received the usual sum of Rs 25 for each piece. This gave me a chance to engage at one remove the Indian military in questions pertaining to defense reform and policy.

During my first and second trips my research was as a historian, albeit one interested in the army's social, cultural, and policy dimensions. I discovered, by accident, that this was part of the movement toward the "new military history." Over the years I have thus interacted with those historians who were interested in Indian military history, including several of my own students. While the standard of historians in India was high in places like the University of Calcutta, military history was a minor field, just as it was in the West. Military historians are often dismissed as the "drums and trumpets" crowd, interested in battles, regiments, and hardware, but not much else. My own self-tutoring in military history uncovered something quite different: a number of scholars, especially sociologists, had written on the social and cultural impact of armed forces, a literature largely ignored by the historians.[13] While none of this group was interested in India, the connection between one of the world's most complicated and subtle societies, the state's use of force, and the emergence of a democratic India was self-evident. The Indian army had been reviled by the nationalists. Some wanted to create a people's army; others wanted to replace it with the INA. Nehru and his home minister, Sardar Patel, wanted none of this: they understood they had to have a monopoly over armed power, and that any group challenging that had to be crushed by any means, including the Raj's army. An analogous situation exists now in Nepal, with the communists eager to replace the regular Nepal army with their own cadres; only in this case advocates of a "people's army" may succeed.

It did not take long for the Indian army to become a patriotic force. Military action in Kashmir against invading tribals and elements of the

Pakistan army enabled India to retain much of Kashmir, and it transformed the army overnight into a national army. The colonial trappings were forgiven, and after the 1962 war, when there were questions raised about the predominance of the so-called martial races, the Indian government simply declared that all "races" or classes in India were martial (see chapter 5).[14] The man who understood this better than anyone else, and who had written the seminal articles on the nationalization of the army and the martial races theory, was Nirad C. Chaudhuri, whom I had the good fortune of meeting several times in his Old Delhi home. His writings on the subject, which date back to the mid-1930s, form the starting point for a small but interesting literature on the relationship between society and army in India.

Despite the obstacles to scholarship and the growing incoherence of Indian universities, there have been some important publications coming out of India.[15] The Punjab, the army's modern heartland, has been studied from the perspective of army recruitment and the impact of military settlements on local society. There has been little on contemporary relations among caste, class, and the army, in part because the subject is deemed too sensitive (the government will not release data), and in part because it would show that Muslim representation has declined steadily over the years in both the officer corps and the other ranks.

In contrast, there was excellent work on the way in which nationalist sentiments were creeping into the armed forces, and the availability of censored letters from soldiers during the First World War provided a rich database. This was mined by DeWitt Ellinwood and other scholars.[16]

1987–88: Phone Taps and Files

There were several important changes between my first research trip to India (1963–65) and the second (1967–68). At the personal level, my family and I were better able to adjust in terms of the mundane problems of housing, transport, and food, but we suffered a culture shock in the second visit. In 1963, before going, we understood that India was synonymous with poverty and we steeled ourselves against the worst. When we first faced it (in the Bombay slums and rural Bihar), it was "not so bad." In 1968 we were unprepared as we had suppressed or forgotten what real poverty looked like. We were angrier at India's failure to grow economically and the attitudes toward the poor of many of our Indian friends. These were also the years in which Indira Gandhi came to power, the years of growing anti-Americanism, and the years of political chaos in India.

The 1967 trip was when I learned that I had accumulated not one but several files, including one sitting on the desk of an Indian official in the Ministry of Defense. All of my publications were neatly stacked, along with notations and minutes regarding what I had written, as well as reports on contacts over the years. The Research and Analysis Wing and Ministry of External Affairs also had their own versions.[17]

Seeing my file, and working in British and Indian archives, also taught me something about government. When I joined the State Department's Policy Planning Staff in 1985, I asked for the file on nuclear dialogue with India. My secretary was surprised: the only files that existed were a few in my locked safe and those held in the secretary's office, chronicling his own statements, actions, and meetings. I was astonished; the much-vaunted American government had a weaker capacity to recall past events than the Indians, who fanatically kept up their files, minuting every conversation (including my interview with the officials I was meeting). Things have improved with computer-based data systems, but Indians are much better prepared for discussions with American counterparts than one would expect. Indeed, there have been instances when American negotiators had to be prompted or corrected by Indian and Pakistani interlocutors regarding America's own position on various issues.

My second trip also enabled me to do some more work on my first book manuscript, aided by some new tools of the trade. For me, burdened with a large manuscript that required constant revision, the great technological breakthroughs were Wite-Out and Scotch Magic Tape, both of which permitted revisions on hard copy (there was no such thing as soft copy, of course, except that which I retained in my memory). More important, the Ministry of Defense figured out how to handle me: as a journalist. I thus went on several press junkets, memorably one by Jeep from Srinagar to Leh. There I was greeted, as often happened, as Mr. Stephens, with the query as to where Mr. Cohen was. I just said he could not make the trip, which seemed to satisfy my army handlers.

This was also the trip when my research topic, the role of the armed forces, became a political issue. Nehru, egged on by Menon, had been suspicious of an army coup, but Indira was even more paranoid, or perhaps more willing to use such fears to advance her own position. Edward Luttwak's imaginative *Coup d'État* became the subject of a parliamentary debate, and the government responded by saying that it would be banned in India.[18] I had purchased a copy in London and anguished over whether I should destroy it or turn it over to authorities. My Indian army book did discuss the possibility of a coup, but it mostly focused on why Pakistan had gone down that road, arguing that one major accomplishment of free India was the containment of the military without lessening military professionalism (a judgment that I might not now make without some qualifications).

Most important, this was also the trip during which I met the indomitable K. Subrahmanyam, an IAS officer from the Madras (now Tamilnadu) cadre, who had developed an interest in security and defense policy, and who was the second director of the government-funded IDSA. My homage to "Subbu" is published elsewhere,[19] but it should be noted that he was as passionate about reforming India's military structure as he was about protecting its option to acquire the most advanced military equipment of the day, the atomic bomb. He was very much like Morris Janowitz: neither man liked small talk, both were obsessed with the issue at hand, and both pressed their ideas relentlessly. IDSA commissioned and published an article by me on caste and recruitment. Since IDSA was to be an Indian-only outlet, I was deeply honored.[20]

Having pretty much mined the subject of the internal role of the military in Indian politics, my thoughts began to shift to broader foreign policy concerns and United States–Indian relations, always a subject of lively debate at Sapru House and IDSA.[21] During World War II an enormous amount of military aid was sent to India, helping build Asia's largest center for the repair of aircraft. Hundreds of thousands of Americans transited through Calcutta on their way to China and to do battle with the Japanese in Burma. There was a moment, after the war, when the United States was prepared to provide significant military and technological assistance to India, but this aid was framed in the context of the Cold War.[22] Just before my first trip to India there was another military supply relationship, with a few hundred American officers helping rearm the Indian army and air force. This relationship cooled as India concluded that China was not the great threat that it had appeared to be in 1962.

Washington refused to change its policy on Kashmir, or break off with a formal ally, Pakistan, concluding that if the price of a new relationship with India was the abandonment of Pakistan, then it was too costly. Just as important, India was seen as increasingly pro-Soviet—the India–Soviet arms deal that provided MiGs to India went through in 1962. Except for a few scholars and the occasional diplomat and developmental expert, most of the Americans I met in India (and in the United States) who were interested in foreign policy issues were focused on Soviet–Indian relations.[23] The ranks of Americans were swollen by those who tracked the various communist parties. Calcutta and Kerala were especially "hot" topics to study.[24] One by-product of the extension of the Cold War to India was that I met, sometimes under hilarious conditions, numerous Soviet "scholars," some who were genuine, others who were KGB operatives.[25]

However, my real tutors were Indians, and a few American scholars, who, not knowing anything about current trends in the field of international relations, told me, in the words of the soft-spoken Paul Brass, "It's domestic politics—that's what determines Indian foreign policy!!!" or words to that effect. Brass (and many Indian academics) had worked on ethnic, state, and regional politics in India, and while they did not closely follow Indian foreign policy, they understood that in India, as in all other non-Western "developing" states, there was an intimate linkage between domestic politics and foreign and security policy. Whether it was trade with neighbors (or its absence), ethnic overlap, migration, cross-border incursions, or the ties of religion, language, and identity, India could not be treated as a black box, where foreign policy decisions were made in isolation of domestic realities. The academic work that formalized this truth came later, and it was done, fittingly, by such scholars as Mohammed Ayoob, an Indian who had worked at Sapru House, SIS, and later in Australia and Singapore.[26] Ayoob's work on "Third World" security policy consolidated and formalized what was obvious, but it was interesting to see how long these ideas were rejected by the American academic establishment, perhaps because they came from an Indian and not an American. The South Asian contribution to the international politics literature has been superbly summarized by Kanti P. Bajpai and Harish C. Shukul.[27]

India Watching from Japan

After publishing *The Indian Army* and becoming involved in the movement to stop Pakistan's brutal military actions in what was to become

Bangladesh, my own research interests shifted.[28] From looking at the impact of society, culture, and politics on the role of the Indian military within India (and Pakistan), I wanted to explore how India conducted its relations overseas and, in particular, how it used force abroad. Alas, in its wisdom, the Indian government decided to punish the most pro-Indian elements in America, the academic India watchers. A scheduled research trip to India in the early 1970s was canceled when India shut off access to American scholars working on "sensitive" (read contemporary) subjects. This was understandable. Governments do self-defeating things. But what was incomprehensible was the attitude of the AIIS apparatchiks.[29] It was: "We won't fight for your visas and academic access now, as long as we can get a few of us in India to study Tamil temple paintings and attend conferences on the nuances of fourteenth-century Sanskrit." This is a close paraphrase.

Thus began the long retreat from an interest in contemporary India, which contributed to a weakening of overall American expertise, just at the moment when contemporary India began to stir. This closing down of India was the confluence of two interests: that of the anti-American elements in the Congress Party, the External Affairs Ministry, and the intelligence services, and that of the few American scholars who were still able to pursue innocuous research in India. There was resistance in the AIIS, but it failed, and we lost a generation of students who wanted to study contemporary political and social issues in India.

The attitude of Indian colleagues did not help. When Rajni Kothari published an article in an issue on "academic colonialism" in *Seminar* he was echoing the Left and anticipating Edward Said.[30] Indian academics were jealous of Americans who had seemingly extravagant resources and used new methodologies (Indian academia was still largely British trained, and many Indians had absorbed British disdain for the American upstarts). Americans were doing actual field research, especially those who were studying local and state politics, which set them apart from many of our Indian colleagues. Above all, I believe Indian academics were influenced by the pervasive anti-Americanism of the Indian government, which had concocted an axis in which the United States, China, and Pakistan were conspiring to keep India from "rising" or "emerging." This anti-Americanism was so pervasive that when I made a brief trip to India as a tourist to see what my chances were of getting a visa, I was taken into an office of two friends at JNU. They locked the door and explained that they had been prohibited from even answering aerograms requesting an affiliation with JNU. It was very sad; even sadder was the decline of JNU's American Studies program, which became the world's only anti-American American Studies program. (Chapter 6, on the military under Indira Gandhi, was written at this time, and during the Emergency I saw banners hanging outside my former bungalow on New Delhi's Janpath proclaiming that "India is Indira, and Indira is India.")

The upshot was that many American scholars contemplated abandoning India as a professional field. I know that several of my contemporaries have shifted to other subjects entirely. Taking the opportunity to spend a year as visiting professor in Japan, I became a long-distance India watcher, and soon established contact with the tiny community of India experts in Tokyo and other cities. Interestingly, this opened up some new research avenues. The Japanese had been the chief sponsor of Subhas Chandra Bose's INA, and there were even some English-language archives pertaining to Bose and the INA. I was also able to meet some Indian and Japanese sympathizers of the INA (I had met many ex-INA officers in India in 1964), but decided to leave the subject to others to write about at length.[31]

For the most part the attitude of Japanese officials and scholars was: "Why don't you study Japan, instead of this backward and irascible state, India?" I asked myself the same question, but I decided that the learning curve of becoming a Japanese specialist, including language training, would be too steep and that India was still an interesting and important country. However, being "Kissingerized" was valuable.[32] I was able to see more clearly how the American community of India watchers viewed the rest of the world through Indian eyes, which was useful but also at times detrimental to objective analysis. The Japanese had their own perceptual problems toward India. It was easy to see how they were easily offended by what they regarded as a poor country acting in such a high-handed and arrogant fashion.

1977: A Detour to Disaster

Sensing that India was beginning to change in important ways, I declined an offer to train up as a Japan specialist and returned to study Indian foreign policy in 1977. Earlier I had been advised by several Indian officials to lie about my research topic, but I have always felt queasy about either giving or taking such advice. However, by 1977 the situation had eased, and I proposed a study of Indian foreign and security policy, looking not at the role of the armed forces within India but their role abroad. Of course, the 1971 intervention was remarkable as the first and biggest (and only successful) military operation of the Indian armed forces outside India after Independence. With a grant from the Ford Foundation (AIIS was still uninterested in funding such research and indeed later turned down one of my finest students working on a similar project), I went to Andhra University, where a former student, C. V. Raghavulu, and a good friend, R. V. R. Chandrasekhar Rao, were faculty members. The Janata government governed uneasily in New Delhi and anti-Americanism had abated, but they still loved Indira in Andhra Pradesh. Her picture remained on government office walls even though she was out of power. I also learned something of regionalism in India, a lesson that was hard to acquire in New Delhi, and how the Telugus regarded themselves as a people apart, not to be dictated to by New Delhi.

An academic affiliation was arranged. Intellectually, this was good, as Rao was one of India's leading foreign policy experts. My project was to look at India as an emerging power, but I never got around to the subject (except for a few articles) as, literally, disaster intervened. My family and I were then living in Visakhapatnam, and on November 19 a powerful cyclone swept into Andhra, just twenty kilometers from us. All thoughts of research and scholarship would have gone out of the window, if we had any.

We were safe, but word of something awful trickled back to campus as students returned from visiting their homes. Probably 10,000–20,000 were killed immediately, and a huge area was devastated. I was no expert in disasters, but I had studied genocide and the role of armed forces in disaster relief, so Raghavulu and I visited the area. There followed a grant from the Indian Council of Social Sciences, a report, a book, and a lifelong interest in the politics and culture of disaster.[33] With one or two exceptions, I know of no foreign scholars who have studied disaster management in India.[34]

This is exactly the kind of subject in which Americans should be interested. South Asia, like other regions of the world, is edging toward greater and greater extremes of weather, which has exacerbated already unpredictable river flows. It is very likely that in several years there will be large population movements due to an increase in both flood and drought, and more areas of the subcontinent may become uninhabitable. Singapore, among other modern states, is planning for this, and it should be a high-priority research topic for Americans. Indian scholars and officials may be more aware of these trends, as shown by several recent articles and the inauguration of the private Emergency Management Research Institute in 2005 to supplement the National Disaster Management division of the Home Affairs Ministry.[35] As of 2015 the structure has been again altered, with the ministry retaining control and a major change in leadership.

As often happens, the unexpected opportunity proves to be more useful than the planned, organized research strategy. Both living in the South and working at the village and district level (I made several trips to the cyclone-affected area) expanded my understanding of India, as did teaching at an Indian university and observing firsthand how casteism had eaten away at a once great institution. Conversely, tours of the district with the Collector, who happened to be from a schedule caste (that is, untouchable or, now, Dalit), taught me about changes in the caste system. If I were to embark on a second academic career in India, it would start with a comparative study of how district governance, where the majority of Indians still live, has changed over the years.

1978: Passage to Pakistan

The 1977–78 trip to India not only offered a diversion into the disaster management field; it also provided me with an opportunity to visit Pakistan for the first time, perhaps the single most important event in shaping my understanding of *Indian* foreign and security policy. I had tried to go to Pakistan during my first India trip, but my visa application was rejected by the government of Zulfikar Ali Bhutto. I went in 1978 as a tourist, traveling by bus and train, staying in two-star hotels, observing the country that was so demonized by my Indian friends. My conclusion was not that Pakistan or Pakistanis were better or worse. They were just different from India. They were similar in many ways (language, food, clothing, and culture), but different in their obsessions, fears, and, above all, their subjugation by corrupt politicians and incompetent generals.

By chance, I gave a brief talk at the American Center in Lahore. I suggested that Pakistanis should not rely on the United States and had to come to terms with India. The press was there, and the story was read by General Zia ul-Haq, which led to an impromptu dinner at Army House with Zia and the junta. The dinner was acrimonious. Not being a diplomat, I impolitely, and in great detail, corrected what I thought were serious misstatements about India and America. When we concluded, I assumed that I would not again be welcome in Pakistan, but to my surprise Zia walked me to my car and asked if I would like to return and write a book on the Pakistan army. He had read *The Indian Army* and liked it. I returned several times, ultimately publishing *The Pakistan Army*, which he promptly banned.[36] Zia subsequently told me that it had to be banned because the Pakistani people were very "emotional" on some issues. He also told me that I should not worry, as more people would read a banned book. The general was not without a sense of humor, although he was a brutal man who did much to weaken Pakistan.

The book on Pakistan created some problems. It was taken in Pakistan as proof of my pro-Indian sentiments (I had earlier published a book on India as an emerging power), and Zia was criticized for giving me access to the army. In India, the book was evidence, especially for those who had not read it, that I was now anti-Indian and had become sympathetic to the Zia regime. I was more surprised at the reaction of some American colleagues, who also assumed that I was somehow "pro-Pakistan" and anti-Indian. They had not read the book either. Their views were simply carbon copies of the attitudes of the country they knew the most about, India, whose prejudices and stereotypes they unfortunately had come to share. With the exception of a few scholars, including the late Leo Rose and Stanley Kochanek, both of whom had done fine work in India, Pakistan, and other South Asian states, our community had become as tribalized as South Asia. While real area expertise is an asset, there is a risk of falling in love with the first country that one studies deeply, handicapping the study of other states and cultures. This is evident in the work of many experts on the former Soviet Union who subsequently turned to India as a second area of expertise, and in the work of the China experts, who still see India through Chinese eyes as a weak and somehow lesser state.

"Emergent" India

My work on Indian foreign policy began in earnest when I was asked by the eminent scholar of Bengal and academic entrepreneur, Richard Park, to coauthor a book on India (see chapter 7).[37] (The intellectual groundwork for this work was laid during my stay in Tokyo, where I not only studied Japanese history but that of China, as well.)

I agreed, and we eventually produced *India: Emergent Power?*[38] The question mark was important: we pointed out that the obsession with Pakistan and the weak economy would cripple India for the foreseeable future. Until India accommodated, defeated, or otherwise removed Pakistan as a regional rival, it would always be "hyphenated" with that country, and until it embarked on the kinds of fundamental reforms that were just getting under way in China, it would always be equated with poverty and misery. This was unfortunate, we noted, because India had accomplished much. Despite the Emergency it was still a democracy, its people were freer than in just about any other Asian state, and India's cultural contribution to the world was self-evident.

From the late 1970s, my focus was more on foreign and strategic policy than the role of the armed forces, although the latter continued as a major theme in my work on Pakistan. The reputational change of India had not yet begun. That was noticeable only after the 2000 millennium software success story. By 2001, India, which was once identified with poverty, Mahatma Gandhi, and, latterly, Mother Teresa, was the place where the "techies" came from.

From the perspective of the American government and many foundations, the sole point of interest was India's nuclear weapons. The 1974 test was not militarily productive, but it transformed official American policy toward India (and Pakistan). With heavy funding from the foundations, many scholars and experts turned to India in the hope of persuading it to forgo a nuclear weapons program. With few exceptions, they neither understood nor cared about the domestic compulsions that drove the Indian program, or the larger strategic and perceptual framework with which Indians viewed the world, and especially China and Pakistan. It was foolish to publicly state, let alone have as policy, that the goal was to "cap, roll back, and eliminate" India's nuclear program. Doing so strengthened the hand of India's nuclear hawks.

I witnessed the Indian nuclear debate from 1964 onward, but I wrote little about it until 1990 (except for the anonymous *Seminar* article). After that date I was able to work with and advise many nonproliferation experts who came to India to study and write about the Indian program. The best, such as George Perkovich, got it.[39] Others were convinced that their logic overrode irrational and uninformed Indian fears, and that India had to concentrate on developing its economy, not on becoming a nuclear weapon state. I edited a book and wrote numerous articles that attempted to explain the gap between Indian and American perceptions, but in the end both sides were driven by deeply held suspicions, in some cases legitimate, and by the myths that had grown up around nuclear weapons.[40] On the Indian side, this included the assumption that nuclear weapons were the badge of a great power, and that their possession would ensure India's rightful place in the world. On the American side, there was a belief that stopping the Indian program was the key to stopping Pakistan and other states beyond the region. (Chapter 9 has as complete a statement of my views on the nuclear issue as I have written.)

The Indian and Pakistani nuclear programs precipitated a new fad, the Track II dialogue, and I was a regular participant for many years. However, by 1992 (when with the Ford Foundation) I decided that gathering the has-beens of both countries and exposing them to the anguished pleas of Americans not to do what America had done was a waste of my time. With the support of Perkovich and others, we launched the summer workshop for younger Indian, Pakistani, and Chinese scholars, now in its thirteenth year, and created the Regional Centre for Strategic Studies in Colombo. These represented an effort to improve the quality and range of the South Asian security debate. The workshop was later extended to include nonmilitary dimensions of security, such as ethnic violence, environmental degradation, gender issues, and migration.[41]

The alumni and faculty of these workshops, and of ACDIS, now include a good percentage of the contemporaneous Indian and Pakistani security communities. These are engaged in a lively debate over issues that were rarely discussed thirty or forty years ago. In Pakistan, this included the role of the armed forces in governance, hitherto a taboo subject for public discussion.

India: Emergent Power? was one of the first overall assessments of Indian power. But it took the 1998 nuclear tests, multiple India–Pakistan crises (1987, 1990, and 1999), and a change in economic policy before India was seen, as it always was, as Asia's third major state. The case for this was made at length in *India: Emerging Power*, which attempted to assess power and reputation along several dimensions: economic, military, and civilizational soft power.[42] The recent trend of books that purport to compare

India and China—the "Chindia" idea—is not always useful and sometimes exaggerates India's potential, but the books are a measure of India's reputational transformation.

A new generation of scholars and experts, many of them Indians (some trained in the United States) and Indian Americans who have done research in India, have it right: this is a complex civilizational-state with expanding power, and its rise is dependent on its domestic stability, its policies toward neighbors (notably Pakistan), the rise of China, and the policies of the United States.[43] The literature that predicts a conflict between the rising powers (India and China), and between them and America the "hegemon," is misguided: the existence of nuclear weapons by all three states, plus Pakistan, ensures that barring insanity, any rivalries between rising and established states will be channeled into "ordinary" diplomatic posturing, ruthless economic competition, and the clash of soft power. In this competition, India has some liabilities and many advantages, and the structure of the emerging world suggests a closer relationship between the United States and India, without ruling out much closer ties between China and India. There remain some questions: Can the present Indian leadership show magnanimity in dealing with Pakistan, and does it have the foresight to look ahead to new challenges, notably environmental and energy issues that require new skills and new international arrangements? Importantly, some of the best work on answering these questions is being done in India itself, and the work of Kanti Bajpai, Amitabh Mattoo, Harsh Pant, C. Raja Mohan, Rajesh Basrur, and others reveals the maturity of Indian thinking on strategic issues. It has not come too soon, as the challenges that India will face are growing, and those of Pakistan are even more daunting.

I also served two years in the Department of State, working for George Schultz, and chapter 14 was published shortly afterward and explains the two reasons why the Reagan administration pursued its opening to India. First, there was an interest in India itself—after all, it was the world's largest democracy, a fact that appealed to many pro-democracy ideologues. However, realpolitik was a second factor—warmer relations with India were seen as protecting America's alliance with Pakistan, and the India gambit had President Zia's support. The strategic opening faltered, but it has been revived in recent years for many of the original ideological and strategic reasons—only now there is an additional economic incentive plus a large and politically important community of Americans who have emigrated from India.

Trying to explain to an Indian audience in chapter 15 the way in which the United States made its South Asia policy, I argued that U.S. military aid to Pakistan deferred but did not end the Pakistani nuclear program—I am not sure if it even deferred it. Cutting aid would have risked the operation in Afghanistan, which was critical; my comment about increased openness in the Pakistani debate was naive.

Lessons

I draw six major lessons from my experience, and contact with India over a forty-five-year period.

First, when given a lemon, make lemonade. Accident and chance play a big role in the research process, but a scholar of India, or any South Asian state, has to have a frame of mind where setbacks are accommodated, and, if possible, turned to his or her advantage. Sometimes they open up new research avenues, as did my detour into disaster politics.

Second, time spent on subjects not central to a research plan can be seen as building intellectual capital. I learned to go into almost every interview with the attitude that I can learn something from even the most foolish person, and often the fools turned out to be shrewder and wiser than I had anticipated. Working on seemingly peripheral subjects may be a distraction, and certainly it extends the time it takes to complete the original research or writing goal, but it does not have to be without merit. I have called this the "doing something else syndrome." When you cannot concentrate or focus on the prime research goal, do something else as long as it is productive in its own right. Type up notes, draft an op-ed piece, clean up your office, or work on your Hindi.

Third, tools that enable a lifelong learning process, such as language skills, are important investments (although I do not claim to be fluent in either Hindi or Urdu). Language provides a window to a world that might not otherwise be accessible (in my case, this recently came in useful in Hindi conversations with a Malayalee noncommissioned officer who knew no English). It also provides clues as to how a civilization interprets the world and how it organizes concepts. At the minimum, it provides access to a popular culture that is shared by the elite as well as the ordinary Indian citizen.

Fourth, India has now built its own strategic community. That community is as diverse as America's, or any other European or Asian state's, and it now produces many of the best experts on strategic issues and the role of the military. Yet it is inhibited still by nationalism and by archaic government practices that restrict information about nonsensitive matters to a degree that seems laughable. The government itself lags behind: there are no more than a few Indian politicians who really understand the armed forces and the use of power, and the expertise among the civilian bureaucrats who serve as the interface between the politicians and the generals is very weak. The official studies of the histories of the 1962 and 1965 wars have been written but have not been published. The same is true of the 1971 war. Indian politicians and scholars are still denied information about the caste and religious composition of their own army, material that the British used to publish regularly. Still, when it comes to insights into what Indian policy and strategy are likely to be, "get me an Indian" is the place to start, although many of those Indians are resident abroad where the working conditions are superior.

Fifth, American scholarship on contemporary Indian matters suffered greatly during the years of no access for those studying "sensitive" issues. This placed American academics at a disadvantage when it came to understanding India's transformation into a major state. Although the general decline of area studies is partly to blame, much of the responsibility rests with those who dominate these programs: the language, literature, and cultural experts who look to the past, not to the future. The Title VI programs need a new injection of money, but their custodians must learn to draw more on the strengths of other disciplines so they can better educate their students, the broader public, and the policy community about this new phenomenon: India as a major power.

Sixth, the distinction between Americans and Indians, and scholars of other nationalities, is increasingly blurred. The cultural gap between younger scholars of India regardless of their national origin is also narrowing. They simply have more in common than my generation did, and the availability of electronic forms of communication makes them world citizens of a sort. This also provides new opportunities for cooperation among scholars. Besides the retrograde hypernationalist websites, there are now books, articles, and websites that are the results of collaboration between scholars across the globe. The Cold War History Project is one model. To a limited degree, the websites devoted to the armed services of India (but managed by civilians) are another. But the best one may be the way in which the global disaster management community has put everyone's "best practices" on the web. The time may be right for a serious, global, interdisciplinary effort that would return to my first puzzle, the role of the armed forces in politics and society. Given developments in Pakistan, Nepal, and Bangladesh, this will continue to be an issue that will preoccupy policymakers for the indefinite future.

TWO

Rulers and Priests

A Study of Cultural Control

The purpose of this article is to shed some light on contemporary Indian problems of defense and civil–military relations through an examination of the role of the military in ancient Hindu society.

Were India a Western nation, the link between ancient and contemporary states and military policy would be historical: the evolution of relevant thought on the subject would be historical and chronological. India, however, is telescoping certain developments such as bureaucratic rationalization, technological innovation, and scientific thought processes in rapid order. It is importing Western thought wholesale and consciously, through the efforts of a thin crust of a Westernized elite. Rationalization of the military was one of the first such innovations to be introduced in India, with old forms and hereditary militant castes being adapted to Western notions of promotion on the basis of ability—a specific instance of the transformation of status hierarchy to contract (by ability) hierarchy.

Two processes are observable: the still continuing one of the rationalization of the military—undertaken by the British and continued by the Indian government—and the adjustment of a traditional society to the Westernized military, an adjustment encouraged and stimulated by the Westernized elite. Thus, an examination of traditional notions of the military in Indian society not only is an exercise in historical reconstruction but should yield some insights into contemporary processes of Westernization. To search for the sources of contemporary Indian defense policy, we should turn to Clausewitz, Sandhurst, and Dehra Dun; to search for the sources of attitudes toward defense policy held by traditionalist Hindu elements in India (which, it can be argued, are becoming increasingly powerful as democratization makes an impact on Indian society), we can more readily look to the Mahabharata and the *Arthashastra*.

It must be stressed at the outset that the following examination is only a partial investigation into the sources of traditional attitudes held today; the literature and the dynasties to be examined fall into the premedieval period of Indian history. For example, the *Arthashastra*'s earliest core is usually dated circa 300 BC, the Laws of Manu and the Gita circa 200–100 BC, and the reign of Asoka circa 269–232 BC. Yet I believe that much of the characterization of ancient Indian politics to follow holds true—especially in northern India—until the great waves of Muslim invasion, and perhaps afterward, as well. Two factors led me to make this assertion: the great reverence of Indians toward the major Hindu scriptures down to this date and the often noted capability of the Indian subcontinent to modify invading cultural-political patterns (with the obvious exception of the British).

The following analysis moves from a general description of the role of the military in classical Hindu society and thought, through an analysis of specific crucial intrasocietal relationships, in a search for factors that seem to have been most responsible for the unique path of development the "political" has taken in India. I then put forward some tentative hypotheses that relate to the causes and consequences of the distinct and original conception of the role of the military held by ancient India.

The Military, Civil–Military Relations, and the Classical Hindu State

The central assumption of this section is that modern Western concepts of the role of the military and the use of organized violence do not adequately explain the significant contributions of ancient India to the art and science of government. Attempts to apply directly Western-derived notions of the state, of government, and of civil–military relations are both misleading and inaccurate, if the attempt rests on more basic principles of society and on hierarchies of values embedded in the Western tradition. The following analysis utilizes as far as possible analytical tools that are cross-culturally derived; in general, comparisons with Western traditions are made for purposes of illustrating the unique and characteristic elements of the Hindu tradition.

Societal Organization and the Military

The most sophisticated and useful concepts yet devised for analyzing the broad relationship of the military in a society are those presented by Stanislaw Andrzejewski, and these will be used—in simplified form—here.[1]

Andrzejewski's single most important concept is the Military Participation Ratio (MPR), both actual and optimum. Actual MPR is defined as the amount of military involvement and activity actually obtaining in a society; optimum MPR is the ratio that, within the given techno-tactical conditions, would enable a state to attain the maximum military strength, other things like morale, leadership, etc., being equal.[2] Ancient Indian kingdoms were generally characterized by an extremely low MPR, with only a single caste extensively participating in military-political matters in large numbers. Social stratification—according to Andrzejewski—tends to vary inversely to the MPR, and the evidence available to us from Indian history supports this hypothesis, for ancient Indian society was, relatively speaking, extremely stratified. I cite as evidence (not proof) of this recruitment policy the following passage from the *Arthashastra*:

> Comming [*sic*] dawn [*sic*] directly from father and grandfather (of the king), ever strong, obedient, happy in keeping their sons and wives well contented, not averse to making a long sojourn, ever and everywhere invincible, endowed with the power of endurance, trained in fighting various kinds of battles, skillful in handling various forms of weapons, ready to share in the weal or woe of the king, and consequently not falling foul with him, and purely composed of soldiers of Kshatriya caste, is the best army.[3]

The linkage between high stratification and low military participation is clearly revealed when one examines the deviant Indian cases. A society or subsociety that allows virtually all its men the opportunity to bear arms will generally regard military prowess as a chief determinant of status; further, since knowledge of military combat is widespread, any group attempting to establish a stratification will have to contend with a militarily skillful potential opposition. In India "wild tribes" such as the famous Pathans, and more recently the Sikhs, both had and have high MPRs and are relatively unstratified. Reference is made in several places in the *Arthashastra* to the "wild tribes who make no distinction between a friend and a foe," who do not seem to fight "fairly," and who were tough fighters not always willing to play the game of war according to Hindu rules.[4] While the research was done in modern times, G. Morris Carstairs's comparison of such a wild tribe, the Bhils, with a group of twice-born (upper caste) Hindus illustrates the striking difference in participation in military-warlike affairs between the two groups.[5] Whereas the Hindu group had specialized itself functionally in such a way that only the village Rajputs participated extensively in political matters and were the chief employers of violence in the village, virtually all members of the Bhil tribes were expected to act violently.

A second important variable in the societal–military relationship is the degree of subordination of the military to the political leadership that obtains in a given society. Several factors contribute to the degree of subordination, and we may briefly mention the following: the intensity of warfare; the size of the armed forces; the availability of technical means of control; the rulers' willingness to use such means of control, especially with regard to equipment and remuneration; the ease of suppression of revolt; and the very existence or nonexistence of separate social roles of "political" and "military." Since the last factor is so obviously crucial to the operation of the others, it will be dealt with separately below. It can be stated here, however, that the written Indian tradition is remarkable in its nondistinction between political and military elite roles, both being assigned to the Kshatriya caste. There appears to be no sanction against commanders in chief who overthrow their rulers and become themselves the new ruler, as long as they are "better" kings than their predecessors.

As for the other factors that affect subordination, they seem to have generally supported the cultural nondistinction between political and military elite. While the armies were large, their infantries were composed in great part of poorly armed (if armed at all) peasantry, and the larger figures given in ancient military histories invariably include hordes of camp followers and servants. The effective fighting units, the well-armed and well-equipped Kshatriya lords, were able to retain effective control over these elements of the Hindu army as long as combat did not involve whole populations and did not become so intense as to challenge the social underpinnings of the military organization. The generally limited objectives of the armies contributed to the retention of control over politico-military matters by the Kshatriyas; any contest over the control of the technical or organizational instruments of war was usually a matter of Kshatriya against Kshatriya, while lower castes remained politically and militarily unimportant for purposes of decisionmaking. Considering the size of the population and the size of the effective fighting forces, ancient Indian states generally had low MPRs. An exception to these generalizations was the occasional Brahminical activity in politico-military matters, usually linked to some regional tradition.

One famous case of military usurpation of kingly power tends to support my argument that the political–military distinction so crucial in the modern Western civic tradition was not made in ancient India. This is the seizure of power of Pushyamitra, who overthrew one of the last of the Mauryan emperors, Brihadratha. Pushyamitra was Brihadratha's commander in chief, and founded his own dynasty, the Sunga, according to the Puranas.

A third variable of Andrzejewski that I examine in terms of the Indian experience is the relationship of the military structure to the degree of political cohesion in a given area. This variable forces us to face directly the level-of-analysis problem as it applies to the Indian scene, for many conclusions as to the relative cohesion of Indian political systems depend directly on the level of organization we examine.

If we examine ancient India as a single geographical unit analogous to modern India, the system seems fragmented, chaotic, "feudal," and decentralized, with only occasional bursts of unity. Its political life would be characterized by dynastic instability and shifting patterns of temporary alliances, readily broken and not cumulative.

While the above may be true for the entire geographical areas called "India," the regional continuity of many parts of India is striking, with many dynasties lasting fully as long as major European governments. And on the level of local administration even greater continuity of government might have existed than in Europe. While our special interest is focused on the regional and supraregional relationship of military organization to political cohesion, it should not be forgotten that in some respects the military affected local government in an indirect manner, at best, largely because of the low MPR of Indian dynasties.

The organization of the military in India was linked to the political stability of the region as a whole through the practice of feudal arrangements for political and military alliances. When an enemy was defeated, the defeated king was usually permitted to rule as a feudal lord; the temptation for renewal of the struggle was always before the defeated territory, because rarely was an attempt ever made to integrate the new feudatory into the conquering polity. Feudal territories were usually permitted to maintain their own military organizations and were expected to provide aid in any major undertaking of the home country. This, of course, was due to the heterogeneous nature of the military force. As long as the military instrument remained heterogeneous and drawn from a narrow stratum of society, no large-scale and serious effort at integration of new states could be maintained.

On this level of interest, the main historical exception is the emergence of the two great Indian dynasties, the Mauryan (circa 322–183 BC) and the Gupta (circa AD 320–540), and their relative impermanence in terms of the political cohesion of all-India. These two regimes stand out (along, perhaps, with Harsha's notable reign) as periods of relatively high political cohesion, but during which the MPR remained constant and the degree of subordination of military subleaders remained low. Cohesion, in other words, was not based on fundamental changes in social life, and not on fundamental changes in the loose-knit military organization of India, in which most kings, after being conquered, were permitted to maintain their armies, with due allegiance to the reigning monarchs. The *Arthashastra* makes a strong attempt to provide for a unified, cohesive, and well-trained army, and advocates a standing army rather than a militia-type system of reservists.[6] But if this work can be taken as representative on these matters, while a great deal of attention was given to organization and technical details, little attention was devoted to the problem of integrating defeated armies in such a way that a military victory would increase rather than reduce the military cohesion of a king. A general failure to integrate defeated kingdoms in a politically and militarily permanent way paved the way for eventual revolt against the central power when the strong hand of the emperor was removed, and a reversion to a system of multiple power centers on the all-India level.

With virtually no exception, it appears fair to characterize Indian politics as being analogous to a multipolar balance of power system, in which several small contenders for supremacy vie with one another, in shifting alliances and periods of warfare, with no single power emerging as permanently supreme for any length of time. When one power did manage to achieve a relatively cohesive system of political control, on a supraregional basis, the fundamental social and military changes that would be necessary to maintain this supremacy were not achieved, even where they were attempted.

Combining the three variables of MPR, political–military subordination, and large-scale cohesion, it is possible to characterize ancient Indian politics in comparison with other social-political systems. Using Andrzejewski's neologisms, we can categorize the small-scale regional dynasty as "ritterian," similar to the medieval European feudal system in which the knights played the principal military role but were not united over any great geographical space. The Indian empires represent successful attempts to increase political cohesion, but failing in attempts to increase the subordination of minor military figures to the central empire. Present-day India, by contrast, is "mortzaic": cohesive with strong subordination of the military to the central political system but still not socially highly militarized. The European powers during the world wars that were so highly militarized are described as "neferic" by Andrzejewski. By way of contrast, the wild tribes of ancient India (and many of them today) were "tallenic": analogous to the American frontiersmen, they were relatively unorganized (noncohesive, nonsubordinate) but highly militarized; the Sikhs (and some tribes) were equally militarized but also more cohesive (although they were not functionally differentiated, and thus remained "masaic" rather than neferic). The British conquest of India accomplished first the political cohesion and then the military subordination of the subcontinent, and India as a whole moved from ritterian through homoic to mortzaic ideal-types of politico-military structures.

The Cultural Role of the Military/Political Leader in Ancient India

Having characterized the place of the military in the social-political order of ancient India on a broad scale, we can now approach the problem of the role of the military and the theory of defense in ancient India as treated in some of the great traditional works of Hindu thought, and by some of the practitioners of the political and military arts in India. Perhaps the first and most famous description of the origin of the military caste appears in the *Rg Veda* in which the rajanya (warrior) is said to have sprung from the two arms of the Purusa, while the Brahmin came from the mouth, the Vaisya from the thighs, and the Shudra from the feet. While we may regard this as an allegory, the allegory assumes importance, as through the millennia the general hierarchy of the source of the castes remains constant (with exceptions later in Buddhist tradition).[7]

The role of the warrior is examined in greater detail in the great insertion into the Mahabharata, the Bhagavad-Gita. The Gita, in fact, can be read as primarily interested in the function of the warrior, especially his resolution of life-taking with the ultimate objective of freedom or release. While it is not our purpose here to enter into a detailed analysis of relevant aspects of the Gita, certain passages of this great classic of synthesis are worth noting.

These relate to the basic rationalization for the taking of life; since everything is Brahman, nothing is really lost by death: "the dweller in the body of every one . . . is eternal and can never be slain. Therefore, thou shouldst not grieve for any creature."[8] So fortified, Arjuna is urged to slay his noble and great enemies, for their death does no real ill: "treating alike pleasure and pain, gain and loss, victory and defeat, then get ready for battle. Thus thou shalt not incur sin."[9] As long as the mind of the warrior is not oriented toward the end of his action, as long as he does not become attracted to the fruits of war, he fulfills the requirements of a yogi, acting as his dharma dictates.[10]

The net impact of the above and other passages of the Gita is that the warrior has his own particular dharma—to fight and to kill, but in a non-attached way—and that he should not consider the dharma of the Brahmin, that is, to abstain from slaying. The Gita does not attempt to determine what a just military action may be, because it is not interested in external justice, but in internal equanimity. The enemy is not in the field, but in the self.[11] The rationalization of violence, in the Gita, thus presents a striking contrast to some of the elements of Western tradition. Both the Indian and the Western tradition (as exemplified, say, in the writings of Clausewitz and the practice of Bismarck) attempt to put some restraint on the warrior, who by virtue of his monopoly of force presents a threat to nonmilitary elements in society. Whereas the Western tradition attempts to achieve a balance between ends and means in the use of violence and objectives of policy, the Gita restrains the warrior-ruler by insisting that he disattach himself from ends entirely, with the social implication that so constrained he will not be interested in domestic repression or foreign recklessness per se. One can, of course, argue that dissociation from ends can also serve to justify any end, but the history of Indian politics seems to indicate that the control has worked, and that relative to the West, Indian warriors have been more restrained by their tradition. What I regard as evidence for such a speculation is presented in later sections, but before this can be done, further elements in the Hindu tradition of military/political behavior must be noted.

The Laws of Manu give us—from a prescriptive viewpoint—a detailed picture of who may and who may not act the role of the warrior, thus elaborating the simple caste/occupation correlations of the Vedas and the Gita.

The general rule of intercaste occupational changes is that one may, if in dire straits, perform the task of a lower caste, but one may never become upwardly mobile occupationally. Therefore, only Kshatriyas and Brahmins (by the force of necessity) may be rulers; Vaishyas and Sudras are disenfranchised politically and militarily.

In addition to the detailed allocation of caste function—the Laws give us a statement of the social obligations of the Kshatriya, the theory of protection of the people. The king is enjoined to maintain the caste structure, to wield the stick of punishment to maintain order in the world, and above all "to protect his subjects, for the king who enjoys the rewards, just mentioned, is bound to (discharge that) duty."[12] Such an injunction on the king-ruler represents another cultural restriction on his potentially destructive actions. He is urged to regard his subjects' welfare as his duty; while he is to achieve personal release on the basis of the purity of his performance and the nonattachment to ends, the content of his actions is nevertheless given a cultural evaluation, as well.

The conclusion that is drawn from the above cursory examination of traditional and authoritative materials is that ancient India did not indeed develop the same theory of civil–military relations as that developed in the West, but created a different theory equivalent in function to that in the West. The main distinctions the ancient Indian tradition makes are whether or not the ruler is from the correct caste, and whether or not he rules in the people's ultimate interest, not whether his background is military or civilian. A cultural control of the elite group specializing in the use of violence exists in both traditions, and both the West and India appear to emphasize such control far more than does the Japanese tradition, to cite an example of the other extreme from the Indian case. The West achieved the control of the military by differentiating the function from that of the political leadership (I exaggerate the case here for illustrative purposes), while the Indian tradition controlled the joint military-political functional elite through the imposition of certain external standards of performance (the welfare of the people) and through internal inhibitions by intimately linking social and religious objectives. The conclusion is drawn here that the latter control over the military caste was achieved in India through the downgrading of the military activity relative to the religious, thus enabling those endowed with religious authority to exercise directly and indirectly control in the name of the entire culture. We turn now to a more detailed statement of this cultural value hierarchy of ancient India.

Cultural Values and Caste Hierarchies: The Indian Case

The proposition to be advanced here is that, relative to most other great world cultures, the Hindu tradition has decidedly de-emphasized the role of the military in its value hierarchy, replacing it not with the civic or political ideal but with an all-encompassing religious/philosophical system. It is not claimed here that this is true of all cases and at all times, any more than similar broad gauge generalizations are true in every case for other civilizations, but I believe that the above characterization is approximately correct. We first examine some of the classic statements of the Hindu value hierarchy, and then attempt to prove the truth of the generalization by noting one major exceptional case: Asoka's reign, which I believe supports my argument.

The Gita, being addressed to a warrior-king, could hardly be expected to glorify the relative status of the Brahmin as compared with a Kshatriya, yet not only is there no statement of Kshatriya superiority; there are passages that can be interpreted as implying Brahminical virtues as superior. Briefly, Arjuna is enjoined to act, but it is not the mere act that yields the state of yogi-hood, but action as it is transformed into wisdom and knowledge that is desirable.[13] The Kshatriya thus does not achieve directly (wisdom) what the Brahmin achieves directly through his study and meditation. This subtle elevation of the Brahmins' virtues occurs in other passages of the Gita, as well, notably 7.16, 7.17, 7.18.

A clear-cut statement of Brahminical superiority—to the point of blatancy—can be found in the Laws of Manu. In the passages explaining the legitimacy of going down the caste scale for an occupation (within limits), the justification for Brahmins in politics is given: the Kshatriya is "next to" the Brahmin "in rank," that is, one lower.[14] Later, the king is told that the best way to achieve happiness is by honoring the Brahmins, in addition to showing bravery in battle and protecting the people. And, of course, it must be remembered that one of the strongest injunctions to the Kshatriya, to uphold the caste order as a whole, is in effect to maintain the Brahminical ascendancy over all castes, including the Kshatriya.

A yet more detailed and graphic statement of caste status occurs in the *Arthashastra* of Kautilya. Brahmins, of course, are exempt from torture, receive easier punishment, and have the sanctity of their kitchens protected on as high a level as the sanctity of the king's person and council.[15] In matters of sons born to a Brahmin father, they share in the ratio of 4-3-2-1 in the inheritance as they are born of mothers of the Brahmin, Kshatriya, Vaisya, and Shudra castes. In the equally important matter of providing prohibited food to the respective castes, the punishment is highest for those who violate the Brahmin's ritual purity, next highest for those who defile a Kshatriya, then a Vaisya, and, lowest of all, a Shudra. In a ruthless passage dealing with the plight of a prince who finds himself the captive of a rival kingdom, the prisoner is urged to employ the utmost cunning to free himself and regain his own kingdom, with a significant exception:

> Having acquired close Intimacy with heretics (pashanda), rich widows, or merchants carrying on ocean traffic, he (the prince in dire straights [*sic*]) may, by making use of poison, rob them of their wealth as well as the wealth of gods, unless the latter is enjoyable by Brahmans learned in the Vedas.

It is worth adding that the probability of the prince being taught by "learned" Brahmins was very high in ancient India. As Kautilya notes (possibly referring to the historical case of Chandragupta Maurya):

> That Kshatriya breed which is brought up by Brahmans, is charmed with the counsels of good councilors, and which faithfully follows the precepts of the shastras, becomes invincible and attains success though unaided with weapons.

The net effect of these classic Hindu writings was to promote intracaste interaction and discourage intercaste equality, to set up a hierarchy of values, place the warrior near but not at the top, and tell him that whatever status he does have can only be held by maintaining the entire structure, including his own inferiority. While many elements of the Hindu political tradition led to wars between Hindu kings, the Hindu doctrine of social organization and Kshatriya duty effectively froze the caste structure in such a way that revolutionary social ideas never emerged, with the exception of Buddhism.

The literature is also replete with references to justified tyrannicide, always an effective check on the king's actions, and an indication of attitudes toward the king (also an indication of who was writing the texts). Unlike the West, where the doctrine did not receive full statement until it was propounded by John of Salisbury at the height of the church–state conflict, India can trace pro-tyrannicide arguments right back to the Mahabharata.[16] The interpretation that Altekar puts on the early appearance of the tyrannicide argument—that in ancient India "sovereignty" ultimately resided in the people—is certainly a remarkable reading into the past of contemporary theories of government; I do not share this view, but regard the doctrine of tyrannicide as indicative of an attempt by the Brahmins as a group to maintain effective control over the warrior-ruler stratum.

While I do not argue here that the relationship between Brahmin and Kshatriya constituted a "theocracy" in the Western sense, I believe that those Indian historians who have attempted to prove that the relationship was not priest oriented have been mistaken. For example: Altekar argues in his *State and Government in Ancient India* that ancient India was not a theocracy, that "religious and philosophical dogmas and concepts did not deeply influence the Hindu political thought, practice or institutions."[17] While admitting the evidence of Brahminical influence on kings, especially in the Vedic and late Vedic eras, he argues that this influence declined quickly, and that India never experienced theocratic regimes of long duration. When one looks for a classic theocracy, as does Altekar, India does indeed provide little in the way of such a governmental system, and Altekar himself contrasts the European church–state conflict unfavorably with the Indian church and the state or the Brahmanas and the Kshatriyas.[18] Unlike squabbling Europe, the two Indian castes realized that they could prosper only if they cooperated with each other, each conceding a qualified divinity to the other.[19] My point here, however, rests on a more subtle conception of "cooperation" than envisioned by Altekar, and argues that priestly influence over the warrior stratum was indeed comparatively greater in Indian history than in the West for all but a few cases in the eighth and ninth centuries AD.

Another noted Indian historian, U. N. Ghoshal, sides with the non-theocratic position on the issue of Brahmin–Kshatriya relations in ancient India, especially as compared with the medieval European situation.[20] He argues that the Brahmin–Kshatriya relationship was not complicated and competitive in the way the church–state relationship was in the Middle Ages, and claims that this is due to the fact that Brahmins were never organized in a hierarchy comparable to the church's. In these circumstances, he adds, the question of the mutual relations of the Brahmins and Kshatriyas never reached the level of strenuous theories of the champions of secular and religious authority in medieval Europe. It did not—it must be pointed out—because the Kshatriyas never developed a group of propagandists, spiritual or secular, comparable to that assiduously cultivated by the European monarchs.

Political philosophy in the West generally arose during or after some great domestic political struggle, usually in an attempt to justify an accomplished fact. In the great church–state conflicts of the late Middle Ages, representative writings can be found defending both positions, as rulers developed their own court philosophers and publicists to justify their actions. In Hindu literature, the very issue of secular versus spiritual was rarely permitted to rise to the level of open discourse, and the assumption of a spiritual sphere pervading all action remained dominant through the millennia. Hobbes, Locke, Milton, John of Paris, Machiavelli, and Bodin were not all necessarily anti-church, but they tended to be in their respective contexts pro-secular. A comparable body of literature supporting the rights of Kshatriyas against Brahmins simply does not exist in Indian thought. I believe it to be a powerful argument in support of my hypothesis that the literature of politics and political/military affairs is Brahminically oriented.

Having examined briefly some of the original and secondary literature on the subject of Brahmin–Kshatriya relationships, let us turn to a case that is deviant in several respects: that of Asoka Maurya, a ruler of unusual talent, political/military success, and religious beliefs.

Asoka as a Deviant and Illustrative Case

If Hindu tradition and practice dictate that the king consider becoming a forest-dwelling ascetic, voluntarily yielding his throne and power in order to fulfill his earthly life cycle, what explanation can be adduced to account for the clearly deviant behavior of one of ancient India's greatest kings, Asoka? This case is one attempt by an exceptional individual to break out of, or at least bend, the confining ideology and court system that gives the Brahmin a key advisory role, and to expand the scope of the assigned kingly role. Thus, where Asoka's support and encouragement of Buddhism can be explained as the resultant of a sincere religious conversion, alternative or supplementary interpretations can also be made from the known historical facts.

One such interpretation views Asoka as a power-oriented ruler seeking a means of circumventing the Brahminical priest class by patronizing an alternative and far less powerful religious system. While other warrior-rulers may have been content to operate within the orthodox Hindu system, perhaps playing off groups of influential Brahmins against each other, Asoka attempted to break out of the old system entirely through conversion, changing his religious orientation toward a still struggling and presumably far more controllable religion. It is not surprising that virtually all commentators (especially Indians) view Asoka's conversion as the exclusive resultant of a sincere religious belief, and there is certainly a degree of truth in such a view. Yet a similar interpretation was long put on Constantine's conversion, and it is only argued here that in both cases greater political freedom for the ruler and control over the population was a concomitant and not unwelcome consequence of conversion.

Perhaps one aspect of Asoka's reign sets him apart from the typical Hindu monarch: his extraordinary effectiveness as an administrator and as a political leader. The best testimony to this effectiveness is the fact that Asoka enlarged his empire without destroying it, but more evidence as to his ability is found in the famous Edicts.

The driving energy and ambition of Asoka is revealed not only by the fact that he created the rock and cave Edicts but in the texts of the Edicts themselves. Rock Edict VI enjoins his aides to notify him wherever he may be and at whatever time when important matters of state business arise: "during all hours and in all places, whether I am dining or in the Lady's apartments, or in the inner apartments, or in the lavatory, or when riding, or in the garden, everywhere, the reporters should report to me the business of the people."[21] Just as important, Asoka indicates that he is to be the arbiter in matters where his officials or council disagree in an emergency. In a classic statement of the duty theory of kingship, Asoka reveals the strength of his personal motivation:

> I am never completely satisfied with my work of wakefulness or dispatch of business. I consider that I must work for the welfare of all people; and the attainment of this is rooted in wakefulness and due dispatch of business. There is no other work for me (more important) than doing what is good for the well-being of all my people. And why do I work as aforesaid? It is to see that I may discharge my debt to beings and that I may make some happy here (in this world) and they may hereafter gain heaven.[22]

Direct support for our interpretation of Asoka's relationship to the Buddhist order, and his motivation for aiding it, comes from certain of the minor pillar edicts. In the Sarnath Edict, the Kausambi Pillar Edict, and the Sanchi Pillar Edict, Asoka expresses his interest in the management of the Buddhist Samgha, and indicates punishment for those who divide a Samgha up, whether they are monks or nuns.[23]

Asoka's support of Buddhism and his extraordinary activity and ability are, I believe, two facets of his politically oriented personality structure. It is to a detailed analysis of the mechanism by which such a personality might be created in the Indian context that we now turn.

Conclusion

Our route to an understanding of contemporary problems of defense and civil–military relations in India has been a tortuous one, and this section attempts to present a linking mechanism by which ancient attitudes and concepts can be fruitfully compared with contemporary Westernizing, traditional, and neo-traditional (modernizing) attitudes. Specifically, we will attempt to account for the basic differentiation in Indian and Western notions of the secular sphere and the religious sphere, and the nondevelopment in the Indian tradition of a separate military elite, distinct from the political leadership of a state.

The explanatory hypothesis can best be described in terms of Harold D. Lasswell's formulation of the nature of political commitment, which was itself derived from an analysis of American politicians.[24] Briefly, politicians are individuals whose personal motivations are projected on the public scene and rationalized in terms of the interest of the public good. The type of personality structure of the individual determines to a great extent the "style" of the individual in the public arena, whether, for example, he will verge toward the administrator or the agitator type. Because of the linkage of their own personality to public matters through their ego involvement, politicians, as examined by Lasswell and others, tend to identify themselves in a nearly total way with their cultural roles. For our purposes, the most important consequence of this personal involvement is a channeling of politicians' life energies into their occupations, a channeling made easier by the Western notion of civic duty, tradition, and loyalty.

It is my contention that a similarly total displacement of personality needs is not as frequently encountered in Hindu philosophy or practice; the people are a means to another, more personal end in both the Western and the Indian traditions: in the former, however, the link is emotional and complete; in the latter, the link is explicit and ineffective. For example, while there are elements of public service and self-fulfillment in both Western and Indian cultures' leadership roles, it is argued here that the relative emphasis of Indian culture is on self-fulfillment through public activity, and on self-fulfillment equaling public activity in the West.

The all-pervasive religiosity of ancient Hindu society—including the political aspects of society—helped define the cultural role of the warrior-ruler in such a way as to create a distinct and unique theory of kingship, and at the same time guarantee that that theory was fulfilled in practice to some considerable extent. It is the nature of the commitment of the king—and perhaps more important, his administrative hierarchy—to the state or civic order that I believe to be the crucial variable in the comparison of Indian and Western traditions. Certainly no large group of people could function for long without considerable attention paid to the associational needs of each individual, but the nature of the attention is a variable of the utmost importance. One can fulfill a civic obligation (culturally defined) because one wants to, or one can fulfill it because one has to. Personal gratification may be assumed to be the motive force in such civic actions, but the gratification can be identified closely and emotionally with the action, or it can be an end toward which the action is explicitly directed. The relative lack of ego involvement of Indian rulers with their states is reflected in their failure to effectively claim divine right or heavenly support. Hindu kings did not style themselves as possessors of a heavenly mandate, or as mediators between heaven and earth, as did the Chinese emperor, or as divinely supported, as the Persian kings preferred to think of themselves.[25] Only fickle Lakshmi (fortune) guarded India's rulers, ready to support another according to the workings of chance and the turning of the wheel of time. Their failure to invoke more powerful gods in the Hindu pantheon was not due to their lack of imagination, but reflects a fatalistic and skeptical conception of their duty.

Zimmer expresses the same idea in his description of the Hindu despot of ancient times:

> He is the actual temporary holder of despotic power, but not borne on by the mission of a new idea, some new dream of human affairs with which his age is pregnant and which he fancies himself as chosen to bring into the world. He stands merely for himself—himself and those whom he can pay or bribe, gain with favor or threaten and bully into his service.[26]

I agree with K. V. Rangaswami Aiyangar's characterization of the ancient Indian tradition and the duty of the king:

> An absolute ruler is one who recognizes no authority above him. In Indian political thought and practice, it is not the king who rules but it is Dharma, helped by the power of enforcing Dharma, termed "Danda" or "sanction." A king has no power to change Dharma. His fiat can not run against traditional Dharma. It is so with both Brahmanical as well as Buddhist rulers.[27]

Some modern evidence deriving from an extended examination of twice-born castes in an Indian village tends to support my speculations concerning the psychic attachment of ancient India, especially the warrior-rulers, to the kingdom. Carstairs argues that the behavior of individuals is derived from the early strong dependence relationship with the guru, the deity, the father, and, above all, the mother. Intense oedipal rivalry with the father results in the necessity of suppressing one's own sexuality and sensual gratification: when confronted with this self-suppression, the guru, deity, and so on, are compelled to help. The universal compulsion to give when asked in Hindu society (according to Carstairs) is related to a feeling of intense discomfort and guilt, not because of a feeling of enjoyment; this could not be due entirely to social pressure either, because this feeling of obligation occurs in private thoughts, as well. The obligation is felt as a duty, with the force of a guilt feeling behind it, not as a right, deriving emotional power from an ego-building act. This is probably the psychic mechanism underlying the invariable commentary that Indian society is based more on an emphasis on duty than right, compared with the West, a statement I regard as tending to support my hypothesis about the relatively weak ego involvement of rulers with their kingdoms in ancient India.

Child-rearing practices of ancient India also tend to support my hypothesis and Carstairs's investigations. If chapter 17 of the *Arthashastra* is reliable, it appears that the king–prince relationship was anything but cordial. According to some commentators, says Kautilya, the princes are like crabs, having "a notorious tendency of eating up their begetter." These commentators are uncertain as to whether the prince should be hidden secretly or publicly punished and banished; the fear of the prince is akin, they say, to that of a lurking snake or a wolf. It is notable—in view of the course of the Mauryan empire, that Kautilya himself does not advocate such severe treatment of the prince. Family quarrels are regarded by Kautilya as "death in life," for "no sooner is a royal family with a prince or princess given to dissipation attacked, than it perishes like a worm-eaten piece of wood." He urges training by "adepts" in childhood, and no attempt at instigating the prince in evil actions which may permanently ruin his character.

In this article I have laid great emphasis on the single variable of personality commitment to political matters on the part of the ruler, neglecting such factors as technological development and bureaucratic innovation in the maintenance of large empires. In truth, technology, bureaucracy, and personality are causally interrelated in any ongoing society, each tending to support (or restrain) developments in the other through extraordinarily complicated mechanisms. Yet I believe the selection of personality for my major focus has not been misplaced. While it is the most difficult to examine in great detail in an historical context, it is the variable that tends to change the least (allowing for deviant cases). Further, I believe it is, in this case, the most important of the three variables. Indian politics frequently developed extremely sophisticated bureaucratic organizations, and for many centuries Indian technology led the world. Yet innovation in these spheres could not be said to have been cumulative and progressive, and the only explanation for this that I can propose is that personality and cultural orientations of ancient India were such as to produce a reversion to the classical system after every major attempt to break out of it failed. Despite the innovations of an exceptional series of rulers under the Mauryan and Gupta empires, the changes proved to be only temporary, for their successors lacked the near-total commitment and political flexibility to maintain the structures they erected. It was not organization and technology that was lacking; it was a large group of men committed personally to these instruments of political control, who could carry on effectively when the exceptional ruler disappeared, that was lacking.

In summary, I believe that it was the interaction of traditional Indian personality structure with cultural emphasis on the sanctity and authority of the Brahmin that combined to severely limit the authority and power of the Indian military/political elite, as compared with Japanese or Western cultures. These factors were probably significantly reinforced by the wide ranging interactions of Brahmins, who shared—as no other caste did—a common supraregional language, Sanskrit. While much in the Indian tradition can be found to support the military or political activity as an ideal—notably the idea of the Chakravartin, and the idea of military duty as a special kind of dharma—I believe that the net impact of the Indian tradition leads to a more religious-oriented conception of duty for the ruler caste than in, say, the West.

Traditional Indian Civil–Military Relations and Modern India

The goal established for this article was the production of hypotheses that could be usefully examined in the light of both traditional and modern Indian contexts; it remains to be seen whether such hypotheses as have been proposed as helping to explain ancient patterns of politics and political behavior are applicable today.

Certainly, the functional specialization of Indian society into military and nonmilitary segments continues to be in the main unchanged, with even today certain castes and subsocietal groups providing the bulk of the military and its leadership for India. Yet under the impact of pressure for mass recruitment and democratic ideology, the old ways are rapidly changing, and the emergence of the military as one of the most Westernized segments of Indian society may make it an attractive career for some of the most ambitious elements in India today, as it has become in many other economically less-developed nations.

Perhaps of greater significance than the raising of the MPR in India has been the sharp Western-derived differentiation between military and political elites, with the former legally and actually subservient to the latter. One might cynically note that nothing has really changed: the warriors are still subservient to the (now) politicized Brahmins, but this would be a misleading reading of the contemporary Indian political process. While it is true that with notable exceptions, the Westernization process has been led for and by the Brahmin caste, it is in the nature of this process that powerful equalitarian ideas have been diffused up and down the caste structure, and it is perhaps only a matter of time before political control is equally diffused.

On the level of political cohesion, it remains problematical whether modern India will demonstrate a greater degree of unity over a long period of time than did the ancient Indian states. To the extent that military organization is a crucial component of subcontinental unity, however, it appears certain that disunity will not come from this quarter. The technological changes in warfare have made military structure a centralizing, not a decentralizing, factor in societal unity.

Despite the structural, functional, and technological changes that have been wrought in Indian political life, I believe that my hypothesis concerning attitudinal and psychological commitment toward the state per se remains applicable to many segments of Indian society. The wholesale infusion of Western notions of politics has done much to create a political elite that thinks in largely Western terms, but no close observer of the Indian scene would assert that these patterns of thought and behavior have permeated very deeply into Indian life. And, paradoxically, the Western-derived notion of social equality and justice may well bring to positions of leadership and authority individuals with greater ties to traditional ways than the present generation of leadership. On the level of the regional and local party organizations, in the communal-oriented Hindu parties, and in the lower ranks of the services, traditional notions of the role of the military in an Indian state may be most important, and may be present in measurable amounts.

1968

THREE

Issue, Role, and Personality

The Kitchener–Curzon Dispute

In 1905 the viceroy of India, Lord Curzon of Kedleston, was forced to resign as a result of a disagreement with his commander in chief, Lord Kitchener of Khartoum. What began as a mild bureaucratic affair soon escalated into a major power battle, and the scene of the struggle shifted in turn from the narrow confines of Indian bureaucracy to the exalted chambers of imperial decisionmakers to the public forum of two continents.[1] The dispute is important for several reasons. Historically, the removal of Curzon from India signaled the end of an era in British India; 1905 was an important turning point in the development of the Indian nationalist movement, and Curzon had done much to stimulate that movement, albeit unwittingly. The triumph of the military might have altered the kind of civil–military relations that had existed in the Indian colony, but curiously it did not. The victory of Kitchener was another important step in his rise to power and influence.

Analytically, there are important questions concerning the description and explanation of the dispute. In particular, what terms and methodologies are appropriate for the examination of a dispute with no single obvious cause? While the political myth that issues, not people, really count may be useful for sublimating conflict in a political system and buffering sensitive egos, it provides no definitive guide for analysis. The issues are important, but, as I hope to show, they were not decisive. This article attempts to explore the Kitchener–Curzon dispute on several levels of meaning and, as far as can be done fifty years after the event, relate them to each other.

The Issues

Most observers of the period agree that the Kitchener–Curzon dispute was an important if not pivotal event in British–Indian history. Yet there was and is disagreement over its significance. At the time some regarded it in terms of the individuals involved, especially as it led to the permanent removal of Curzon from India.[2] Another view emphasized the damage done to the principle of civilian control,[3] and still another view held that on grounds of good military practice Kitchener's victory was to be welcomed.[4] In truth, according to one's angle of vision, any number of triumphs and disasters can be read into the events that occurred in 1904–05.

The overt point of dissension between Curzon and Kitchener was the relative power and influence of the two highest military posts in India, the commander in chief and the military member of the viceroy's council. The theoretical division of labor allotted to the former actual operational control over the military and to the latter the support, supply, and organizational function. The commander in chief was second only to the viceroy in precedence, but the military member—who was usually junior in rank to the commander in chief—had the right of direct access to the viceroy, had control over much of the military's organizational branch, and was able to criticize the commander's proposals before they reached the viceroy. Even before Kitchener came to India he had set his mind on abolishing the system of dual military control and centralizing all military matters in one man's hands. Upon his arrival, Curzon persuaded him to wait before making any drastic changes, but Kitchener revived his proposals in discussions with his officers and in letters (written without Curzon's knowledge) to important individuals in Britain. He was eventually able to get the home government to consider his proposals for doing away with the military member, and when they proposed a compromise solution that would have retained the member but drastically reduced his power, Curzon resisted and was finally forced to resign. However, behind this conflict over the position of the military member there were two important policy disagreements. These linked the question of the military member's power to broader and more difficult issues. Rather than consider in detail the arguments that related to the power of the military member—important as they are in themselves—we examine the two more fundamental issue conflicts between Kitchener and Curzon: their disagreements over the nature of the empire and over the role of the military within a component of that empire.

The Nature of Empire

The Kitchener–Curzon dispute sprang in part from different views of the nature of India's connection with the empire and the proper ordering of official relationships within that empire. Conflict over the nature of the imperial connection between Curzon and the home government worked against Curzon in two ways: it weakened the confidence of Curzon's superiors in his judgment and it found Kitchener on the government's side in terms of the principles that they felt should guide them in such a crisis as the conflict between Curzon and Kitchener. The problem of reconciling home and Indian interests, which were not always complementary, was a regular feature of the imperial political system. In this period, the home government was conservative (as indeed were both Kitchener and Curzon). The prime minister, Balfour, saw the perennial imperial problem in terms of a conflict between the rulers in outlying portions with great local knowledge but "no responsibility and little thought for the general situation" and the home government naturally reluctant to overrule the man on the spot on specific issues, but nevertheless charged with the ultimate responsibility.[5] Before the clash between Kitchener and Curzon had reached its climax, there had already been considerable conflict between Curzon and the home government over the handling of the Afghanistan negotiations and the Tibetan expedition.[6] The substance of Balfour's argument—that Curzon's responsibility was small, his vision relatively local, but his power great—was elaborated and expanded as the conflict with Kitchener mounted. It was put to Curzon directly at the peak of crisis by Sir Arthur Godley[7] and linked to the doctrine of ministerial responsibility: "after all is said, this fact remains, and cannot be got over—the fact that the responsibility for every one of your acts, great and small, lies with the S[ecretary] of S[tate], the Prime Minister, and the Cabinet, and that where the responsibility is absolute and unshared, there must be a corresponding right of control, absolute and unshared."[8] One conclusion Godley derived from this statement is that "the real government of India is in the H[ouse] of Commons," a statement to which Curzon strenuously objected.[9] For the government, the chain of responsibility thus went from the Cabinet to the House of Commons (as the ultimate representatives of the people), and from the viceroy to the Cabinet: a viceroy who cannot obey and carry out Cabinet policy should resign, just as a Cabinet minister who cannot agree with government policy must resign; this is the case even if the viceroy is right and the Cabinet wrong (a situation that Godley conceded might occur). Ultimately the Cabinet must be obeyed, for it alone can take into account all factors.[10]

This was the British doctrine of ministerial responsibility as applied to the position held by Curzon, and he was neither temperamentally nor intellectually ready to admit that it applied to him.

When confronted with the argument, which was sometimes wreathed in compliments and sometimes put forward with great frankness and bluntness—Curzon reacted by shifting the focus of the argument from the responsibility of the superior authority to that of the necessity for trust of the subordinate, and pressed his argument with an intemperate vigor, which usually succeeded in confirming any suspicion in his correspondent that the original charge was correct. Curzon's own attempts at defining the nature of the Indian connection were unsuccessful in their immediate objective of convincing the home government, and they only revealed how far apart the parties to the quarrel were. Curzon saw a division of labor between India and Britain; he dissented from the proposition that the government is *in* the House of Commons: "for everyday purposes the Government of India is the Secretary of State and the Cabinet at one end . . . and the Viceroy and his Council at the other."[11] For purposes of the direction of foreign policy involving other powers, Curzon acknowledged the supremacy of the home government, whatever that policy might be; he was not one to deny the principle of a firm hand on foreign affairs. But, in internal matters, it was the man on the spot who should decide, and military administration was for Curzon primarily an internal matter.[12] Within this double-ended imperial framework, there was a profound change occurring, according to Curzon, which, if anything, was making the "man on the spot" even more important: "I believe that history will recognize myself as having done much (whether wisely or unwisely) to accelerate . . . India . . . from the level of a dependency to the position which is bound one day to be hers, if it is not so already, Namely that of the greatest partner in the Empire."[13]

As befitting the greatest partner in the empire, Curzon saw India in possession of its own "constitution" by which he meant a body of norms and rules established both by Parliament and unwritten tradition. And, also befitting such a great partner, India was developing its own "public opinion" that had to be considered, gauged, and generally taken into account. It was impossible for a viceroy now to act in complete disregard of public opinion in the way Lord Lytton did, argued Curzon, for "public opinion has been growing all the while, is articulate, is daily becoming more powerful, cannot be ignored."[14] In defense of his own bold techniques, Curzon claimed that it was impossible for men in England to appreciate this change and to attempt to rule India through the telegraph.[15] Ironically, the same argument of changed circumstances was used even more effectively by Kitchener in rebutting those in England, like Roberts and several ex-viceroys, who opposed him but had been out of contact with India for some time.[16]

Kitchener's view of the nature of the empire was strongly colored by his previous military experience in Egypt, South Africa, and the Sudan; he certainly regarded India as an important component of the empire, but hardly viewed the rest of the empire as mere guardians of the route to India. They were important in their own right, and certainly the fact that Kitchener had made his reputation in battles to gain some of these lesser components of the empire made them more significant in his eyes.

His non-Indian background and his own concern for centralized direction led him to argue that Indian military policy should be controlled by the Committee of Imperial Defence, not the government of India.[17] This was necessary, he could argue, because of the intimate connection between imperial needs and Indian needs: where Curzon saw every such connection as necessitating more power for India, Kitchener saw the necessity for imperial, that is, British, direction.[18] He placed his own dispute with Curzon in the imperial context, sidestepping the question of viceregal control in favor of the broader imperial control. This was always one great strength of his position, for it put him on the side of Curzon's superiors. Many of their arguments were shared, making Curzon's own position irrelevant to their main concerns.

It is not surprising, in view of their different constitutional positions and different relationships to India, that the parties to the Kitchener–Curzon dispute differed in their very concept of what "imperial" meant. Here again, it was a question of shift in emphasis: everyone began with the same "facts," but they weighted them unequally and drew divergent interpretations. All agreed that India was the brightest jewel in the imperial crown. From this Curzon deduced that the jewel was properly the most important object to defend, and he therefore had a degree of autonomy in many matters that was only occasionally surpassed by British interests. In short, India was the empire, or at least the focus of imperial interests. For Kitchener, Godley, Brodrick, and the home government, "imperial" was more often equated with "British" than "Indian" when it came to the question of defining imperial interests; certainly, India was the most important single part of the empire, but this was an empire ruled by Britain.

But, despite these divergent views, the system had worked fairly well up to the clash with Kitchener, and other viceroys had had the same arguments with their secretaries of state and home governments.[19] All the parties to the dispute were certainly experienced enough in imperial matters to realize that their conduct could never be guided by one principle alone, whether that principle was the responsibility/power doctrine or the "man on the spot" doctrine. All of them seemed to have realized that government demands compromise in fact, if not in principle. Yet in this case few of the parties were willing to compromise on the basic question of the distribution of power, and consequently refused to yield any ground in the parallel debate over the justification for the exercise of that power.

Control vs. Efficiency

Within the context of those divergent but not necessarily divisive views on the nature of the Imperial relationship, there was a conflict between Curzon and Kitchener over the role of the military in India, and the relationship of the functions of civilian and military. Perhaps it was not surprising that a conflict should occur in this policy area, for the military function is one of the most ambiguous and sensitive in any political system, whether imperial or national. Both Kitchener and Curzon dealt directly with a general problem of civil–military relations, reconciling the principle of civilian control with the demands of military efficiency, but they approached it from opposite ends of the argument. As the controversy increased in intensity and as the personal and political stakes rose, each became more extreme. While neither man denied the legitimacy of the other's principles, they presented their own arguments in such a way as to bypass each other completely. Indeed, the very problem was phrased in totally different terms.

Curzon claimed that by destroying the position of the military member without substituting a civilian in his place, Kitchener's plan was in reality "not one to disestablish an individual or even a department, but to subvert the military authority of the Government of India as a whole, and to substitute for it a military autocracy in the person of the Commander-in-Chief."[20] The charge of subversion of civilian control and the potential establishment of a military autocracy was repeated continually by Curzon's supporters. Lord Ampthil, writing to Brodrick, regarded Kitchener's attempt to abolish the military member as symbolic of a greater attempt at constitutional change—it is "the thin edge of the wedge."[21] Even Lord Roberts, who was Kitchener's close friend, sensed the importance of this aspect of the dispute when he cautioned Kitchener on assuming that the Indian political system was similar to the Egyptian system. In fact, he warned, it was closer to the British system in the separation of civilian and military and in the need for civilian control over fiscal aspects of military administration.[22]

But Kitchener would have little to do with the military autocracy argument. He was frequently confronted with it, and he invariably dismissed it:

> I am said to aim at establishing a military autocracy, and the use of this term seems to have terrified not only my civil colleagues but the Viceroy himself. But the autocracy at which I aim is but the autocracy exercised in his own sphere by every commander of a regiment, a brigade, or a division. I desire . . . to put an end to the existing divorce between responsibility and control.[23]

He argued that it was the ultimate check of the secretary of state for India and not the existence of two high military officers sharing authority that was the real bulwark against the creation of a military autocracy (reflecting in this argument his view of the structure of imperial politics).[24] Kitchener gave scarce credit to Curzon's argument for dual control and derided Curzon for wanting "a buffer behind which he can screen himself from the terrible 'military autocrat' that rises up in his visions. It is the bogey in a different form."[25] Even though he won his argument with Curzon, the charge of military autocracy kept reappearing, and annoyed Kitchener considerably. He defended himself to Curzon's successor, Lord Minto, by arguing that those who used the phrase "military autocracy" were responsible for creating "dangerous" rumors in India, and that it was only the "ignorant and idle" who thought his intentions were evil.[26] When the new liberal prime minister (Campbell-Bannerman) stated that his party would not weaken that "sacred principle" of "the subordination of the military to the civil authority," Kitchener's friend Sir George Clarke sent an extract of the speech reassuring him that it had been made for the "edification" of the liberals, and that the government desired no change in Kitchener's position.[27] Curzon's raising of the constitutional issue would, Clarke wrote, have an appeal to civil officials of all classes, and to "the civil mind in general," but Kitchener had little to fear.[28] Aroused, Kitchener immediately prepared a memo to deal with the speech, stating his own views on civilian control. He was "as fully imbued with, and as strong a supporter of the principle that the Army should be in complete subordination to, and under the supreme control of, the Civil Government as any of my opponents can be."[29]

From Kitchener's own defense and from his behavior throughout his career—especially during World War I—it is difficult to believe that he was not sincere in his refutation of the charges that he wished to subvert civilian authority and establish some form of military autocracy. His motivation in the dispute with Curzon was far less grandiose than that attributed to him by his opponents, but it was none the less as powerful for Kitchener as, say, Curzon's ambitions were for him.

In India Kitchener was guided by a desire to make as good a record as he could in his area of responsibility, and to him this meant reforming the Indian military establishment along modern lines and making it capable of meeting both imperial and Indian obligations. In a word (and a word he used incessantly), Kitchener's goal was to make the army efficient, and for the purposes of "the efficiency of the Army both in war and peace" he was guided by three "Principles": (1) to do away with dual military control and duplication of work, (2) to give the chief military adviser direct access to the viceroy so that he would not be constantly misinterpreted or distorted by an intermediate channel, and (3) that "under the supreme authority of the Viceroy and Government of India the power of military control should be given where responsibility is held to lie."[30] Kitchener rarely referred to his objective vis-à-vis the army without employing the criterion of efficiency. For Kitchener, either the military member or the commander in chief would have to be eliminated organizationally for "the efficiency of the Army as a whole."[31] And, when the military member's power was curtailed, "we have made an immense stride towards efficiency by the new arrangements."[32] The cavalry was urged to make their men more efficient, the viceroy was praised for being the only one who cared for efficiency (1904), and the Indian army's officers were similarly praised for desiring "progress towards efficiency" (1905).[33] Haldane's reforms of the British War Office were criticized for misguided energy, and the situation would remain "hopeless" as long as "the civilian Secretary of State hunts political shadows and allows the real efficiency of the Army to go to pot."[34]

It was not by chance that Curzon emphasized the constitutional side of the conflict while Kitchener stressed the limited goal of military efficiency. While these arguments were intrinsically important, and carried considerable weight with various participants in the crisis, they were only the reflection of a fundamental disagreement over the very roots of military and defense policy. Curzon's argument for the strict subordination of military to civilian was based on two premises: the primacy of political direction and a distrust of the military. As a parting shot, when he left India, Curzon had his supporters in the military department prepare this statement as a preliminary to a summary of his military administration:

> The Indian army exists for the purpose of enabling the Government of India to enforce upon its own subjects, or neighboring communities, compliance with such standard of conduct or demands as may constitute the essential factors of any general policy which it may desire to pursue.[35]

During his administration Curzon enforced this principle of political supremacy as thoroughly and as persistently as his considerable personal powers permitted. There are innumerable examples of Curzon's direct involvement in detailed matters of military administration such as promotion policy, troop disposition, discipline, and the conditions of service. On several occasions this created a great deal of resentment among the military, and Curzon's actions had partially alienated the upper ranks of the Indian army by the time the final crisis came.

When told that his position antagonized the military, Curzon did not really mind. In fact, he held such a low opinion of his military organization (and of military men in general) that he offended them without misgiving.[36] He had an especially low opinion of those British serving in the lower ranks in India, the "inferior class of Englishmen in this Country," whose insolence, lust, drunkenness, and racism were responsible for nineteen out of twenty clashes between the British military and the hapless Indians.[37] Only Kitchener, in the early years of his tour in India, and a few other officers (when Curzon finally realized how formidable Kitchener was) were excepted from his condemnation of the military. If Kitchener was a "militarist," as his opponents claimed, then Curzon epitomized the "civilianist" approach an insistence on the primacy of political direction over all aspects of military matters: in India that meant Curzon's direction. Whether or not Curzon was justified in distrusting the military in India in general is uncertain, but there is little doubt that Kitchener did give Curzon genuine grounds for anxiety over the acceptance of his version of the proper role of the military in a political system.

Kitchener never denied the correctness of the principle of civilian control, but he defined the purpose of the military in such a way as to whittle down the scope of that control and to place the military man in a more central position on matters of defense and war. Not surprising for one who measured a military organization by a standard of "economical efficiency," Kitchener held that the main purpose of a modern army was not national or individual aggression and aggrandizement but was simply insurance against national disaster. It being so, the money and energy spent on maintaining the military could be compared with private expenditures on similar precautionary measures.[38] As this statement stands, there is nothing that would indicate an unusual concern with the prerogatives of the military, but in private correspondence he was considerably more frank. Kitchener felt not only that the military should be considered and evaluated along these lines (which are admirable standards of administration) but that it was the military itself which was best fitted by training and temperament to carry out the evaluation. In short, Kitchener was a devotee of expertise, and he argued that if trusted and given power, officers could be counted on to achieve the goal of efficiency.

Just as Curzon distrusted the parochial outlook and limited mental acuteness of the average run of military men, Kitchener certainly distrusted and scorned the politicians in matters of military administration. The British were regrettably "the most un-military nation in the world," who he feared would face serious difficulties should they meet a "really military enemy."[39] Kitchener questioned whether it was just the remnant of a fear of an Oliver Cromwell that caused the lack of British military spirit, rather than that "the civilian authorities are jealous of any independent military administration."[40]

In India, Kitchener combined his argument that the military were the best suited group for their own administration and direction with the powerful argument that an officer (such as the commander in chief) should not be in a position in which he had to accept orders from or have his orders questioned by an officer of inferior rank (the military member). Kitchener claimed that the dual authority was an insult to him as an officer, for it impugned his motives; if in fact he was brought to India to reconstruct the military—he argued—he should be given all means to fulfill that objective. Curzon's argument that the dual control system kept down the power of the commander in chief only annoyed Kitchener, who continually professed that this was not his real interest: "as to power, I do not want any more power outside the army, but I do want power to do good in the army; why keep on a dead level of inefficiency or drift backwards because you won't trust the person you appoint to do good."[41]

This nicely sums up his position: since there was little reason to doubt Kitchener's sincerity, Curzon's attacks on the grounds of a threatened military autocracy may well have strengthened Kitchener's position with the home government, which did not believe there was a threat to ultimate civilian control. Kitchener's argument that the military are the best suited group to judge their own competence went generally unchallenged; Kitchener was the military hero of the period; who could doubt his competence in military matters? Only in the First World War was the point effectively realized, at a disastrous cost, that military rank alone does not qualify an individual for competence in politico-military matters, and only in the next great war was the lesson vigorously applied, by Winston Churchill.

Issue and Personality

In analyzing any major political struggle it is always difficult to relate the issues that have been developed during the course of the conflict to individuals who hold particular views. It is easy to draw up a list of which opinions are held by particular individuals, but why they are held is another problem, and to establish a causal relationship between types of individuals and kinds of issues is a still more hazardous venture. There are, I believe, enough data to enable me to push the analysis of the Kitchener–Curzon dispute beyond the level of issue conflict. Since the participants are dead and certain kinds of data are destroyed, the analysis must necessarily be incomplete, but some links between personality and issue do emerge. Before these can be noted, however, it will be necessary to examine in more detail some characteristics of the participants and the nature of their personal interactions.

Paralleling the confused and bitter debate on public policy described above was a tangle of extraordinary personal relationships. These involved many motives and ambitions: Curzon, Brodrick, and Kitchener, for example, were each looking beyond their immediate positions to the future. It is hardly surprising to encounter ambition on this level of political life, for men who had come so far might well be expected to crave for higher office. But personal ambition alone does not "explain" the dispute, for while each participant carefully considered future steps in his own career, in no case did this necessarily mean that one man felt that another's reputation had to be destroyed. Of these relationships, that of Curzon with St. John Brodrick is at once the most puzzling but also the most instructive. Curzon and Brodrick had been lifelong friends; they had corresponded and shared their hopes and problems with each other since their days together at Eton. Until 1903 they were on the best of terms with each other, but from that point onward their relationship deteriorated rapidly as the crisis with Kitchener grew. After the crisis they exchanged only the most urgent and necessary official correspondence. Curzon protested, for example, that he was not being given the prerogative of the most ordinary criminal because India's case was not being fully heard "in the constitutional way." Later he complained that Brodrick had never commented on the "merits of the case," and that while he had written all to Brodrick, Brodrick had not had the decency to write of everything to him.[42] Brodrick in turn criticized

Curzon's behavior toward himself and the government. He claimed that Curzon could get his own way more often by listening to advice, by being more tactful, and by taking into consideration others' problems.[43] The break in this personal relationship paralleled a growing policy disagreement, but it did not come about because either of the parties wanted to wreck a friendship or made no effort to avert it. One major attempt to smooth over the antagonism between Brodrick and Curzon was made by Sir Arthur Godley, who wrote with Brodrick's approval and showed Curzon's letter to his chief. Godley repeatedly rebuked Curzon for emotionalism in a series of witty, frank letters, far more cordial than those between Brodrick and Curzon. Godley urged Curzon not to form his judgments so quickly and express them so firmly, and above all, not to attribute to individuals (especially in England) hostility of a personal sort.[44] He pleaded with Curzon to be more friendly to the government and expressed his anxiety that Curzon was "alienating and wounding" those he must work with.[45] Finally, Godley begged Curzon to frame his communiqués to the government in such a way as to obtain his own (Curzon's) goals; he strongly advised Curzon that if he kept on antagonizing, he would get nothing.[46]

Curzon's reaction to Godley's moderate and friendly intercessions was extraordinary. In a savagely self-pitying letter he asked Godley to put himself in Curzon's place: racked with pain, conducting all his business from a sickbed, faced with a hostile native public, and receiving a critical letter from 6,000 miles away. How did Godley think Curzon felt? Convinced of the justice of his case, Curzon informed Godley that "I have torn up your letter and I hope to forget that I ever received it."[47] The momentous split between the viceroy and Brodrick—the one man most responsible for Indian affairs in the home government—parallels closely the split between another statesman and his close friend that occurred twelve years later. The close friendship between Woodrow Wilson and Colonel House was due largely to House's capacity for enhancing Wilson's self-esteem; when House was given an official status (at the Paris Peace Conference) and began to give Wilson some unwelcome advice (significantly, concerning treatment of the Senate's ratification of the Versailles treaty), a break occurred between them.[48] Similarly, the more Brodrick attempted to give Curzon official advice—especially on the matter of handling Kitchener, a task Brodrick had when he was war minister—the more hostile Curzon became toward him. At one point Curzon accused Brodrick of being contaminated by contact with the military. The more that advice was tendered, the more hostile Curzon became, until a point was reached where no advice was listened to unless Curzon felt sure that the person involved was absolutely above suspicion. The underlying psychodynamics of the two situations may or may not have been identical, but the development and fruition of hostility is remarkably similar. Curzon's behavior during his break with Brodrick was not unique for him. There seemed to occur during his career in India a pattern in which he oscillated between a craving for affection, admiration, and praise, and a blind rushing toward conflict with those who dared to show hostility, or who slackened their flow of praise toward and compliments of Curzon.[49] Crucially for Curzon, this pattern appeared in his relationship with Kitchener.

Curzon was at first confident that Kitchener would fit into his official "family." As noted, he went out of his way to obtain Kitchener for India, and once in India, many offers of friendship and companionship were extended by both Curzon and Lady Curzon. Kitchener refused these offers and went on with his own plans, for he was the last person in India willing to place himself and his reputation under Curzon's influence. Curzon's attempt to establish a dominant–dependent relationship vis-à-vis Kitchener failed entirely. In Curzon's mind Kitchener may then have been transferred from a potential dependent and a source of affection and compliments (on a personal level) and a source of strength for Curzon's public reputation (on the political level) to a hostile figure who exuded neither affection nor praise and who was a rival for general public esteem. Curzon's involvement with Brodrick, Kitchener, and Indian public opinion seems to be closely related to his general outlook on the external world. As long as affection and praise flowed in without pause, Curzon was the epitome of gratitude and understanding. But if the slightest challenge to his superior position appeared (or even if he thought there was such a challenge), his reaction was an excessive hostility that could create antagonism where there had been none before.

The interesting question is why Curzon was unable to extricate himself from difficult and embarrassing situations once he entered the downward turn of a friendship-suspicion-hostility cycle. It was certainly not because he was ignorant of potential disaster or because he was ill advised, for his closest friends frequently warned him of the consequences of his behavior.

As one explanation we can hypothesize that Curzon's self-defeating actions at this point in his career were in a sense deliberate. He took such actions consciously or unconsciously aware that they were leading to disaster, but also, perhaps, because he wished to face adversity and then triumph after going to the edge. It seemed that at times Curzon sought political punishment, confident that sheer ability would permit a quick recovery. He delighted in raising the stakes of a dispute to the highest possible level, for this involved broader and grander issues, the kinds of issues that he was most interested in. He turned administrative quarrels into matters of high principle not because he was an unskilled administrator (he was a good one) but because the larger stage permitted him a greater scope for his undoubted flair for the dramatic, the bold, and the imaginative.

Were Curzon dealing with a more pliable opponent, his outbursts and theatricisms might well have succeeded. But Kitchener, guided by his own powerful drives, resisted Curzon's attempts to integrate him into their official "family" and immersed himself in his professional work. Following a pattern that went back at least as far as his Sudan campaign, he surrounded himself with a small, devoted band of officers, demanding and receiving absolute loyalty. Social activities beyond this tight circle were painful for him. His immediate object in India was to consolidate power in one place for purposes of military administration, and he attacked with all his considerable energy anyone or anything that stood in his way. Kitchener's administrative objective was the achievement of "economical efficiency," a vague enough ambition, but one that apparently motivated him deeply. While the dominant characteristic of Curzon's behavior during this period was an incapacity to yield or compromise, matched only by a facility for antagonizing those who were his most likely allies, Kitchener's behavior seems to indicate a completely different pattern. His was an obsession with acquiring and maintaining control over everything that related to the administration of the military, coupled with recurring periods of self-doubt and depression.[50]

As in the case of Curzon, these behavior traits may be symptoms of a distinctive personality working out its own inner struggles. In Kitchener's case his cycles of depression were manageable, and his ego was active enough to at least maintain the impressive public image and retain the loyalty of a small group of intimates.[51] In any case, Kitchener's behavior during the struggle with Curzon was effective enough to achieve his goals, although he never ceased complaining to friends of the difficulties and trials he encountered. Regretfully, there is little data about Kitchener's early years (he destroyed all written material), and speculation about his personality structure must remain just that. But, in summary, he can be characterized as a man of great introversion, with sharply and narrowly defined interests. He avoided public audiences beyond the military, and had a strong dislike of sharing his authority over matters of military administration. On each of these points of issue and personality, the contrast with Curzon could not have been greater.

Given the issues described above, and the unique personalities of the participants to the dispute, a link that relates the two causally (or at least dynamically) is suggested in the works of Harold Lasswell.[52] Kitchener and Curzon obviously shared one psychological characteristic: they both filled and were gratified by political, public roles. They both displaced personal and private motives onto public objects. But these objects were slightly different: for Kitchener they were the military and the British Empire, for Curzon they were the empire and India. And not only did they displace their personal motives on different objects; the rationalizations for this involvement and displacement differed. In Kitchener's case efficiency was the main theme; for Curzon it was the greater glory and grandeur of the empire and its brightest jewel, India. So, there was a potential for conflict based on differences in loyalties and interests or differences in the rationalizations of these loyalties. In this case the difficulty of fully employing Lasswell's paradigm stems from the lack of data pertaining to "p." To find out what the personal and private motives really are, we need clinical or extensive historical data, especially on an individual's early years. Nevertheless, there is enough evidence, some of it cited above, to hypothesize some special correlations between the personalities of Kitchener and Curzon and their public roles.

Kitchener and Curzon resemble fairly closely Lasswell's "compulsive" and "dramatizing" types, respectively.[53] Kitchener did indeed select less varied objects for displacement and rationalization than did Curzon; his obsession with efficiency was well suited to a displacement on the military hierarchy. He did incline "toward carefully defined limits and the well-worked-out ordering of parts," and tended to desubjectivize a situation.[54] Curzon's political style was almost the exact opposite on each of these points: he was renowned for exhibitionism, provocativeness, indignation, and the stimulation of other people;[55] he saw the psychological nuances of every personal relationship, and in fact saw some where there were none. Thus there was a real difference in political style or character between the two men, a difference that was perhaps exaggerated by their confrontation, as each man sought to present a consistent, powerful image to the other and to their superiors sitting in judgment in London. Given the data available, it is impossible to accurately order the sequence of the development of the conflict. We do not know precisely whether personality differences triggered a latent issue conflict, or whether pressures for the defense of a particular institutional role led to a personality conflict that was justified on the grounds of certain issues that were convenient. It can be said, however, that the conflict reached a genuine crisis state when issue, role, and personality were all involved. Had the conflict been confined to one or two levels, it would have been much easier to resolve. But when a move for reconciliation or compromise was made on one level, it was often perceived as a trap on another level: too often the participants viewed an attempt at issue compromise as a personal insult or a threat to their institutional role. It was this linking of issue, role, and personal involvement that gave the dispute its extraordinary bitterness, intensity, and importance. It points up again not the truth but the function of the myth of the separation of political man and political issue.

Conclusion

What are the implications of the foregoing analysis? Does our interpretation of the interaction between role, personality, and issue have any broader application, and do the issues raised by the Kitchener–Curzon dispute have any relevance outside of their historical context? One obvious use of the above characterization of Kitchener and Curzon is as an interpretive key for other phases of their careers. If my judgment of Curzon's political style and personality is accurate, his behavior in other disputes may be more comprehensible. While they were "irrational" in terms of what ordinary politicians may have done, they were "rational" in terms of his particular personality structure. Similarly, Kitchener's behavior at other points in his career might be better understood in the light of what little we know about his character and political style. His periodic attacks of self-doubt and indecision were the most obvious symptoms of a deep mental conflict. Detailed examination of other phases of his career may help us to better understand both the cause and effect of such symptoms.

I am not implying that traditional methods of scholarship are obsolete, but I do believe that in some instances an unorthodox methodology may be useful for the understanding of otherwise inexplicable behavior. Even when the personality approach is used, however, this does not mean that the issues involved are not important in their own right. It is obvious, however, that in this case they were not decisive. Another implication of the importance of a personality clash in triggering or sustaining an issue or role conflict is in the area of preventive politics.[56] While it would be difficult if not impossible to formally screen civilian or military elites for their ability to cooperate, it is possible to accomplish the same end informally. In many states civilian bureaucrats and politicians take a particular interest in the selection, training, and promotion of officers not only to ensure their quality and professional capability but to see that their views and methods of operation are compatible with those of the broader political system. The fact that there were virtually no quarrels between civilian and military elites in British India after Kitchener's departure was due in large part to the selection of more pliable military men to the upper grades of the army.[57]

A final implication of my case study pertains to the effect of structural ambiguity on civil–military relations. In colonial systems there are frequently dual channels of authority and communication back to the home country, or at least some ambiguity about the legitimacy of such channels. Many earlier civil–military clashes even in British India stem in part from the opportunity offered the military to protest or appeal a local Indian decision. The Kitchener–Curzon dispute had been preceded in India by civil–military quarrels in 1683 (Keigwin's Rebellion),[58] in the eighteenth century (against Clive),[59] in 1809 (the White Mutiny),[60] and just before the 1857 Mutiny (Dalhousie vs. Napier).[61] Each of these disputes was resolved, as was the Kitchener–Curzon affair, by a test of political strength between civilian and military. And, not surprisingly, the chances of victory in an appeal to higher authority frequently determined the kinds of arguments and political principles a group or individual would employ. When an individual or group (usually the military) was likely to win an appeal to higher authority (as was Kitchener), they tended to stress the ultimate control of the British government; when they were likely to lose, they argued the relative independence of India as a political system analogous to but separate from Britain. In their appeal to higher authority the military had an unusual advantage. They formally accepted the principle of civilian control, merely reserving the right to choose the level of civilian authority that was to control them. However, even given structural ambiguity as a constant variable, civilians and the military were not eternally quarreling over the almost three hundred years of British Indian history. As in the Kitchener–Curzon dispute, peaks of conflict seemed to occur when the intersection of important political roles was not predetermined or regularized, and when in addition personal antagonism either initiated or stimulated conflict between the individuals who filled these roles. This leads me to suggest that for a more thorough understanding of these and of similar disputes between powerful political figures, where data are available, as much attention should be paid to socialization in political roles and the personality structures of key individuals as to institutional arrangements and issue conflict.

FOUR

Subhas Chandra Bose and the Indian National Army

This article attempts to reassess the impact of the Indian National Army (INA) and its leader, Subhas Chandra Bose, on the democratic future and political stability of an independent India. The analysis concentrates on the relationship between Bose and the INA and two important institutions of India that are to a great extent responsible for its present democratic orientation and political viability—the nationalist movement and the Indian armed forces.

The Relevance of the INA

The reevaluation of certain crucial events in the transitional period in which India obtained its freedom from British rule is not merely a matter of historical concern, for it was during this period that both the nationalist movement that today governs India and the military organization that today defends India came into their own, each being subjected to prolonged and severe challenges and each emerging substantially in the form in which they exist today. The major component of the nationalist movement successfully transformed itself from an agitational, divided, and powerless organization to the democratically committed leadership of free India—a profound accomplishment, considering the fate of many nationalist movements of other ex-colonial areas. The transformation of the Indian armed services from a colonial tool to a national instrument, while maintaining high standards of professionalism, has been a no less remarkable achievement. When one compares the behavior of the officer corps of the Indian armed forces in the postwar period with that of such countries as Burma and Pakistan, one is impressed with the fact that not only is India not dominated by the military but the channels of advice and influence of the military have been institutionalized and regulated in a way that is compatible with a democratic policymaking process.

The first section deals with the impact of the INA on the Indian army in the 1940s, and special attention is paid to the motivations of those who fought with the INA and those who rejected it. In the next section, the relationship of the INA and its leader, Subhas Bose, to the nationalist movement are examined and an attempt is made to separate out the impact on the component elements of the nationalist movement. The concluding section presents an evaluation of the net impact of Bose and the INA on a crucial aspect of the politics of free India—the structure and content of a civil–military relationship compatible with a democratic political process.

One of the most important but least examined aspects of the Bose–INA episode in Indian politics derives from the relationship of the INA to the Indian army and the attitudes of both British and Indian soldiers toward the INA movement. The attitude of most nationalist Indians was relatively sympathetic toward the INA and Bose, whereas that of most British Indian officials was resolutely hostile (especially those in the Indian army officer corps), but in between were a group of men who were committed in varying degrees to both the nationalist movement and the British-led Indian army: the Indian officers. The INA was organized and led by men in the latter group who had been in the Indian army. Below we examine their motives for enlisting in the INA and the reaction to the INA by their British ex-commanders. Unfortunately little information is available on the attitudes of the one group of individuals who retained power in free India toward the INA, those Indians who did not join the INA and inherited the leading command positions from the retiring British.

It should be noted that the "INA" mentioned above was one of three forces bearing that name. One INA (originally the Indian Legion) was made up of Indians recruited in European prison camps and was led by Bose during the period he was in Germany. A force of approximately 3,500 men was actually organized, although they never saw any serious action and ended in an ignoble capture while attempting to enter Switzerland at the end of the war. Thirty specially trained men were sent to Asia, reaching Singapore at about the same time Bose arrived.[1] While Bose was organizing captured Indians in Europe, the Japanese succeeded in forming another INA made up of Indian army troops surrendered (by a British commanding officer) at Singapore. This INA movement was apparently active immediately after the fall of Singapore but did not attract a large or enthusiastic membership; its initial leader was Captain Mohan Singh, an officer of very short service. Mohan Singh and the Japanese quarreled, and he was arrested in December 1942. There then followed a reorganization of the INA with Major-General Shah Nawaz Khan playing a prominent role. Bose's arrival in Asia radically transformed the INA's position, and late June 1943 marks the origin of the third INA with him at its head. Little is known about the maneuvering and influence of the Japanese upon the creation and organization of the INA during the period Bose was its commander; the interpretation of the INA that follows is based necessarily on sources with strong personal interests in any judgment on their motivations. Nevertheless, the inclusion of detailed Axis sources, if they exist, would probably change the picture only slightly.

When the island of Singapore fell to the Japanese, there were approximately 100,000 Allied troops stationed there, including 33,000 British and 17,000 Australian. The other 60,000 were Indian troops, serving in the Indian army. Of these some 20,000 joined one or the other INAs formed at Singapore.[2] Most of the 20,000 who joined the INA were merely obeying their superior officers and probably gave little thought to any moral or political implications of fighting in the INA. The officers' motivations are more important, however, and it is these that have raised most bitterness among the British officers of the Indian army, who were the superiors of the INA's leaders before Singapore. Also, it was the treatment and present condition of INA officers rather than that of the regular troops that raised the greatest political problems for both the retiring British and the new Indian governments.

Motives for Joining

From testimony given at the INA trials, from memoirs, and from critics, three broad categories of motivation seem to have caused the massive transfer of allegiance of the Indian army officer corps in Malaya and Singapore.

Several connotations can be put on each motivation, and other points of view (notably the British) will be discussed. Here, however, the motivation of the officers is described largely in their own terms and in their own words whenever possible. They fall in the categories of personal benefit and gain, nationalist feelings, and the charismatic appeal of Subhas Bose. The distinctions are for purposes of exposition only; most officers freely admitted to multiple reasons for their membership in the INA. The following interpretation was developed independently from, but parallels, Philip Mason's foreword to Toye's *Springing Tiger.*

Certainly some of the defecting officers foresaw rich monetary rewards for themselves and their families by switching allegiance to their former enemy, and to the extent that this was true, the British label of "treasonous rabble" was accurate. No INA officer was ever likely to admit of such motives, and we can only assume that some of them deserved the charge. But probably a more significant reason for the attraction of the INA lies in the internal policy of the Indian army under the British, particularly in such matters of prime concern to professional military men as promotion policy, devolved authority, trust, and personal treatment by British fellow officers.

Indianization

A brief, somewhat divergent comment on British policy toward Indianization of the Indian army is relevant at this point. Before the war Indian nationalists had pressed the government of India for Indianization, but after 1939 the government exerted the greater effort to attracting qualified Indians into the services, with increasingly poor results as Congress opposition to aiding the British grew. In October 1939 there were only 396 Indian officers in the combatant sections of the army and the proportion of British to Indian officers was ten to one.[3] As the war progressed, the number of Indian officers grew rapidly but not so rapidly or with high enough quality to please the British. By January 1941 the number of Indian officers had reached only 596, and the British-to-Indian ratio had risen to twelve to one. (By the end of the war the ratio had dropped from 4.1 to 1 and more than 8,000 Indians served as officers.) The Indian officers who were surrendered at Singapore had never served in the Indian army when the ratio was considerably lower than its peacetime level; in 1939 the

Indianized units consisted of roughly one-eighth of all Indian army units and less than one-tenth of the prestigious combatant units.[4]

The above figures give only part of the picture, for the British had rigged the structure of the Indianizing units before the onset of war so that the odds for promotion of an Indian were considerably smaller than for his British counterpart.[5] Other techniques used by the British to retard Indianization could be listed, as could the complaints of the nationalists urging speeded up Indianization, but the major point is that Indian officers in the Indian army were acutely aware of their newly won and generally precarious prestige. When confronted with an opportunity to rise quickly in rank, to command Indian units in actual combat (a rare event for Indian officers in World War II), it is not surprising that many Indian officers renounced their Indian army commissions.

The differential treatment in the Indian army accorded its Indian and British officers was cited by Major General Shah Nawaz Khan as one specific reason why he joined the INA. In testimony at his trial he said that, in the Indian army, "not a single [Indian] officer was given the command of a Division and only one Indian was given the command of a Brigade." He concluded that, since there were highly competent Indians, "it appeared to me that lack of talent could not have been the reason for more Indians not getting higher commands."[6] There is no doubt that general suspicion in the Indian army of Indian officers—particularly a growing fear that they were being "captured" by the nationalist movement—caused the British to be extremely cautious in their Indianization program; many later saw justification for this caution in the creation of the INA. But it can be argued that devolving more authority to Indians would have made them more loyal, even when captured. The conflict between factors, their relative importance, can probably not be accurately evaluated today; Independence and total Indianization has settled this particular problem forever, although a variant of it still exists with the problem of the class and communal representativeness of the Indian armed services.

A second important attraction of the INA for the Indian army's officer corps was the opportunity to act in the interests of India or at least to attempt to protect those interests. Many Indian officers, particularly those who were recent recruits, were strongly attracted by the nationalist movement and saw the INA as an opportunity to use their profession to eliminate the British from India forever. An extreme statement of this position was given by Colonel P. K. Sahgal in his autobiography: "My father had taken an active part in the 1920–21 non-co-operation movement and from him I inherited an intense dislike for the alien rule. Added to this my own study of History and Political Science taught me that complete freedom was the birth right of every human being and it was the sacred duty of every Indian to fight for the liberation of the motherland."[7] Other officers appear to have been influenced by a wish to protect India from the Japanese should they win as much as to liberate it from the British. Shah Nawaz Khan claims to have originally opposed the INA but joined it to better protect his men from Japanese cruelties. Before Bose's arrival in Singapore, Khan writes that he was active in the INA for this reason and to make sure that anyone joining the INA would realize that they might eventually have to fight against the Japanese, after fighting the British.[8]

The third, and probably decisive, factor in the adherence of large numbers of Indian army personnel to the INA cause (especially in Singapore) is found in the character of one individual, one of the few Indians of his time qualified to assume the role of militant director of the INA. Running through all writings on the INA is an appreciation of the singular role played by Subhas Bose in turning it into an actual fighting force. Of the conditions for the attraction and motivation of Indians to join that force, Bose's charismatic leadership was undoubtedly a necessary if not a sufficient one; with him a force was actually put into the field and engaged in several battles, even with dubious results. Without him it is doubtful that a force could have been deployed at all, and the INA personnel would probably have joined the many other Indian prisoners of war on forced labor projects.

Bose's "magnetic personality" and his "hypnosis" of the INA have been described by his propaganda minister, S. A. Ayer, in a panegyric to his "Netaji" (leader); if we are to believe both Ayer and other INA accounts, Bose's effect on both the officers and men of the INA was instantaneous and electric. In all probability these accounts are true, if somewhat exaggerated, but other factors that contributed to Bose's attraction may be noted. The Indians in the INA were truly cut off from their native land, surrendered by their British leadership to a cruel and ruthless opponent. Bose was an individual with enough international prestige to deal with the Japanese and regain some independent status for the INA officers and men; his leadership offered them some hope of obtaining moderate treatment for their men and even a chance for military success, however slim.

Consequently, any charismatic or personal appeal he had was magnified by this desperate position of the captured Indian troops.

Of the three leading factors involved in Indian participation in the INA, the latter—Bose's personal leadership—was the crucial one for turning the INA affair from a footnote in history into enough of a threat to create serious concern among the British. To the British evaluation of the INA threat to their rule and to India's interests, we now turn.

The British, both in England and in India, were understandably hostile to the INA as a movement and to its members, particularly its officer corps. Their antipathy toward the INA ranged from tolerance born out of necessity to bitterness derived from hostility. The greatest official tolerance among the British to INA came from those who were working toward the independence of India as expediently as possible, notably the upper political and military leadership; the greatest hostility came from the British officers who had both a personal and a professional interest in seeing the INA punished as heavily as possible. For both groups, the trial of the INA officers served as a focal point and test of their relative strength.

Taking first the most extreme, but none the less important, position of many of the British regular Indian army officers and some of their bureaucratic counterparts, the issue of internal bureaucratic discipline and stability looms as their most important argument, and their personal distrust and dislike of their former subordinates their main motive. From the memoirs of one of the most senior British officers in the Indian army, Lieutenant-General Sir Francis Tuker, one can sense the importance put on discipline by the British and their bitter chagrin at the overt and violent challenge to that discipline by the INA. As for the discipline, Tuker wrote:

> With that all things are possible of achievement in peace and above all, in war. Nothing is possible for a battalion which has not got it: it becomes worthless and a waste of the country's money, for an army exists to fight the wars of its country and if it is not fit for that, it is fit for nothing and can be disbanded. It is worse than useless: it is dangerous. The weapon may turn in the hand at the critical time and the nation be lost.[9]

On a more personal level, Tuker attacked the officer corps of the INA as being poor men and poorer soldiers; he described Shah Nawaz Khan,

Mohan Singh, Dhillon, and others as "rabble," and attributed to the leaders of the INA both cowardice and a fascist ideology.[10]

One can readily understand Tuker's bitterness when account is taken of his initial opposition to the INA as an enemy military force, followed by its glorification and virtual acquittal under the pre-Independence British regime. He and others apparently demanded severe treatment of the captured INA, but the whole affair had become too great a political weapon for the Indian nationalist movement to allow of "routine" treatment. Azad mentions the attitude of an unnamed civil servant: "He suggested that the Congress should take no interest in the affair of the Indian National Army, for he argued that this would keep the trial out of politics."[11] It is significant that Azad gave no consideration to the disciplinary problem that so concerned Indian army and civil service officials, treating the INA affair in terms similar to those used by the INA officers themselves during and after their trial. This contrasts strongly with the severe concern expressed by Tuker over the dissolution of India's and Pakistan's armies.

Tuker argued with great vehemence that the results of the trial of the INA officers was a great mistake for it tended to erode the discipline of the Indian army by lightly punishing those who had "cashiered" themselves from that army and turned against it; he castigated those who lightened the sentences passed on the few INA officers who were tried, and he attributed the minor uprisings of the Royal Indian Navy and Royal Indian Air Force partly to a breakdown in discipline brought on by the results of the trials.[12]

Certainly the results of the trial contributed to a breakdown in discipline, but they must be placed in the context of other powerful influences within the Indian services. One of these, a renewed nationalistic fervor, was intensified but not created by the trials; another, the existence of genuine grievances, affected men in the British services as well as Indian (one of the first of the service rebellions took place at the Royal Air Force base at Dum Dum near Calcutta). In evaluating these forces, Tuker, along Churchillian lines, disparaged the nationalists' motives and tactics; he was in a political sense a true child of the nineteenth-century tutelage period, ill equipped to recognize anything but the faults of nationalists, particularly Congress.

The views of such men as Tuker did not prevail on a national level. The trials of the INA officers were not conducted on purely military lines; if they had been, punishment would undoubtedly have been extremely severe.

Under Viceroys Wavell and Mountbatten, suitable compromises were attempted between the extremists of the military and the extremists of the nationalists concerning the treatment of the INA. The final crisis involving the INA officers illustrates the general positions taken by the important parties involved on the British side. A few officers were being tried for specific war crimes. The Indian army commander in chief, Sir Claude Auchinleck, according to Campbell-Johnson, had threatened to resign if they were released with no punishment. He was under strong pressure to not back down on this case, as he had on earlier cases. The viceroy, Lord Mountbatten, succeeded in bringing nationalist and military leaders together and effecting a compromise. Auchinleck was dissuaded from resigning, on one hand, and a renewal of widespread popular clamor was averted, on the other. An amusing incident is related by Mountbatten's biographer of an attempt by a nationalist extremist to use the INA issue in the assembly in order to attack the British; after a short outburst he promptly lapsed into silence, presumably after a warning from the Congress leadership.[13]

The overall handling of the INA affair by the British stands to their own credit for, while they were not able wholly to satisfy any single group, no severe dislocation of opinion of any group occurred that would be likely to hurt a free India. If anything, they hastened the advent of Independence by the handling of the trial. It was held in the historically significant Red Fort of Delhi, and the first three defendants were a Hindu, a Muslim, and a Sikh. The British could not have deliberately created a better stimulus to nationalist public opinion, and the nationalists were given a golden opportunity to rail against the British. Within the Indian army, there were grave misgivings about the lightness of the punishment but, by refusing INA men readmission to the army, many potential troublemakers were kept out of the service. Only those senior British commanders such as Tuker, who had been having their own way in disciplinary matters in the Indian army, were extremely disappointed; it was this very group whose future in a free Indian army was most in doubt, and, as events turned out, great numbers of them soon terminated their official relationship with India. Indian officers were promoted to the highest positions of command as quickly as they could learn their British seniors' jobs.

The analysis of the reaction of Indians in the Indian Army Officers Corps to the INA affair is based on the circumstantial and secondary evidence available to an observer in America, but enough material is nevertheless available to permit sketching the broad outlines of their reaction.

First of all, despite the jailing of many important nationalist leaders, and despite the dramatic appeal of the INA to many Indians, the bulk of the Indian officers remained loyal to their British commanders and performed their duties with generally high distinction. We have evidence of anxiety among high British officers that dissatisfaction existed among the Indian officers, but this never manifested itself in overt rebellion. Even in the Eastern Command, where contact with the INA was made, and members of the same family fought each other, the Indian army showed no sign of disloyalty.

While they were performing their duty, both during the war and during the extended trials of the INA, the Indian officers of the Indian army were under several kinds of cross pressures. While these are listed here, no attempt is made to evaluate them quantitatively. One group of pressures concentrated on the nationalist and patriotic feelings of the officers and involved particularly the question of the proper means to seek India's freedom from foreign domination. I here leave aside the "pure" mercenary type (who fought for anyone, including foreign rulers) and consider only those Indians concerned with their nation's independence. Against the immediate appeal of the INA as an instrument to get rid of the British, there were set two counter-considerations that could be, and probably were, held by a great many nationalist-oriented Indian officers. First, there was some question as to whether the INA, if successful, could have successfully resisted Japanese dominance and, if not, whether Japanese rule might not have been less tolerable than the British (especially to those who were fighting the Japanese). A second consideration was one related by Gen. K. S. Thimayya's biographer: many Indians realized that their military-trained countrymen could best serve India in the long run by learning as much as possible from the British in the arts of war. Humphrey Evans related an account of a discussion between Motilal Nehru and several non-British Indian army officers (among them Thimayya) held around 1929; the elder Nehru urged the officers to remain loyal to the British until the day of Independence came. Undoubtedly the same logic held during the war for it appeared most likely that the British, not the Japanese, would grant Independence.[14]

Another set of cross pressures is related to this last point: from the position of a professional soldier, there existed several military reasons for and against sympathy with the INA. One important factor that probably operated against such sympathy was the fact that all officers joining the INA had broken their oath of loyalty to the Crown and to the viceroy, and the breaking of such oaths by a soldier cannot be regarded lightly. We have the testimony of those that did join the INA that breaking the oath of loyalty was not readily done. Another such factor was that as the war progressed, it became apparent that, while the battles might continue, Japan could not successfully invade India; thus joining its side had proved to be a strategic error on the part of the INA officers, however appealing its chances might have seemed when Singapore fell.

A final factor that is more complex than either of the above, and that probably operated powerfully during the INA trials, was the problem of promotion policy. As long as the British retained control over the Indian army, there was little doubt as to where loyalty should be directed and what kinds of loyalty were rewarded with promotion (along, of course, with factors of skill and talent). But, when the Indian nationalist movement defended the INA as patriots and true loyalists, how did the Indian members of the Indian army react? There was undoubtedly great fear that not only would the INA officers be let off lightly and perhaps rejoin the ranks of the Indian army but also that they would be favored over those who remained loyal to the British, should a virulently nationalist policy be followed by a free India in her military promotion policy. By and large, of course, the fears of Indian officers with regard to their professional future did not materialize, for the problem was clearly recognized by their British superiors and no wholesale reinstatement of INA officer personnel was carried out, by either the British or the new Indian government.

The above cross pressures on Indian officers in the Indian army produced little or no change in actual behavior toward either British superiors or the Japanese enemy but did result in an undercurrent of misgiving about fighting those who had recently been close comrades, particularly when only chance had dictated which particular units fell into Japanese hands. The precise extent of any misgivings during the war and of any fear of reinstatement of the INA after the war must remain conjectural because it is not the kind of subject that was freely discussed publicly by either the British or the Indians involved. For our purposes it suffices to say that neither qualms over opposing the INA nor fear of its reinstatement reached a critical stage; this aspect of the INA's impact on India was handled adroitly enough by both the British and Indians responsible so that an open conflict was avoided.

The INA and the Politicians

Despite their vigorous defense of the INA at the end of the war, an undercurrent of doubt existed among Indian nationalist leaders, particularly Congress, about the meaning of the INA viewed in both the Indian and international context. Here we may first briefly examine some of the non-Congress Indian views toward Bose and the INA and then turn to the attitude of two of the most influential Indian figures, Nehru and Gandhi.[15]

The Indian communists' position is the easiest of all to outline: they were completely opposed to Bose and his army, just as they supported the British war effort when it became clear where the Soviet Union's interests lay. Despite their extremist ideological affinity (or perhaps because of it), the communists called Bose a "lackey," a fascist tool, and applied other stock accusations. Their attacks on Bose were later turned against them by such opponents as the Society for Defence of Freedom in Asia, which has reprinted communist wartime attacks on Bose.[16] The CPI policy toward Bose and the Forward Bloc had to make several twists and turns as the "line" altered through the years. The British communist "adviser" to the Indian communists, R. Palme Dutt, argued that against a free India, Bose's "hypocritical pretense" would have no effect but, against a subject India, it did have some influence.[17] Dutt was thus able to recognize a fact of Indian politics: that Bose and the INA had had an enormous impact on the Indian people during and after the war (particularly during the INA officers' trial); yet he could still class Bose with the Axis powers. While his treatment of Bose was undoubtedly convincing to most CPI members, the vast number of Indians thought otherwise.

The Muslim League varied in its attitude toward the INA. At first it remained aloof from expressing the general support given it by other nationalists. Later however, when it became apparent that the INA trials were to become an important issue in the jockeying between the British and the nationalists, the League joined with Congress in a wholehearted defense of the INA. In coming to the defense of the INA, the League shared in the popular acclaim given to INA defenders and obtained another lever of negotiation to use against both Congress and the British.

The view held by the socialists, or at least by one of their most prominent leaders, Jayaprakash Narayan, was that Bose's motives and those of the INA were the highest possible: they wanted to free India of British control. Narayan himself was working underground during the war toward this end, as were many socialists, but he nevertheless expressed grave doubts over certain practical aspects of the INA movement. He was not at all impressed by the size of the INA or by its efficacy as a fighting force. If India were to be invaded, Narayan wrote, it would be by the Japanese, and he was not impressed by their treatment of the Burmese.[18] Citing Machiavelli and Kautilya, Narayan cautioned Bose against seeking help from a stronger ally in his otherwise praiseworthy undertaking; he concluded that India must be strong enough to free itself from British control, that external aid would only perpetuate India's subjugation.[19]

Most Congress members agreed with the general argument put forward by Narayan. They shared Nehru's 1946 evaluation that "the men and women, who had enrolled themselves in this Army and worked under Shri Subhas Chandra Bose's guidance, had done so because of their passionate desire to serve the cause of Indian freedom," even though they may not have been sure "as to how far the formation and activities of this Army had been justified, keeping in view the wider scheme of things and the implications of the World War."[20] Congress leaders put forward the argument that worthwhile people should not be punished because of their INA activities; their motives had been good, if their aims perhaps misguided, and India in any case needed their help.[21] Nehru did yield to the British, particularly Auchinleck, on the question of treatment of those accused of specific brutalities and war crimes—a move that did not please extremist nationalists, particularly the Bengalis, where pro-INA sentiment was extremely strong.

The entire INA affair, under Bose's leadership, raised a direct challenge to Gandhi and those of his nonviolent persuasion. The way in which Gandhi reacted to this challenge is most revealing, and it was not at all a "pure" or consistent reaction, particularly during the early years of the war. Azad records that Gandhi became more and more doubtful about an Allied victory during the war and that Bose's dramatic escape to Germany "had made a great impression on Gandhiji. He had not formerly approved many of Bose's actions, but now I found a change in his outlook. Many of his remarks convinced me that he admired the courage and resourcefulness

Subhas Bose had displayed in making his escape from India. His admiration for Subhas Bose unconsciously colored his view about the whole war situation."[22] Azad claimed that this admiration was one factor that affected Gandhi's position during discussions with the Cripps Mission. At the time Cripps arrived, a report was circulated of Bose's death in an air crash; the message of condolence sent by Gandhi to Bose's mother was in such glowing terms that Cripps complained to Azad that he had not expected a man like Gandhi to speak that way about Bose.[23]

When the war ended, and Bose's death was fairly certain (rumors that he is still alive have circulated throughout India periodically), Gandhi drew the lessons from the INA both in articles in Harijan and in interviews with ex-INA officers.

Like the socialists and most of Congress (as well as most of India), Gandhi praised both the INA and Bose for their patriotism and for demonstrating lessons of "self-sacrifice, unity irrespective of class and community, and discipline."[24] But these virtues must be employed in the service of nonviolence, not the bearing of arms, and Gandhi highly praised the declaration of Shah Nawaz Khan that he was going to be a soldier of nonviolence in Congress ranks.[25] He challenged the INA to replace their martial attitude of violence for a more difficult one of martial nonviolence; he asked them to take to ahimsa as had the Pathan Badshah Khan. Gandhi said this did not mean yielding to the Japanese had they invaded India, and in fact he outlined his own plan for dealing with such an eventuality.[26]

Gandhi supported the defense of the INA officers by Congress, praising their courage but not their violent means. He in fact drafted the Congress Working Committee Resolution issued to reaffirm the Congress creed of nonviolence; that part of the December 1945 Resolution that deals with the INA indicates clearly an attempt to capitalize on the INA's popularity without associating Congress with its actions:

> Whilst the Congress must feel proud of the sacrifice and discipline, patriotism, bravery and the spirit of unity displayed by the Azad Hind Fouz, organized as an independent force in the foreign countries under unprecedented conditions by Shri Subhas Chandra Bose, and whilst it is right and proper for the Congress to defend the members of that body, now undergoing trial, and also to aid its sufferers, the Congressmen must not forget that this support and sympathy do not mean that the Congress has in any way deviated

from its policy of attaining independence by peaceful and legitimate means.[27]

Throughout the reactions of almost all nationalists to the INA affair runs a sense of doubt of the possible results of allying with the enemy of the enemy; yet when the trials began, Congress, the League, and many communal groups came to the INA officers' defense. Many reasons for this have been given already: there was a desire to protect many able men from undue penalties; many of the INA had had genuinely patriotic motives; and the INA had caught the imagination of great numbers of Indians and it was politically expedient to defend it. Another explanation may be offered, which probably accounts more for the fervor of the defense of the INA than any other single factor: to almost all but the communists, the INA symbolized a united India struggling against British colonialism; it was the first truly cross-communal, united nationalist movement to gain prominence, even though it would have been an impossibility without Axis aid. That this unity should have arisen from the Indian army only added to its interest for the Indian people because the army had been the one group most sheltered by the British from nationalist sentiments; the INA seemed to prove the British wrong when they said India was not really a nation and Indians could not work together. That the unity of the INA had been a major theme in Subhas Bose's propaganda war against the British does not seem to have been recognized by the British when they made the major blunder of putting a Muslim, Sikh, and a Hindu on trial together in the Red Fort. But to many Indians the INA, not the Indian army, was the true object of devotion. As K. M. Panikkar notes, it was not until the Indian army's swift and decisive action in Kashmir that it was generally venerated and vindicated of British leanings.[28]

In summary, it seems ironic but accurate to say that the INA was easier to defend with Subhas Bose dead than with him alive. He had been a genuine threat to Congress leadership before the war and had attracted a large Sikh and Muslim following during the war. But dead, he could be interpreted and used to suit the nationalists' purposes.

Political Implications

The matters discussed in this article raise questions that cover a broad area ranging from Gandhian speculations on the use of force to the dynamic personality of Subhas Bose. These concluding pages focus on only one relatively small area of interest, the impact of the INA episode on postwar civil–military relations in India.

In the period in which the INA was recruited, fought, and collapsed, three major models of the proper relationship between the civilian and military components of a free India vied for attention and adoption. One of these departed with the British.[29] In the first flush of national Independence it was hardly a tenable political position to urge the maintenance of the British connection on anything but a basis of national equality. Once those military men such as Tuker had departed from India, no important group was left that wished to see a military relationship between India and Britain maintaining intact the former intimate connection between the armies, and through them, the ultimate basis of power.

A second model foresaw the military of a free India carrying on in the pattern of the English-speaking democracies: its officer corps would be a professional body with no explicit political ideology, or at least no ideology in severe conflict with a democracy, and would be kept out of domestic politics. Adoption of this model would involve the maintenance of a strong sense of duty and honor in the military as well as the retention of traditions and customs peculiar to the military; these are steps that help ensure attention to preparedness, not politics, as the military's first objective.

Three important groups supported this model, albeit for divergent reasons. The responsible British military and (especially) civilian leadership, the overwhelming number of Indian officers of the services who had been recruited in the prewar period (and who were just reaching positions of high command and became the leaders of the Pakistan and Indian armies), and the dominant elements in the nationalist movement—all were able to agree on the model and on the steps necessary to ensure its success. While the British may have been committed to transplanting their own system, the Indian military to the maintenance of their own status and professional futures, and the Congress Party to the responsibilities of national leadership (and hence standing in need of the skills of the military), these divergent objectives were complementary in their implications in the area of civil–military relations. It was nevertheless an act of great political skill that smoothed over the conflicts in their positions that were raised by the INA affair.

The final model is based on the premise opposite to that of democratic civil–military relations as known in the English-speaking democracies:

the military is regarded as the center (or one of the main centers) of politics in the state. In the first variation on this model, it is the army that embodies the main values of the state, and the latter exists to serve the former, through which it in turn is glorified. The second variation, derived not from Prussian militarism but from Nazi and Soviet practice and theory, regards the military as the instrument of the dominant political movement, although no less politicized than in the former variation. In the wartime and postwar period, several plans for a "peoples' army"—for a military truly "representative" of the nation, for a military as the focus of national attention, or as the servant of totalitarian ideology—were put forward.[30]

Bose's remarkable political philosophy and political activities enabled his image to be cherished by extremists of both left and right in India, and the memory of the INA to be equally venerated by them.[31] He constantly and consciously borrowed from both Nazi and communist ideology, sensing no contradiction and displaying a brilliant talent for buttressing his own activist and authoritarian inclinations. For example, in the period after his dramatic escape from India, he demonstrated his doctrinal autonomy by seeking aid from both the Soviet Union and the Axis powers.

The demise of the man and the decline of the movement made the task of those who envisioned a pattern of civil–military relations along the second model a great deal easier but foreshadowed several problems in this area of politics.

What are the implications for contemporary civil–military relations in India that can be drawn from these models and particularly from the fate of the INA example? These are best divided into two broad areas of importance: the impact of Bose and the INA movement on postwar Indian military and political elites and the net impact on the viability of the present Indian political system.

In the realm of political parties and movements, Bose's supporters have made little progress. The demise and splintering of the Forward Bloc, the pre-INA movement in which Bose attempted to unite leftist opposition to Congress, has been traced elsewhere.[32] It need only be noted that the Boseists remain a regional force at best in Indian politics, lacking above all the leadership of a figure of Bose's stature, for without this they are neither ideologically nor organizationally powerful enough to expand their influence beyond West Bengal, and they are hardly thriving even there. On occasion the days of past glory are revived, as when Bose's daughter recently visited India, or when there is a notable commemoration of Bose, but the strength of the image is weakening as Bose joins the pantheon of departed Indian nationalist heroes. Had he lived, and maintained his position as one of the two serious alternatives to Nehru's leadership, there is little doubt that a serious schism would have been created, with extremists rallying under Bose's unquestionably effective leadership. In view of Bose's own stated philosophy, it seems probable that at the minimum Bose and Nehru would have split politely. The two had little in common other than a desire to get rid of the British and possession of widespread personal followings. One need only read the accounts of the resignation of Bose from the Congress presidency in 1939 to realize the depth of the ideological split between Bose and either Nehru or Gandhi.[33]

As for its influence on the armed services of India, particularly on the theories of professionalization and political involvement that dominate the services, the INA affair has had little lasting impact beyond the initial one described earlier. The Indian armed services are dominated by officers trained in the British tradition of high professionalization and low politicization, but this is hardly due alone to the exclusion of the INA from the Indian army in 1946. The momentous events of recent months have profoundly altered the composition of the personnel of the upper leadership of the military, and in any case, a whole new generation of military leadership has been trained within India.

The effect of the INA episode on the political involvement and political attitudes of the younger members of the officer corps is impossible to calculate precisely. Those who follow the tradition of the "Thimayya school" will regard the INA leaders as misguided patriots who betrayed their oaths to the Crown. Others, less imbued with the notion of a strictly nonpolitical professional officer corps, may view the INA more leniently and reinforce their own attitudes by emphasizing more favorable aspects of the INA officers' dilemma. In either case the memory of the INA will serve as a contributory factor in the complex equation of professionalization and political attitudes; as time passes and the memory of the event becomes dimmer, the actions and the fate of the INA will probably join that of Bose in the ever-renewed struggles for power within the Indian political system.

On the broader problem of the meaning of the INA episode for India's political stability and continuing democratic government, two tentative conclusions may be advanced.

First, when assessing the impact of such a military organization on a democratic civil–military relationship, a multivariate analysis is necessary to give the military organization its true place in the civil–military equation. Just as important as an obedient military is to the maintenance of the liberal democratic model of civil–military relations is the existence of a competent, respected, and democratically committed political elite; the mere repetition of the slogan "civilian control" is not enough to guarantee its existence: that the civilian leadership must demonstrate its capability to rule is no less important than that it maintain the tradition of apolitical professionalism in the military. India's success in maintaining democratic rule, while its neighbors (among so many others) have failed, is due to no single factor alone, such as obliterating the INA, but to relative success in several factors in the civilian–military relationship.

A second and equally important conclusion is that the INA episode was in many respects symptomatic of the difficulties in making a democratic system work in a newly independent country, and that recurrences of a proto-military extremist movement are to be expected as a consequence of some kinds of disturbances of the Indian political system.

While Bose's INA movement may be politically dead—except in rhetorical reminiscences—it may well serve as the prototype for future movements that follow the third model of civil–military relations, especially those that may be military oriented and not party oriented. Such movements might share the following features with the INA movement. First, they may arise, or become mass movements, in time of severe military crisis, threatening the most essential base of national power and challenging the resources and popularity of a civilian regime in a way in which no domestic crisis could. Also, in time of military crisis, the recruitment and control of masses of individuals for military purposes may become a task beyond the capabilities of the existing governmental machinery, opening up the way for regional or fractional military forces beyond the effective control of the central civilian leadership (just as Bose became a threat only when he was granted access to captured Indian troops). Second, such movements may share with Bose's movement an attraction to groups of the Far Left and Far Right, uniting them in an appeal based on violence, quick action, and disciplined dedication to a national cause. Bose demonstrated that doctrinal purity is not a precondition for popularity in Indian politics (and may become a handicap) when a leader has a clear-cut popular goal and demonstrates a willingness to act. Third, it is conceivable that future proto-totalitarian movements in India will emulate Bose in appealing for aid and help from a foreign power while posing as an independent indigenous nationalist movement. Bose's opportunity for powerful support came from the ambiguous position of the nationalist movement with regard to the prosecution of World War II: he effectively emphasized anti-British sentiment among the nationalists while playing down the dangers of Axis influence. Some signs exist that this strategy is being employed in India today by the Left and the Right in the context of the Cold War. Finally, such movements may (perhaps they must) have as a focus of attention a leader of unimpeachable patriotism and charismatic popularity, serving the same function as Bose in the INA.

Several movements, or followings of prominent individuals, share some or all of the above characteristics. Some are independent organizations with a militarist orientation, such as the Rashtriya Swayam Sevak Sangh;[34] some are followers of individuals such as V. K. Krishna Menon (former minister of defense) and Biju Patnaik (former chief minister of Orissa and an adviser to Prime Minister Nehru on military affairs).[35] Given a continued precarious military position, the weakening of Nehru's authority (or his departure from active politics), such groups as these might expand their contacts within an already divided military and base their claim to more power on the argument of special expertise in the military-political field. Following the pattern of Bose, they might at the same time find it expedient to suppress or moderate their ideological appeal for the sake of attracting a following on the basis of national unity.

Among students and observers of Indian politics, several forms of factional or group government have been regarded as the most likely alternatives to liberal democracy. Regional breakaway, communist takeover, and even the military coup have been considered as among the more serious threats to democracy, each of them leading to bitter struggles along geographical or ideological lines. If the analysis of Bose's popularity in this article has been correct, a profound threat to democracy in India could arise as much from too much unity as from too little; under the pretext of a national front, or as the incarnation of the national will, a movement following the Bose–INA prototype might successfully dismantle India's substantial democratic structure, in the name of the nation, and possibly in the name of democracy itself.

1969

FIVE

The Untouchable Soldier

Caste, Politics, and the Indian Army

Military establishments are omnipresent if not everywhere omnipotent. While these costly bureaucracies are the bane of finance ministers around the world, they do provide an important opportunity for comparative analysis.[1] This paper examines a military system—the Indian one—through time, and attempts to demonstrate the changing relationship of that system to Indian politics and society in general, and to the low-caste communities of India in particular. I select the low-caste untouchables because they represent an extreme challenge to the integrative capacity of both political and social systems, and because they have recently been the subject of intensive political and academic concern.[2]

An examination of the military draws our attention to several questions pertaining to democratic ideology. Every democratic system invokes one or more theories governing the relationship between army and society. At the one extreme, democratic equalitarianism implies that each individual in society is equally liable to military service: the levee en masse during wartime, universal conscription during peacetime. Citizenship is not complete without at least the possibility of such service, and the systematic exclusion (or inclusion) of any particular group implies a warping of the democratic ideal. At the other extreme lies a doctrine of expediency and efficiency: those who are most willing or best qualified to serve should be called to the colors; all others are a needless drag on the efficiency of the military.

Military organization also has important social implications. The military can be viewed alternatively as a national school or as a form of punishment: military service may be praised as a worthwhile, status-acquiring task or regarded as a useless waste of time that is dangerously militarizing the youth of the nation. The composition of the military may or may not be held up as a model for society: the "military virtues" are as often praised as they are damned.

In societies with caste or caste-like social systems, the problem of the social implications of military organization becomes even more complex. Whether the society is highly stratified horizontally, or vertically divided, or both as in the caste system, the problem remains: Should the military mirror this caste system or attempt to change it? How appropriate is the military as a channel for social mobility and advancement for the most depressed groups within a society? What cultural or traditional barriers exist to the use of the military as such an instrument of change? The rest of this paper examines these and related problems as they have appeared in India. After noting something of the history of the untouchable soldier, we turn to several variables that seem to be particularly relevant for an understanding of the role of the untouchable in the military, and concurrently attempt to place the Indian case in its comparative and cross-national context.

When political systems are engaged in warfare, they tend to draw more heavily from low classes and low castes for manpower according to the intensity and duration of conflict.[3] War may provide a great, albeit unintended, opportunity for social mobility for such groups, although with the onset of peace such opportunities rapidly fade away. This cyclical pattern characterized recruitment in India both before and after the creation of the modern Indian army. Pre-British peacetime Indian military establishments were dominated by aristocratic warrior elites; when a campaign was undertaken, the peasantry volunteered or was conscripted for the duration of the conflict only. They returned to their peacetime occupation when hostilities were terminated.[4]

When the European powers arrived in India they imitated this indigenous pattern of recruitment. Relatively weak and powerless, and desperate for manpower, they took into their armies any Indian who was willing to serve. At times their ranks included large numbers of tribals and untouchables. Only when the sepoy system was introduced in the eighteenth century was there any attempt to regulate the kinds of Indians taken into the military.[5] Once this occurred, the numbers of low castes and classes dropped, for several reasons. First, the benefits of associating with the British became more obvious to many high castes with military traditions, and they volunteered for service in increasing numbers. Also, it was easy to permit those men actually serving to recruit relatives and friends, making the units more homogeneous. Finally, the British themselves gradually adjusted to the caste system and identified more and more with the higher strata of Indian society. This was especially true in Bengal, where one British observer saw the recruiting officers gradually confine their choice to the "largest, handsomest, and cleverest looking men, who are undoubtedly the high castes."[6]

Although many different low castes and tribes saw military service the years before the 1857 Mutiny, the Mahars of western India were probably the most heavily recruited. In Madras all "pariahs and Christians" constituted no more than 5 percent of the army, and in only a few units did the percentage of these groups rise to 10 percent between 1780 and 1880.[7] In Bengal a few low castes constituted a similar percentage of the presidential army, although Chamar leaders today claim that the figure was significant. But the Mahars numbered between a quarter or a fifth of those units in which they were recruited and perhaps a sixth of the entire Bombay army.[8]

The 1857 Mutiny led to a major reorganization of the Bengal army and the consequent termination of Chamar recruitment. They were in effect replaced by another untouchable caste, the Mazbhi Sikhs, a change that reflected the growing Punjabization of the Indian army.[9] The Mazbhis were Chuhras (a sweeper caste) who had converted to Sikhism following a dramatic and historic event in Sikh history.[10] The Mazbhis were patronized by Ranjit Singh, who tried to recruit them for the Khalsa army. High-caste Sikh communities objected to their integration into the Khalsa and they were formed into separate companies, one attached to each high-caste battalion.

After the defeat of the Khalsa, the Mazbhis saw no military service for several years. They had strong caste traditions of violence and aggressiveness and were classed as a criminal caste by the British. Eventually, the Dogra Maharaja of Kashmir, Gulab Singh, recruited them as pioneer troops for his own army. Pioneers were infantry trained for road, canal, and construction tasks; when attacked they could defend themselves, unlike ordinary laborers. In addition, these tough untouchable Sikhs were useful to the Maharaja for "overseeing his Mohamadan subjects."[11]

When the mutiny broke out, the Mazbhis were drawn into the British Indian army and formed the First Pioneer Sikh Regiment. According to the unit biographer, the Mazbhis were intended to provide a balance for high-caste Bengal Army sepoys, then in open revolt.[12] They were soon put to good use: marched to Delhi, they were instrumental in breaking the resistance of the mutineers. A second regiment was raised in 1858 by John Lawrence, and a third followed shortly. The three Pioneer units saw extremely varied service; at one time or another they were employed in China, Africa, Europe, and the Middle East. By the 1870s there was ample evidence to indicate that caste was not a vital determinant of a man's fighting ability. Untouchable caste units, when properly led, had given a good account of themselves for more than a hundred years. Despite the generally favorable commentary on their quality, low-caste units were gradually reduced in size and number between 1870 and 1914–18.[13] They (and other important classes of Indians) were the unwilling victims of the theory of the "martial races."

Martial Races

There were at least three different views of the "martial races" theory: a military, a racist, and an environmental (climatic) perspective. In India all three were employed as criteria by which various classes were evaluated for purposes of recruitment to the Indian army. In addition, these theories were used to justify new and rationalize old shifts in the recruiting base. The first such shift came immediately after the 1857 Mutiny, with the addition of large numbers of Jats, Gurkhas, Sikhs, and Pathans to the Bengal army. These groups were found to be trustworthy in quelling other military classes in revolt, and were also tough and hardened by recent military experience. Their numbers in the Bengal army grew rapidly, and they became more "popular" among British recruiting officers of the Bombay and even the Madras armies. Ultimately, Bombay recruited heavily from these classes and the size of the Madras Presidency Army gradually shrank. This shift was hastened by the increase in military activity in the northwest, and later by the growing threat of Russian hostility, and a corresponding decline of military activity in the southern, western, and eastern areas of India.

Thus, both region and caste were involved in the shift in the military's recruiting base. The first two theories noted above involved regional differences; the third involved caste. Although only the racial theory of recruitment is theoretically relevant to untouchability, untouchables were affected by the popularity of the first two theories, as well.

The military view of the martial races theory attempted to judge the reliability and ability of different military classes according to their recent combat experience. A central figure in the development of this approach and in the termination of low-caste recruitment was Lord Roberts, who served as commander in chief, Indian army, from 1885 to 1893. Roberts argued that simple inactivity had lowered the efficiency of many classes of Indians, and that it was useless to recruit them.[14] There was some truth to the argument, for many south Indian military classes had not seen battle for years; however, there was as much a decline in the quality of the British officers commanding these troops as in the troops themselves, and Roberts's theory was designed in part to get rid of these incompetent officers.[15]

Unsurprisingly (in the late nineteenth century), pure racist theories of military competence were also invoked. Some classes came to be regarded as inherently unfit for military service, just as others were natural soldiers. A typical view was that untouchables were by birth and varna (a caste category) inherently unmilitary and therefore were of little use to the British and of insignificant threat to the enemy. Why bother to recruit the "dhobi [an untouchable washerman caste] battalions," one series of articles in the Pioneer argued, if they could not be trusted against the formidable Pathans?[16] Untouchables were docile creatures, perhaps suitable for internal guard duty or labor battalions, but otherwise useless as soldiers. As the memory of the mutiny faded, so did the obsessions with trustworthiness and the need for a balance of both caste and region within the military. A final view of the martial races theory, emphasizing climate, was developed later in the century, although traces of it had always been present. One commander in chief of the Indian army, General Sir O'Moore Creagh, held that:

> In the hot, flat regions . . . of India . . . there is no winter cold. In the hot regions are found races, timid both by religion and habit,

> service to their superiors, but tyrannical to their inferiors, and quite unwarlike. In other parts . . . where the winter is cold, the warlike minority is to be found, but its component peoples vary greatly in military virtue. Nowhere, however, are they equal in that respect to Europeans or Japanese.[17]

Creagh also thought it absurd that Indians would ever become seafarers since they were innately incapable of manning ships; he either ignored or was ignorant of the long history of Indian naval exploration. The climatic view allowed a twofold rationalization: it explained the recruitment of North rather than South Indians, and it justified the rule of the British who were from an island located in a northern clime.

Both world wars tested these theories of the martial races as guides to the recruitment of adequate numbers of competent troops. In both wars, especially World War II, it was clearly demonstrated that such theories were irrelevant to the actual problems of recruitment, and in fact these two conflicts demonstrated that the martial races theory could retard recruitment efforts.[18]

In both conflicts untouchables were at first greatly underrepresented in the military, but were then hastily recruited to meet enormous manpower deficiencies. This turned out to be an inefficient process for there soon developed a severe shortage of noncommissioned officers and skilled technicians of the required classes.

In 1914–18 the Mahars were once again permitted to enlist in the Indian army. After a brief period under two Madras battalions they were given their own unit, the 111th Mahars, which was disbanded after the war.[19] The Mazbhis were also recruited heavily during World War I but were afterward "retrenched" and gradually reduced in numbers until in 1932 the last unit was disbanded. The men were either prematurely retired or transferred to the new Sapper and Miner units, which were replacing the technologically obsolete pioneers. The unit historian records that Mazbhis were happier in British units—attached to them as drivers—than with other Indian units where they were looked down on regardless of their individual skill.[20]

The greater intensity and scale of combat in World War II had the effect of drawing even large numbers of untouchables into the conflict. More than 10,000 Mahars and 33,000 Mazbhi and Ramdasia Sikhs were taken into the combatant forces. A Chamar Battalion was raised as part of the Second Punjabis. Its officers were at first Punjabis but these were gradually replaced, and in March 1943 the community achieved the independent status of the First Battalion, the Chamar Regiment, and served in Assam and Burma. In addition to these three castes, of course, many other scheduled castes and tribes, as well as "non-martial races," were recruited.[21] Available figures do not indicate the communal breakdown of noncombatants recruited to the army, but a good percentage of the more than 460,000 were scheduled castes because much of this work was menial and manual labor.

Historically, the ebb and flow of untouchables in and out of the Indian army seems to confirm the hypothesis suggested by several scholars: participation in military affairs is closely related to the intensity of warfare.[22] High intensity demands greater numbers, and lower castes eventually get the opportunity to serve in the military that is denied to them during peacetime. My data indicate that this process occurred and reoccurred in India for more than a hundred years.

While further historical research into this or analogous systems might prove fruitful, we are here interested in exploring some of the political, social, and moral implications of a caste-based recruitment system.[23] Data on the numbers of lower-caste individuals in the military do not tell us much about the effect of their presence on either the military or the individuals and groups in question. We therefore shift from a historical perspective to an examination of some of the intervening political and social variables.

The political, economic, and social impact of military service on low-caste groups can be evaluated by examining two complex sets of relationships. The first revolves around the social payoff of military service for low castes. What is the utility of military service to such a group? Why are some groups attracted to the military and others are not? How does the general position of a group in society affect its interest in military service, what social and political benefits may be derived from recruitment, and, above all, how does military service affect the group's drive for status and influence? The second set of relationships are those between the low-caste group and the ongoing organizational format of the military. Different patterns of recruitment have different social, political, and ideological implications. In many ways, the qualitative position of low-caste individuals in a military organization is as important as sheer numbers.

Power and Status

Andre Beteille has argued that in terms of defining their interests and identity, low-status castes are torn between the conflicting demands of power and status. "Considerations of power lead them to define their identity in opposition to the advanced sections of society," while considerations of status prompt the low-status castes to "merge their identity with the higher strata."[24] Such groups have two strategic alternatives: to emulate high-status groups, and perhaps lose group cohesion, or to emphasize cohesion at the cost of acceptance and status. In practice the alternatives are not quite as stark. Mixed strategies are followed in India, and even in their approach to the question of military service low-status castes can and have followed both paths in search of their identity. As I show, under certain circumstances such mixed strategies may be optimum strategies.

On a tactical level military service may yield important material and status benefits for low-caste groups. This is so because of the governmental character of military service as well as because of the nature of the military itself. Employment by the government implies a channel of communication between low-status groups and the central government, perhaps circumventing intermediate levels of authority dominated by antagonistic groups. Governmental service may also carry with it important material benefits, such as regular employment, pensions, insurance, and welfare benefits. If nothing else, such service (and especially military service) may help individuals in their relationships with local authorities, especially the police. This is an especially important consideration in rural India. Even service in a noncombatant, menial labor or a service unit may bring a measure of stability and security to an individual or group hitherto entirely dependent on local higher-status castes. The British established an extensive paramilitary network of district and local officers separate from regular civilian administration that looked after the interests of families with serving members. This program has been continued and extended in independent India.

However, although they are both government agencies, armies are not post offices. The *military* training low-status castes might receive raises important questions concerning the general strategy of low castes in pursuing both status and power. Low-status caste leadership in India is seriously divided on both regional and ideological lines over the desirability of military training.

For any particular group, especially in India, status is largely a function of regional traditions. The Punjabi Sikh community well illustrates the effect of regional exaltation of the military on the aspirations of low-status castes. The bulk of the community are descended from Jat peasants. Sikhism underwent an early transformation from a pacific, devotional sect into a martial religion in large part because of Muslim persecution. The British first fought the Sikhs and then took them into the Indian army in large numbers (and may well have preserved Sikhism in the process). Simultaneously, significant numbers of scheduled castes turned to Sikhism to escape their position in the Hindu community. Many Sikhs, proud of their material accomplishments and martial ideology, actively sought low-caste converts.[25]

As indicated above, the Mazbhi and Ramdasias Sikhs have had a long if tenuous affiliation with the military. As Sikhs they share with their higher-caste coreligionists a militant, equalitarian ideology, as well as an interest in the military. Both of these factors seem to be contributing to a decrease in discrimination against the Mazbhi and Ramdasias communities; upper-caste Sikhs retain a strong respect for military service, even though Jat Sikhs are rapidly diversifying their interests in fields other than the military.[26] Lower-caste groups had always upgraded their occupations on becoming Sikhs, and joining the military is in many cases the supreme proof of their "arrival," at least in the eyes of the more liberal elements of the Jat Sikh community. Indera P. Singh relates a striking example of the consequences of military service: in the village of Daleke the first (and only) Mazbhis to be allowed to use the village temple for a marriage were military men.[27] Daleke illustrates the broadening, educational effect military service can have, especially on those who have served overseas (thirty of the sixty-five villagers who had gone overseas in four decades were military men). A large majority of the recruits to the army from Daleke are now Mazbhis.[28] In another Punjabi village, Jitpur, military service had been confined to Jat Sikhs. After the 1962 Emergency, Ramdasia Sikhs were recruited from the village for the first time. This recruitment was part of a broader trend of untouchables seeking employment outside the traditional village economy, but it was doubly valuable to the Ramdasia Sikhs because of the high esteem of the military among village Jats. The rate of increasing interest in military service as a "blue-collar" pursuit will undoubtedly grow as education spreads and aspirations rise among the low-status Sikhs of Jitpur and other Punjabi villages.

While the military may be a prime objective of such communities as the Mazbhis and Ramdasias Sikhs (and the Mahars of Maharashtra, and to a lesser extent the Chamars of UP), many other low-caste groups have no strong regional military model to emulate. Should they actively pursue an enhanced military role, serious conflicts may be created. Their problem—or rather the problem of their leadership—is to strike a balance between the advantages and disadvantages of military service when there is no serious social recognition of the military as a suitable vehicle for mobility.

The appeal of the military as a vehicle for low-caste social mobility is further complicated by the historical relationship of the Gandhian movement to Harijan uplift.[29] Aside from the philosophical and moral appeal of nonviolence, demands for increased military recruitment and training may heighten fears of a violent revolution. Police and military service provide the kind of military discipline and training in weaponry that low-status castes lack and are unable to get from any other source except militant political and paramilitary associations. Arming low-status castes is a radical step in a system that has traditionally relied on the police and the military for the suppression of social discontent.

In summary, military service can be of considerable importance for a low-caste community. It may change the image of the group, not only in the eyes of others, but among its own members. Pride, self-reliance, and increased cohesion are especially important to untouchables. Not only does military service help to legitimate a claim to higher status; it may carry with it official governmental encouragement or approval.[30] This claim to status is especially important when the military is a highly "visible" and prestigious career in the region of origin of a particular caste. These symbolic rewards are added to the considerable material benefits of military service—training, regular pay, and pension benefits may add up to a significant increase in disposable wealth and assets. For an economically depressed group of low social status, it is difficult to tell whether material or symbolic rewards are more important. Both kinds of rewards will be greatly affected by another variable: the actual distribution and location of members of a group within the military itself.

Representativeness

All military systems can be evaluated in terms of their "representativeness." By *representative* I mean the degree of congruence or "fit" between the broader social system and the military subsystem in terms of the distribution as well as numbers of particular classes of individuals or groups.[31] The two separate variables of general social stratification and military representativeness can be combined to yield four ideal types. One of these, unstratified society and unrepresentative military, is a logical impossibility. Our interest is primarily in social systems that are stratified and served by military systems that are either representative or unrepresentative. In the former case, if low-status groups are recruited to the military, they will be found occupying positions roughly equivalent in status (and perhaps task) to those they occupied in civilian life.

In India low-status groups have always held a disproportionate number of the menial and service jobs in the military, although this disproportion "fits" their traditional and customary occupational patterns.[32] In a "representative" system the number of low-status individuals drops off sharply as one moves up the military hierarchy. Conversely, in a military organization "unrepresentative" of its supporting society, there would be greater numbers of individuals of low-status background in intermediate- and upper-level military positions than appeared in corresponding positions in civilian society.

In addition to horizontal stratification, representativeness also has a vertical dimension. At any given level, there may be a greater or lesser degree of segregation. In the extreme case (approached in the U.S. military during World War II) of perfect representativeness of a segregated society, entire military units composed of low-status individuals will be maintained alongside high-caste units. Individuals performing identical functions—but of different caste or group origin—will then be found in their own segregated units.[33]

Historically, absolute unrepresentativeness of the military—particularly in its vertical dimension—has not necessarily been a high-priority demand of Indian untouchable leadership. Up to a certain level of social and technical modernization, and up to a certain horizontal level of the military hierarchy, segregation may on balance be more attractive than integration for a variety of reasons.

First, the existence of separate, segregated, low-status military units provides an opportunity to develop a group esprit and enhance a group image. Many such groups boast of their superiority, and seek recognition of it:

> The Sikh Light Infantry is a real fighting unit, the Mazbhi Sikhs are a real martial race, the Mahars do not compare with us for

> fighting ability. But we are discriminated against both in and out of the army: there are no Mazbhi generals or even colonels. . . . I would not want the Mazbhi Sikh unit to be broken up, or the Jats mixed in with us or we with the Jats. It is good to have separate units of Scheduled Caste Sikhs together, this way we can show our martial qualities to the Jats and to the rest even better.[34]

Similarly, Mahars claim they are the most "robust, adaptable, intelligent, fighting, brave, virile and leading" untouchable community in India,[35] and Chamars demand the creation of a separate Chamar Regiment.[36] To the leadership of low-status groups symbolic victories in the form of "named" or easily identifiable units may be as important as material gains for the group.

Second, many officers and politicians of all castes feel that the system of separate "caste" units avoids "incidents" and makes it easier to handle both upper-status and lower-status caste soldiers.[37] Scheduled caste politicians have argued that if mixed with high castes, their young jawans (soldiers) would be continually reminded of an inferior status. The strong desire to produce noncommissioned officers from one's own community reflects this fear of discrimination in detail.[38] If, however, a whole community is segregated, this danger is eliminated. While the unit as a whole may be regarded with disdain by other soldiers, individuals within it are more sheltered from abuse.

The notion of a military "representative" of a segregated or stratified society can be challenged from two different directions. First, society itself—or important components of society—may reject the notion of the military only *matching* or reflecting the stratifications of an inequalitarian society. The proposal that the military be unrepresentative of society as it is, but an image of society as it should be is a familiar one.

The struggles to desegregate a caste-based system—the American—in effect to make it unrepresentative of American society as it actually is and to make it representative of what, in the eyes of many Americans, America should be, are well documented.[39] Analogous efforts regarding the Indian military establishment are less well known, even within India and inside the military. In two services the question of "fit" does not immediately arise: the air force and the Indian navy have always chosen recruits largely on the basis of aptitude. Because of the technical requirements of both services, they tend to draw more heavily from communities with relatively advanced socioeconomic levels and from urban India, especially Bombay in the case of the navy. The army constitutes the bulk of the military, however, and it has always been more or less segregated by caste and community. Exceptions to this rule have been the various technical branches of the army. Even in the infantry, the heart of the establishment, there have been important exceptions to the caste principle. Certain units recruit on a regional basis; they may include untouchables as well as high-caste individuals from a particular region.[40] One unit, the Mahars, bears the name of a low-status group but recruits from other castes, as well.[41]

Another important exception to the caste principle is (or, rather, was) the Presidential Guards. As reported by one of their officers, these select units deliberately mixed individuals and castes down to the squad/platoon level, so that Sikhs, Jats, Gurkhas, Muslims, scheduled castes, Christians, and tribals might be found fighting, dining, and sleeping as a group.[42] Various informants indicate that the experiment has been modified after the 1962 Emergency. The system was harshly criticized by some officers and has not found any important political defenders. As noted above, politicians interested in scheduled caste recruitment seek separate, named units, rather than the anonymity of an integrated force, and they fear the possibility of being submerged among higher castes. They remain reluctant to abandon their reliance on government assistance, perhaps fearing the outcome of open competition.[43] A second flaw in the principle of a military that is representative of a stratified society derives from certain modern military practices. A rationally organized military hierarchy chooses its members on the basis of open competition: it seeks to fit the best man to the job regardless of social origin. The efficient application of this principle may make it more difficult for low-status groups to gain or even retain a foothold in certain military systems (especially those undergoing technological modernization) or in particularly technical sectors of those systems. As noted above, low classes and castes are likely to be underrepresented in the higher military grades, especially in the officer corps, and military systems are often thus "representative" of stratified societies. Historically, the officer corps were closed to lower classes and castes in preindustrial societies with representative military systems, and officers were drawn from aristocratic or neo-aristocratic sectors of society. While notions of noblesse oblige still find some echo in remote corners of the Indian military, the army is overwhelmingly "rationalized" in its rank and promotion structure, even though it retains caste-based units. Such rationalization is a powerful force against large segregated units, such as the all-Negro divisions of World War II. If a caste unit is large enough so that an officer spends most of his career in it, he will be ill equipped for higher command; his range of roles and experience will be too limited for complete professional development.

Paradoxically, insofar as the rationalization of military hierarchies has weakened the principle of vertical segregation and removed many barriers to the horizontal mobility of individuals from lower-caste backgrounds, the parallel development of increasingly sophisticated technologies may well warp the actual pattern of recruitment of low castes so that the final structure of the military remains relatively representative. It is often more efficient to recruit a civilian with a high educational level than to train and educate a total illiterate. Thus, when technical services and technically oriented armies choose their recruits on universalistic criteria of ability and education, there is likely to be a serious underrepresentation of low-status castes in the most "modern" branches and the officer corps because of their poorer opportunities for education.[44] The process seems well advanced in the American military establishment; the lower level of military technology in India would make it possible to draw from a wider range of society, were it not for the relatively lower levels of literacy and education. Indian technical units (engineers, signals, and so on) tend to draw heavily from regions of India with limited "martial" traditions but with important traditions of learning and literacy, such as Bengal and Madras. To compensate for the generally low level of literacy and education, the Indian army has an extraordinarily long period of basic training even for its infantry recruits (forty-two weeks), which includes a compulsory literacy program.

In summary, the role played by untouchables in the Indian military establishment seems to be undergoing a complex, gradual transformation. Political pressure, social change, technological development, and the legacy of the Indian military establishment itself all influence the pattern of recruitment of untouchables, their place in the military, and, ultimately, the impact of recruitment on the untouchable communities themselves. These pressures for change (or for maintenance of the status quo) do not all operate in the same direction: within the military quite "modern" and quite "traditional" modes of organization are found adjacent to one another, vertically, and horizontally. In a developmental sense the coexistence of modern and traditional modes indicate that the military is truly "representative" of an Indian society that is undergoing rapid technological, social, and political change. As within the society, one finds institutionalized within the military remnants of traditional patterns of social relationships as well as patterns based on modern theories of organization.

One must not overestimate either the prevalence of "modernity" within the military, or the contradiction between modern and traditional modes of organization. Marion Levy Jr., M. N. Srinivas, and others have argued that the military is a powerful force for Westernization or modernization; Levy asserts that it may be the most important such force.[45] The Indian case, however, would seem to indicate that in its relationship to society the military is not necessarily a consistent force for social change. Military organizations seem to be very "modern" at least in their external appearance, and—as in India—become increasingly rationalized when they adapt to new technologies. However, as they do this their connection with society is not necessarily made firmer. We must differentiate a purely military output from an impact on the ideas and attitudes of individuals who serve in the military, or any civic action (nation-building) tasks the military undertakes.

The military may draw *from* society, but it may contribute little *to* it in terms of ideological or material change. It is significant that historically the Indian army has paid little attention to civic action programs. It has often engaged in short-term emergency relief or police actions but strenuously resists a more permanent entanglement. There is a strong tie between the military and those regions that contribute large numbers of soldiers, but this is justified on military, not social, grounds. This aloofness may yet change if the army continues to broaden its base of officer recruitment and more politically active and socially conscious segments of Indian society contribute more heavily to the officer corps.

Even if this happens, there may still be no significant erosion of caste as the dominant criteria for recruitment and as an organizing principle for infantry units. There is great support for and belief in caste for this purpose among "modern" officers, let alone those drawn from conservative or landed aristocratic families.[46] Unlike the American military, where caste based (all-Negro) units were ideologically resented and militarily inefficient, the caste principle finds general acceptance within India. Units based on caste hold constant a large number of nonmilitary variables: region, language, religion, sect, and status. If there is any trade-off between effort expended on learning new military skills and effort devoted to adjusting to radically new social situations, then at least in the Indian context caste-based units are militarily efficient. They will probably remain so until general social disapproval of caste as an organizing principle becomes significantly greater, or until a rapid rise in the technological sophistication of the army requires higher educational levels for recruits. Both developments seem unlikely in the next decade.

Conclusion

I conclude by hypothesizing a model or paradigm to describe the process involved in the social mobilization of low castes as this is related to the military. Although abstracted from the Indian case study, such a model might be used to describe other caste-based social systems.

Stage One

In a premodern, preindustrial system, the structure of the military reflects the structure of an inequalitarian or caste-based system: it is "representative." The military is less likely to be organized for the functional purpose of victory than the functional purpose of mirroring, complementing, or elaborating the status system of society. Low-status castes find a place in the military corresponding to their inferior position in society, although the conditions of service may be somewhat better in the military, and the idea of promotion or reward on the basis of performance and skill may trickle down to the lower reaches of the hierarchy. Still, except in times of actual warfare (when low-caste military leaders may radically change their position in society through energetic military action), the military provides little opportunity for either political power or social mobility for low castes.

Stage Two

Given a slight increase in resources available for political action, and the desire for mobility and increased status, low-status groups may enter a stage of "Kshatriyazation." They emulate indigenous martial traditions, and put forth a claim for separate but equal status within the military establishment. They are especially likely to turn to the military for assistance in the drive for status if there are highly visible regional martial traditions.

If the low-status group seeks entry into a military system undergoing modernization, it must conform with contemporary organizational doctrine. If the military is concerned with system output—military success—the group must somehow show that it is especially well qualified to contribute to that success. If scientific manpower evaluation is imperfect or does not exist, then various pseudo-rational criteria will be developed to judge the competence of ethnic and caste sub-groups in society; low-status castes may thus find themselves creating or reviving such themes as the martial races theory.

Stage Three

A further transformation of a military organization is likely to occur when the idea of individual equality of opportunity, of promotion by ability, is introduced. Whether the idea is introduced because of pressure from society or because of the military's own search for more modern theories of organization, it is likely to be a far-reaching event. Generally, notions of individuals' achievements are most likely to be introduced in the officer corps, and even then within the technical branches. As the military itself becomes more technologically oriented, universalistic criteria will spread to other branches and to lower ranks. The related developments of increasing equalitarianism and more sophisticated technologies may create a trap for low castes. Although racial or status-based criteria may be eliminated, educational requirements may rise faster than the rate of social development of low-status groups. Any system at this point of development faces some difficult choices between important values. Recruitment solely on the basis of ability and military cost-effectiveness is likely to lead to an underrepresentation of low castes or to their virtual segregation into nontechnical services and branches, including the infantry. The notion of compensatory favoritism has been introduced in India (although not in the military) to help "make up" low-caste deficiencies, but this reverse discrimination may conflict with equalitarian theory. The conflict, fundamentally, is between two theories of equality: that of the group and that of the individual.

Stage Four

Once its manpower problems are solved, or at least brought under control, the military may be asked to serve other, broader, values than its own operational efficiency. First a mirror of society, then a mirror image of other "modern" armies, it may ultimately be requested or required to act as an agent of social change—an explicit force for social mobilization and modernization. In only a few nations has the military undertaken such a challenging task. Israel is the most striking example. Turkey has had such programs, the American military has been under pressure to serve as a national school, and very infrequently the Indian military has made gestures in this direction. While the idea of using the military as an instrument of social change may appeal to politicians eager to get full value for their defense expenditures, it holds little attraction for most professional soldiers. Left to itself, the military in most nations will recruit the cheapest, most available, and most willing soldiers, regardless of social payoff. But, in a sense, not utilizing the military for nonmilitary objectives is a waste of resources. By selective recruitment (or at least a quota system involving reserved places—a principle already embodied into the Indian constitution) and through the medium of the total military environment, it may be possible to make an impact on even hard-core areas of social and economic impoverishment.

SIX

The Military in Indira Gandhi's India

The Indian military played no direct role in the arrest of thousands of political figures, scholars, MPs, journalists, intellectuals, and "miscreants" on June 26, 1975. Neither were they responsible for the imposition of press censorship, the expulsion of foreign journalists, the state of emergency imposed that day, the suspension of civil liberties, or the continuing reinterpretations of the Constitution of India. Yet the integrity of the Indian military was used as a major justification for all of these actions—and perhaps others yet to come. In her defense, Indira Gandhi and Indian government spokesmen have repeatedly stressed that the arrests, censorship, and emergency were necessary at least in part because of appeals made to the military (and police) to revolt and mutiny.

The sole basis for this serious charge appears to have been the statements of various opposition leaders, especially Jayaprakash Narayan; these leaders have not been accused of direct contact with uniformed forces. Narayan did raise the issue of military obedience several times before and during June 1975. For example, in a speech at Suri, West Bengal, "J. P." was reported to have "appealed to the armed forces not to carry out illegal orders."[1] A few days later, in New Delhi on the eve of a planned mass civil disobedience campaign, he repeated the appeal, calling on army, police, and government employees "not to obey any orders they considered illegal." Narayan added that "the Army act lays down that the armed forces must protect the Constitution. If the Constitution is changed legally it does not matter. But the Army must oppose any unconstitutional changes."[2] Mockingly, he dared the government to try him for treason.

While J. P. may have believed he was within both the law and the norms of Indian politics, Gandhi thought otherwise. Even before the arrests, she had responded to Narayan's suggestion that the armed forces disobey illegal orders. On the evening of the twenty-fifth, just before J. P.'s appearance at the mammoth rally in New Delhi, she claimed that "if a soldier began doubting whether his superior's order was right or wrong or started referring to the rules book then the war would be lost." After ordering the arrests of thousands of Indian politicians (including Narayan himself), she charged that "certain persons have gone to the length of inciting our armed forces to mutiny and our police to rebel."[3] Parenthetically, this is not the first time Gandhi has made such a charge. In 1967 she accused one of the parties (Communist Party–Marxist) that was to support Narayan in the 1975 crisis of sowing disaffection in the Indian army.[4]

I return to the substance and implications of Gandhi's accusations later in this chapter, but the essential point is that the military became an issue in the momentous events of 1975, although there is no evidence to indicate that it ever became a participant. Nor is it likely to in the foreseeable future. The inaction of the military will be its outstanding quality in Indira Gandhi's India, a passivity that contrasts sharply with an obvious potential for intervention. With the suspension of civil liberties and the closing of the political system, the military becomes one of the very few institutions that could—at a single stroke—terminate Gandhi's experiment with new forms of democracy; yet, we would argue, this is not apt to happen. The soldiers are likely to continue to disappoint those who expected them to heed Narayan's call; they are also likely to disappoint those who expect them to join Indira Gandhi's revolution.

To understand the basis for these conclusions it is necessary to draw back and examine the military in its larger social and political context. It relates to this context both as an institution and as an idea or model. Armies as institutions are bound in time and place, are functionally specific, and have fixed patterns of recruitment, training, and action.[5] They also share many characteristics with other armies, although no two are identical. This applies to their political as well as their military behavior. But the military as an idea is quite different.[6] It is functionally and organizationally diffuse, may take quite different forms in different societies, and—

above all—can be held by civilians as part of their belief and value structure. Belief in the military as a model or ideal is voluntary, and not derived from any particular organizational format or performance standard. Those who adhere or appeal to the military virtues may do so in whole or in part, and may view the military as either an end or a means.

India has had a long and striking history of the military as an institution. The French, and then more successfully, the British, adapted Western military forms to Indian conditions as early as the eighteenth century, and these hybrid institutions have flourished in South Asia. This chapter is primarily devoted to examining the relationship to contemporary political developments of the military as an institution.

However, we must not ignore the impact on Mrs. Gandhi's India of a different and perhaps equally important facet of the military: glorification of military values and practices. We turn to this first.

The Military as Ideology

Military rule, militant or aggressive foreign policies, the militarization of society, the praise or emulation of so-called military values and virtues—all of these can be called "militarism," but they are really quite distinct phenomena.[7] They also appear as significant strands in the fabric of recent Indian history. No discussion of the military in India today would be complete without at least a brief look at these phenomena. Two areas seem to be of special importance: the military as a model for domestic politics and the martial spirit as a style in foreign policy.

Indira Gandhi's father, Jawaharlal Nehru, detested the military. He had no particular interest in military matters, and wrote of the profession in scathing terms.[8] He hated the automatic discipline and the mindless obedience that he associated with the military and abhorred the carnage of war. Yet, in a moment of extraordinary self-revelation, he did speculate on the relationship of war to Indian society:

> Much as I hated war, the prospect of a Japanese invasion of India had in no way frightened me. At the back of my mind I was in a sense attracted to this coming of war, horrible as it was, to India. For I wanted a tremendous shake-up, a personal experience for millions of people, which would drag them out of that peace of the grave

> that Britain had imposed upon us. . . . The war was not of our seeking, but since it had come, it could be made to harden the fiber of the nation. . . . Vast numbers would die, but it is better to die in war than through famine.[9]

This view reflects a subordinate but recurrent theme in Indian thought. Trial by combat might be tragic or unfortunate, but it could have beneficial consequences. Although Mahatma Gandhi rejected war in all forms (and urged nonviolence on the British in their resistance to the Japanese), he spoke sympathetically of the military as an organization, praising its discipline and order. Gandhi advised young Indian officers to become soldiers of nonviolence, applying their (admirable) military skills to domestic problems, becoming a peace army.[10] Thus, in the attitudes of two of India's greatest leaders, there was a place for the solidarity and dedication that emerges from conflict, or for the martial virtues of discipline, obedience, and order that were thought to characterize the military.

However, the apotheosis of the martial spirit was more clearly evident in a third major Indian figure, Subhas Chandra Bose.[11] He was Nehru's major contemporary and chief political rival within Congress, styling himself Netaji, or leader. Bose fled India at the outbreak of World War II, eventually leading the Indian National Army (INA) against British and Indian troops. Militarily he was a failure, but politically he proved to be enormously popular. Had Bose not died in 1945, it is highly likely that he would have returned to India as Nehru's chief rival. A fine speaker, he, rather than Nehru, articulated the undercurrent of militant, aggressive nationalism that has always existed in India and that appears to have resurfaced. It is in the political philosophy and appeal of Bose that we see one historical precedent for Indira Gandhi's popularity.

Bose was nonsectarian and attracted a broad base of support among different regions, castes, and religions of India. He was also an extremist of the center, in Lipset's terminology.[12] He never ceased stressing discipline, order, and obedience as national virtues. Finally, Bose maintained an abiding interest in military and national security symbols, beginning with an early interest in uniforms, drills, and riflery and culminating in the leadership of the INA.

Although the comparison may not be exact, some of Mrs. Gandhi's appeal would seem to be due to the similarities rather than the differences between herself and Bose. She is certainly a secularist and professes faith in democracy, although perhaps democracy of a special variety. Her speeches are dominated by references to the need for discipline and order, and she has not disowned the slogan "India is Indira, and Indira is India."[13] Finally, there is no doubt she believes that internal and external enemies require continual vigilance, militancy, and preparedness. In the face of such enemies, even the enemy poverty, civil liberties are expendable, and in fact might obstruct progress. These themes are important components in her political style, and no opposition group has yet to develop an effective reply. Although India lacks a garrison state's discipline or resources, Indira Gandhi attempts to use internal and external threats and enemies to mobilize those resources and that discipline in the ultimate hope that, once India is fully mobilized, the threats can be allowed to wither away.

If this is the direction in which she is heading, it should not come as a surprise to observers of the Indian scene; nor is there a lack of comparative data to help us define the emerging character of her regime. Analyzing predictions of the fragmentation and disintegration of India, I wrote earlier that "a profound threat to democracy in India could arise as much from too much unity as from too little; under the pretext of a national front, or as the incarnation of the national will, a movement following the Bose-INA prototype might successfully dismantle India's substantial democratic structure, in the name of the nation, and possibly in the name of democracy itself."[14] This appears to be occurring, and not without considerable support within India. For a nation beset by severe economic difficulties, political instability, and social disorder, the emergence of an all-powerful leader has come as a temporary relief. The historical precedents of a strong, dominant leader exist in Mahatma Gandhi, Nehru, and Bose (although the first two often expressed self-doubts about their unique roles). Indira Gandhi can claim to be heir to this tradition.

A second facet of the military as an idea in contemporary India is the role that military and security problems play in Indian politics. The most striking development here has been the importance of such issues in legitimizing an unprecedented concentration of power in Mrs. Gandhi's hands. Such issues—threats from the United States, threats from China, threats from Pakistan—have periodically become the object of publicity campaigns designed to remove an issue from the opposition parties and reemphasize Gandhi's mastery of the situation. If poll data are any measure of success, the strategy seems to work; the prime minister's popularity has consistently soared in conjunction with such events as the 1971 invasion of East Pakistan and the detonation of a "peace bomb" in 1974.[15] While I cannot attempt a full analysis of the reasons why such appeals are popular in India (and, indeed, in most other states), some elements of this appeal can be noted.

Contemporary Indian political elites grew to political maturity during a period of extraordinary foreign policy activity. India's foreign policy, created and guided by Nehru, was reasonably successful abroad, far more so at home. For years, India was the dominant nation in the Third World, was courted by both superpowers, and participated in a continuous exchange of foreign visitors and delegations. Indian intellectuals, journalists, administrators, and politicians came to believe that their nation's international role was quite special and distinct, and recognized as such by the rest of the world.

When Nehru's foreign policy was discredited by the Himalayan border fiasco in 1962 and the continued ability of Pakistan to pose a threat to India (at least as perceived by Indians), the nation turned elsewhere. If military weakness was the source of extreme shame, then India would pursue a policy of overwhelming military strength, turning to several outside sources for assistance. Defense studies burgeoned, realpolitik became the guiding star, and the military was elevated to a place of honor, despite its defeat in 1962. Indians discovered that they could have nonalignment and use their expanding military power to support their foreign policy; indeed, they have come to believe in recent years that military might is the basis of any sound relationship between them and the military superpowers, let alone Pakistan and China. Hence the continued development of an arms industry and an active nuclear program.

A second way in which national security issues have been utilized by Indira Gandhi to build political support is exemplified by her stress on the danger of penetration by foreign powers. Her argument has been that such powers (and their intelligence agencies) regard India as a threat and wish to destabilize or otherwise weaken it through cultural, political, or military action. The informed reader can independently judge the validity of such arguments, but they do have a profound political impact within India. To argue that this perception of foreign (especially American) hostility is incorrect verges on treason for an Indian citizen, since the government of India claims to have substantial evidence of foreign intervention. In fact, Mrs. Gandhi claimed that opposition to her and to her views on Indian security problems may be taken as evidence of such foreign influence.

In an environment of fear and suspicion of foreign intentions it is easy for Indira Gandhi and her supporters to stress reliance on her as an incorruptible, unassailable leader. When an insidious threat exists, democratic institutions themselves (such as opposition parties, the press, and other nongovernmental groups) become channels of foreign influence and must be limited for their own good. Only the leader and her incorruptible associates can be assumed to be free of foreign control and can defend the security of India.

We do not know how long such arguments will continue to persuade in India, nor whether they will be advanced in years to come. However, we do believe that they have been effective in mobilizing support for Mrs. Gandhi and are not likely to be relinquished soon. The crowds that applaud her militant style in foreign policy may not represent all of Indian opinion, or even a majority of that opinion, but they are a base on which she can build at least the appearance of mass support.

An Institutional Perspective

Any inquiry into the actual role played by the military in the Indian political system immediately encounters the problem of restricted information. Evidence about the attitudes of the military, their role in central Indian politics, and their ties with civilian elites is almost entirely indirect, and direct evidence is often unreliable or ephemeral.[16] Such matters are among the most secretive in Indian political life, though there was a temporary relaxation in this restriction on information during the years 1962–71, when India needed outside assistance to meet the Chinese challenge and to rebuild its military establishment. However, difficulties in gathering information about the military in India are balanced in two ways. First, the Indian military as an institution has a long and important history; this institutional history can contribute to our understanding of contemporary issues and attitudes. In fact, as many Indian officers have noted, the Indian military is one of the least-changed institutions in the country, a state of affairs that they regard with mixed feelings.[17] Second, the military is a universal profession that invites comparison across national boundaries. In the case of the Indian Army we are particularly fortunate in being able to draw comparisons with the Pakistan Army (and, perhaps, the Bangladesh Army), especially in the army's relationship with political institutions and personalities, although we are not intimating that what has happened in Pakistan or Bangladesh is likely to happen in India.[18] Such comparisons are particularly easy to make in areas such as the professionalism of the military, its external defense role, and its contribution to the maintenance of internal tranquility.

The remainder of this section deals sequentially with these issues, drawing inferences, first, from the visible past of a well-established institution.

The British Legacy

In British India the role of the military in politics was a live issue for almost 150 years: it took that long for the British to conclude that civil–military relations in India were to follow the British pattern as closely as possible.[19] India had been a military preserve in many ways, and elements of this lingered on through Independence. But the military no longer dominated after 1910. The turning point was the notorious Kitchener–Curzon dispute of 1905. Despite the victory of the military in this crisis (or, more accurately, because of it), civilian officials in India and Great Britain obtained effective control of Indian affairs, civil and military.

This was fortuitous because selected Indians soon joined the British Indian army as commissioned officers. (Indians had already entered the Indian Civil Service as early as the nineteenth century, but did not appear there in substantial numbers until the 1920s and the 1930s.) As in the case of their civilian counterparts, these Indian officers were carefully chosen by the British. However, whereas the criteria for entry into the Indian Civil Service were largely objective, those applied to Indians seeking entry into the officer corps were quite special. Not only were candidates required to pass the standard intelligence and physical examinations; they were carefully screened according to their caste and social background.[20] The British were interested in recruiting the "right type" of officer. This right type was quite conservative; he was not outspoken; he was obedient; he came from a wealthy, landed, aristocratic background, which eased his adjustment to the semifeudal Indian army; he came from a "martial" ethnic group such as the Sikhs, Jats, Punjabi Muslims, or Rajputs; he was a "gentleman."[21] Of course, recruitment to the officer corps from such martial groups guaranteed neither martial character nor political loyalty. Many of the finest officers of the Indian army (and its postcolonial successors) came from Bengal, Madras, or Maharashtra, or from castes not usually associated with martial prowess; conversely, many of the key officers in the INA movement were Punjabi Muslims and Sikhs.

The training given the young Indian officers reinforced their conservative social predilections. Many were initially sent to Sandhurst, where they underwent the same course as the British. Later, when this became politically and administratively impractical, Indians were given an even more rigorous military education at the Indian Military Academy (IMA) in Dehra Dun.[22] This education stressed loyalty to the regiment, to the officer corps, to the king, and to the viceroy. Once in their units, this process of formal and informal socialization was continued. Young Indian officers were frequently reminded of their obligations and duties in various service courses and, above all, through the institution of the officers' mess. By and large this socialization process was successful. Given the hypocrisy and racism of a number of British officers, it is surprising that few Indian officers defected to the Germans and Japanese during World War II.[23]

While the substance of an officer's education specifically excluded consideration of "political" matters, it must not be thought that Indian army officers—British or Indian—were in fact apolitical persons. It is true that they were taught to be nonpartisan, favoring neither one political group nor another. The British did not talk about Conservatives or Labor, the Indians did not talk about Gandhi, Nehru, or Bose.[24] But they were all aware that British rule ultimately rested on the loyalty of an army almost entirely Indian in composition. Further, the Indian army had always been used for a variety of political tasks, ranging from de facto governance of frontier regions to internal security.

The present generation of Indian military leadership was recruited, trained, and commissioned during the hectic days of World War II.[25] However, like most of their predecessors, they suppressed whatever political feelings they had and served the British well. Young political activists of that period were in the Congress or various underground and revolutionary groups, fighting the British, but Indians in the military performed no acts of revolution or insurrection (with the exception of those who had been captured by the Japanese and joined the INA). Unlike Burma, Indonesia, Algeria, and China, India achieved its freedom without an armed struggle and without the assistance of the military, factors that made it possible later to establish strong civilian control.

The Military in Independent India: Constraint and Restraint

As in other areas of public life, the leaders of an independent India sought to reshape for their own purposes what the British had left. Rejecting the model of a radical, politically attentive military, on the one hand, and the Gandhian alternative, on the other, the Indian leadership quietly achieved their central objective of establishing firm, effective control over the military. While Nehru and his political and administrative colleagues have been faulted for their decisions in agricultural and industrial policy or population control, they were flawless in their choice of constitutional, administrative, and political restraints on the military. In fact, no other new nation has established as effective a system of civilian control, and in many established democracies the military wield considerably more power than they do in India. Since virtually the entire network of restraints, controls, and manipulative devices remains intact today, and since the network would seem to suit the interests of both the military and Indira Gandhi, it is worth careful examination.

Constitutional and Legal Constraints

Following British practice, formal control over the military rests in the monarch substitute, the president, although de facto control is exercised by the elected prime minister and cabinet.[26] Under the Constitution the defense of India is reserved exclusively to the central government, and no Indian state has ever seriously contemplated the development of even a paramilitary force without union permission. There is no opportunity in the system for ambitious officers to create their own satrapy outside central government supervision. This fact alone makes meaningless any direct comparison of post-1947 India with pre-1949 China. India will not readily fall victim to warlordism or to the rivalries of competing armies, unless some unimaginable catastrophe were to destroy the cohesion of the Indian military.

To ensure dominance of civilians, steps were taken after Independence to create a balance of power among the three armed services. Under the British, the Indian army was numerically and politically more powerful than the Royal Indian Air Force and Royal Indian Navy combined. The commander in chief of the army had a special advisory function vis-à-vis the government of India, and was a member of the cabinet. Not only did the Indian government make the three services legally equal after Independence; it has exaggerated the relative influence and power of the chiefs of the two weaker services—the air force and the navy—at the expense of the numerically dominant army. The three service heads are all designated chiefs of staff, and the Indian government abolished the position of commander in chief, held by the senior-most Indian army general, whose responsibilities included all three services. Further, the chairman of the Chiefs of Staff Committee is always the officer with the longest period of tenure, which has often been an air force or navy officer.[27] In brief, this has meant a partial redress of the natural imbalance between the army chief and the heads of the two other services, providing civilian leadership with substantial leverage over the army.

Structural and Organizational Factors

Recruitment to the officer corps in India is entirely on the basis of standardized written and oral examinations: there are no formal regional, class, or caste quotas or restrictions. However, the medium in which the recruitment and examination process takes place is the English language, and, since it is a volunteer military, the services must select from those who choose to apply. These two factors have led to an officer corps somewhat unrepresentative in terms of class and regional origins, being skewed toward an urban and northern recruitment base.[28] Officer candidates are trained via the English language, and are encouraged to adopt a lifestyle and professional environment closely resembling that of the Indian army of forty years ago, complete with swagger sticks and British accents.[29] All of this, which has often been criticized in Parliament as being un-Indian, serves to encourage differences between the officer and his Indian environment, making it difficult for him to build alliances across the culture gap.

Even more surely to forestall the development of monolithic power in the army, some attention has apparently been given to ensuring that officers from "nonmartial" regions of India are overrepresented in higher commands, especially the position chief of the army staff (COAS). No caste, region, or religion, even the numerically dominant Punjabi Hindus and Sikhs, can hold a proprietary view of any position with the Indian army.[30]

When senior positions do open up there is a natural amount of lobbying on the part of various groups within the army, but final decisions are made by civilians, although custom has usually been that the senior-most general becomes COAS. Recently, to control promotions, the tour of duty of two serving chiefs was extended. This meant that several experienced officers reached retirement age without opportunity for promotion, ultimately paving the way for the promotion of Lieutenant General T. N. Raina. The fact that Raina is a Kashmiri Brahmin (and the two superseded officers had excellent credentials) has led to some speculation about Indira Gandhi's motives. The episode was reminiscent, to many, of the rapid promotions given to B. N. Kaul (another Kashmiri Brahmin) by Krishna Menon and Nehru in the years and months just before the Chinese–Indian conflict of 1962. These promotions created an uproar in the Indian army, the press, and Parliament.[31]

A structural factor that has enhanced civilian control has been the large size and moderate sophistication of the Indian military.[32] This has meant that Indian officers can be trained almost entirely within India itself, the only exceptions being routine exchange programs or training in specialized or advanced equipment.[33] Thus, an Indian military career is highly self-contained; most officers, whatever their service, encounter military officers from major powers. This accords with express government policy. Indian civilians did not miss the point that the ties Pakistani officers had to the American military were used as a resource in their attempt to gain control of the state. Foreign military personnel consequently find it difficult to mix with Indian officers except on the most superficial basis; this was true for Americans even during the period when the United States was providing substantial amounts of military equipment to India (1962–65).[34] There have been strong public protests over brief contacts between Indian and Pakistani generals during border demarcation talks. Indian civilian officials are sensitive about the entire issue: they fear "informal penetration" of their own system through military links and the subsequent political contamination of their own officers.

This operational deployment also has some impact on the military's potential for political intervention. On the crudest level the division of the Indian army into four major regional commands, each in turn divided into areas and subareas, would seem to be an obstacle to a coup.[35] No single regional command contains a preponderance of armed forces; a coup would require collusion of all four regional commanders (officers of lieutenant general rank). Further, there are major cities located within each command, even within the Southern Command, which is primarily a training organization. Were any one or two regional commanders to continue their support of a particular government, they could serve as regional foci of resistance to the coup, and the military would immediately be confronted with a civil war. This might even occur were one or two area or subarea commanders to refuse to go along with a coup.

One additional feature of the military's structure is worth noting. Air force and navy units are controlled by their respective headquarters, and there is no unified military command structure in India. The three service heads are chiefs of their respective service staffs. As noted, they stand in rough equality to each other and meet together, with collective responsibility, as the Chiefs of Staff Committee. There is no substantial "Joint Chiefs" organization or staff, as in the United States, nor is there a supreme head of this committee who can act on behalf of all three services. This problem has been discussed in Indian military circles for years, although exclusively in military terms.[36] However, it might well be that the numerous proposals that have been made to streamline the command structure at the center have been sidetracked by civilians because of the political implications outlined above. The present system certainly does enable civilians to play a major role in the decisionmaking process, and makes it difficult for the military to act in unison against civilian authority. A comprehensive system of checks and balances, dividing power against itself horizontally and vertically, is as evident in the Indian military as in the American federal constitution. The intent was the same: to contain power deemed dangerous.

Foreign Policy and the Direction of War

India has been involved in armed conflict from the first days of Independence: three wars with Pakistan, one with China, military intervention in

Hyderabad and Goa. Of these conflicts, one remains of overwhelming importance for the Indian military, from the perspective of their relationship with civilian authority. The war with China still rankles: in it the Indian army suffered a dramatic and humiliating defeat, and Indian civilians played a major—if not dominant—role in the events that led to that defeat. From the army's point of view they were betrayed by civilian leaders (and a few of their own generals who collaborated with such civilians), a betrayal that will not be forgiven save with the passage of time and the retirement of the participants who remember the events of 1959–62.[37]

From 1965 onward the Indian military have openly discussed the management of succeeding wars in comparison with the 1962 fiasco. Their overwhelming concern is twofold: that there be adequate preparation for war, and that the conduct of the war be left to the generals, subject to stated political objectives. Thus, the Indian military see the conduct of war in terms of a fairly clear-cut division of responsibility: politicians and civil servants provide the needed materials and set reasonable goals; the military is left to win the war according to its best professional judgment.[38]

The resource base of the Indian military is bifurcated: while India's own ordnance factories produce many varieties of weapons, most of these have imported components, and many vital weapons are manufactured abroad (as are all of Pakistan's advanced weapons systems).[39] This heavy reliance on foreign sources in both India and Pakistan has meant that these two states' foreign policies are oriented toward actual or potential weapons suppliers.[40] In Pakistan one important factor in domestic politics has always been the ties a particular individual or group has to a potential arms supplier; this was the case with both Ayub (the United States) and Z. A. Bhutto (the United States and China). Until now, in contrast, ties with a potential arms source have not been a major factor in Indian politics. The Indian military has not developed links to a particular arms supplier. While Indian officers were said in the 1960s to be partial to Western-manufactured aircraft and tanks, they apparently raised no objection to the creation of a heavy dependency on Soviet and Czech sources for these weapons. Nor, in fact, is there any evidence that association with Eastern European arms suppliers has made the Indian military "pro-Soviet" in any ideologically meaningful sense. It must be concluded that from a political point of view the development of an extensive arms industry within India has lessened the country's international dependency, although the quality-cost ratio of some weapons indigenously produced does not compare favorably with that of weapons imported or even indigenously manufactured under foreign license.[41]

The conflict with the Chinese represented far more than a simple defeat to the Indian army. In the North East Frontier Agency (NEFA) whole units simply disintegrated. These units—some of brigade strength—had not been crushed by superior forces or equipment in a direct confrontation; they were psychologically disarmed before they ever saw the enemy.[42] The worst possible fate—to a military man—had overtaken the Indian army in the NEFA. At each level there was a loss of confidence in superiors, and a sense of chaos and impending disaster swept down through the ranks.

The origins of this chaos are clear. There were important differences in strategy and tactics among Nehru, Krishna Menon, the bulk of the military leadership, civilian intelligence, and a new breed of so-called political generals.[43] An attempt to play a game of positional chess with the Chinese backfired, and yet the politicians could not bring themselves to completely hand over conduct of the war to the military (who favored large-scale retreat into India proper). The official military inquiry into the NEFA disaster concluded that there were grave mistakes made at the highest levels of the decisionmaking process, with civilians and the military fully sharing the blame.[44]

From their perspective, the military feel that the 1965 war with Pakistan demonstrated that it had largely overcome most of the inadequacies of 1962. The Indian army showed little genuine military inspiration, but there were no serious lapses, and large numbers of officers died in combat (a standard measure of military machismo). From the military's point of view, the brightest side of the 1965 war was the relative freedom of action that they were given by the prime minister, Lal Bahadur Shastri.[45] Shastri was completely naive in military matters, and none of his political colleagues fancied themselves as fledgling field marshals.

The army has been even more exultant over the skillful invasion of East Pakistan in December 1971.[46] The generals who planned and led that invasion have been lionized, receiving full credit from civilian officials for their management of the war.

If there were any difficulties in the Bangladesh operation, they occurred earlier. There is evidence to indicate that the Indian army had been deeply involved in supporting Mukti Bahini guerrillas for several months before the final invasion.[47] There were a number of casualties during that phase of the struggle, and before the final invasion came it appeared that the war might drag on for months or years at a low but bloody level. Would the Indian army leadership have tolerated such losses for much longer? Would it have agreed to keep large numbers of troops tied up on the East Pakistan border indefinitely? One suspects that the joy in victory was enhanced by relief that its involvement in a nasty and costly guerrilla struggle was over.

Aid to the Civil

Second only in importance to the external defense function, the military in India has a responsibility that is, in its argot, called "aid to the civil." Such activities as assistance during natural calamity and famine relief (including air dropping of food to isolated villages) fall in this category.[48] The Indian armed forces welcome such challenges, recognizing that they are vital and lifesaving, as well as good public relations. But they do not welcome other aid-to-the-civil tasks, which are becoming increasingly burdensome. The military has been called on to maintain essential services (telephones, roads, railways, power) during political and economic disturbances, indirectly serving as strikebreakers. Even more difficult and onerous are the requests to restore law and order. This aspect of aid to the civil has a long and inglorious history, and is worthy of detailed analysis, for it has powerful political implications.

The Indian army still bears visible traces of its colonial heritage in the location and character of the military cantonments. These were deliberately sited on the outskirts of major population centers and insulated from local political control (they still have separate governments, statutes, and regulations).[49] The cantonment isolates the military from civilian society, but its proximity to that society permits rapid intervention.

This intervention is scrupulously controlled by statute and regulation. The military must obey any request for assistance from the highest-ranking magistrate present at the scene. The commanding officer cannot refuse to give aid, "but the action he takes in pursuance of meeting this requisition is left to his sole discretion."[50] Once authority has been transferred to the military commander, a civilian magistrate cannot issue orders to the military or order that fire be opened. But the magistrate can make the determination when military assistance is no longer required, and the military officer in command must refrain from further action, except to protect his own troops. Such troops, when engaged in the restoration of civilian authority, are required to use the minimum necessary force.

This system has proven workable over the years, with only a few notorious exceptions such as Jallianwala Bagh. However, it was designed to handle local disturbances. In the years since Independence the number of civil disturbances seems to have increased dramatically, and in the period 1961–70 the army was called out on 476 occasions to restore order.[51] There are no data available as to the nature of these disturbances, the magnitude of the army's efforts, or the duration of what is in effect martial law. What we do know, however, is that the use of the army has expanded far beyond the historical, localized aid-to-the-civil role. Whole states have been blanketed by a variety of security forces (including the army) after the imposition of president's rule. Some states have been literally occupied by the military for two decades (Kashmir, Nagaland, Mizoram), although these are special cases, with either disputed borders or active guerrilla movements.[52]

What is startling about the army's internal security role is that it continues despite a dramatic increase in the size and quality of police and paramilitary forces. The Public Accounts Committee of Parliament noted in 1974 that expenditures on police forces had increased by fifty-two times since Independence and had doubled between 1969 and 1971.[53] Most of the increase took place in such units as the Border Security Force, Indo-Tibetan Force, and Central Reserve Police, all organized along paramilitary lines, housed in barracks, subject to military discipline, and often commanded and manned by ex-army personnel.

One clear-cut lesson of Pakistan's experience was that excessive or ill-conceived aid-to-the-civil operations will be resisted by the military and may become a cause for their displacement of civilian rule.[54] This lesson was not lost on the Indian officials most responsible for such matters.

It is certain that the expansion of the police apparatus was partly intended to lessen the need for regular Indian army units to come to the aid of the civil, although it also gives the central government an enhanced capacity for coercion. There remain a number of points of conflict. The military are obsessed with the need to retain their own identity, separate from that of the police. This sense of separateness extends to the color of uniforms the police and the military wear, as well as to the superior armament of the military.[55] Above all, the military resists being divided into "penny-packet," police-size units; it usually insists on retaining its regular military formations.

The basis for this desire to distinguish itself from the police forces is quite pragmatic. The military is not called in to restore order unless the police themselves have failed in this task. To increase its effectiveness, it wishes to demonstrate that it is qualitatively different from the police, and that it is prepared to use more potent means. Often, the mere rumor or sight of military units is enough to restore order.

One recent and momentous incident deserves special mention. On May 21, 1973, the Indian army was called in to disarm and relieve the Provincial Armed Constabulary (PAC) in Uttar Pradesh. In the process, it suffered substantial numbers of casualties. The police had rebelled, joining with the students that it had been sent to quell. The sources of that rebellion were very poor pay and working conditions, the development of union-type organizations within the police (banned by law), and an apparent weakness on the part of the politicians.[56] Except for minor police protests in Delhi and Calcutta, this had been only the second time since 1857 that a military or police force had rebelled in India.[57] The significance of the rebellion lies not only in what it tells us about the deterioration of the morale of the police and paramilitary forces and the difficulty of maintaining large numbers of such forces but in the fact that it occurred in the Hindi heartland area. Threats and disturbances in this area are likely to have a greater impact on the central government than similar outbreaks in states more distant from New Delhi.

A by-product of the army's periodic excursions in the law-and-order business is that regional commanders are required to develop a profound knowledge of local political, religious, and economic problems. Contacts with local administrators are important, but so are these with local political parties and religious leaders, the heads of National Cadet Corps units, students, and village and labor leaders.[58] Such groups are most likely to be involved in any civil disorder, and the military tries to maintain its own channels of communication with them. It is not unusual to encounter an army officer who, in one breath, disclaims all knowledge of or interest in politics but in the next outlines with great perception the local balance of political forces and likely sources of instability.

Realization of Civilian Control

While many ex-colonial states attempted to impose civilian control over the military, few have been able to realize this objective. Such control requires, in the long run, civilian authorities who are not only determined to control the military but are competent to do so. India has been fortunate in possessing a corps of civilian administrators and politicians who have built on and strengthened the pattern of civilian control established during the last thirty years of British rule.

As before, fiscal responsibility is strictly within civilian hands via the Finance and Defense Ministries. The military is routinely called on to account to civilian administrators for the smallest deviation from budgetary allocations. (Perhaps apocryphally, military officers cite the example of the brigade commander who was asked why his unit exceeded its routine ammunition allocation—during the 1965 war with Pakistan.) More important, all requests for new weapons, force expansion, and structural adjustments are routinely evaluated by civilian bureaucrats from the very earliest stages of the decisionmaking process.[59] The general competence and intelligence of these civilians are high. While they are outnumbered by their military counterparts, they can draw on an extraordinarily rich tradition of civilian administrative control.

This raises the fundamental question of the capacity of nonmilitary elites to supervise and dominate in that hazy area where civilian and military interests overlap. Not only must the military be taught that civilian control is the norm but civilians must demonstrate that they are effective. The original Clausewitzian justification of civilian control was, in fact, that political considerations were so important in war that the purely military outlook was inadequate.[60] It is never the absolute magnitude of an external or internal crisis that alone determines a realignment of political forces in a state, but the relationship of such a crisis to the will and determination of key elites. In a state with a vigorous and alert political elite—and, as in India, an attentive civilian administrative cadre—quite severe setbacks will be tolerated by the military if it has confidence in the ultimate good judgment of civilian leadership. However, quite trivial incidents can trigger off a coup in systems where such confidence and respect are lacking. Paraphrasing the aphorism, leadership not only must be competent; it must be seen to be competent.

Since the late 1950s there has been a clear-cut pattern in the appointment of the minister of defense, one of the most sensitive and important positions in the Indian government. Krishna Menon, appointed minister in 1957, was one of Nehru's most trusted associates. Menon's successors have shared this characteristic, especially under Indira Gandhi. Her appointees (Jagjivan Ram and Swaran Singh) have been her political supporters; where there has been an indication that support has wavered (as in the recent case of Swaran Singh), they have been replaced. Her most recent appointee, Bansi Lai (a man of no apparent expertise or interest in defense matters), is one of Mrs. Gandhi's most fervent and useful political allies. It remains to be seen whether he will be trusted with such politically sensitive decisions as the promotion and assignment of senior military officers.[61] If a parallel situation is relevant, these decisions may be made by the prime minister's secretariat (under her personal control), just as decisions about the promotion and assignment of senior civil servants were shifted from the Home Ministry to the secretariat.

Obedience and Authority

The above discussion leads us directly to what must be speculative conclusions about the relationship of the military to the momentous political changes occurring in India today. Such conclusions are based on our knowledge of the nature of the Indian military and the character of Indian politics, and must be at a general level of analysis.

Ultimately, the question of whether or not the military will intervene in the current situation is decided inside the minds of a set of officers. It cannot be reduced to a formula. But it centers on a calculation of gains versus losses.[62] The military compare the costs and gains of acquiescing in an ongoing system with the costs and gains of meddling in it, or even transforming it. A professional officer corps is not immune to temptation, but the kinds of issues and pressures that will lead it to intervene are different from those that tempt a politicized military establishment. We can therefore rule out a wave of sympathy with J. P. Narayan, the Jan Sangh, or the CPM propelling the Indian military to action against Indira Gandhi; we could probably do so even if the opposition groups were less ideologically splintered or more pro-military than they are.

There is little doubt that to the extent that they have recalculated the costs and gains associated with intervention the Indian military has at least temporarily rejected greater political involvement. It will continue to see itself as outside politics, neither supporting nor opposing the present government, content to carry out its assigned military tasks.

However, I do not believe that the present situation is of no interest to the military. Its concerns probably lie in three areas, each of profound importance to the professional soldier: the legitimacy of central authority, the nature of the challenge to that authority (and to the federal principles on which India is built), and the potential for conflict between Indira Gandhi's rule and the values and goals of the officer corps.

The Legitimacy of Authority

When J. P. Narayan called on the military to disobey "illegal" orders, he was appealing to the military to examine the nature of Indira Gandhi's authority, and to reject it as illegitimate. For a soldier, the accusation and its implications are profoundly disturbing. Armies function at the margin of moral behavior: they willingly perform acts that are, in any civil society, questionable, the more so if performed against one's fellow citizens. The legitimation of such behavior is therefore essential, and if the institution that performs the legitimation function for the military is itself called into doubt, the military also becomes suspect.[63] Thus when Mrs. Gandhi stresses her popular mandate, the illegitimate tactics of the opposition, and her adherence to constitutional proprieties, she has a clear purpose in mind: to persuade the military (and, of course, other bureaucracies and groups) that her rule *remains* legitimate and that their obedience to her authority is morally as well as pragmatically correct. In such circumstances, the military is told, nothing really important has changed. On its part, the military is probably eager to hear such reassurances. Hardly devoted to civil liberties, parliamentary niceties, or a free and open press, it is undoubtedly willing to ignore Gandhi's zestful exercise of power as long as she can make a reasonable claim to legitimacy and as long as there are no more attractive political alternatives. It is difficult to carry my analysis much further. Presumably, if the Indian Constitution were rewritten to create a presidential form of government the military would acquiesce—again, not having much of a political alternative, and certainly not tempted to seize power itself. However, if such a transformation of the Constitution were perceived as having been done simply to enhance the power of a single individual, or if Mrs. Gandhi's arguments about the legitimacy of her recent actions begin to wear thin, one significant barrier to military intervention would be removed. It may have been weakened already.

The Challenge to Authority

The other side of the legitimacy coin is the nature of the challenge to civilian authority. The military in any state, including India, will maintain its obedience to civilian authority that lacks legitimacy if it neither wishes nor is able to seize power itself or if civilian alternatives are unpromising. The latter point is worth considerable emphasis.

The Indian military has always identified itself with national, all-Indian perspectives and images.[64] It is, in fact, a truly national institution in India, as representative as and yet more unified than the civil services. In the military, Indians from all castes, regions, linguistic groups, and classes work in extraordinary harmony and unity. The officer corps, drawn from all over India but speaking a common language, is particularly sensitive to the difficulties and problems encountered in maintaining an all-India organization, but not less proud to have done so since Independence.

Because it and its troops are drawn from the entire nation, and because it is reliant on that entire nation for material, transportation, funding, and moral support, the officer corps is highly sensitive to regional disputes and conflicts that threaten the integrity of the state. While it may look on a particular regional demand as just or legitimate, it tends to support the central government in generally opposing regional pressures for autonomy or greater independence.[65] Its attitude toward caste-based or ideological demands is similar: while conceding the occasional just claim, its perspective is unshakably that of New Delhi.

Although some of the groups arrayed in opposition to Mrs. Gandhi are stridently pro-military, even these (such as the Jan Sangh) have a pronounced regional base. And Gandhian elements in the opposition are hardly regarded as pro-military. Some opposition groups favor a reconciliation with the Chinese, a position still unacceptable to many officers. Thus, from the military's point of view, the very groups that attack her authority lack the credentials themselves to assume power. Were a significant challenge to her authority to develop from within her own ranks, this situation might change. Both Y. B. Chavan and Jagjivan Ram, perennially mentioned as alternatives to Gandhi, are "national" leaders in the sense that the military can understand and appreciate, but they—and others—appears to have been effectively neutralized by her.

The Challenge from Authority

A third area of strain in the civil–military balance might be the growth of conflict between the military and the present leadership itself. If a military organization is confronted with tension between the roles it is asked to perform or if there are discontinuities between its self-perceived status and role demands, it will seriously question civil authority regardless of the latter's legitimacy. Much of this occurred in Pakistan, and more recently, Bangladesh, when the military were in each case asked to carry out distasteful aid-to-the-civil tasks without the full authority to see them to their conclusion.[66] In Bangladesh, the military's position was further compromised by the growth of a highly politicized paramilitary force, the Rakhi Bahini.[67]

In view of the skill and intelligence with which military matters have been handled in India since Independence, we would not expect such developments to occur there, Attempts to create a political youth corps were as unsuccessful as attempts to perpetuate the Indian National Army.[68] Nor is Mrs. Gandhi likely to ask the military to engage in civic action tasks, or even to subscribe to her ideological program, except in the most general way. In terms of her political interests, a neutral and politically inert military is inadequate.

However, strains might develop if the army is asked to perform quasi-military tasks without adequate resources, or without a clear termination date. It has already been engaged in a sometimes brutal campaign against Naga rebels for many years, but India has been restrained in the means it may employ.[69] This has been a difficult if tolerable situation because of the dominance of Indian forces vis-à-vis the Naga rebels, but one can imagine a similar situation occurring elsewhere on a much larger scale.

As I wrote several years ago, the deterioration of Bangladesh politics may force a new Indian intervention.[70] A rise in border incidents, large numbers of refugees, a stridently anti-Indian regime in Dacca, or an impending civil war are all conditions that could prompt it, especially if they were coupled with public pressure on the Indian leadership for "action."[71] Yet, as the Indian leadership knows, any intervention is likely to vastly complicate the situation and may not succeed. The burden of such intervention would fall on the shoulders of the military, and in this case it is not likely to be equal to the task.

There will be no clear-cut "enemy" forces, but only a vast, resentful, and uncooperative population. Indian military power might be sufficient to temporarily tip the balance of power in Dacca, but it can never rule Bangladesh for any length of time without deteriorating into a glorified occupation police force. Thus, unless involvement in Bangladesh were limited in time and scope, severe conflict between the military leadership and their civilian masters would be bound to arise, perhaps with momentous consequences.

If India can avoid involvement in such a Vietnam-like situation, the only likely area of disagreement between the military and Gandhi's government will be in budgets and weapons, traditional arenas of conflict. Such disagreement will be especially likely if Indira Gandhi is serious about her development plans and were to seek substantial new resources. She could not then overlook the burden of defense spending that India has carried for more than a dozen years.[72] But because of the rise in prices and a revision of military pay scales, the defense budget (which has grown slowly in recent years) probably cannot sustain present force levels, a problem India has in common with the United States. Additionally, pressures are mounting from the military for replacement of obsolete weapons systems and for acquisitions (such as high-performance attack planes) to fill in certain glaring gaps.[73] These are deficiencies that are obvious and clear, and they cannot be balanced by continued development of the nuclear program. In fact, were India to "go nuclear" militarily, the experience of other nations seems to indicate that no less attention could be given to nonnuclear weapons systems.[74]

Clearly, the one way out of pressures for increased defense spending would be to redefine Indian foreign and security policy requirements. Some Indian observers have suggested that reconciliation with China would enable India to maintain a smaller military.[75] Here, Mrs. Gandhi and the military would seem to have a common interest in not making major changes in present Indian security policy: she for foreign policy and domestic political reasons (antipathy to the People's Republic of China is a precondition for the Soviet tie), the military because of its distrust of the Chinese and a desire to maintain as large and as powerful a force as possible.

The Most Likely Future

Assuming the continuation of the political pattern established after June 1975, it is possible to project the likely role of the military in Indira Gandhi's India. Other scenarios could be written (some features of them have been touched on earlier in this chapter), but the following is the most likely future.[76]

First, the relative power of the military will be enhanced, if only because other centers of power and influence in Indian political life have been destroyed or reduced in stature. As argued, it is highly unlikely that the full potential of military power will be exercised, but it will become more visible and politically more sensitive. In brief, the military finds itself to be one of the few giants left, and inevitably it will become more political, at least in the eyes of others.

Second, the officer corps does not yet have a proper model for a coup, and any enhanced political involvement on its part is likely to be indirect or subtle. The catastrophic examples of Pakistan and Bangladesh in recent years have convinced the Indian military not only that a coup would be difficult to carry off under Indian conditions but that military rule is not likely to be successful.

Third, subversion of the military by opposition groups is not likely to be successful unless economic and security conditions deteriorate considerably.

Fourth, the ties between the military and Indira Gandhi's regime will become more explicit. As it becomes clearer to everyone that the military comprises one of the few genuinely important institutions in India with some autonomy and integrity, the connection between its tacit support of Mrs. Gandhi and her continuation in power will be perceived by everyone (she has certainly made the connection, as indicated by her public remarks). As in other aspects of her rule, this will represent a return to an arrangement once encountered in British India.

Fifth, greater dependence on the military, even if such dependence remains implicit, will weaken Mrs. Gandhi's bargaining position vis-à-vis requests for weapons, funds, and symbolic rewards. If India follows the pattern established in a number of other states, this will be the price to pay for military subservience, and it is likely that she will be willing to pay it. Defense budgets are not likely to decline, and ties to foreign weapons sources will remain important.

Sixth, the military will remain content with this arrangement. Personally and as professionals, its members will be well treated, and there will be no difficulty in rationalizing away any political excesses committed by the government. This situation will be stable as long as no attempt is made to interfere in what the officer corps regards as its natural sphere of responsibility, and as long as the army is not deeply involved in quelling domestic disturbances nor bogged down in a no-win war with one of India's neighbors.

1980

SEVEN

Toward a Great State in Asia?

States strong *enough to do good are but few.*
Their number would seem limited to three.
Good is a thing that they, the great, can do,
But puny little states can only be.
—Robert Frost, *"The Planners," 1946*

In Bismarckian Europe the presence of a great power could be readily determined. It was a state that was able to decide on its own whether or not it would engage in warfare.[1] The remaining nations were subordinated to the will or whim of the great states of Europe. With the qualified exception of imperial Japan after 1905, the suggestion that great powers existed outside of Europe was laughable. Retrospectively, the widespread notion that only within such a great power could the individual achieve true self-fulfillment is of equal interest. The greatness of the state was believed to enhance the quality of citizenship, a conviction that dates from the Greek city-states.

One hundred years later such views are simply not uttered in polite society. All states—great and small—are deemed equal, at least before the UN Secretariat. Universal democratic egalitarianism encompasses relations between most states (if not within them) and all, large and small, are equally great powers—a nonsense that may be marginally functional in taming the excessive pride and ambition of some of their numbers.

The determination of great-power status has not advanced much beyond Treitschke's cynicism. Outside of the two superpowers no state can apply its military power at will, and there are serious (and increasing) limits on even their capacity to intervene.[2] Some would ask of what use is military power in an era of nuclear stalemate, exploding populations, fragile economies, and disintegrating societies? How can third world states, in particular, rationally (let alone morally) contemplate the acquisition of enhanced military power—when such power will probably be used by the military against the government in power or the population in the streets?[3] In sum, great powers as we have known them—as military powers—are said to be obsolete, if not more dangerous to themselves than to others.

Some, however, still maintain the old arguments about the necessity of force and power. Morton Kaplan has recently tried to revive Mackinder's geopolitics, and there has been a curious effort to quantify various aspects of "perceived power" by Ray S. Cline.[4] Both Kaplan and Cline argue for the existence of critical regions surrounding the global heartland, and Cline suggests a new "Athenian Alliance" to the United States and the Western European powers, who must associate themselves with at least one great power in each major "politectonic" region.[5]

Without completely rejecting the utility of such approaches to the analysis of great powers, this volume grows out of quite a different perspective and should not be confused with this new school of regional-power politics. Between the superpower and the smaller (or fragile) state there are perhaps a dozen or so middle powers.[6] At least three of these middle powers are in Asia and appear to be increasing their relative advantage over both immediate neighbors and distant states. Collectively, the chapters in the Marwah/Pollack volume raised the question of the emergence of one or more of these states—China, India, Japan—as a latter-day version of Europe's great powers. Even while accounting for the differences in the international system in which they function, the presence of two dominating superpowers, their internal weaknesses, and the uncertain impact of military technology, they will ultimately be regarded as qualitatively different from the next order of states. In Asia these states include Indonesia, Iran, Pakistan, and Vietnam. In this volume we did not make the collective claim that China, India, and Japan form the core of their regional systems, although some analysts do and others still may. If this (Marwah/Pollack) collection of essays has a shared concern, it is that the influence and power of these states be neither overestimated nor underestimated, hopefully avoiding such grotesque estimates as Cline's ranking Pakistan ahead of India, the hysteria surrounding the construction of an "anti-Chinese" ABM in the United States, the still-heard belief that Japan could and should be pushed into the world as an independent power center, or the exaggerated hopes and fears surrounding the future of Iran.

What does the term *great power* mean in contemporary Asia? At the very minimum, it implies regional hegemony or rough equality with a neighboring great power. It may further include continental or global influence—although not necessarily dominance. The attainment of such power can come about only if a number of conditions are fulfilled. Most, but not all, pertain to the enhancement of national capacities:

—The capacity to manage the domestic processes of economic development and national integration

—The capacity to resist outside penetration

—The capacity to dominate regional competitors

—The capacity to deter outside states (especially superpowers) from lending support to regional competitors

—The capacity to achieve autarky in critical weapons systems, or at least to be able to bargain successfully for them during crises

—An awareness that the above capacities exist for, or are within the reach of, a state increasing its relative strength and influence

Great power status thus implies the existence of local military preponderance over neighbors through the spectrum of force and the means to maintain that dominance. It may also include the availability of nonmilitary instruments of statecraft, the ability to manipulate the domestic political weaknesses of rival states, and certainly a willingness to conduct a diplomacy that places power and status over other objectives. Finally, if necessary, a great power is willing and able to make external political commitments and has the resources to fulfill such commitments. I do not refer to the commitment of the weak alliance partner to the strong, but of the strong to an equal or a weaker state.

Do China, India, and Japan fulfill these criteria? It is an assumption of the Marwah/Pollack volume that they do, at least in part. The individual-country chapters will probe the accomplishments and deficiencies of each state in greater detail in terms of its great power potential, but we can first offer some general and comparative observations. These observations are of two kinds. The first pertain to the general and shared characteristics of China, India, and Japan as legatees of diverse Asian traditions, which also possess some of the material and political requisites for great power status. The second type of observation goes beyond the individual-country chapters, which are largely straight-line projections of recent historical trends, and identify areas of uncertainty and instability in the prediction process. These include the influence of technology on military balances, trends in the nuclear proliferation and arms control process, and the perception and behavior of the great powers.

Three Great Powers—or None

Great powers have a special view of their own history, they have substantial material assets, and their elites believe that they can manage the strategic environment.

On Having a History

The meaning of history is a subjective matter, determined as much by present reflection on the past as by the actual course of events. As Adda Bozeman has written:

> What once was actual and real often loses its poignancy for later generations, and what is only dimly discernible in the present may assume clear contours sometime in the future. . . . Memories that control the thinking of the Arabs may not suggest significant recollections to the Chinese or the French. Each nation, then, has a different image of the past, and each generation a different perspective over the passage of time.[7]

The fact that the three states we are examining are Asian is important both because of certain historical traditions and because of their self-perceptions and the perceptions of outside states toward them.

The relevant historical legacy of China, India, and most recently, Japan, is that they were once triumphant states or empires with a continental reach. This is as critical to their emergence as great powers as any "Asian-ness" that might exist. Each of these states has a great tradition of imperial or continental power, and in each case this tradition stands in sharp contrast to more recent subservience, humiliation, and vulnerability.

The vulnerability of Asia to the West (and much of Latin America and Africa, as well) was twofold. First, Europe and Asia developed only the most rudimentary common diplomatic language. From their earliest contacts there were ready exchanges of technology and material goods, but there was no growth of a shared view of an ordered world system. Second, in the absence of such a shared view, power and force became the ultimate arbiter of differences, and the dialogue between the Orient and the Occident was essentially a "dialogue des sourds" (dialogue of the deaf).[8] In this dialogue the various Asian powers were extremely vulnerable to the numerically inferior but highly motivated and very well-organized military forces of Portugal, France, Great Britain, Holland, Germany, the United States, and Russia. Through bitter experience it has become clear to the elites of these Asian nations that their military vulnerability was the critical factor explaining their weakness, not any inherent failure of their society or culture. While compromises had to be made to accommodate Western military technology (including major changes in their societies), this did not imply the destruction of indigenous values or the abandonment of idealized models of the past.

In China, India, and Japan, military power and technology became an obsession as a result of contact with the West, and the individual country chapters necessarily focus on this issue. To the elites of these states (with the special exception of Japan, which had passed through this phase by 1945), the liberation of their countries from Western influence or dominance, the reestablishment of former imperial or hegemonical relations, as well as the establishment of control over their own societies even today require substantial military power. Ironically, such power was and still is often derived from the West, leading to a troubled relationship between these states and potential Western arms suppliers. The recent histories of these states, unlike that of a number of other Afro-Asian states, have as much to do with ambivalent military relations with the West as with economic dependencies. For if a state has even a token interest in restoring something of its historical position, it must inevitably treat economic power as a means to military power, and use the latter in the service of a diplomacy whose goal is the shaping of a desired regional or world order.

Material Basis of Power

If Western Europe and the United States were the proper models for great power or superpower status, then only Japan would approach the standard, and then with some difficulty. India and China are not rich or developed in the Western sense. Yet because military power is relative and takes several forms, these states do begin to fulfill some of the material requirements for great power status.[9] While their economic systems differ greatly, as do their populations (in terms of education, skills, health, and social organization), they do share one characteristic: they are able to generate large surplus funds, manpower, and/or advanced technology to enable them to support a substantial military effort. Japan alone has not done so and spends less than 1 percent of its GNP on defense, but it has the material capacity to develop into a great military power in the future. The inhibitions that limit defense spending in Japan are political and psychological, not economic, which does not imply that Japan will necessarily increase its defense burden.

Available data show both the enormous magnitude of forces and the defense effort of which a number of Asian states are capable, and points up their structural differences. Only India and China are similar in their economic base: large, poor peasant societies with relatively small (but in absolute terms, substantial) industrial sectors. The enormous populations can be organized into huge infantry forces at relatively low cost; the industrial sector can turn out sufficient weapons for such forces. They can also produce limited quantities of large-scale or advanced weapons—ships, tanks, aircraft, communications, and logistics support facilities—although until recently, this could only be done with external assistance.

It is commonly assumed that because of the extreme poverty of China and India, heavy defense spending will be economically dysfunctional, and therefore regarded as deferrable. The limited work concerning Indian military expenditure and economic growth indicates that the opposite may be true. Emile Benoit and his associates determined that there was a positive relationship between defense spending and real economic growth; the most likely explanation being simply that the increased discipline and improved organization associated with the crisis triggering an increase in defense spending also lead to greater efficiencies in the productive civilian economy.[10] In a more efficient or developed economy the relationship may not hold. China's defense burden is much greater than that of India, but there are many ways in which its military units are linked to economic production, and here also the raw figures may not indicate actual defense burdens.[11]

The material base of Japan is quite different from that of China and India but may also qualify it for great power candidacy. Japan's strengths and weaknesses are obvious to even the most casual observer. Already an economic giant, it is nevertheless vulnerable to disruptions in raw materials sources and access to markets for its middle-range technologies. Undoubtedly, Japan could, if it chose to, quickly establish an indigenous arms industry of some sophistication; it has a large well-trained population base.[12]

The Strategic Environment

Unless one is a firm believer in classical geopolitics, there is nothing inherently distinctive or strategic about the location of China, Japan, and India. Their physical existence becomes strategically important only as a function of their relations with the superpowers (especially the USSR), prevailing military technologies, and the time period in which strategic political objectives are pursued. With the advent of nuclear weapons no state can rationally pursue absolute security, but a lesser degree of insecurity can be achieved vis-à-vis threats that are not thermonuclear. What does distinguish these three states is their capacity (or potential capacity) to manage nonthermonuclear military and economic threats from neighbors and both superpowers. There are also common features of the three states' strategic environment.[13]

While they do not share a common external threat or enemy, China, India, and Japan do interact with the superpowers in similar ways, each possessing a particular strategic and military importance. Each country has received military assistance, weapons, or military technology from at least one of the superpowers. Each country has been regarded as a potential (or actual) ally or adversary and has been subjected to pressure from one or more superpowers to join a mutual security pact. Despite this, India and China (unlike other Asian powers) have some ability to resist such pressures and, within the context of alignment, Japan has the ability to retain the option of strategic autonomy. This is a goal utterly beyond the reach of, say, Pakistan, which must stand by while India is courted by the two superpowers.[14] Pakistan is unable to play off one major power against another, for it has lost even its capacity to balance India, retaining only a nuisance value against India. Militarily weak and strategically indefensible, it has been relegated to minor power status for the foreseeable future. (2016: This passage underestimated Pakistan's capabilities and its desire to match India militarily, as well as its willingness to trade strategic access for weapons and material support with the United States, China, and other states; see the chapters below on Pakistan for more recent view.) Both Koreas, Taiwan, Thailand, and Indonesia are other Asian states with only marginal international bargaining power.

Another shared characteristic of the great powers is the close linkage of status and security. Weak states pursue whatever measure of security that they can achieve within the limits of their resources, and must be prepared to either subordinate their autonomy to powerful neighbors or allies, or engage in an extraordinarily skillful balancing act. For China, India, and Japan, however, the pursuit of status is as important as the pursuit of security. These are states that have a larger conception of purpose than mere survival; their diplomacy is at the service of this broader ideal or ambition. Thus, they may well choose strategies that seem to be self-defeating and needlessly expensive, and that may not even maximize security. One such strategy is the active defense of disputed borders, even at a high cost. Defending such borders is an act of will or self-assertion; should a state fail to defend itself as in the manner of a great power, then it will ultimately lose the status properly accorded to such a power, and its actual security will decline, as neighbors probe for additional weak spots. Smaller or weaker states do not carry this "big power burden."

Finally, these three states share a structural similarity within the hierarchy of nations. Neither global nor regional, they regularly interact with the two superpowers, with smaller neighbors and, in some cases, with one another. These experiences should have sensitized them to the tender feelings of smaller powers and may have done so. (China, of course, has made a fetish of international egalitarianism between large and small states, but the behavior of India and Japan toward their smaller neighbors has also been, on the whole, judicious.) In their different ways each also makes a claim to some form of global influence and each seeks to dominate its immediate region, although in pursuing the latter objective it is vulnerable to the balance of power game. As argued above, one prerequisite of great power status is the capacity to deter outside powers from supporting regional rivals. Much of India's diplomacy revolves around cutting Pakistan's access to U.S., Russian, and Chinese weapons. China seeks to discourage the West and Japan from helping the Soviet Union develop both the advanced and extractive sectors of the USSR's economy. The Japanese have settled for a strategy of dependence on superpower involvement, but only to keep the other superpower at bay.

Strategic Pressures

China, India, and Japan can all claim security problems that require substantial levels of modern weaponry. Unlike Western Europe, where an alliance structure exists to ensure conventional defense and the involvement of the United States, these states operate in a disorganized and transient strategic environment with little or no regional cooperation. Only Japan can anchor its security policy to a superpower although some circles of American opinion have advocated that Japan pursue a more independent or autonomous policy.

China and India perceive the existence of immediate military threats to their integrity and have armed accordingly. They trust neither superpower and often state so publicly. Furthermore, they are not linked to each other in any coherent strategic framework, and efforts to do so have repeatedly failed.[15] Their policies are likely to be pursued in terms of a strict construction of national interest, not regional accord or "stability." Discussions about an independent policy are naturally more muted in Japan, but even supporters of the U.S. tie are aware of and have discussed the alternative of strategic autonomy.

Two areas of military and strategic uncertainty common to all three states are of special interest. One stems from the confused historical pattern of border determination, the other from the logic of regional dominance in a world of superpowers.

China, India, and Japan each have a disputed or threatened border or territory with a power of equal or greater size. These border and territorial disputes, growing out of settlements between earlier regimes as a consequence of nation creation (or even as the residue of World War II), are of vital importance to the leadership of each state above and beyond its role in the international balance of status and power. They generally have two important internal political consequences. First, India and China have rebellious or incompletely integrated populations on or near their borders. Border disputes are an open invitation to subversion, rebellion, and an assistance to guerrilla movements. Great distances and difficult terrain also facilitate such activities. Second, the leaders of these states are no less vulnerable to the "national security" issue than those of the superpowers, and more so than those of small states with limited military ambitions. Even in Japan, the central leadership must demonstrate continued toughness on territorial questions, which transcend the Left–Right politics in any nation. Border disputes are a central domestic political issue in India and China.

Security requirements also flow from the intermediate position of these states in the hierarchy of nations. Because each is militarily powerful enough to exert regional influence, their smaller neighbors seek outside assistance in balancing them. This has led to superpower calculations of the wisdom and feasibility of "balancing" China, India, or Japan, versus a strategy of accommodation. In all cases, calculations of small-state survival, middle-state dominance, and superpower competition come into play, leading to a complex multilevel diplomacy. This process is most developed in South Asia but can be seen in operation in the Gulf region, Northeast Asia, and in superpower diplomacy toward China and its smaller neighbors (especially Taiwan and Vietnam).

Additionally, these three states have reached a level of military power that is of concern to the superpowers themselves, as well as their small neighbors. Because of their concern about regional dominance they have all developed some capacity to resist superpower intervention or raise the costs of that intervention.

This diplomacy of insecurity has produced a ratchet effect in the military inventories of China and India. As they move to meet perceived threats from regional competitors (including each other in some cases), their capacities vis-à-vis smaller regional states become overwhelming, and they enhance their capacity to resist, threaten, or deter the superpowers. The most dramatic example of this is in South Asia. India began an armament program to meet the challenge of Pakistan (which was being supplied with weapons by the United States after 1954). This program helped to some degree in meeting the Chinese threat, and in turn, the major arms acquisition program undertaken after 1962 enabled India to ultimately achieve near-total dominance over Pakistan in 1971. The momentum of that armament program has also given India a substantial capacity to meet naval threats from the sea, a capacity that it did not have during the *Enterprise* mission in the Bay of Bengal.[16]

Image and Reality

Asie, Asie, Asie,
Vieux pays merveilleux des contes de nourrice,
Ou dort la fantasie comme une impe'ratrice
En sa foret tout emplie de mystere.
—ASIE, Tristan Klingsor, *1901*

Two different conceptual frameworks are of special importance to an understanding of perceptions and misperceptions of China, India, and Japan. The first derives from the false assumption of their "Asian-ness," the second from the role accorded to the larger states of Asia by the classical geopolitical model.[17]

John Steadman, Harold Isaacs, and others have noted that the accuracy of Western images of Asia has not progressed much beyond the romantic poetry of Klingsor or the rough-and-ready realism of Kipling. Treating Asia as an entity is to engage in myth creation. As Steadman points out, "The largest significant unit of an Oriental society is not Pan-Asian but 'sub-Asian.'" The term *Asia* designates no single society, as does the term *Europe*; *Eastern*, unlike *Western*, cannot be employed to identify a single community.[18] Despite this fact, stereotypes of Asia as a whole and of individual Asian states persist at the highest levels of public life.

This is not to deny the numerous ties between India, China, and Japan. Many of these were of great historical importance: Mongol invaders sweeping down through Persia to gain control over the South Asian subcontinent from the thirteenth century onward; earlier, Buddhism being carried from India to China and ultimately to Japan, which was only one element of massive Chinese cultural influence on Japan. These and other connections are of significant interest to the linguist, religious historian, and cultural anthropologist. Added together, however, they are of less political importance than the fact of geographic coincidence. Being "of" Asia has often provided an excuse for initiating relationships that were marginal at best; being "in" Asia has also meant that these states are often viewed by non-Asian powers as having something in common, and they have each had to adjust and readjust to similar stereotypes. Such transient and superficial images of Asian states cover a wide range, but they are notable for their shallowness and their interchangeability. One such convertible pair of stereotypes is the cruel, rapacious, barbaric warrior-horde versus the soft, effeminate, and weak state. Another pair is the industrious, antlike, mass society versus the indolent, diseased, and lazy peasant. Whole nations are readily pigeonholed and then recategorized. Such stereotypes originated with the contact between expansionist European states and the states of Asia, and grew out of desire to rationalize colonial or hegemonic relationships. The stereotypes made it easier to legitimize the protection of weak Asian states from the strong or (within a region, such as South Asia) the weaker communities from the more warlike and militant.[19] Thus, such stereotypes were applied to relations between as well as within the states of Asia.

A second source of the perceptual errors that punctuate even recent contact between the various nonregional powers and the states of Asia is the dominance of geopolitical models. Whether it is the earlier incarnation as a control over the "heartland," or one of the latter-day versions (such as the zero-sum approach of the Cold War), they share one feature: the imposition of a grand strategic pattern on the Asian map, and the reading of that map according to the overlay.

In each case Asian states—unlike their European counterparts—are judged by and large unable either to determine their own interests or to protect them. Their "true" interests are deemed compatible with those of the outside power, an assumption that the Soviet Union's projected Asian collective security system shares with its CENTO and SEATO forerunners. A multipolar model, such as that briefly floated by Henry Kissinger, did recognize the strategic importance and political integrity of two Asian states, China and Japan, and elevated them to the level of Europe, the United States, and the Soviet Union as two of the five great world power centers. But the classic geopolitical model, although sometimes modified to include Japan as a special case, regards the rest of Asia as weak, fragmented, and vulnerable to pressure from the central landmass. It is composed of states with no value except as victims, which require outside protection from the West, whether they wish it or not. Further, the real issue is not their growth, prosperity, or even security but their position in the global tug-of-war. The foreign policies and strategic objectives of these Asian states are thus evaluated within a framework of a superpower struggle. On more than one occasion this superpower involvement has far exceeded any conceivable security or economic value of the state itself, because what is at issue is a broader strategy. As Isaacs notes, the most tragic and prolonged military calamities in Asia have been the result of the interaction of a geopolitical model with stereotypical images of Asia.[20]

Other chapters in the Marwah/Pollack volume provided ample evidence to show the fallacy of the belief in the incompetence of Asian states in general, and of China, India, and Japan in particular. These are not confused or erratic states—or at least, they are no more confused or erratic than their non-Asian counterparts. Nor are their interests necessarily in harmony with one another or with outside powers, especially in such areas as arms acquisition and nuclear weapons.

It can be argued that an insuperable obstacle to the emergence of China, India, and Japan as great powers is their own domestic weakness. India and China are societies with large ethnic and religious minorities, and they both have enormous regional diversity. India shares with Japan highly pluralist democratic politics. This ethnic, religious, regional, and political diversity could have a restraining influence on foreign policy, at the very least, and may lead to internal dissension, revolt, or even civil war.[21] Thus, some of these states are likely to turn inward, ordering their domestic political affairs before they seek a global or even a regional strategic role.

There is merit to this point of view, and such a course of events cannot be ruled out. Yet despite the growth of regionalism and ethnicity in many states around the world, such a development in India and China still appears unlikely. They seem to have mastered the succession crises that might have provided the opportunity for such a fissioning of society to occur. In India, the most complex of the three states under consideration, the process of accommodation or suppression of subregional and ethnic minorities is particularly well established. Japan, despite its great power and industrial capacity, is the most problematic in terms of the development of a broadly supported, outward-looking foreign policy that seeks to match the status acquired as an economic superpower in military and diplomatic arenas. Thus, even acknowledging the obvious domestic problems facing China, India, and Japan, we should not assume that they face inevitable disintegration, weakness, or fragmentation. Nor are their domestic disorders an insuperable barrier to expanded international influence.

My argument can be summarized at various levels. To begin with, these states each draw from both Western and indigenous models of great power behavior. Their foreign policies are likely to be a synthesis of the two: some degree of emulation of the classical model and some degree of creative adaptation of their own imperial tradition (or cultural memories of that tradition). Furthermore, the three states possess much of the material base associated with powerful states, although the nature of that base varies considerably among them. In each case, however, the critical requirement is that surplus manpower, talent, and funds are generated and can be put to the service of political and strategic objectives. Finally, these states have legitimate security needs, derived from both their location in an unstable Asia and their intermediate position between the superpowers and smaller neighbors. At least two of these states maintain substantial levels of forces in relative terms, and the third, while spending very little on defense on a percentage basis, has great potential for a rapid expansion of arms levels and military technology. Finally, perceptions of these states are subject to more than the usual distortion. Stereotypical images of their capabilities and intentions are widely held and highly transient in content.

Thus India, China, and Japan all share a potential for great power status, and quite possibly near-superpower status. Very few other states in the world fall into this category. Within Europe, one would include Germany and France; outside Europe, perhaps only Brazil, Nigeria, and possibly Argentina. Each of these states has, or might be able to develop, the capacity to exert dominance in its region. They have or are developing capacities to influence international economic, political, and military systems, and they can each draw on national traditions and ideologies of imperial grandeur. They represent prime candidates for careful scrutiny as we look forward to the strategic balance of the 1980s.

Toward the 1980s

With respect to the immediate future, there are areas of uncertainty in any judgment about the emergence of China, India, or Japan as great powers.[22]

These include major changes in outside perceptions of these powers, the influence of new military technologies, and the problematic relationship of these three states to arms control and proliferation processes.

Perceptual Discontinuities

A sharper discontinuity between self-image and external (especially superpower) perception involving either China, India, or Japan is likely to have important political consequences. Such a discontinuity is most likely to involve an underestimation of their power, influence, or ambition. This would be one way in which an action–reaction cycle might begin, with the regional power attempting to demonstrate its true interest or capability and the outside power interpreting this as either insignificant (thereby prodding the regional power into further displays of power) or threatening to regional stability (thus challenging the regional power).

There are a number of possible sources of such perceptual errors. One is change in the internal political structure of a state. A vivid example of this was supplied during the nineteen months of Indira Gandhi's "Emergency." During that period opinion in the West swung away from India in general and Mrs. Gandhi in particular; what was only a feeling of discomfort with India's earlier nuclear explosion turned into active opposition, as Gandhi's new regime was now thought to be irresponsible and dangerous.[23] A regime change in Japan would also harden distrust in many sectors in the West, even if (as in the case of Mrs. Gandhi) there were no substantial changes in either nuclear policy or foreign policy.[24]

A second major source of perceptual change would be an exacerbation of international economic problems. Even in the relatively favorable economic climate of recent years, Japan has become increasingly regarded as a state that is inimical to particular Western economic interests. Informed Western observers of Japan, as well, have mixed feelings on this issue. There is not only a feeling that Japan could carry a larger defense burden but also that its small expenditure on defense is an indirect Western subsidy of Japan's remarkable economic growth. There are feelings of envy and admiration for the society that produced that growth, and a sense of being hostage to Japan's implicit threat/capability to rearm. Japanese rearmament might raise strategic problems but it would also slow the process of economic expansion, which is perceived by some as a greater threat than military expansion.

Third, the role of these states in the international strategic system may be further exaggerated or misperceived. Given the desire to reconcile containment with lower defense budgets in the Nixon, Ford, and Carter administrations, it is natural to look to these states as "balancers" of the Soviet Union. To the degree that they perceive their interests and integrity as threatened by the USSR, this is a perfectly sound policy, but traces of impatience have already emerged, especially with Japan and India. In the former case, Japan is perceived as a state that fails to carry its full share of the mutual defense burden; in the latter case, India is seen by many as a state that not only fails to "balance" the USSR but actively consorts with it. The perception of China has been equally vulnerable to rapid change. The present regime or some future one may decide to achieve a formal rapprochement with the USSR; this will in turn be seen as a positive threat to American interests by many, especially if the United States has extended material and military commitments to China.

In all of these perceptions and misperceptions there is a common assumption of the "emerging" or marginal character of the state in question. There is a belief that such states are flawed or in some other way unable to determine their interests. There will be an oscillation in outside perceptions of these states, first exaggerating and then deprecating their might, alternately wishing that they would join the international system as full-fledged powers and fearing that, once part of the system, they would become unmanageable.

Weapons Acquisition and Technological Change

Weapons acquisition can serve many purposes. Aside from legitimate security needs, as defined by a state's own military and political leadership, it is a process that has important economic, political, and symbolic consequences. Of the three states under consideration, one (Japan) can afford to acquire sophisticated weapons in large quantities without evident damage to its own economy. In fact, purchases of foreign weapons by Japan is seen as an important device for easing the balance of payments problem of major Western arms exporters, especially the United States. It is more difficult to judge the economic impact of weapons acquisition by India and China, for their domestic developmental requirements are visible and pressing, although there is some evidence that defense spending is less upsetting to real growth than one would expect.

The political consequences of the weapons acquisition process are no less complicated and equally important. Dependence on foreign weapons sources has proven a costly policy for such diverse states as Pakistan, Iran, Israel, and South Vietnam. Each profited by receipt of weapons from the United States, but each was subjected to pressure from the donor, their patron, or a change in policy that left them with insecure or unreliable support.[25] Yet, as India and China have demonstrated, it is difficult to establish a domestic weapons industry without having it lapse into obsolescence. Japan's strategy is probably optimal: it produces most of its own weapons, but often in association with a foreign manufacturer, thereby gaining the latest in technology while retaining some degree of autonomy. In addition, with Japan's powerful economic infrastructure it can, of course, contemplate autarky more readily. Finally, the symbolic meaning of weapons acquisition should not be ignored. Are India's large forces merely a sop to militant nationalism, symbols of national pride and achievement? Is Japan's light defense burden a product of realpolitik, or a necessary concession to antimilitary and antiwar sentiment in the Japanese population? If, in fact, a weapons program (or the absence of one) is based on symbolic considerations such as these, it may be no less real than if it grew out of a consideration of security and insecurity, but it certainly might be more transient and changeable.

According to the authors of the country chapters in this volume, the weapons acquisition process is determined largely by rational calculations of security requirements. They tend to support the "political" side in the debate over technological versus political causes of arms races.[26] Weapons themselves are not the cause of conflicts that grow out of clashing interests and ambitions. Nevertheless, the possession of weapons—their numbers, location, disposition, and readiness—can exacerbate such conflicts, and in particular circumstances may indeed be a major contributor to international conflict. The India–Pakistan dispute would be one major case where weapons themselves have assumed a symbolic and political existence beyond their military utility.[27]

An area of particular concern to all three states under examination is the complex effect that new weapons technologies will have on their security and international status.[28] Several new kinds of weapons systems are being introduced into the inventories of the technologically advanced states. Of the three Asian powers we have examined, only Japan is able to even keep up with the research and development in this field.[29]

One class of weapon, precision-guided munitions (PGMs), is especially disruptive to conventional military estimates. PGMs are distinguished by their high degree of accuracy (better than .5), their relatively low cost (compared with likely targets such as aircraft, tanks, bridges, and other vulnerable structures), their simplicity of operation, and their versatility. (PGMs can be carried on land-, air-, and sea-based platforms, although what may realistically distinguish between them is their intended target, not their launch vehicle.) Some hope has been raised that such weapons will tilt the offense–defense balance in favor of the latter, ushering in an era of a military status quo, in which present boundaries and political structures of all sizes are able to defend and protect themselves without threatening their neighbors.[30] It seems more realistic that on land, at least, offensive operations will still be possible—using these defensive weapons—but that they will be more tentative and protracted, with blitzkrieg tactics being discouraged. It also seems likely that massed armed forces are going to be seen less and less frequently as the optimum size for independent operation grows smaller and smaller.

Such small units, combined with high weapons technologies and a need for advanced communications networks, may in fact work to the overall advantage of the superpowers, at least when facing a state of the second rank. At sea, however, PGMs would work against the fleets of the superpowers. Incursions by major naval units in areas such as the Persian Gulf, the Bay of Bengal, the Sea of Japan, or off the coast of China may become too dangerous when PGMs are in the vicinity. PGMs would seem to have an uncertain effect on the vulnerability of China, India, and Japan to air attack or airspace penetration. Unless a state has access to the latest in PGM technology (which probably means access to one of the superpowers), as well as a very sophisticated air defense command and control network (which India and Japan do have), there would seem to be no effective way of stopping penetration at will by a superpower.

In summary, lacking a consortium of middle-level powers, it would seem to be absolutely vital that such states maintain some ties with either superpower in order to retain access to PGM technology (and to other new technologies, such as laser weapons). Lacking such an association, they will be especially vulnerable to two characteristics of some PGMs noted above: their cheap cost and simplicity of operation. A middle power faces not only the risk of falling hopelessly behind the superpowers in terms of keeping up (that is, more than one generation of weapons technology in arrears) but also the risk of its smaller neighbors gaining access to such weapons, thus altering regional balances.

Arms Control and Proliferation

It is difficult to estimate with much precision the likely course of the arms control and nuclear proliferation processes in Asia, and the roles of China, India, and Japan with regard to these processes. China, of course, already possesses nuclear weapons, and India has demonstrated a capacity to produce them—halting short of a military program. Japan certainly has the necessary nuclear technology. Several of these states could help others become nuclear weapons powers, or their example might force others to develop such weapons. What is critical is not the capacities of these states to become nuclear weapons powers or to improve the systems that they already possess but the calculations that would support a decision to do so. Before discussing these calculations, which are vitally important yet often misunderstood by outsiders, some terminological clarification is necessary.

Even superficial examination of the problem reveals at least three objectives normally subsumed under the phrase *arms control*: prevention, limitation, and control.[31] *Prevention* refers to the initial acquisition of a weapons system, nuclear or conventional. Of the three states in question, China is a nuclear weapons power and India is only a nuclear power, with demonstrated weapons capabilities. *Limitation* as an arms control objective denotes restriction in the qualitative and quantitative levels of weapons. The Indian example of self-restraint after initial acquisition is particularly relevant here. It has demonstrated the ability to build a stockpile of weapons, but has apparently not done so as part of the "nuclear option" strategy.[32] *Control* as an arms control objective refers to the disposition, deployment, use, or command and control arrangements associated with a particular weapons system. Declaratory statements, such as China's "no first use" pronouncements, would fall into this category. Dealing with prevention, limitation, and control can be regarded as separate but necessary components of an arms control arrangement.

Arms control efforts must recognize the diversity of motives behind acquisition. These range from classic arms races (in which nuclear weapons are only a further step in a mutual escalation process) to the impetus of technology (because it can be done, it will be done). In addition, weapons may be acquired for purposes of strategic bargaining with other nuclear powers, or as a symbolic expression of national achievement (directed toward either domestic or foreign audiences). To complicate matters, once acquisition takes place, other considerations may shape levels and control arrangements.

Enough is already known about the politics of nuclear proliferation in these three states to make a few general statements about their role in the proliferation process. First, if India or Japan acquire a military nuclear system, it is likely that the Chinese pattern will be followed. In this case, strategic vulnerability and political conflict with a superpower encouraged the development of a modest retaliatory capacity that was coupled with public assurances of restraint and moderation. None of the three states face a major threat from a smaller neighbor (although their nuclear acquisition might be dysfunctional if it forces states such as South Korea and Pakistan into a nuclear program); it will be their relations with the superpowers that are likely to force them into a military nuclear program.

Obviously, none of these states, including China, can hope to have an effective strategic deterrent against the United States or the Soviet Union for many years without improvements over the kind of system already possessed by the Chinese. A first-strike strategy would be suicidal for them. At the very best they can achieve a limited capacity to destroy a few population centers in retaliation. But the major significance of a nuclear capacity for these countries would be the ability to conduct nuclear strikes or demonstrations against the equipment, military facilities, and allies of a nuclear-armed enemy, without being forced to attack major population centers. This form of limited nuclear war is ideally suited as an intermediate strategy for states with great power ambitions; it gives them the status of a nuclear program and permits the development of relevant technologies without unduly provoking the superpowers. Later, missile delivery systems could yield an advanced second-strike capacity, although there will necessarily be a gap between initial acquisition and the establishment of such a secure capacity. This produces a powerful incentive to defer initial acquisition until a rather sophisticated system can be developed—as long as strategic deterrence is handled by some friendly power (the United States in the case of Israel and Japan, and the Soviet Union in the case of India). Maintenance of explicit or tacit guarantees of deterrence must be a high priority for any state serious about acquisition of nuclear weapons in Asia. Withdrawal or weakening of such guarantees is likely to hasten proliferation, although there may come a point when a middle-rank state (probably India) decides that external deterrents are no longer credible or worth the political price, or are even no longer required. In the end, the proliferation of weapons in Asia (and in certain other regions, as well) will depend on the willingness of the existing nuclear powers to manage their relations with the near-nuclear powers in such a way as to satisfy both the reasonable ambitions and security requirements of the latter. These relations will necessarily include inducements and punishments on behalf of the superpowers, and implicit blackmail—involving the threat to develop nuclear weapons—on the part of the near-nuclear and new nuclear powers. For the latter, the threat may be to expand and refine levels and qualities of weapons or to promote the spread of nuclear weapons to other states and regions.[33]

Conclusion

In his study of the international hierarchy, Steven Spiegel singled out the secondary powers as critical for the future of the international system. Neither superpower is likely to decline, nor are the minor powers and regional states likely to change their role as "ideological and adventurous upstarts." The secondary powers, however, will determine whether or not "an advanced form of the present system continues or whether a considerable transformation occurs."[34] Such a transformation would involve the creation of several additional centers of powers, presumably complete with nuclear forces, exerting influence within one or more regions of the world. A more radical prospect has been advanced by Rajni Kothari, who argues for twenty or more regional centers, smashing the tacit division of the world by the two superpowers.[35] In this plan, states such as India, Japan, and China would naturally dominate their regions, but no superpowers would have worldwide influence.

While I have argued the likely emergence of China, India, and Japan as great or near-great powers, forming a separate and identifiable class of states, this does not necessarily imply concomitant changes in the international system. What may emerge is a "managing agent" world, in which such regionally powerful states as India are conceded local dominance, and superpowers refrain from supporting regional rivals, let alone engaging in direct confrontation. Other states, such as China and Japan, are accorded a specialized global role (political in the case of the former, economic for the latter) without recognition as a full-fledged superpower.

These developments would challenge the superpowers' global strategies, which were based on such general policies as containment, or more recently, the application of ideological, political, or developmental standards. These new middle-rank states would not be seen as prizes in a contest, but as autonomous actors, full components in a restricted geographic or functional sphere of activity.

Awareness of such a change in the international system is bound to come slowly.[36] However, conceding a new status to these states (if, indeed, they seek such change in their international role) is not only compatible with superpower interests but may be the best way to restrain their military expansion and control the issue of nuclear proliferation. A strategy of preemptive recognition still runs two risks. It may lead to the abandonment of smaller regional states in granting hegemony to powers with regional or subcontinental ambitions. In some cases (such as the Arab states of the Gulf region, or the two Koreas) this may be dangerous and unsettling; in others (Pakistan) it may lead to serious internal disorder. Second, according enhanced status to the emerging great powers may tempt them to reach beyond their capabilities.

As long as the world was dominated by two superpowers, the three major states of Asia have had to function in a relatively hostile world, but one in which there were natural opportunities to exploit the superpowers. The years of bidding and bargaining over the favors of these states may be over, and replaced by a focus on their own capabilities, ambitions, and objectives. Much of our argument implies a certain pessimism about the capacity of the United States and the Soviet Union to accommodate to this new reality. The inevitable influence of distance, perceptual distortion, and ideological obsessions will all make an accurate assessment of these states difficult. It is hoped that chapters in the Marwah/Pollack volume will to some degree assist in the process of understanding the strengths, weaknesses, ambitions, and limitations of the three major states of Asia, thereby helping global adaptation to their likely emergence over the next decade.

1992

EIGHT

The State Is Dead

Long Live the Armed Ethnic Group

August 14 is the first anniversary of the KGB-led coup that tried to preempt the new Union treaty in the Soviet Union. The failure of the coup led to the discrediting of the KGB, the downfall of the Communist Party, and the dissolution of the USSR. The entity that was both feared and misunderstood for so many years came to a symbolic end when Mikhail Gorbachev, already stripped of his party chairmanship, resigned as president of the (former) Soviet Union on December 24, 1991.

Because the world still saw things in terms of an ideological struggle between West and East, many of us in the West were justifiably excited by the collapse of communism. However, insufficient attention has been paid to the broader implications of the breakup of the Soviet state. This was the second instance since the end of World War II of a modern multiethnic state collapsing—the destruction of Pakistan in 1971 (midwifed by the armed intervention of neighboring India) was the first. (Ironically, Pakistan itself was evidence of the difficulty of state-making—it was conceived in violence when the British left India in 1947.)

With separatist movements cropping up throughout the Middle East, Southern and Central Asia, and parts of Europe, it is important to understand that the Soviet Union disintegrated not only because of the political and economic collapse of communism, and the enfeeblement of its security forces, but because the Soviet state was under extraordinary pressure from within and without. It may turn out that the crisis of the multiethnic state, not the disappearance of communism, will be the most profound political event of our generation.

This breaking-up process has far-reaching implications for U.S. foreign policy. In recent decades, Americans seem to have a special problem in determining if, where, and how Washington should intervene in a world made up of states of unequal power, stability, and importance.

Americans under sixty have lived their entire adult lives during one of two titanic struggles. The first was against the Nazi and Japanese empires in World War II, the second against Leninist structures and Stalinist expansionism in the Cold War. Yet traditional American isolationism survives, most recently speaking with the voice of television commentator and presidential candidate Patrick Buchanan. For some conservatives, the United States, as God's chosen country, can only be contaminated by contact with a corrupt world and scheming foreigners.

But nowadays, the conservative Right has a new ally: the burnt-out Left, still obsessed with the noninterventionist "lessons" of the Vietnam War. They think that America is corrupt—that it has failed to live up to its own ideals. To them, Washington cannot act abroad without creating victims.

Together, the two isolationisms threaten the rational conduct of foreign affairs. Without a significant, dramatic international threat, internationalisms of all varieties face tough going in the next decade. This could be dangerous to world peace. The fate of the political entities that develop and control nuclear weapons, that oppress or liberate their own people, should be of central concern to policymakers. But it is hard to think about (and even harder to make policy about) such entities at a time when the state is disintegrating in so many parts of the world, and isolationist rhetoric shadows political discourse.

What is eating away at the legitimacy and power of the state—the entity that was the building block of international politics for the past two hundred years? Five factors have undercut the moral, economic, militant, and political foundation of the modern Western-style state.

First, the state has lost its monopoly over information. Galloping technologies have weakened the ability of the state to control the information flowing to its citizens. The two revolutionaries of our era are not Marx and Lenin, but Bell Labs and the Boeing Corporation—inventors, respectively, of the transistor and the wide-bodied jet. The transistor and its solid-state progeny have put modern communications receivers in the hands of individuals, families, and small groups. State broadcasting systems everywhere are forced to compete with the BBC, CNN, and the private Singapore-based Star radio and television services.

Meanwhile, jumbo jets make it possible for people and goods to move cheaply and rapidly across frontiers. In some cases this has meant new horizons and new ideas; in others, it has enabled older ties and linkages to extend across the world. Terrorists of all nationalities, for example, not only blow up jumbo jets but ride in them, commuting between target state and safe haven.

The electronic and air travel revolutions have enabled ideas and people to move over and through iron and bamboo curtains. Although modern police states have used advanced electronics to spy on and control their own populations, the race has been won by the "offense." At least temporarily, the bureaucracies of bugging and terror have been outmaneuvered by VCRs, cassette tape recorders (crucial in overthrowing the Shah of Iran), small transistor radios, shortwave and satellite broadcasting systems, and discounted air tickets.

Second, the state cannot protect its citizens in wartime. When Ronald Reagan said in 1985 that a nuclear war could not be fought, and, if fought, could not be won, he kicked away one of the most important props of the state since the mid-eighteenth century: the argument that it protected its citizens from the depredations of foreigners.

Ironically, the spread of nuclear weapons after 1945 at first seemed to strengthen the hand of the state. At no time in history did any state command such enormous military power as did the United States and the Soviet Union during the period of American and Soviet nuclear hegemony from 1950 to 1990. Even today, hawks in India, Pakistan, Iraq, North Korea, and other near-nuclear states seek nuclear weapons for statist, not strategic reasons. Yet, the breakdown of the Soviet Union suggests a different lesson: mere possession of nuclear weapons is not enough to prevent the breakup of a state, let alone to ensure the physical protection of its citizens from external attack—except by mutual suicide.

Indeed, as a state appears to become strong through the possession of nuclear weapons, its citizens become vulnerable, undefendable targets of the nuclear weapons of other powers. Short of developing a perfect strategic defense system, no state can ever again promise its citizens physical security. Reagan's staunch support of the Strategic Defense Initiative was no whim. He understood that nuclear weapons had transformed the role of the state, and only through a miracle of technology might the modern state regain one of its key functions.

Third, the state no longer ensures economic prosperity. States once claimed, sometimes erroneously, that only they could ensure economic growth and justice within a given territory. The nineteenth-century model of the self-contained state embodied an evolution from basic agriculture, through a trading economy, to industrial self-reliance—dramatically symbolized, in the last century, by steel mills and rail networks, and today, by aircraft industries and nuclear power plants.

But the nineteenth-century model has been supplanted by a new model. Subnational regions and territories try to link up with larger economic entities: a multi-national corporation, or a Japanese auto firm, or an American clothing retailer. Mayors and governors from Kansas to Guangzhou compete with one another for the favor of Mitsubishi or Motorola. They demand that their national governments either subsidize the process or get out of the way.

And, if the weather and geography are suitable, some regional leaders calculate that they can become stand-alone "tourist destinations." All they need is a beach or mountain scenery, and the jumbo jets bearing German and Japanese tourists will come, just as soon as the concrete hardens at the spanking-new international airport.

Kashmiris, for example, looking at Nepal and Sri Lanka, have calculated that a regular air link with Europe and Northeast Asia could quadruple their income from tourists—and payments would be in hard currencies, not in Indian rupees. Only the Indian state—controlled by a New Delhi elite—seems to stand in their way.

Fourth, the state has lost its monopoly on justice. Aristotle taught us that the object of politics is justice. Until recently it was understood that the state—a Western invention—provided the context in which individuals and groups achieved justice. Further, it was also assumed that a large and powerful state could best guarantee justice within its borders, and secure justice vis-à-vis potentially hostile neighbors.

That is no longer true. International organizations, human rights groups, and self-appointed spokesmen for democracy all challenge the state's claim to be the moral arbiter of its citizens' lives. When backed by the power of international lending institutions, or by the Japanese Export-Import Bank, or by U.S. Congress, these arguments carry unprecedented weight, and they have the unintended consequence of giving aid and comfort to some who would destroy certain states.

Earlier this year, all the South Asian states jointly challenged the linkage of human rights and international loans. India and its neighbors are democracies with fairly good human rights records, but they resent—as violations of sovereignty—the application of human rights criteria by foreign institutions. They also fear that separatist groups will see this as an international endorsement of their aims and methods.

And, from a new quarter, Islamic movements not only challenge the dominance of secularized Western notions of justice and freedom; they undercut the grounds on which many rulers govern in secular Muslim-majority states or in states (such as India and the Philippines) that have large Muslim populations.

Finally, the state is being attacked from within. Multiethnic states are everywhere trembling in the aftermath of the breakup of the Soviet Union and the civil war in Yugoslavia. A once-heretical question is again being raised: Why should there be one China? Or one India? Or only two South Asian Islamic republics—Pakistan and Bangladesh? Or one Iraq, or one Sri Lanka? Why not three, or four, or five, or twenty?

Three generations ago, the great nationalist leaders forged anticolonial movements by arguing that if India, or the Dutch East Indies, or the Gold Coast, could achieve "unity in diversity," that they could manage their complex societies better than foreign imperialists could.

Today, separatist ethnic, regional, linguistic, and religious groups have turned the argument inside out. Contemporary Nehrus, Nkrumahs, Jinnahs, and Titos argue that there can be greater economic progress, military security, and political justice in diversity—that the big-state apparatus is irrelevant in an era of global economic linkages and unusable military power. And the new subnational leaders see foreign lending agencies and human rights groups (which in America includes the Far Right as well as elements of the Left) as allies, not enemies, as they press the case that the parts of the state are greater than the whole.

Implications

What does the crumbling of the state hold for the future? Four points seem to be crucial for the international community to keep in mind.

1. The classical state is not dead, even in those cases where new states rise from the corpse of the old. The state remains the model for those who would destroy it. We are not likely to see the new states of the world pass up the opportunity to acquire all of the trappings of sovereignty: their own airlines, armies, navies, and even nuclear weapons programs.

But the new rulers will be sabotaged by the same forces that brought down their predecessors: an emerging global economy, new international standards of state behavior and human rights, and populations that cannot be easily controlled. Thus, there may be more states (the breakup of the Soviet Union and Yugoslavia has alone created twenty new ones), but their governments will be weaker. The entire foreign office of Kazakhstan consists of eight people, yet it is a republic that nominally controls hundreds of nuclear weapons.

2. The proliferation of states, either through the voluntary reorganization of existing entities (the Soviet pattern) or through civil war and chaos (first Pakistan, and more recently Yugoslavia, Ethiopia, and possibly Iraq) will interact with a second proliferation process—the rapid spread of weapons of mass destruction. Nuclear weapons and missiles are, respectively, fifty- and sixty-year-old technologies. These technologies have been mastered by thousands of scientists and technicians around the world.

The more unstable and nervous of the new state entities will reach for such weapons technologies and hope that they will ensure the survival of the regime and of the state. But the lesson of the Soviet and Iraqi cases should not be forgotten: the disposition of these technologies is not solely dictated by old notions of national "sovereignty"; these weapons are of widespread concern beyond the state borders, and their spread may justify international or unilateral intervention.

Establishing nuclear nonproliferation as a firm international norm is important now, and it should be a factor that determines the conditions under which the United States supports—or refrains from supporting—states under attack.

3. It is unlikely that the state will be replaced by either global or regional political institutions as the unit of international politics. For better and for worse, we will have a world of states, not a world of effective international or regional organizations. The United Nations and one or two regional organizations may play a useful role in cushioning the impact of state breakup, or in some cases preventing it, but they will not attract the loyalty of great numbers of people, nor can they meet basic economic, moral, and political needs of sizable numbers of people.

While it is important to support nascent regional organizations, such as the South Asian Association for Regional Cooperation and the Association of Southeast Asian Nations, these groupings are no substitute for great-power engagement in regional security matters. The involvement may be intrusive and even violent in cases where some states are trying to destroy others (the Middle East, certainly), or advisory in regions where there is a prevalence of vulnerable multiethnic states (South Asia). And great-power involvement may be vital in areas that lack any regional organization—especially Northeast Asia, the most dangerous area of all, where a divided state, Korea, interacts with a volatile combination of nuclear-weapons powers, advanced economies, and historical antagonisms.

4. It is time to abandon the deceptive vocabulary used to classify large numbers of states. In the 1950s, the euphemisms "developing" and "emerging" replaced "backward" and "undeveloped," which in their day were polite substitutes for "wogs" or "natives." But in the 1970s, another term arrived, further corrupting the discourse on state building. "Third world" began as a euphemism for the "nonaligned," but then it acquired a vague social, political, and moral content.

To the Right, third world states were somehow poor, somehow threatening, and generally a danger to the rest of us when they fell on one another or acquired weapons of mass destruction. On the Left, there was an effort to create the illusion of a class of states with shared moral qualities, a group that represented more than the sum of its parts. However, while the first and second worlds have conceptually vanished, the third world remains, still shaped by Cold War constructs.

Thus, virtually every public figure today proclaims the existence of a "third world" located somewhere along the Mexico-Bombay-Manila axis. Weirdly, China is not a "third world" country, but India—with two hundred of its eight hundred million possessing a European living standard—is.

Western leaders, steeped in Cold War visions of strong enemies, long ignored the transformation of weak states into stronger states. Our understanding of the deeper destructive processes at work in many states around the world (and not all of them are poor, southern, or nonaligned) may have been compromised by such terms as *third world*, *South*, and other euphemisms.

State Building

In the United States, academic and government strategists who speak enthusiastically of a new world order need to look more carefully at the friable and imperfect material they are working with.

In a speech last November, John Reichart, a member of the State Department's Policy Planning Staff, characterized the "new world order" as an era of hope based on "cooperative diplomacy," adherence to human rights, and the spread of market economies. The deplorable "old world order" was epitomized by containment, "a negative strategy." Containment was "what we were against"; the new world order is "what we are for."

But policymakers need to devote as much attention to an understanding of the units out of which we are constructing a new world order as they do to the nature of that order. The fall of communism was an astonishing event, but so, in its own way, has been the breakup of the Soviet state. Other than China, there are no more communisms of consequence left to fall.

Nevertheless, the state in many parts of the world is under attack and most will not go as quietly. Their leaders have not lived under the shadow of nuclear terror for two generations, as did the leaders of the United States and the Soviet Union. Further, in most cases these leaders see the West as a threat, not as a potential friend. For the leaders of such states, and for those who would challenge them, weapons of mass destruction are likely to be seen as part of the solution, not as part of the problem.

The cliché of the day in the Pentagon and among its friends on the Right is that our unstable new world is "more dangerous than ever." Meanwhile, on the Left, there has been a convenient rediscovery of "human rights" violations and a growing indignation over state violence, coupled with virtual silence about the separatists, narco-terrorists, and murderers who are trying to tear apart a number of states. But between those who assume that there is nothing wrong with the state, and those who argue that there is nothing right with most states—between threat-of-the-day thinking, on one hand, and indignant liberal isolationism, on the other—there is a prudent center.

Chester Bowles, a New Dealer who became an undersecretary of state in the Kennedy administration, understood that state building was an important national security interest of the United States. But Bowles failed as a strategist because he was not single-minded enough for the pugnacious Cold Warriors who surrounded him. They saw Bowles's interest in state building in Africa, Latin America, and Asia in a purely Cold War framework, not as an important aim in itself.

But Bowles was right. Today, many years after Bowles left the scene, multiethnic states are fragmenting, and the United States must make the best of it. Rather than observe from afar, we must have a foreign policy that takes this into account, especially when many of these states (or their successors) will have access to instruments of mass destruction. These states, in particular, need our understanding, assistance, and perhaps direct intervention to achieve the kind of stability that benefits them individually, and the world collectively.

1989

NINE

Solving Proliferation Problems in a Regional Context

South Asia

This essay suggests ways in which the United States can prevent, limit, or contain the proliferation of nuclear weapons in South Asia. While concerned about the immediate future, it also reviews past policies and regional realities, before proposing a comprehensive short- and long-term American regional nonproliferation policy and explaining how such a policy should be implemented.

The exact nuclear status of India and Pakistan is a matter of conjecture. It is my understanding that neither state has a working nuclear weapon but that both could quickly convert existing stocks of fissile material into a deliverable device. Given time, both could produce sufficient nuclear weapons to deploy a small first strike nuclear force. Certainly, India (with its large stocks of plutonium) has the capacity for a much larger force. Both states also possess adequate means for delivery in the form of advanced fighter-bombers. Both have recently tested short-range missiles, and on May 21, 1989, India launched the Agni, a medium-range missile—offering no pretense that it was engaged in purely peaceful research or testing.[1]

First India and then Pakistan moved close to acquiring a nuclear weapon. The overall Indian nuclear program is mature and well developed. Indian nuclear research began in the 1940s, a bomb program was widely discussed and studied in the 1960s, and a so-called PNE—peaceful nuclear explosion—was tested in 1974. Despite this history of nuclear research—and predictions of imminent weaponization—the Indian leadership has crept slowly along the nuclear path. This was not the perception of some Pakistani leaders. Misjudging Indian intentions, they pressed for a Pakistani program as early as 1964.

Thus there are two states in South Asia unconstrained by strong outside alliances, beset by a range of internal and external security problems, engaged in a long-term political struggle with each other, and close to two other nuclear powers. They now possess the means to acquire military nuclear systems. That they have not done so is no less significant, and provides American policymakers with both an insight into Indian and Pakistani nuclear politics and an entry point into their nuclear decisions.

This essay takes a frankly regional perspective. Few in the larger nonproliferation community have a firm grasp of the political calculations that have driven India and Pakistan toward weaponization. Since 1964 regional proliferation dynamics have often been misunderstood when they have not been ignored. While America's regional specialists sometimes line up uncritically behind the Indians or the Pakistanis, a different angle of vision—even a little clientitis—might be useful in the debate over coping with regional proliferation. While we must be concerned with the impact of South Asian nuclear events on proliferation elsewhere, with the importance of preserving the Non-Proliferation Treaty (NPT) and with the virtue of policy consistency, South Asia now constitutes so much of the proliferation problem and the regional outcomes are so uncertain, that a strong case can be made for taking the narrow view. A comprehensive and consistent American nonproliferation policy that works only where there is no danger of proliferation and that has no impact or even accelerates the weaponization process in South Asia does not strike me as much of an accomplishment.

South Asia will demand close and constant attention in the next few years. We should not be optimistic just because India and Pakistan have not yet plunged into overt nuclear programs. Both states are not only driven by the logic of technology, their own interactive relationship, and other strategic and political considerations; they are running out of alternatives to weaponization. The central goal of American policy should be to see that attractive alternatives exist. Failing that, there is an even chance that the slow, measured pace that has characterized nuclear decisions in the region will become increasingly interactive and threatening.

Past Policies: Six Strategies

America's nonproliferation policy in South Asia has always been to oppose the acquisition of nuclear weapons by regional states. Over the years the United States has successively deployed six different strategies in an attempt advance this South Asian nonproliferation policy. These have been pursued with varying degrees of energy and success. Many of these strategies complement each other, and some have overlapped. A comprehensive American policy for the 1990s will have to incorporate several elements of these strategies.

Sublimating the Nuclear Mystique

Initially, America's nonproliferation policy in South Asia assumed that by channeling regional interest in the atom toward civilian uses, the desire to acquire nuclear weapons would wane. Since the United States (or another responsible power) was the sole source of nuclear technology and fissile material, local programs could be carefully monitored. The Atoms for Peace program eventually led to the construction of power and research reactors in India and Pakistan (including East Pakistan, now Bangladesh) and the training of thousands of regional scientists in American labs and universities.

The NPT: Potlatch or Condominium?

When it became clear that spreading peaceful nuclear technology was a policy that had begun to work too well, the United States turned to a comprehensive plan that would link civilian nuclear ambitions to arms control, and link each to important concessions to be made by the major nuclear powers—the NPT.

This treaty was to be a great exchange, a trade, between the nuclear haves and nuclear have-nots. The West and the Soviets would reduce their nuclear forces if the non-nuclear states would give up any attempt to acquire them; the reward for the latter would also include civilian nuclear technology. The NPT was offered as a kind of superpower potlatch: they would give up something substantial, destroying and trading away their most destructive systems. The non-nuclear world would become more secure and would reap a bonus in the form of power reactors.

This was a perfectly acceptable arrangement for almost all nations, and the NPT has been signed and ratified by more than 130 states. Most of these states either belonged to a superpower alliance or they had no interest in acquiring nuclear weapons. Indeed, most states who were not alliance members had no need—or lacked the capacity—to go nuclear. The NPT made it easy for both classes of states to avoid doing what they did not want to or could not afford to do. In several cases (South Korea, Taiwan) states were able to parlay their adherence to the NPT into enhanced commitments from a superpower.

But for two other classes of nations the NPT was a bad deal. For states with real enemies and threats that lacked superpower guarantees, the bomb seemed quite attractive (South Africa, Pakistan). And, for states that had regional aspirations of their own, the NPT was certainly restrictive (China and India fall into this category). Such states most strongly protested against the "Yalta syndrome," since any such international arrangement as NPT places severe limits on their regional and extraregional ambitions.[2] They will continue to hold this view as long as nuclear weapons are linked to great power status.

Technology Denial

For the states that stayed out of the NPT, particularly Pakistan, the United States turned to a policy of strict technology denial in the mid-1970s. Formalized in the London suppliers club, elaborate covert and overt mechanisms were developed to monitor and limit the flow of nuclear technology to Pakistan, which was highly dependent on outside suppliers. Even where an item or a technology could not be kept from such states, it was possible to make it more difficult or costly to acquire it, presumably slowing down the pace of a nuclear program. The Nuclear Non-Proliferation Act of 1978 (NNPA) placed greater restraint on American nuclear contacts with non-NPT states, banning all nuclear exports, requiring full-scope safeguards, and even banning talks on nuclear safety (the United States now has nuclear safety talks with countries such as the Soviet Union and China, but not with India and Pakistan).

Buying Influence: Aid, Trade, and Technology

In contrast, the main effort with regard to India seems to have been to use aid, trade, and technology to acquire influence in nuclear decisions (the difference between the strategies for Pakistan and India can be traced in part to the stronger evidence of a military nuclear program in Pakistan, but also because India could absorb, and had sought, a wide range of dual-use technologies that—in the minds of American officials—offered some influence over nuclear decisions). If nothing else, aid and dual-use technologies put a foot in the diplomatic door: on several occasions after 1982 American officials traveling to South Asia to discuss proliferation matters were provided with a military item for Pakistan and a piece of dual-use technology for India.

Enhancing Security

By 1981 it had become clear that Pakistan's price for giving up its nuclear program was too great. Pakistan wanted NATO-like guarantees from the United States against an Indian attack as well as from a Soviet/Afghan attack. U.S. policymakers refused to offer such guarantees. Instead, they proposed to Congress that American military aid to Pakistan would, in addition to providing Pakistan with the means to defend itself against threats from Soviet-occupied Afghanistan, enhance Pakistan's overall feeling of security, thus reducing Pakistan's desire for a nuclear weapon.

While this was the first time that military aid was positively and publicly linked to nuclear proliferation in South Asia, there were other regional examples of this policy. In South Asia the Soviet–Indian arms relationship must have been seen in Moscow (if not New Delhi) as one way of limiting India's nuclear ambitions. The Soviets have never encouraged an Indian nuclear program—besides adding another state to the nuclear ring surrounding the Soviet Union, an independent Indian nuclear program would reduce Delhi's dependence on Moscow and would probably increase the prospects of Sino-Indian normalization. Elsewhere, the United States–

Israel and United States–Taiwan relationships also provide the recipient state with enhanced security and, presumably, make less important the need for nuclear weapons.

A Regional Approach

Finally, American policy has tentatively turned to the regional approach. From about 1985 (marked by the special mission of NSC staff member Don Fortier and Undersecretary of State Michael Armacost in September) American officials came to see South Asian proliferation as an interactive problem that had to be dealt with in both regional capitals. Subsequently, it was realized that on two counts China was part of the region as far as nuclear matters were concerned; first, there was the suspicion that China had provided nuclear assistance to Pakistan, and, second, some old hands remembered that the Indian program was originally triggered by the 1964 Chinese test. The Soviets were informed about this regional approach to South Asian proliferation, although there is no evidence of any cooperative action.

Successes and Failures

Most of these strategies and policies met with some success, otherwise we might now be talking about a fully proliferated South Asia. American policy did make a difference since the United States was the only state that combined excellent intelligence and technical capabilities, good ties to India and Pakistan, a legitimate interest in nonproliferation, and an array of incentives and disincentives that could be deployed to support its nonproliferation policy. However, each approach also had certain shortcomings.

For example, the earliest, best-intention American efforts to help the nuclear programs of South Asia seem now to have been excessive, and perhaps harmful to nonproliferation interests. They transferred nuclear technology, skills, and often critical materials to states that might not have needed them for legitimate energy or research needs. Second, these programs provided the pretext for later military or dual-use programs: all the suspicious Indian and Pakistani programs have been justified as "peaceful" or "civilian." Finally, these early programs expanded or created Indian and

Pakistani nuclear bureaucracies that were then exposed to what was essentially a Western and American double standard: "Our programs can be military and peaceful since we are responsible people; yours must be only peaceful, since we do not know whether we can trust you with these devices."[3]

Atoms for Peace thus convinced many South Asian scientists that they could be admitted to the outer hallway, but the living room and dining room were reserved for the "great" powers. Thus was planted the equation (reinforced by a great deal of public hand-wringing over how heavy a burden it was to be a nuclear weapons state) that great power equals nuclear power.

The NPT was even worse. It rang hollow in Delhi and Islamabad, where it was seen as a double betrayal. The nuclear states were not going to disarm, nor were they really serious about transferring nuclear technology at a price that poor states could afford. The NPT was likened to one of those false pledges of freedom that the British had repeatedly offered and withdrew. Promises were cheap; while no Indian or Pakistani leader of any significance wanted to go nuclear in 1964–65 (except for the very junior Zulfikar Ali Bhutto in Pakistan and one of India's foremost nuclear scientists, Homi Bhabha), few Indians or Pakistanis saw the NPT as advancing their national interests. Indians and Pakistanis were in agreement on this, and both were genuinely surprised when few other states joined them in opposing the NPT.

With the collapse of the NPT as a nonproliferation strategy for South Asia, the sticks of technology denial, on the one hand, and the carrots of aid and technology, on the other, were only stopgaps. They did buy access and time. In 1981 my own view was that the U.S. aid package to Pakistan would have a marginal impact on the Pakistani nuclear program and that the U.S. tie would defer, but not terminate, Pakistani weaponization.[4] The Soviets must have come to the same calculation in the case of India. Aid as influence had its role and its limits; we would only pay so much to be heard, and in exchange, India and Pakistan would, at best, postpone critical decisions (or slice them thinly) while we were talking.

The shortcomings of the Reagan administration's regional approach are well known. It was at first driven by Afghan-related considerations. The United States could not continue to supply the Mujahideen through Pakistan nor could it arm Pakistan if Congress were to cut off assistance because of Islamabad's nuclear program. But Pakistan itself was driven to a nuclear program in part because of its India-related fears; during this period, in an attempt to bury the idea of an "Islamic bomb" (which indeed was one of Zulfikar Ali Bhutto's original objectives in beginning the program) all Pakistani officials stressed, rather disingenuously, that the threat from India lay behind their own nuclear program. Thus, New Delhi had to be brought into the American effort to save the Pakistan aid package. The Indians were perfectly aware of this but saw an opportunity to move closer to Pakistan's chief patron. They also wanted the opportunity to embarrass Pakistan, and constantly used their closer ties to Washington to point out Pakistan's errant nuclear ways.[5]

Despite important shortcomings in conception and implementation the regional approach had (from an American perspective) a positive impact on Indian and Pakistan nuclear policies. American officials may have underestimated the impact of their efforts on Indian and Pakistani decisionmakers. Thus, while there were sporadic discussions and plans for a comprehensive regional nonproliferation policy, such a policy was never fully staffed out.[6]

If nothing else, the new regional approach may have encouraged India and Pakistan (as they competed for American favor) to run up a whole series of proposals for regional nuclear and conventional arms control. Most of these were not to be taken seriously, and at the very moment Delhi and Islamabad were gushing with suggestions for mutual inspection, verification, and force reduction, the two states almost slipped into war. Nevertheless, American interest in a regional approach did influence regional officials and strategists. It caused them to think about regional arms control and nonproliferation, and it began to shape a common vocabulary with which to discuss and talk about such issues (one important stage in the evolution of U.S.–Soviet arms control negotiations was the emergence of such a common vocabulary, including agreement on shared definitions of key terms and phrases).

The regional approach met with opposition from two important American groups.[7] One included those in the nonproliferation community who had advocated a consistent, global, American nonproliferation policy. They saw the regional approach as a fig leaf for a continuing relationship with Pakistan and a sellout of nonproliferation objectives. In their view the regional approach was aimed at persuading Congress to avert its eyes, not at persuading India and Pakistan to give up their nuclear programs. This is too harsh, especially since their own alternative of a get-tough policy would have pushed both India and Pakistan into the nuclear weapons column.

The other opponents of a regional approach were the advocates of a strong alliance with Pakistan. They saw Pakistan as the pivot of a larger Middle East strategy; some may have privately seen a nuclear Pakistan as a more effective protector of American interests (we may yet hear more of "nuclear surrogates" and of the need to get the new nuclears "on our side"). There are good arguments for moving closer to a regional nuclear power, but there are equally persuasive ones for keeping one's distance from such states.

This review of recent American nonproliferation strategies in South Asia suggests some of the ingredients for a long-term policy:

—While a new policy will have to be built from the ground up, we can build on many past accomplishments.

—The NPT has reached its limits as far as South Asia is concerned.

—The South Asian proliferation problem is beyond the reach of technical harassment and only with difficulty, and careful planning, amenable to a mixture of political, military, and economic inducements.

—We know that we cannot provide the kind of security guarantees that Pakistan wants nor will we or the Soviets provide wide-ranging guarantees to India (certainly, if we or the Soviets were to provide such assurances to one regional state, it would trigger a nuclear program in the other, quite possibly placing Washington and Moscow on opposite sides of a regional nuclear competition, with China holding the wild card).

—A South Asian nonproliferation policy must rest on a regional approach, even if there are inconsistencies with a global strategy based on the NPT.

Regional Realities, American Misperceptions

Before moving to a discussion of current American interests and policies, it is essential to review several regional realities. Misperceptions of the region tend to cluster around three points: the motives and nature of the India–Pakistan "arms race," the internal politics of these programs, and the likely outcome of this competition.

An India–Pakistan Arms Race?

Most American officials believe that the Indian and Pakistani nuclear programs are driven by competition between the two states. It would be foolish to argue that their nuclear policies do not influence each other, but it is wrong to characterize their relationship solely—or even primarily—as an arms race. India's PNE program was, initially, a response to the Chinese test of 1964 and Beijing's subsequent weaponization. It was also a way to demonstrate to both the United States and the USSR that India was a power to be reckoned with; recently, China has again figured in Indian strategic and nuclear calculations, and informed Indian hawks now speculate that the Sino-Soviet summit of June 1989 means that the Soviet "umbrella" over India, epitomized in the Indo-Soviet Treaty of Peace and Friendship, has been furled.[8] The Pakistan program has been important in Indian calculations only since the late 1970s, and even then they were made in the context of the broader (if shifting) strategic picture.

While the Pakistan program began as a response to the Indian nuclear debate of the 1960s, and was accelerated by the 1974 Indian test, it also was conceived in larger terms.[9] First Zulfikar Ali Bhutto, and then Zia ul-Haq (and thus the military, which was opposed to nuclearization under President Ayub Khan) saw Pakistan as a stable, advanced and Islamic state; a Pakistani bomb would not only deter the conventional and nuclear threat from India; it would put Pakistan in the forefront of the Islamic world. Note also that the Pakistanis early came to an appreciation of extended deterrence; here they were following the Israeli and NATO examples, not India's.[10]

A Peoples' Bomb?

Americans have also consistently misjudged the intensity of support for nuclear weapons in India and Pakistan. This has led some to a fatalistic view of the inevitability of proliferation. But public opinion polls in India and Pakistan have consistently shown a majority against weaponization in both states. These figures were overwhelmingly antinuclear in the 1960s and 1970s; they are still marginally antinuclear. Yet when asked whether India or Pakistan should possess a nuclear weapon if the other has it, or if their country were to be threatened by another outside power, virtually all respondents indicate strong support for a bomb. In other words, regional public opinion has reservations about nuclear weapons but stronger reservations about being taken by surprise. This is, as one would expect, the view of most Indian and Pakistani politicians.

The armed forces in neither state have pressed for the bomb. Ayub Khan rejected Bhutto's suggestion that Pakistan go nuclear and fired him as foreign minister. Pressure for a nuclear program came from Pakistani civilians, not the armed forces. The same was true of India. None of the Indian armed services favored going nuclear until recently—each was afraid that the nuclear program would divert resources from conventional arms purchases and each was concerned that another service might gain control over the bomb.

If the public did not favor nuclearization, and the armed forces were neutral, at best, then how did these two states move to the edge of a military nuclear capability? There are different answers to this question for India and for Pakistan.

In India's case, a coalition of hawkish scientists, bureaucrats, and strategists have kept the pressure on successive governments. All Indian leaders since Nehru's have resisted "the next step," but most have moved further down the nuclear path in the absence of a good reason to freeze or to dismantle their nuclear programs.[11] Since Lal Bahadur Shastri's term as prime minister (1964–66) this deferral of the go–no-go decision, while simultaneously allowing research and development to move ahead, has acquired the label of the "option" strategy.[12] As a result, a wide range of programs have been authorized, started, and allowed to mature without a clear policy decision about their consequence.

In the 1960s the option strategy was invented in response to a perceived threat from China; in 1971 (when work on the PNE was authorized) India came under pressure from both the United States and the USSR in conjunction with the newly minted NPT and in the context of heightened tension with Pakistan. By maintaining a nuclear option Delhi could at least assert its nuclear independence (even as its dependence on others for conventional arms was growing). By the late 1970s the option strategy was firmly embedded in Indian policy.

The news of Pakistan's nuclear program almost precipitated a weaponization decision (there was also talk of a takeout of Pakistan's enrichment facility at Kahuta), but it was decided to continue to broaden the technical base of the nuclear program and speed up missile development. Only in 1974 (and the actual decision to test the PNE) did domestic factors play a role: Indira Gandhi was in deep political trouble, and the test may have impressed some Indians. What we see now (in the shape of the missile tests, statements about uranium enrichment, and other examples of a broad-based Indian program) are the result of decisions taken many years ago. Still, there is no strong evidence that the Indian leadership has committed itself to a full-scale, deployed nuclear and/or missile program.

Pakistan has been more purposive. From the beginning Bhutto wanted a nuclear weapon. He saw the bomb as a way of balancing India's conventional superiority, neutralizing the Indian nuclear threat, and reviving Pakistan's shattered strategic reputation. This policy met with near-universal support in Pakistan, and enabled Islamabad to operate one of history's most sophisticated industrial espionage programs.

The American connection may have modified Pakistan's plans, but it did not fundamentally alter them. Pakistan, also, wants to have an option, but one with a short fuse. It models itself after Israel—ambiguity about its own nuclear program brings it many of the benefits of nuclearization yet allows it to retain a tie with its major outside weapons supplier, the United States.

2016: The following underestimated the Pakistani conviction that a nuclear weapon was vital, yet they waited ten years until the Indian tests to have their own on May 28, 1998. Unlike India, where support for the nuclear program has broadened over the years, it has weakened in Pakistan. When Pakistan was an isolated and threatened country, the bomb seemed attractive. But as Pakistan has emerged from the Zia years as a respected, reasonably stable, and militarily more impressive state, different Pakistani groups have had second thoughts about the nuclear program. The military still see it as problematic, the diplomats are fully aware of the strains that it has caused in Pakistan's relations with the United States and other Western states, and no Pakistani politician today has the experience and skill of Zulfikar Ali Bhutto. They are more like their Indian counterparts—in the absence of a clear-cut alternative, they are willing to tolerate the nuclear program. Only the scientists involved in the program are true believers—although there are reports of a peace movement among some Pakistani scientists not directly engaged in the enrichment and weapons programs.

A Stable or Unstable Region?

Finally, outside observers have had trouble judging the stability of a proliferated South Asia. They tend toward two extreme views. One is the alarmist position that India and Pakistan, driven by racial and religious hatreds, are locked into a deadly arms race that could (at worst) lead to regional and/or global nuclear war, or (at best) produce a nuclear accident, nuclear theft, or the transfer of fissile material and sensitive technology to other near-nuclears. The perception is widespread that regional governments are unstable and insecure, that they cannot be trusted with nuclear weapons.

On the other hand, there is a minority view that nuclear weapons themselves generate their own logic—that of deterrence. This position holds that any pair of nuclear antagonists, such as India and Pakistan, will replicate and evolve on a small scale the peaceful deadlock that has characterized the American–Soviet relationship.[13]

Perhaps the most honest conclusion we can reach about the stability of a proliferated South Asia is that we do not know what will happen. One of the unknowns about the future of proliferation is the degree of evolutionary congruence between technology and strategy. It took decades and billions of dollars for the West, the Soviet Union, and China to integrate strategy and military technology. But the new nuclear states (especially India) are likely to be born with fully mature military systems. Will their nuclear doctrine be as developed? What kind of doctrine will be adopted by nonaligned nuclear states that also have complex conventional military threat? Looking at the problem in the abstract, Brito and Intriligator note that as the number of nuclear states are increased then there are more weapons, targets, and decision-centers. Further, the chances of an irrational or crazy state appearing are also increased. This may be balanced—once again, in the abstract—by the power of deterrence logic: increasing the number of nuclear states also increases the number of partners available for deterrence.[14]

But we do have some evidence about the crisis behavior of Indian and Pakistani decisionmakers. This evidence, like the theoretical analysis, is inconclusive. India and Pakistan have gone to war four times, and India fought a war with China in 1962; further, there have been a number of border crises, most recently in 1987, when India confronted both Pakistan and China. Pessimists can point to the growth of ethnic disturbances in all three states, to their propensity of such conflict to spill across borders, to the misperceptions and stereotypes held by leaders in each major state, and to the strong influence of domestic politics on the foreign policies of India and Pakistan.

Yet South Asia's two major military powers have reached significant arms control agreements with each other. They have also managed to exclude outside states from their own bilateral relationship (formalized in the 1972 Simla agreement between Bhutto and Indira Gandhi), and regional leaders are increasingly aware of the impossible costs of a major war.[15]

My own speculative view is that nuclear proliferation will stabilize the Indo-Pakistan relationship about to the degree that nuclear weapons have introduced caution into U.S.–Soviet and Soviet–Chinese relations (a judgment that does not imply much enthusiasm about proliferation's beneficial side effects). India and Pakistan have, in fact, been engaged in a kind of nuclear diplomacy for several years, and there is strong evidence that in 1987 (during the height of the crisis caused by Exercise Brasstacks) both sides understood this perfectly. President Zia stated the obvious when he told me in July 1988 that India and Pakistan had achieved deterrence stability because of uncertainty as to whether each possessed nuclear weapons and how many they might have. More recently, nuclear and conventional arms control agreements between India and Pakistan may have been made possible by the knowledge in both states that escalation could lead to nuclear war—or at least the overt display of nuclear capabilities. For these reasons, proliferation may have a calming, even stabilizing regional effect.

On the other hand, there is the possibility of accident, misunderstanding, or misperception. We know of one missed signal: during India's Exercise Brasstacks Pakistan sent a message to India via an Indian journalist who delayed publishing his story for purely commercial reasons. We also know that neither India nor Pakistan has done much work on nuclear doctrine, and both will face formidable command and control problems. How will they move beyond the present stage of nuclear ambiguity, bluff, and gamesmanship to the world of stable, second-strike deterrence? Will such a progression be as smooth as it apparently was for the United States and the Soviets? Will the cost and complexity of a stable, mobile, and reliable deterrent be beyond their capacity (especially Pakistan's)? Will outsiders step in with technical assistance—possibly leading to a slippery slope of their involvement in regional nuclear calculations? Finally, will India and Pakistan duplicate the behavior of almost every other nuclear weapons state and provide assistance to other states that wish to go nuclear?

These and other questions suggest how complex are the motives and processes that will determine whether or not India and Pakistan acquire nuclear weapons. They also suggest something of the difficulty we face in constructing an American policy that can cope with regional proliferation and its associated consequences.

Toward an American Policy

What are American interests in the South Asian nuclear complex, how do they match up with Indian and Pakistani concerns, and what criteria should be applied to policy?

American Interests

America's South Asian nonproliferation interests fall into or touch on three different areas. First, there are purely nonproliferation-related interests. These include the following:

—Slowing down or controlling regional nuclear military nuclear programs by stemming or stopping the flow of nuclear materials and technology to India and Pakistan

—Ensuring that India and Pakistan do not aid other states with their military programs

—Seeing to it that the South Asian example of creeping proliferation is not emulated or admired elsewhere

—Protecting the NPT (due for renewal in 1995), especially since it has recently come under Indian attack

Second, there are two American strategic/global interests associated with regional proliferation:

1. Containment of Soviet (and, earlier, Chinese) influence in South Asia has always interacted with our regional proliferation policy—usually to the detriment of the latter. However, with the Soviet withdrawal from Afghanistan, proliferation becomes one area where further cooperation with the Soviets, and even the Chinese, makes sense, and might enhance both nonproliferation interests and the remnants of containment policy.

2. Looking ahead to a world of five great powers (Japan, the European Community—with its two independent nuclear systems, China, the Soviet

Union, and ourselves), we want to ensure that if regional proliferation occurs, it will not destabilize what will already be a complicated nuclear world.

Finally, there are a number of regional interests at stake:

—American policy has, since 1947, favored the emergence of a stable and cooperative South Asian regional system based on Indian and Pakistani cooperation so that all regional states might better solve their pressing economic and developmental problems.

—Our bilateral relationship with Pakistan has become something of a limited partnership, since we have parallel interests with a moderate, Islamic, Pakistan in the Persian Gulf and Middle East; these interests will remain important even after the Afghan crisis is resolved, and justify a limited strategic connection.

—In the case of India we are dealing with a strategically unique state. India is emerging as more than a regional power but less than a multiregional or global power. Not only will India dominate the rest of South Asia (raising particular problems for our Pakistan connection); it could challenge China and other large powers (including ourselves) in the Indian Ocean and nearby regions if it feels its economic, ethnic, and strategic interests are threatened. Since Indian strategists are divided as to what those interests are, India's behavior could be especially unpredictable.

A South Asian nonproliferation policy must meet four tests. First, it must address and balance the wide range of American interests outlined above. Second, it must be consistent. Any new policies must be linked with and evolve out of past efforts, and not involve any sharp or sudden turns. This is not a matter of policy elegance as much as bureaucratic politics: nonproliferation touches on so many different bureaucratic and political concerns that a successful strategy must co-opt numerous veto groups in Washington that are poised to shoot down new policies.[16] Third, the policy must be simple, flexible, and capable of implementation in a system notorious for its fragmentation. Finally, it must not require substantial new financial resources.

An Enhanced South Asian Nonproliferation Policy

An enhanced South Asian nonproliferation policy can meet these criteria. The policy outlined below would build on current policy in that it focuses on the regional security calculations that motivate the Indian and Pakistani nuclear programs. It will also draw on a wide range of incentives and disincentives to influence regional actions. This policy differs from current thinking in that it refines and differentiates the approach to Indian and Pakistani elites, draws on new regional and extraregional partners, and defines *region* in a broader context than presently used.

The immediate objective of this enhanced regional policy should be to seek a regional standstill or nuclear freeze, either tacit or explicit, ensuring that India or Pakistan will not plunge ahead into a military nuclear program by miscalculation. Simultaneously, the United States should develop a policy that looks to the future. Its approach should be to influence the assessments of influential Indians and Pakistanis concerning their nuclear programs.

In order of increasing difficulty, the objectives of a long-term strategy should be to: (1) constrain India and Pakistan from helping others obtain nuclear weapons, (2) ensure that they do not damage the global NPT regime, (3) encourage Islamabad and Delhi to further stabilize their nuclear "option" posture and avert an all-out nuclear arms race, and, possibly beyond the reach of any strategy, and (4) persuade them to give up the option altogether. Achieving these goals will require an array of incentives and disincentives and the cooperation of a number of regional and extraregional powers.

The Short Term: Getting through 1991

Aside from the fact that India and Pakistan have nuclear programs that could be quickly militarized, there are a number of critical events and dates that suggest that the United States and other interested governments move quickly to address the most pressing regional proliferation issues.[17]

The United States should immediately declare as a regional nonproliferation goal that it encourages a freeze or standstill in regional military nuclear programs. It should simultaneously begin the public monitoring, or verification, of such a freeze while inviting the two regional states to separate discussions over freezing or leveling off their nuclear programs. At this stage the United States should offer no incentive other than the argument that a precipitous arms race between India and Pakistan is in the interest of neither state.

Actually, the United States has for years provided a de facto verification service for Indian and Pakistani officials. Through our formal and informal statements to the press, Congress, and to regional leaders themselves, the United States has not only commented on but has influenced regional nuclear decisions. Washington should formalize and expand this de facto proliferation watchdog role. Whether through official U.S. channels, through some international, binational, or multinational forum (or a private group), the United States can provide assurances to regional decisionmakers that both sides have not crossed the weaponization line. Ideally these assurances will be given in cooperation with other interested states, especially the Soviet Union. This arrangement would be publicly resented but privately welcomed in New Delhi; Pakistan would probably support it, since we now provide detailed public statements about the Pakistan program as it is. In effect, the United States (with, one hopes, other countries) would engage in intelligence sharing between two rivals, providing timely alert to either concerning events in the other state.

Such a "verification watch" would buy some time. While it would become the subject of controversy, it would also strengthen the hand of groups in both countries that wanted to move slowly on weaponization since it would provide assurances that neither state has a covert supply of deliverable nuclear weapons.

Without a comprehensive follow-on policy a nuclear standstill would be a mere gimmick. Pursuing a regional freeze is clearly an effort to buy time, and in that sense does not differ significantly from many past efforts. America's long-term objectives should be to use this time to help regional states and others to build a stable, non-nuclear South Asian security regime at minimal cost and risk to ourselves. But such a detailed policy will take time to plan and implement. The following are the broad contours of such a policy.

An effective regional nonproliferation policy must, first and foremost, address the ambitions and concerns of potential nuclear states. In South Asia the United States should address those concerns that affect India and Pakistan together and separately.

India and Pakistan

The core of American regional policy should be the argument that going nuclear (or even maintaining an unstable and precarious option) will decrease, rather than increase, security. If India and Pakistan go down the complex path of nuclear deterrence, local conditions may create unusual risks and greater costs than they anticipated. Their systems will threaten each other, and in turn they will be threatened by other regional and global nuclear systems. Further, their example will likely cause other states to go nuclear, increasing sharply the risk to their own security. Finally, while overt nuclear programs will probably reduce the likelihood of conventional war between the two states, the example of every other nuclear power indicates that it will not reduce the need to acquire and deploy vast amounts of conventional forces.

Until recently, it was difficult for Americans—who have built and deployed more than 20,000 nuclear weapons—to make these kinds of arguments. But with historic agreements already behind us and more to come, our credibility and that of the Soviets has been greatly enhanced: we need to help informed South Asians draw the correct inferences about the relative cost, risk, and gain of being nuclear weapons states. Right now, the hawks are dominant in India, but opinion remains divided in Pakistan and India about the wisdom of actually becoming a nuclear power, and there is still a strong residue of antinuclear feeling in both states. These moderate views can be strengthened in various ways. One would be an array of "negative" assurances offered by existing nuclear weapons states. The United States, the Soviet Union, and China could declare, or restate existing pledges, that they would not use nuclear weapons against a non-nuclear regional state. Such pledges would be largely symbolic in nature, but they could acquire more meaning if they were linked to the consideration of positive assurances to non-nuclear states threatened by nuclear states.

Besides weaponization, there are other American nonproliferation interests embedded in our relations with India and Pakistan;

—Chief among these is obtaining agreement not to transfer sensitive materials and technologies to other states. This may require agreement outside the framework of the NPT, or it could be based on a series of bilateral agreements between both states and other nuclear powers. In either case, the United States should discuss with other significant states the possibility of coordinated sanctions against a non-NPT signatory that pursued such policies. While there may be political or economic reasons for India or Pakistan to help others acquire military nuclear technology, their security will, in the long run, be adversely affected by the addition of new nuclear states in their own region. In this sense, nonproliferation is very much in Pakistan's and India's interests.

—The NPT regime itself has come under attack from India—it is conceivable that Pakistan might join the effort. I discuss below some specific steps to organize an international effort to advance such policies, but our regional policies and regional nonproliferation interests must both be tied to and used to enhance our support for the larger NPT regime.

—Nuclear safety should become part of an extended U.S.–South Asian dialogue. The NNPA prohibits discussions on nuclear safety with India and Pakistan, presumably as punishment for their refusal to sign the NPT and to open up all facilities to full-scope inspection. This is a self-defeating policy that blocks an important channel through which Americans can influence key South Asian nuclear officials.

To Pakistan

The United States should restore its earlier policy of proportionate incentives and disincentives in its relationship with Islamabad. This policy was implied in the 1981 decision to link the provision of conventional weapons to Pakistan to that state's overall sense of security, and thus to make nuclear weapons less attractive. As long as the Soviets were in Afghanistan, American officials (including many in Congress) were reluctant to enforce their own policies with regard to Pakistan's nuclear program. The Reagan administration considered, but rejected, a policy of proportionality: cutting or limiting military aid to the degree that Pakistan's nuclear program itself was militarized. This policy should now be reinstated.

Such a policy would be more credible today than in 1981–88. Pakistanis knew that we were less concerned about their security than their role in containing the Soviet Union; now that containment is a declining issue our commitments to Pakistan as a regional partner may, paradoxically, carry more weight than our links to Pakistan as a partner in containment. American policy should provide Pakistan with a choice: a reduced, but long-term relationship with the United States, on the one hand, or further movement down the nuclear path, on the other. The latter policy might, ironically, worsen its own security situation.[18] Should it move far enough down that path, it will also encounter American sanctions. If Pakistan were willing to freeze its nuclear program at existing levels, then the limited strategic partnership between the two states could be extended.

On the other hand, hard evidence of a standstill in the Pakistani program, and progress toward a regional freeze should be rewarded. In 1989 there were rumors of a Pakistani proposal to trade concessions on their nuclear program for the supply of civilian nuclear reactors. This was not the first time this proposal was floated: in late 1985 President Zia proposed what he called a "wild idea" to senior U.S. officials. An unimaginative, negative U.S. response only referred to obligations to meet U.S. law, and so forth. If Zia's successors are serious, the issue should be pursued further.

There are several other arguments that the United States can deploy in dealing with Pakistan. One pertains to the internal political role of nuclear weapons in Pakistan itself. When Zulfikar Ali Bhutto began the bomb program, he saw nuclear weapons as one way of trimming the size of the military budget and reducing the importance of the army in Pakistan. Today, however, it is clear that the bomb program itself has little to do with controlling the generals, but it has created a powerful political lobby. Further, nuclear weapons might themselves become caught up in Pakistani domestic politics during a crisis—central policymakers will not only have to worry about the loyalty of army units deployed around Rawalpindi, but the loyalty of PAF units that would, presumably, have operational responsibility for these devices.

To India

The core of American policy toward India should be to link strategic accommodation with New Delhi in exchange for its continued non-nuclear status. Indian ambitions, while still poorly defined, extend well beyond South Asia. But India is not an Iran, a Vietnam, or even a China. Delhi does not have messianic or dangerous hegemonic ambitions. India seeks to be a great power, although it is unsure exactly what that means. The United States should not try to challenge or "contain" India, but it does want to see a newly powerful India emerge as a responsible regional leader.

A condition for American support can be the continuation of India's non-nuclear status. India, like Japan, should be encouraged to enter that class of states that combine military power and moral stature—the latter in part because they have renounced nuclear weapons, not because they intend to acquire them.[19]

There are many ways the United States can convey to India its broad, strategic support. One symbolic act would be to back India's admission to the UN Security Council; another would be to take seriously Indian interest in disarmament. Rajiv, from the beginning, saw himself as pursuing some of Jawaharlal Nehru's broader disarmament goals. Through disinterest and neglect, the United States has angered senior Indian officials by their studied disregard of well-intentioned Indian disarmament proposals. Even American regional experts were cynical about Rajiv's "six nation" initiative, or his later "three tier" scheme for global disarmament, or his statements to American officials that India was seriously interested in the disarmament elements of U.S.–Soviet talks. Some of these Indian proposals contain ideas that can be turned to the advantage of a nonproliferation policy—for example, India has expressed a willingness to allow verification devices to be placed on its territory in order to detect violations of a test ban agreement.[20] Could such devices be used to verify a regional nuclear agreement? The United States needs to attack directly the widespread Indian view that regional arms control agreements cannot be verified. Recent agreements with the Soviets and Rajiv's own proposals provide the ideal opportunity to join the issue with Indian officials and strategists.

While a policy of positive incentives that helped India achieve its broader ambitions might just make an Indian nuclear program unnecessary, the United States should also be willing to increase the costs of an Indian nuclear program, especially one that destabilizes regional or Asian nuclear balances. America should consider assisting those countries—especially non-nuclear states—that might be threatened by offensive Indian nuclear forces. Washington should make it clear that its goal is not to contain or surround India—but that the United States has legitimate interests in the security of other major states, especially those that have forsworn a nuclear weapons program. The positive way to put this argument (which applies with even greater force to conventional arms balances) is that we want to assist India in avoiding an arms race with itself: if Islamabad, in particular, wants to maintain a 1:3 arms balance, it will be New Delhi, not Islamabad (which has number of external supporters), that will be faced with a disproportionate defense burden.

Implementation

While the policy outlined above will not require much in the way of financial resources, it is very demanding in terms of time, thought, and management. In particular, it will require close contacts and discussions with a wide range of states. Chief among these are India and Pakistan: the United States must revive the dialogue on proliferation issues with both countries—the first step toward solving the regional proliferation problem must be taken in South Asia, not Geneva or Vienna. But this policy will also require extended discussions with important nonregional states—especially Japan—and even with some of the smaller states of South Asia.

In all of this, the guiding principle should be to exploit existing elements found at the regional, Asian, and global levels to reinforce and strengthen a regional nonproliferation strategy.

India and Pakistan: Establishing a Dialogue

Because of ten years' close cooperation on Afghan-related matters, there are excellent contacts between American and Pakistani officials. While anti-Americanism still runs deep in Pakistan, a dialogue has been achieved. This is not the case with India. For a number of reasons—including cultural and stylistic differences—Washington has been unable to sustain an extended dialogue on proliferation and nuclear matters with Delhi, let alone foster discussions between Islamabad and Delhi. Ironically, random visits by individual Americans (for example, Congressman Stephen Solarz) have been helpful at times, but they are not part of any larger strategy. As noted earlier, the Armacost-Fortier trip of 1985 was to be the first of several visits to the subcontinent, but Fortier's death and anxiety over the aid package to Pakistan limited the number and effectiveness of subsequent trips.

This is the moment to encourage a sustained regional discussion on nuclear proliferation between the United States and both India and Pakistan.[21] This can be achieved through a number of channels: in conjunction with the next NPT review conference, at talks about a regional freeze or verification agreement, and as part of a discussion about the spread of many types of advanced weapons and technologies.

Ironically, the essential ingredient now missing is effective coordination and management of the American side of this dialogue. Nonproliferation is a subject divided among many bureaus and departments, and its recent transfer from the undersecretary of state for political affairs ("P") to the undersecretary of state for security assistance ("T") moves it further from the Department of State's regional experts, although it does bring nonproliferation policy closer to one of the few effective forms of leverage: arms aid. A region-specific working group that included defense, ACDA, and other bureaucratic interests would be helpful in coordinating policy, and even in remembering what that policy is.[22] Equally important would be close consultation with Congress, if only to reduce the opportunities for India and Pakistan to exploit differences between executive and legislative branches. One problem with enhanced executive congressional consultation is that so few members of Congress are either interested in proliferation or knowledgeable. The best-informed and most articulate senator (John Glenn) is also a strong critic of recent regional nonproliferation efforts.[23] But no organizational arrangement can substitute for sustained, high-level administration interest in the linked tasks of advancing American nonproliferation and regional security and political interests.

Japan, the Soviet Union, and China

The most effective long-term innovation in present U.S. policy would be to associate Japan with our regional nonproliferation efforts in South Asia. For years American officials, fixated on the Soviet Union, have pointed to Moscow's "good" record on nonproliferation and have waited for significant Soviet efforts in the region. In fact, the Soviets have been only marginally helpful on proliferation issues (beyond their NPT obligations), and in my judgment, positively harmful in past nuclear threats to Pakistan and unrestrained supply of military hardware to India.

There are also good reasons to be skeptical about the role that China might play in freezing a regional nuclear arms race. While it makes sense to include China when talking about "regional" South Asian nuclear matters (a position always taken by the Indians, and now just being accepted in Washington), China is more likely to be part of the problem than part of the solution. The road to obtaining Chinese cooperation (especially vis-à-vis India) runs through Islamabad; Beijing is likely to be guided by Pakistani wishes on such matters as an Asian INF agreement, negative assurances, and restraint concerning provocative or threatening statements.

In an increasingly multipolar world, the United States should cast around for partners whose interests match up closely on important issues. In the case of South Asian proliferation, Japan is well suited to become such a partner. It is an Asian state, it has been subjected to nuclear attack, it is unlikely to ever acquire nuclear weapons, it has unquestioned status as a world power, and it now plays an important economic role in both India and Pakistan. From Japan's strategic perspective, a more active role on nonproliferation is potentially rewarding and nonthreatening to significant friends and neighbors. However, associating Japan with a regional nonproliferation strategy is not a one-time effort. It will require patience and expertise, but it would be the most promising long-term step the United States could take.

Other South Asian States

India and Pakistan's smaller regional neighbors should not be neglected. None want to see the region go nuclear, several (Nepal and Bangladesh) have publicly spoken out against a regional nuclear arms race, all have signed the NPT, and all think that as hard as it is now to live with New Delhi, a nuclear neighbor would be a more difficult neighbor. Proliferation, testing, and nuclear war would affect several of these states directly; they might even be dragged into a nuclear arms race if India or Pakistan wanted to use their territory to deploy nuclear weapons.

The diplomatic weight of these states may not individually amount to very much, but both India and Pakistan are sensitive to their concerns. The new South Asian Association for Regional Cooperation should not be burdened with a regional security issue—it lays outside the scope of the organization—but regional leaders can be encouraged to speak publicly and privately with India and Pakistan. They might be the key to a regional agreement that allows these two states to level off or even reduce their nuclear programs.

Conclusion

To summarize our analysis and argument, the following points are central:

—An enhanced South Asian nonproliferation policy, supplementing the NPT regime, fits both American nonproliferation and regional interests.

—A short-term strategy should emphasize a regional nuclear freeze or standstill, possibly in conjunction with others that might join the United States in monitoring it; long-term strategies directed toward India and Pakistan should emphasize the net decrease in regional security of weaponization or an arms race.

—As a halfway house outside the NPT regime, the United States should encourage India and Pakistan to join the prohibition against the transfer of sensitive materials and technologies; a reasonable quid pro quo would be resumption of discussions on nuclear safety.

—To encourage a regional dialogue we might begin with subjects where there is congruence between regional and American views (chemical and biological weapons); this would also further the development of a common language and terminology and facilitate further arms control discussions.

—To Pakistan, the United States should restore its 1981 policy of proportionate incentives and disincentives; the United States should also emphasize the changed domestic political implications of a runaway nuclear program.

—To India, the core of American policy should be the linkage of strategic accommodation with New Delhi to continued non-nuclear status; while the United States should pay greater attention to recent Indian proposals for arms control, it should also confront directly the Indian argument that regional arms control agreements cannot be verified.

—The internal U.S. government mechanism for development and coordination of an enhanced regional nonproliferation policy needs to be strengthened.

—We must plan for 1995 and beyond. If India and Pakistan do go nuclear, there will still be important regional and nonproliferation interests that will engage the United States in South Asia.

—In the long run, active Japanese support for a South Asian arms control regime would be especially significant; Soviet and Chinese support is likely to be contingent and partial.

—The smaller regional states, Nepal, Bangladesh, and Sri Lanka, should not be overlooked: they have moral, if not military leverage over India and Pakistan, and would be adversely affected by a nuclear arms race, nuclear accident, or nuclear war.

South Asia, American Policy, and the Future

This essay has only outlined a comprehensive proposal to cope with nuclear proliferation in South Asia. There is no certainty that it will work, but it is unlikely to do harm, whereas doing nothing may be damaging to important American interests.

I emphasized that in the long run what counts the most are the deeply felt feelings of Indian and Pakistani leaders about their own nation's security. The United States must focus on those feelings in a manner that draws on rather than rubs against the regional context in which they are made. We will need the cooperation not only of the Soviet Union but of major Asian powers, notably Japan and South Asia's weaker states, to erect and preserve a South Asian security regime that makes unnecessary the need for nuclear weapons.

If India and Pakistan do not go nuclear, it will be in part because of U.S. encouragement and policies; if they do, there is no less need for American influence on regional nuclear decisions, including those that might affect proliferation and nuclear strategy elsewhere. Over the past ten years, South Asia has attracted our attention and anxiety as it has moved from a pristine non-nuclear status to that of the nuclear option; this concern will greatly intensify if and when the region makes the transition from option status to weaponization and from weaponization to doctrinal development and deployment. There are better and worse ways of managing each stage; our own experience may not be relevant to the South Asia case, but South Asia is likely to be important for other states and regions that proceed down the nuclear path.

Whether or not the policies discussed in this essay are seriously considered, the United States will be tied to nuclear decisions in South Asia for many years to come. Regional proliferation is a long-term problem that affects our own national security; we should not be confident that we can do very much to halt the process, but we should not let ambivalence concerning nuclear weapons incapacitate our thinking and behavior.[24] Nuclear proliferation in South Asia is not a function of supplier policy, nor is it a technical problem, nor is it even an "arms control" issue: it is a process that will be increasingly central to vital U.S. national security interests and to the interests of many states around the world. The spread of chemical weapons will, in several years, be seen as a sideshow compared to the acquisition of true instruments of mass destruction by fragile and even irresponsible states.

America is learning how to cope with issue complexity in a world of many parts and of powers of unequal size. We have proposed a "mix and match" strategy to deal with proliferation in South Asia. This is not an exceptional suggestion; regional proliferation is typical of the complex challenges that will face American diplomacy in years to come. In this sense, as we grapple with the Indian and Pakistani bombs, we have already put one foot into the future.

1986

TEN

State Building in Pakistan

Pakistan remains a state on the verge of disorder. Even though it inherited a coherent set of administrative institutions from British India, the idea of Pakistan was firmly held before the state was created, and Pakistan always had adequate material and human resources to sustain itself.

Contemporary Pakistan is the complex product of historical invasion, colonial rule, communal strife, forcible partition, and civil war. In this chapter I focus on this "new" Pakistan, the state that once constituted Pakistan's West Wing, and primarily on those institutions in Pakistan normally associated with the state such as the bureaucracy, the political party system, the courts, and the armed forces.[1] I make several assumptions about the role of such institutions in the state.

First, their contribution is not necessarily positive. Some political institutions can corrode and destroy the very structure that gives them purpose.[2] Neither the "state" nor its constituent institutions are value-free. States and their institutions everywhere serve some interests better (or worse) than others. They also influence and shape perceptions of what these separate and common interests are. As Aristotle argued—and as President Zia ul-Haq firmly believes—the state and its apparatus have a duty to mold its citizens.

Second, politics everywhere—but perhaps more visibly in Pakistan—rests on a mix of consent and coercion. This may take the form of the threat of withdrawal of consent—or the threat of the application of force—but the two are omnipresent. When consent is absent, coercion shows its face, usually in the form of the application or threat of military power. The military or police forces are only faintly removed from the center of political life in any state. As Katherine Chorley wrote, "the position of the army in almost any society is the pivot on which that society swings," a statement that is unquestionably true for a Pakistan that has been under military rule for more years than civilian.[3]

Third, the institutions of the state are not autonomous but rest on a broader political culture. When that political culture is mixed or is changing, then institutions may come into conflict or become ineffective. This is so because a change of the structure of state power will usually favor one institution over another, and important ideological, ethnic, regional, religious, or other groups are linked to particular institutions in the pursuit of their interests. In a multiethnic society such as Pakistan, it has proven impossible to manage the relative power of state institutions—especially the military versus parliamentary structures. Pakistan was unable to function as a British-style parliamentary democracy because inter-wing and interethnic conflicts were too powerful to be contained in polite structures; it was later unable to maintain even a halfway-house "consociational" democracy, in which linked elites governed in concord.[4] But the ensuing military rule carries with it imbalances and may have the further consequence of damaging the military itself as an institution.

Finally, it is important to note the Janus-faced nature of the state itself. States "always exist in determinant geopolitical environments, in interaction with other actual or potential states," and this can be—and in Pakistan repeatedly is—a crucial factor in domestic politics.[5] State rulers use external threats (real or imagined) to shore up their own position or, as in the case of the Pakistani military leadership in 1971, to prevent the coming to power of groups (such as the Awami League in East Pakistan) that are thought to be soft toward hostile neighbors (such as India). Nowhere is this factor more striking than in Pakistan, whose military, police, and bureaucratic elites have been united in their concern over internal weakness vis-à-vis external threat and over external involvement in internal affairs. These state bureaucracies have generally been opposed on these issues by other important institutions, such as the parties, the courts, and the educational establishment. A more complex issue is whether particular state institutions, which were created to serve one end and that reflect one national value or goal such as security, can be adapted to serve another. Or can such institutions survive when sister institutions decline or disappear? This question was particularly pressing in a state ruled by military professionals who seemed to be dismantling those very professions and political and administrative institutions that give the modern state its purpose and direction.

Comparative Perspectives

In comparative terms, Pakistan is unique in certain ways, and it shares certain qualities with other countries. I return to some of the shared qualities below, but it is important to note three special features of the Pakistani state: its ideological underpinning, its physical integrity, and its traumatic truncation in 1971.

Islamic Pakistan

Islam is potentially an important unifying force in any largely Muslim society. Muslims gather for organized prayer, assemble in Mecca during pilgrimage, and partake in a holy war against unbelievers or enemies of the faith. Islam, more than other religions, is a religion of what Elias Canetti calls crowds, which unite the just in opposition to the unjust, the saved against the damned, the believer against the unbeliever.[6]

Though Pakistan is the only country explicitly formed as an "Islamic" state, modern Pakistan is not a throwback to the caliphate or even a religious state run by clergy. In Pakistan, Islam as an ordering principle of state structure is fostered by men who are themselves the product of Western secular institutions, and yet many who fought for Pakistan were not themselves orthodox Muslims. They did not want to see Pakistan guided and structured according to Islamic principles, but saw Pakistan as a state where they would be free from the domination of their more numerous Hindu neighbors. Others opposed the idea of Pakistan, in particular, the conservative and orthodox Jama'at-i Islami.[7] The Jama'at's leader, Maulana Maududi, argued that an independent Pakistan would be incomplete as it would leave millions of Muslims within a largely Hindu India. After Partition in 1947, however, Maududi changed his mind and migrated to Pakistan. His Jama'at movement has strongly supported the recent wave of Islamization in Pakistan.

The shift from the concept of a state run largely along British Indian secular principles to a Pakistan serving as a laboratory of Islam occurred after Independence. This renewed concern with Islam as an organizing principle of state structure has led to the same problems faced by analogous states. While Israel is the most interesting contemporary example, Pakistan officials point out the difficulties faced by the Catholic states of Europe. Like Pakistan, the Catholic states had to adjust the relationship between church, religion, and state apparatus; they had to deal with the problem of nonterritoriality; and they had to face the phenomenon of two or more religion-based states pursuing different policies with different state structures. Pakistanis, for example, are aware that their "Islamic" practices are often at variance with those of Saudi Arabia or Iran.

A considerable amount of state-supported research is now devoted to the problem of creating an Islamic state in Pakistan. If earlier efforts in Pakistan are any guide and if the experience of the Catholic states and Israel is relevant, this research will be inconclusive on major issues. Islamic law itself is divided in some matters by the Shi'a–Sunni schism, and in other areas it is unlikely to displace well-established and effective codes derived from British Indian practice. Nor does Islam provide many clues to structural changes that would allow Pakistan's many and unequal ethnic groups to achieve elite consensus.

Territory and Destiny

Not only is Pakistan unique among states in its explicitly Islamic origins; it is practically unique in its territorial configuration. The "old" Pakistan was for many years divided into two disparate and physically separated parts. Paraphrasing Freud, territory is destiny, and had a hostile India not been interposed between East and West Pakistan, it is unlikely that the breakup of 1971 would have occurred despite severe stresses. Pakistan's Eastern wing, which subsequently became Bangladesh, was relatively homogeneous ethnically. Although predominantly Bengali, East Pakistan had a small non-Bengali immigrant community known as the Biharis (although not all were from the Indian state of Bihar), who generally allied themselves with West Pakistan against Bengali demands for greater autonomy within Pakistan.[8] Further, there was an important Hindu minority in East Pakistan, a minority viewed with great suspicion by West Pakistani elites. But

East Pakistan tended to vote and act en bloc, whereas Pakistan's West Wing was more diverse, composed as it was of four major language groups (Punjabi—spoken by 60 percent of the West's population—Sindhi, Pashtu, and Baluchi). In the old, two-wing Pakistan, Bengalis generally had their share of administrative positions and made an active contribution to Pakistan's intellectual life. They were, however, underrepresented in the military and complained bitterly that their own relatively underdeveloped economy was being exploited by West Pakistani firms. While Bengalis were not at the center of power in Pakistan and while they occupied only 15 percent of the territory, they were close enough to sense their relative powerlessness compared with their numbers—for they constituted slightly more than 50 percent of the entire population. East Bengal was part of Pakistan—a majority of the state, in fact, not an appendage. Bengalis felt less than equal when they were more than half.

Ethnicity and Rebellion

Ultimately, accumulated grievances and mismanagement led to the 1971 separation. Physical separation multiplied the impact of ethnic diversity on the state. More crudely stated, the Pakistan government was unable to apply the necessary force to suppress Bengali discontent simply because of the distances involved; there is no doubt that it would have done so if Bengal had been contiguous to West Pakistan or if Bengal could have been insulated from Indian influence.

The geopolitics of the "new" Pakistan is quite different from the old. Ethnic divergences that seemed minor when East Bengal stood as a counterweight to the entire West Wing are not new but are newly important. The example of Bangladesh is now available as a precedent for the non-Punjabi groups,[9] even perhaps for other states with troubled ethnic or religious groups.[10] This precedent cannot be exaggerated: before the formation of Bangladesh, separatism for the North-West Frontier Province (NWFP), Sind, or Baluchistan (which did not even become a province until 1971) was thought to be highly improbable. Bangladesh showed that Pakistan's neighbors could and would support separatist movements if the opportunity were there.

Yet history has a way of foreclosing certain opportunities as well as creating them. The lessons of Bengal are deeply imprinted on the minds of those who have ruled Pakistan since 1972. By sensitizing the new Pakistan's leadership to the possibility of regional, ethnic, or linguistic separatism, Bangladesh has also made it harder for such a movement to succeed. Although not a military man, Zulfikar Ali Bhutto applied brutal force against the Baluch armed rebels in the mid-1970s (too much force—he and his military advisers could not forget Bangladesh, where some thought that not enough force had been applied). Bhutto's successor, Zia, has adopted a more conciliatory approach, although some Baluch leaders regard this as merely a tactical difference and argue that the ultimate end is Punjabi dominance (as some Bengali leaders argued that Yahya Khan's regime was merely serving West Pakistani and Punjabi interests). These internal linguistic, ethnic, and cultural divisions still present a challenge to the integrity and very survival of the new Pakistan. Such divisions can still be exploited by surrounding states, and the combination of internal dissent and external support could once again be a fatal blow to the physical integrity of the Pakistani state.

Commonalities

If Pakistan presents some striking features in its ideological and physical makeup, it shares certain qualities with other important states. In terms of religion, Pakistan now has an almost entirely Muslim population, but, as in other Muslim countries, the differences between Sunni and Shi'a have an impact. Sunnis dominate in Pakistan, but there is a large Shi'a community. Various problems have arisen with regard to the enforcement of Islamic laws of taxation since Sunni and Shi'a legal codes differ in several important respects. The small non-Muslim communities have been relatively unaffected and in fact have usually found representation in Cabinet and Parliament,[11] although the presidency of Pakistan has been constitutionally reserved for a Muslim. More problematical has been the treatment of the Ahmadiyya, a sect that has been declared non-Muslim.

As a multiethnic and multilingual state Pakistan also shares a number of characteristics with Iran, India, and other states in the region. Each major grouping in Pakistan (Punjabi, Pashtun, Sindhi, and Baluch) has its own provincial assembly, governor, educational system, and administrative cadre. However, the imbalance between the Punjab and the other three groups is more akin to Persian dominance in Iran than anything found in India; this Punjabi dominance is exacerbated by a predominantly Punjabi military establishment.

Further, many of Pakistan's ethnic groups spill over across state frontiers. Pashtuns, Baluchis, Kashmiris, and Punjabis are found in Afghanistan, in Iran, and in India, and subnationalist movements are not far beneath the surface in the case of the first three groups. This ethnic overlap has one overwhelming implication for the Pakistani state: its foreign policy, especially vis-à-vis its neighbors, is to a great degree a function of domestic politics. Similarly, Pakistan's treatment of its own population (especially in Kashmir, Baluchistan, and the North-West Frontier Province) is necessarily a concern to its neighbors.

Finally, Pakistan shares with several states a British legacy of constitutionalism and civilian rule despite functioning as a state without a constitution for most of its history and having been run by the military more often than not. While there are those who argue that Pakistan is destined to be like Iran, Iraq, or Syria—oscillating between bondage to the military and chaos—one critical difference is that among those institutions still functioning in Pakistan (including the military) there remains a deep commitment to constitutional civilian government.

The repeated displacement of civilian institutions by a military bureaucracy again raises the question as to whether an institution which has been established and organized to fulfill one narrow task (national security) can effectively perform functions (executive, legislative, and judicial tasks, control over the media, redirection of educational priorities, and even formulation of religious and cultural policies) normally associated with other major state institutions. And how does it affect the triangle of state, Islam, and ethnicity? To answer these questions, we must first examine the adjustments in power and influence between the major institutions of Pakistan, especially the political parties, the judiciary, and bureaucracy, on the one hand, and the ever-powerful military, on the other.

Civilian Institutions: Broken or Merely Bent?

The historical trajectory of Pakistan's major civilian political institutions would seem to describe a downward curve. Pakistan was a country that began with a full complement of parties, effective bureaucracies, a comprehensive system of laws and courts, a vigorous press, and a small but burgeoning system of higher education. Until recently all of these institutions were in disrepair: the parties were banned, the bureaucracy was held up to ridicule, the press was subject to censorship, the civilian courts were supplanted by a martial law system and a new Islamic legal system, and Pakistan's universities were the literal battleground for opposing political forces, few of which have great regard for higher education itself. Except for the still affluent military, Pakistan was undergoing deinstitutionalization.

This image is only partly true. The several excellent surveys of Pakistan's political institutions emphasize this political decay, but it is vital to add that from a comparative perspective Pakistan remains an institutionally developed country.[12] Politics is still thought to be a legitimate vocation—although the politicians have difficulty plying their trade—the bureaucracy has shown considerable capacity for regeneration, the press manages to work around a sometimes obtuse censorship, and the universities continue to produce students and scholars that compete effectively in the West. Even the judiciary is capable of making its voice heard although it is much weaker than even under Bhutto. Let us look more closely at three major civilian institutions—the political parties, the judiciary, and the bureaucracy—and see how they have adjusted to the successive crises that have punctuated Pakistan's political history.

The Political Party System

Political parties are everywhere multifunctional institutions. They serve not only as "transmission belts" for public opinion and group interests but also (especially in communist countries) as mobilizing agents for the state and instruments of change. Pakistan's parties have never been able to fulfill either of these functions. The party movement that created the state—the Muslim League—was most influential in those areas of British India that did not become Pakistan. While many of the Muslim League's leaders emigrated to Pakistan, their mass base remained in India and this, coupled with the incipient personalistic quality of the party, led to the League's rapid decline as a political force. Yet no other mass party took its place, and the political system of Pakistan was dominated by groups that were parties in name only. Some were vehicles for local leaders and others were never far from their feudal roots. The notions of a legitimate opposition, of parties as permanent institutions rather than as instruments of individual power, and of consensus on vital issues were all absent. Nor was the ideology of Islam widely attractive except as a common ground on which to declare a non-Indian identity.

The prospective fragility of Pakistan's party system was recognized by Jinnah before the state became independent. Unlike Jawaharlal Nehru (who served as India's prime minister under a governor-general), Muhammad Ali Jinnah chose to become Pakistan's governor-general. "In this way," according to von Vorys, "he proposed to rise above parliamentary responsibility and direct from his own heights the evolution of Pakistan's political institutions."[13] But Jinnah died shortly after Independence, and the parliamentary path was pursued by his successor, Liaquat Ali Khan, and other politicians for nearly ten years, until Ayub Khan's coup ended democracy in 1958.

Ayub moved because the system was not working. There were no restraints of individual or institutional loyalty, party organization, or public responsibility on individual ambition. "The only guide to action, which remained by default, was individual self-interest," according to von Vorys. "Holding office became the highest goal.[14]

From the perspective of the civil service, the military, and most other professionals and institution builders in Pakistan, the army's first coup came both as a relief and as an opportunity to reshape Pakistan's political institutions. Ayub Khan eventually turned himself into a political leader (with some initial success) and ruled until 1969, only to be displaced by his army commander in chief, Yahya Khan.

Ayub's reign was important in the prominence of civilian advisers, and it was in fact more a bureaucratic–military alliance than simple military rule. In a very real sense Ayub's regime more closely resembled the British Raj in its strong central direction and an assumption of bureaucratic omnipotence. His government did provide several years of stability and economic growth and continued the work of building such institutions as the educational system, but Ayub was ultimately brought down by mass protest. The fact that the generals (especially Yahya) were unwilling to trust the politicians only contributed to the irresponsibility of the latter. Pakistan was simply unable to evolve strong political institutions that made military intervention unnecessary—or military institutions that were capable of governing without reliance on these fragile political institutions.

The ultimate failure of military nerve took place in 1971 when Yahya refused to allow Sheikh Mujib to form a government after his Awami League had won a majority in the 1970 elections. Had Yahya done so, Pakistan would have survived intact, albeit in a different form. But again personal ambition and regional affiliations were too great to resist, and Zulfikar Ali Bhutto shares responsibility for the breakup of Pakistan and for the decline of party institutions by his unwillingness to see Mujib as prime minister.

With a few exceptions, Pakistan's political parties have not had strong organizational roots. Of the parties in the "old" Pakistan the largest ethnic/linguistic party was the Awami League, whose support was entirely in the East Wing; it was nearly equaled in size by the Pakistan People's Party (PPP), which was unashamedly a West Wing party, with strongest roots in the Punjab. After the deaths of their leaders (Sheikh Mujibur Rahman in the case of the Awami League, Bhutto in the case of the PPP) these parties tended toward factionalism: in both cases the cult of the leader has been less effective in death than in life. Despite a strong ideological thrust in both cases, party organizational politics tended to be overwhelmed by personalities.

Bhutto and Mujib introduced mass politics in a country that had never experienced this phenomenon, and together they opened up new (for Pakistan) political choices. But even if they had been able to contain their own ambition and maintain organizational coherence, these new choices frightened many in Pakistan (and in Mujib's case, in Bangladesh). Could Bhutto continue to control the mobs? Could he be displaced by a worse rabble-rouser? What if he turned on those institutions (such as the business community, the military, the bureaucracy, and other parties) that had not been the PPP's enthusiastic supporters? No one was more aware of this discontent than Bhutto himself, and after 1972 he tried to gain leverage over such groups through an adroit mixture of bribery, demagoguery, and—where these did not work—coercion. He ultimately lost control, although in 1977 it was not so much a failure of institutions as the failure of an individual who sought to rise above the very structures he created.[15]

The PPP's policies toward Pakistan's ethnic/linguistic groups and Islamization were both crucial in its rise and ultimate fall. While professing a popular socialism, epitomized by the slogan "bread, clothing, and shelter," the PPP was from the first a predominantly Punjabi party (although Bhutto was himself a Sindhi and the party had deep roots in Sind). But Bhutto was obsessed with regionalism, and he brutally suppressed Baluch armed rebels after they protested his attempt to impose PPP control over the provincial legislature. He also reacted to the post-1971 revival of Islam by introducing his own program of popular Islamization. Bhutto's notoriety as a Westernized secular Muslim undercut this effort, although it did anticipate many of the Islamic programs pursued by Zia.

Between 1977 and 1985 political parties ceased functioning in Pakistan. While they regularly announce "campaigns" or movements to displace the military from power, none posed a serious threat to the regime. Some political activity has been channeled into an appointed federal advisory council, the Majlis-i Shura, a large number of whose members were active politicians.[16] One of the few groups allowed to function freely was the Jama'at-i Islami, whose conservative Islamic ideology overlapped with that of Zia ul-Haq. Lending its support to the military regime at first, the Jama'at now distanced itself from Zia, but it still exercises considerable influence on university campuses against both moderate and radical student groups.

Rumors abound that the Majlis will become a partially elected body in its next sitting, or that the provincial elections for local bodies will be expanded, or that general elections will be held.[17] Such rumors, however, have been circulating since 1977, when Zia first promised elections "within three months." National elections will be held only when the military is sure that the results will not threaten its own position, the changes introduced in Pakistani society, or Pakistan's foreign policy. If PPP support withers, the chances for an election increase, although the regime will certainly remember the miscalculation of Yahya, who had not expected the Awami League to win in 1970.

The Judiciary

Up to 1985 three different legal-judicial systems functioned in Pakistan: the British-derived civil courts that trace their structure from the Government of India Act of 1935 and have roots deep in Anglo-Saxon Law; the martial law courts, also derived in part from the British experience but greatly elaborated and refined under successive Pakistani governments; and the Sharia (the sacred law of Islam). One might also add such codes of behavior as Pashtunwali (the traditional tribal code of the Pashtuns), which function in some areas of Pakistan (especially NWFP and Baluchistan) and in certain matters take precedence over civil codes.

The civilian court system is analogous to that found in India and features a Supreme Court, four high courts (one for each province), district courts, and lower courts. From the first years of Pakistan the courts served as a protective agency for those who were in difficulty with the government, and held Pakistan to a reasonably high standard of Indo-British law. Even the military regimes have been concerned that martial law be retroactively sanctified by the Supreme Court.

The judiciary has become the battleground between those who seek to expand the role of Islam in Pakistan and those who wish to maintain the codes, court systems, and legal profession inherited from the British. It has not, unlike other institutions (such as the military), been regarded as an arena of ethnic conflict. Most judges in the respective high courts come from provinces they serve in: the exception is Baluchistan, which has not produced many ethnic Baluchi lawyers (Baluchistan did not even have its own high court until 1971).

Until recently, the lawyers and judges who comprise this civilian court system were under siege from two directions: the military and the Islamizers. The military introduced its own parallel system of martial law courts throughout Pakistan and simultaneously encouraged the development of the Islamic Sharia courts.

The martial law courts were of two types: summary and regular. The summary courts are created to handle specific disturbances (riots, crime waves) and are disbanded when the emergency ends. The "regular" martial law courts were located in most cities and districts and handled violations of the various martial law regulations. Under Zia's regime various activities (gatherings of politicians, defamation of the martial law system, and so forth) were prohibited; these went immediately to the martial law court system, where they were ultimately passed on by Zia, who presided over the system as chief martial law administrator. However, some activities (violent crimes that may have a political origin) were also justiciable in the regular civilian courts. Local police officers were regularly bribed so that their first information report steers the case into the "proper" court. In some cases, individuals preferred to be tried before the summary and often secret martial law courts, where opportunities for bribery were greater than in the open civilian courts. However, all political cases went to the martial law courts, and all arrests of politicians were under the martial law regulations. They were not bailable, nor could the civilian judges issue writs of habeas corpus in such cases; this important restriction on civilian judges was introduced in 1975 by Zulfikar Ali Bhutto.

In March 1981 a Provisional Constitutional Order further modified the 1973 Constitution and completed the subordination of the superior civil judiciary to the martial law authorities, giving the latter the power to determine whether or not a case would be held before the martial law courts or the civil courts. Theoretically, an army major on martial law duty had more power than the chief justice of the Supreme Court of Pakistan. Recognizing the implications of the 1981 Order, the chief justice and three colleagues from the Supreme Court and eleven justices from the Sind, Punjab, and Baluchistan high courts either refused or were not allowed to take the oath under this Provisional Order and lost their jobs.

The Sharia courts have raised more controversy in Pakistan, partly because it was a crime under martial law regulations to criticize the martial law courts. If a case is registered under Islamic law, it will go to an Islamic court at the magistrate or district level. A case can also go to the regular civilian court and will then also be tried under Islamic law (by regular judges). Appeals in such cases go to the Sharia court, located above the high courts but below the Supreme Court.

Zia first established Sharia Benches in 1978, promising to set them up at each high court and a Sharia Appellate Bench in the Supreme Court. Their function was to declare a law invalid if it was repugnant to the Qur'an and Sunna. However, these courts cannot deal with matters concerning Muslim personal law (which differs among Shi'as and Sunnis), the procedures of the martial law courts, the Constitution itself, or fiscal matters. Critics of the Sharia system argue that it is a mere sop to the Islamic parties and makes no real impact on civil or military court systems. Nevertheless, the Sharia system is being expanded. In 1983 additional legislation was passed in the Majlis-i Shura to establish 150 qazi (religious judge) courts in the districts.[18]

While some have criticized the martial law courts for being lawless, the Sharia system may be vulnerable to the charge that there is too much Islamic law. The Sharia courts (and civilian courts that handle cases based on Islamic law) have the difficult task of not only administering justice based on a legal code developed in the broader Islamic world but administering it in the face of hostility from many Westernized Pakistanis, especially the lawyers and judges trained in the Western legal tradition. In 1983, when the Islamic legal codes were being prepared, protest marches were held in major Pakistani cities by women who protested that the Evidence Act did not treat women equally. A cable of protest signed by a number of prominent Pakistani women, including the wife of one Cabinet member, reflected wider unease that under the new Islamic codes women would be systematically treated as inferiors in the courts, and ultimately outside them, as well.

Their fears are well grounded. While it is not surprising to find the Islamic clergy supporting a reduced status for women in Pakistan in accordance with their reading of the Qur'an, this position is also held by some in the military, including President Zia. His government dismisses the protests to the laws of evidence as Hindu inspired, or un-Islamic, although this event did lead to a slowing of the pace of Islamic reformation.[19]

One consequence of Pakistan's new emphasis on Islam and Islamic courts has been that some opponents of the 1977–85 martial law regime have resorted to "Islamic" arguments and used these courts when other avenues of protests were shut. In appearing before military court in early 1983 Benazir Bhutto, daughter of the executed former prime minister, argued that the martial law court itself was both un-Islamic and impermissible according to the 1973 civilian constitution of Pakistan.[20] More recently, the All-Pakistan Newspaper Society (APNS) pleaded before the federal Sharia court in Islamabad that continuation of the Press and Publications Ordinance of 1963 was "repugnant to the Holy Qur'an and the Sunna" because under Islam a person has an absolute right to independent adjudication in a dispute with authorities. Citing chapter and verse of the Qur'an, various newspaper editors and lawyers have argued that the same person cannot be party and judge in the same dispute, precisely the situation held by government newspaper censors.[21]

In both cases there was a mixture of cleverness and desperation in the appeal to Islam by individuals and groups not noted for their past orthodoxy. In a sense, such appeals were a victory for the government's Islamization drive since Islamic symbols and criteria are invoked, but few would believe that in these instances interest in Islam is anything more than tactical and expedient. Those in high places in Pakistan, including Zia, joke about straightening the *qibla*—direction of prayer toward Mecca—of the secular, Westernized opponents of Islamization, but express confidence that these secular Muslims will eventually bring themselves into conformity. The latter have done this superficially, but one suspects that if the regime should falter, there will be a strong middle-class reaction against the Islamic courts, Islamic codes of dress and conduct, and restrictions on women in the name of Islam. But the advocates of Islamization are counting on time and the growth of a middle class rooted in more traditional Islamic values and beliefs. The divisions are already apparent within the political party system, the judicial system, and even the military.

The Bureaucracy

Pakistan inherited its bureaucratic structure from British India, and this structure has been virtually preserved intact over the years. Each province has its own locally recruited cadre, but these are inferior to the various central services. In the "old" Pakistan recruiting for these central services initially met no great difficulty, as recruitment, training, and most operations were carried out in English. Problems arose only at the district level when some knowledge of local languages was important, but such difficulties were in themselves not a barrier to the normal functioning of the state bureaucracy. Difficulties did arise in the "old" Pakistan when a disproportionate number of senior civil posts fell to Muhajirs (mainly Urdu-speaking refugees originating from India) or Punjabis, and the situation persists today in Baluchistan where most administrators, even if born in Baluchistan, are non-Baluch. To overcome the continued predominance of Punjabis, Bhutto introduced a quota system for regional representation and tried to encourage Sindhi recruitment, apparently with little success.

However, the imbalance in recruitment to the civil service has never been as great or as politically consequential as the imbalance in recruitment to the army (discussed below). The members of the Civil Service of Pakistan (CSP) were strong advocates of highly centralized regimes in Pakistan and, beginning with Ayub Khan, served the various military regimes with enthusiasm and skill. This was not always reciprocated by Ayub, who introduced the first of a series of measures designed to dilute the power of the CSP. Ayub made lateral entry possible, and a number of army officers resigned their commissions to enter civilian service. The attack on the CSP was intensified under Bhutto, who formally abolished it, creating a Central Superior Services (with heavy lateral entry) and a District Management Group that had greatly reduced privileges. Some of these changes were reversed by Zia, who relied heavily on senior civil servants (as well as a large number of retired generals) for a variety of sensitive administrative tasks. Zia, for example, appointed Ghulam Ishaq, a retired Indian Civil Service (ICS) officer, as finance adviser to reorient Pakistan's economic policies, in shambles after Bhutto's attempt to create an instant popular socialist economy.

While restoring some of the prestige and perquisites of the senior civil services in Pakistan, Zia insisted that the civilian bureaucracies conform in externals to his Islamization program. After 1982 all officials working in the secretariats were required to wear "national" dress, time and space had to be set aside for daily prayers (although performing *namaz* is not compulsory), and Islamic history has been introduced as part of the general training and indoctrination program for all services.

None of these steps can be considered radical, although they have changed the physical appearance of the typical Pakistani government office. Bureaucrats who had to invest in a new wardrobe have now come to accept such attire. The major complaint comes from a few military officers on deputation in civilian positions who lament the unmilitary garb they must wear and the loose fit that makes it easier to inadvertently gain weight. The average bureaucrat sees such practices as a small price to pay for national solidarity or—more important—furthering his own career.

The three civilian institutions that we have briefly examined—the party system, the courts, and the civilian bureaucracy—each exhibit a different relationship to Islamic ideas and to Pakistan's diverse ethnic/linguistic composition. The party system reflects the diversity of attitudes toward Islam and Pakistan's heterogeneous social structure, but its historical failings are also due to the absence of experience in democratic politics, the inordinate dependence on strong political leaders (three of whom, Jinnah, Liaquat, and Bhutto, met early or untimely deaths), and the inability of party elites to forestall party fissuring. The bureaucracy has its own failings and successes, but these are not closely related to Islam or ethnicity; the senior bureaucrats of Pakistan remain willing to serve whatever civilian or military government holds sway and have thus retained their organizational identity, if not their power. The courts, however, have become a central battleground between "secular" Muslims who resist Islamization and the Islamizers who have succeeded in establishing a parallel set of religious courts in addition to supplanting civil codes with Islamic ones.

I have frequently alluded to the power of the armed forces. Pakistan has been under military rule for most of its history from Ayub's coup in 1958 to the resignation of Yahya Khan in 1972, and again under Zia ul-Haq from 1977 to the present. Military rule, however, has always had a strong civilian component, as senior politicians and bureaucrats have played an important role in all periods of martial law. Nor has "the military" been a monolith: there have been important dissenters to martial law and particular policies within the military among retired generals. But the military has in fact been the most important political institution in Pakistan for much of its history and has repeatedly attempted to practice corrective surgery on other important governmental and political institutions. It is important, therefore, to examine closely the armed forces' relationship to Pakistan's ethnic diversity and Islamic ideology. What we see in this regard is that ethnic imbalance has always been a critical political factor in state politics, and that the army's new interest in Islam may yet prove to be its most important achievement.

Military Institutions: Power and Policy[22]

Of Pakistan's institutions, only the military has remained untouched. It was too powerful for civilians to tamper with and virtually ran itself without outside interference. Only when it was defeated by the Indian army in 1971 were there attempts by Bhutto to restructure it, and some of these attempts may have only hastened his own downfall.

Our primary interest in the armed forces lies with the Pakistan army (the politically most powerful service), and, within the army, the officer corps. The attitudes, professionalism, regiment or branch origins, and shared formative experiences of its young officers are likely to shape Pakistani politics beyond the year 2000, just as the experiences undergone by Zia ul-Haq in the 1940s shape his behavior today. Our focus is on four linkages: between the army and Pakistan's ethnic groups, the army and Islam, the army and other important state and political institutions, and the army and foreign policy.

Ethnicity and Representativeness

The maintenance of proportionate representation of important ethnic groups in the military has important symbolic and practical dimensions. The symbolic dimension of military service is self-evident: if a Pakistani cannot fully share the obligations and rewards associated with such a central state institution as the military, he is not a citizen in the full meaning of the word. Conversely, the dominance of a particular region within the military is often seen by others as a potential threat.

The practical dimensions of ethnic representativeness are no less important. In dealing with conflict within a region (such as Baluchistan) it is essential to have within the military and security forces individuals from that region who understand the local languages, terrain, culture, and aspirations. Yet there are dangers associated with such a practice. First, the military trains its members in the art and science of violence, and a continual flow of veterans from the army back to a rebellious area may strengthen the capacity of the rebels. Second (and apparently of great importance in the Lahore riots of 1977), disturbances in a particular region are quickly felt in military units drawn from that region. Such forces cannot be trusted to control a crowd possibly made up of their own kin.

The British who ran the old Indian army strongly believed that India was a series of disparate, segmented societies, an agglomeration of "nations" with different characteristics and attributes. They concluded that not only were some ethnic groups inherently more martial or warlike than others but that such groups had to be counterbalanced to ensure that they would not unite against the British or exploit regions and castes and religious communities that were "weaker." The idea of the "martial races" had complex origins, some based on myth, some rooted in South Asian tradition—which antedates the British—of ranking different ethnic groups according to their military-like qualities, including not only ferocity (in which the Baluch excel) but also adaptability to discipline and organization. But this view of "martial races" did partially reflect actual regional, religious, cultural, and ethnic differences among Indians. It also led to a serious imbalance of recruitment in the old Indian army and to the dominance of Punjabis in the sepoy ranks and later in the officer corps. The British found that Punjabi Muslims made very good soldiers, and often good officers. Punjabis took to discipline better, recruitment among Punjabis was easier, and the nomadic Baluchi had the disconcerting habit of decamping without notice. By the beginning of World War II the largest single class in the Indian army was Punjabi Muslims.

Upon achieving Independence, Pakistan found that it had something like 60 percent Punjabi Muslims as sepoys and in the officer corps. The second-largest group was drawn from the Pashtun Muslims of the Northwest Frontier Province (one of the few ethnic groups Punjabis respect). Pashtuns, although a minority, play a major role in the officer corps. (Zia, in fact, is the first Punjabi to serve as head of the army, all of his Pakistani predecessors being Pashtuns.) From the beginning Punjabi and Pashtun officers claimed a special position in the new state of Pakistan: they stressed that the virtues of Pakistan were their virtues and that the Islamic character of Pakistan was reflected in the Islamic character of the military. In popular publications as well as in the military schools the history of Pakistan was traced to Muslim dominance in South Asia, and Pakistanis were portrayed as the natural conquerors of the region by virtue of their purer religion and their martial characteristics. These assumptions led to the grotesquely inflated belief of the martial superiority of Pakistan's army over "Hindu India." The Indians had within their ranks some near-martial races—Sikhs, Gurkhas, and Rajputs were shown particular respect—but the Indian army was "contaminated" by such nonmartial groups as Tamils, Telugus, Gujeratis, and, fatally, Bengalis.

No regular Bengali Muslim army units had been raised during World War II. The Pakistan army immediately raised two battalions of the new East Bengal Regiment in 1948. These and subsequent Bengali units were organizationally significant because they were the only single-ethnic units in the new Pakistan army and were officered entirely by Bengalis. After Independence the Pakistanis had systematically mixed different army units—but not Bengalis. While Bengali units were slowly expanded, there was strong resistance within the Pakistan army to greatly expanding East Bengali representation in the military, and considerable distaste for the quality of Bengali officers and other ranks.

We now know the consequences of discriminatory treatment against Bengali officers and soldiers. They became the backbone of armed resistance to the Pakistan army during the civil war in the East Wing; despite warnings, the Pakistan army leadership never could make up its mind as to whether the Bengali units should be expanded into full partnership or completely eliminated. Since the army was running the country, the exclusion of East Pakistanis also had very broad political implications.

This discussion of the military origin of the old Pakistan's destruction is offered as a reminder of the central symbolic and practical importance of ethnic representativeness within the military when it dominates the politics of a country. It raises the question: Could it happen again? The question is relevant and worth examining since the present Pakistan army's units and officer corps are hardly more representative than the old one, with a few districts of the Punjab and NWFP still as dominant.

Before Independence, more than 77 percent of the wartime recruitment from what became Pakistan had been from the Punjab, 19.5 percent from NWFP, 2.2 percent from Sind, and slightly more than 0.06 percent from Baluchistan (and of this number, 90.7 percent had served in the army). Today, the percentages have not changed dramatically. Seventy-five percent of all ex-servicemen come from only three districts in the Punjab (Rawalpindi, Jhelum, and Campbellpur) and two adjacent districts in NWFP (Kohat and Mardan), so the army as a whole is still ethnically unrepresentative. These five districts are part of or adjacent to the Potwar region of Pakistan—very poor, overpopulated, underirrigated, and on the path of countless invasions of South Asia—and between them, they contain only 9 percent of the male population of Pakistan.

Since the departure of the Bengalis, all regular units of the "new" Pakistan army are now integrated in that they are supposed to contain a fixed ratio of Pakistanis from several regions.[23] Each of the four major infantry regiments (Punjab, Baluch, Frontier Force, Sind) recruits on a national basis through a central system of recruiting officers. However, because of the large numbers of Punjabis, some units (even in the Baluch Regiment) have no Baluchis and very few Pashtuns or Sindhis. The problem is further complicated in that quotas are by region, not by ethnic group. Thus a Pashtun living in the Punjab is counted as a Punjabi, and a Punjabi living in Baluchistan is counted as a Baluch.

The disproportionate representation of ethnic Punjabis in both the officer corps and the other ranks has changed greatly since 1971, in that very few Bengalis served in the military although they were half the population. Still, while exact figures are unavailable, it is likely that Punjabis remain slightly overrepresented at both levels, Pashtuns receive about proportionate representation, and Baluchis and especially Sindhis are underrepresented. Since there is no conscription, little can be done to draw in reluctant or uninterested ethnic groups.

There is now more awareness of the dangers of an ethnically unrepresentative army. A predominantly Punjabi army is particularly sensitive to political unrest in the Punjab itself. Large numbers of Baluch or Sindhis in the military would mean a better-trained and disciplined population in two provinces with separatist sentiment. Moreover, if ordinary citizens from Sind or Baluchistan do not make good soldiers—or if they were not interested in participating in the defense of the country as soldiers—what does this imply about their loyalty to the state of Pakistan, and the loyalty and officer-like qualities of Baluch or Sindhis who join the officer corps? What lesson is to be drawn by such groups in the face of Punjabi dominance? The former chief justice of the Supreme Court raised this issue in the army's professional journal. Justice Hamoodur Rahman reminded his readers that the main culprits in the disintegration of the old Pakistan were Punjabis and that this gave rise to a feeling of Punjabi domination that in its turn propelled into prominence "regionalistic and parochial aspirations."[24] The dilemma was recently summed up from a military perspective by a senior retired lieutenant general who had been a close associate of Ayub Khan: "The idea is to get more Sindhis in and the response is not there! It is like the Bengalis—the attempt to do it was there, the response was weak, but as I saw it, the attempt [to bring in Bengalis] was late—but there were those who could say, 'See, if you had done it earlier, see what happened later?' Had we rushed it, would things have been worse?"[25]

The Army and Islam

After Independence there was little detectable concern about the relationship among the military, Islam, and the state of Pakistan. Other than trivial steps such as replacing British slogans and symbols with Islamic ones, no outward change in the appearance of the officer corps and various military establishments took place. Primary attention had been given to building an organization and the development of strategic doctrine. The close relationship first with the British and then the United States military encouraged deferral of the issue of Islam: it was enough that the army served an Islamic state.

In time, however, the failures of the Pakistani political system coupled with the recruitment of officers from more traditional sectors of Pakistani society increased the salience of the question of the relationship between army and state in an Islamic country. Officers began to ask what other national models might be more relevant to their army than the secular British or American patterns, and the military has started to take seriously Islamic history and Qur'anic doctrine, although the basic institutions of the army still follow Western lines. The present army is an uneasy blend, especially in matters of doctrine. The Shi'a–Sunni schism does not play a major role within army politics, although it certainly has been a factor from time to time. It was rumored, for example, that Yahya Khan was particularly vulnerable as commander in chief because he was a Shi'a, and Shi'as are somewhat resentful that certain foreign training posts are closed to them (most importantly, Saudi Arabia). The army is, however, increasingly "Islamic" in that regulations against drinking are now seriously enforced, although prayer is left up to the individual and technical military subjects remain untouched.

Comparatively, the most relevant model is the Israeli defense force. Pakistanis respect the mix of democracy, religion, and fighting qualities that they see in Israel (although they certainly oppose Israeli policy) and would like Pakistan to emerge as a kind of Islamic Israel. There are other analogies. One distinguished retired general argues that Pakistan "cannot have an army and a political system which is derived from secular, Western models. The comparison should be with the Catholic states of Europe: how long did they take to work out a relationship between the army and the state?"[26] This view more closely resembles Muhammad Iqbal's philosophy of autonomous Muslim states than Jinnah's semisecular Pakistan, and it seems to be accepted by the present military leadership.

Under President Zia, there is a systematic attempt to construct a state and an army along Islamic lines, yet still to be "modern" and efficient. In the years since he has come to power Zia has extended and reinforced the Islamization of Pakistan, introducing a number of banking and commercial practices based on Islam, punishments drawn from the Qur'an, and the "Islamic" reform of many parts of Pakistani society.

The central question is the following: Why has the military pursued this policy of Islamization of the state when many of its own institutions are quite un-Islamic in origin? Is Islamization merely a diversionary tactic used by the generals to keep the most Westernized segments of Pakistan off balance? Or is the policy due to the religiosity of Zia and his advisers?

Neither answer seems to be exactly correct. Zia is a devout Muslim but no fanatic, yet he and others take Islamization quite seriously. The view of the senior leadership was best expressed by one senior retired general, who provided this analysis of the weaknesses of Pakistani society and how Islam serves as both a goal and a corrective:

> We [the leadership] are progressive and enlightened individuals. But Islamic laws have been brought in [chopping off hands, lashes]. Are we hypocrites? Well, there are good laws, but they require a good society; the two things have to go side by side. The development of the world has not been uniform: within certain countries also the development has not been uniform. In the West, for example, law can be enforced uniformly; it will be acceptable practically to everybody as being the law at the time, because the whole society has grown upward simultaneously. In the East it is not so. In Pakistan, for example, you find people who live in caves! You can find people living by centuries, till the twenty-first, leave alone the twentieth. So, a law which a man of the twentieth century considers to be modern and civilized is considered to be uncivilized for a man living in the fourteenth century. And there are people here living in caves, in a prehistoric period!
>
> I think we are trying to civilize people here, whereas in the West the people are becoming animals, going toward the other direction; for me, homosexuality is such a big crime against humanity. Chopping off hands for stealing in Pakistan, I do not consider to be against humanity. You consider such things [liberation of laws concerning homosexuality] to be a step forward; we consider it to be against human nature.

And, he concluded, expressing the view of virtually the entire leadership of Pakistan in the Zia years:

> We do not accept that the West goes out to impose its views on us. We do not cry or shout about what Sweden has done—they have authorized their children to go to court against their parents—

> now this is destroying human civilization which has been developed by this race of human beings over centuries. It is wrong, totally wrong, but if we had done it, the whole of the West would have started shouting, "Look how uncivilized and backward those Pakistanis are." You people have a friend in Pakistan. You can always find fault, but you will destroy us, with what result? The West is looking for an ideal society, but is an imitation of that ideal for us? I think it would depend on the situation: you cannot impose a proper type of culture, civilization, without considering the basic structures of that society.

The inner tensions and contradictions in this view are clear. The typical officer is highly Westernized in appearance and in his values, yet he is Muslim and Pakistani and rejects much of what he believes to be the degradation of the West. More officers come from devout families than in the past, and more believe that religion and public life should mix. Fewer and fewer come from secularized Muslim families who believe that religion and public life should not mix, and young Pakistanis who hold this view tend to go into professions other than the military. Further, those officers who do not feel strongly about the mixing of religion and reform have been swept up in the wave of Islamization as part of a general search for ideology within the military after the disaster of 1971. This defeat persuaded some officers that Pakistan was being punished for not being true to its original (Islamic) purpose; other officers do not feel quite this strongly but recognize Islam as an important unifying factor in maintaining the integrity of the army and the state and as a link between these institutions.

Islam does not provide a complete model or pattern, certainly to the more well-informed and highly trained officers. The Pakistani military is trying to work for an amalgamation of two cultures. Their approach is to draw on their own professional experience and careers: if good government works within the military, if it can be imposed by adherence to regulations, law, and tradition, then the broader society should be amenable to the same kind of ortho-social control. Zia and some around him who hold these views know that they have not been able to persuade many Western-educated Pakistanis of their correctness, but this only confirms their view of un-Islamic rot in Pakistan and the need to persevere.

The Army and the State

When Zia ul-Haq assumed power in 1977, he promised that he would hold elections within ninety days. The promise was repeated and only recently fulfilled. Zia has rejected the suggestion that he enter politics, aware that Ayub's experiment along these lines ended in disaster and a second coup. Zia's power rests on his command of the army, and it would not permit him to play a partisan role while remaining chief of the army staff.

Two contesting theories have been offered to explain not only Zia's coup, but earlier intervention by the military in Pakistan. On the one side, many academic and civilian critics regard the Zia martial law regime as the latest in a series of military governments, which themselves are a cover for Punjabi/West Pakistani dominance, or antidemocratic values held by the generals, or both. On the other side, the military defends its actions by pointing to civilian incompetence and misrule and believes that the military—the soldiers—may be the only truly national, patriotic, and efficient institution left in Pakistan.

There is evidence to support either view. We need not rehearse these arguments again, as ample literature already exists on the subject.[27] However, two further arguments are important in understanding how the military came to power, how it continued to rule, and how it might yet fully withdraw. The first relates to the notion widely held in Pakistan of "democracy," the second to the military's ambivalence about governing the state.

In Pakistan the confrontational dimensions of democratic government are emphasized: democracy thus seems synonymous with hostile and uncompromising opposition to established governments, even legitimizing outrageous and destructive behavior. This kind of "democracy"—unscrupulous campaigning, public libel and slander, betrayal of party loyalties, misconduct in government, and so forth—is seen as a threat to the state itself. Accordingly, security and bureaucratic elites regularly support repressive measures in the face of such behavior, and they also tend to exaggerate the dangers of such behavior.

The image of democracy gone berserk is widely held within the military and civilian bureaucracies of Pakistan. As in the case of the general quoted above, it is often argued that Pakistan is not yet ready for democracy—that Pakistanis lack the necessary level of education, culture, or maturity to make democracy work, and that the military must therefore stand by as guardians ready to intervene. This narrow conception of "democracy" has its origins in the colonial experience when British officials made the same argument. This theory of democracy and cultural/political backwardness has dominated Pakistani elite military and bureaucratic thought since Independence.

A second vital point in understanding military rule concerns the moral and legal ambiguity felt by the armed forces toward governing the state. The military ruled in the name of the 1973 Constitution (albeit virtually transformed by various martial law decrees) and continued to promise elections. The martial law regime offered this symbolic compliance with democratic politics not only to humor its American allies or to hoodwink gullible Pakistanis but because it was concerned about the legitimacy of its own rule, just as previous martial law regimes saw to it that successor civilian governments legitimated their actions. The military did not want to be accused of treason by a successor civilian government bent on revenge.

The military was and is nervous about its own power. While there has been some public discussion of a system that would give the military a formal constitutional role (as in Turkey), there is still no consensus within the senior ranks about the propriety of such a role and its compatibility with "democracy," that is, civilian rule. Further, some openly oppose such a role as incompatible with their notion of military professionalism and likely to damage the military itself by association with corrupt or incompetent civilian regimes.

The ambiguity of the military toward state power and its extreme sensitivity toward internal security problems in turn are clearly demonstrated in the ill-fated attempt to create a paramilitary force in Pakistan. Such paramilitary forces have been created in a number of new states.[28] They generally serve two vital purposes: they act as a buffer between the regular armed forces and society, allowing the military to concentrate on professional matters, and they can be used to balance the armed forces politically and make a coup harder to plan.

Unlike India, where civilian governments raised a number of parliamentary forces after 1968, Pakistani leaders did not consider the issue until 1972. Ayub and Yahya were army men, their power rested on the support of the army, and they felt confident that the army could and should be ready to handle domestic law and order problems. More than its sister army in India, the Pakistan army inherited something of the paternalist autocracy that characterized the Punjab school of administration of British India. Although some of the perquisites of such a system included opportunities for corruption and bribery by the officers, the army stood by to help civilian authority when necessary, and even supplant it.

This pattern was broken when Zulfikar Ali Bhutto created the Federal Security Force (FSF) in 1972 as both a buffer and a counterweight. The army, shattered by its defeat in East Pakistan, accepted the FSF, although some senior retired officers refused to accept Bhutto's offer of appointments in the force. Tolerance turned to fear, however, and then to hatred. Bhutto used the FSF as a private police force and began equipping it with arms that rivaled those of the military—some retired officers now characterize the FSF as an incipient Nazi SS. When Bhutto was overthrown in 1977, one of Zia's first acts was to abolish the FSF. The army is again the second line of defense against internal disorder and remains highly sensitive to domestic law and order problems. It has a domestic intelligence service of its own and interacts closely with local police and intelligence services. Virtually all army units have some secondary law and order assignment since they are generally stationed within marching distance of some important civilian population centers (most of the army is in the Punjab, as are most of the cities of Pakistan).

The recent spell of military rule was certainly not "democratic" politics, but Zia and other generals (and not a few civilians) would defend it as "good government." Economic stability and law and order have returned to Pakistan and foreign policy is well managed. The system allowed consideration of slightly divergent points of view, and public discussion of important issues in the press and in the Majlis-i Shura. Unlike previous martial law regimes, however, the military has tried to share the implementation of martial law with civilians and has kept the various civilian ministries functioning. Zia, in his capacity as chief martial law administrator, was known to issue an order to a particular ministry, which in turn has either appealed this through the martial law hierarchy or taken it back to him via the Cabinet (in his capacity as president). Then, as president, Zia has at times reversed the martial law directive he originally approved. The same process occurred in the four provinces where the governors were also martial law administrators. In the eyes of many Pakistanis, this was a poor substitute for popular democratic government, but it was not quite the draconian rule often associated with military governments elsewhere.

The Army, External Relations, and Power

The foreign policy dimensions of domestic politics cannot be ignored in the case of a state recently dominated by the military and facing substantial external threats, especially when that state has many dissident ethnic groups with ties abroad and when the armed forces are dependent on foreign powers for their military hardware. Politics in Pakistan is linked to foreign policy in at least five ways.

The first is the connection between dissident ethnic and linguistic minorities and foreign governments. Pashtuns, Kashmiris, Baluch, and Sindhis must be placated, for they do have a limited option elsewhere. The Pakistan government may find itself pressed at home if one or more of its neighbors decides to meddle.

Second, Pakistan's heavy defense expenditures affects not only the growth of the entire economy but also the distribution of resources among the provinces. Sindhis and Baluch in particular see little economic benefit from Pakistan's heavy defense burden, and they and other minority provinces often encounter the military only as a hostile force.

Third, the army has continued Bhutto's efforts to place Pakistan in the Islamic world. Bhutto was seeking a way back into the international community and saw an opportunity to gain access to the rich resources of the oil states. But the military added its own perspective to Bhutto's Islamic foreign policy. The military sees itself as the strategic center of the Muslim world, having the best training facilities of any Muslim state and maintaining military missions in more than twenty countries. These operations have brought it great prestige and considerable financial rewards, a neat conjunction of personal, bureaucratic, and Islamic interests.

Fourth, if Pakistan does go nuclear, the stakes in domestic politics in any future coup or transfer of power are raised. Not only will there be a struggle for control over such weapons but foreign governments will feel that they have a direct and vital interest in such a struggle. Indeed, the emergence of an unstable and disorderly Pakistan as a nuclear power may be too great a provocation for some neighbors. Although some believe that once states acquire nuclear weapons they become reasonably trustworthy, no one familiar with Pakistan's violent tradition of political succession would share this optimism.

Finally, despite a major attempt by Bhutto to build a domestic arms industry, Pakistan remains dependent on foreign nations for its hardware and financing. Virtually all air force equipment is Chinese, American, or French in origin; most armor is Chinese or American; and other weapons, ships, and equipment come from these and a few other sources. If the armed forces fully yield power to civilians, they are likely to want a veto over foreign policy decisions, particularly those affecting weapons suppliers, and they are unlikely to tolerate a civilian leadership which dramatically reduces arms levels.

Conclusions and Prospects

Pakistan came into existence as the expression of an idea with a very short history. Yet it was born with a developed set of state institutions that had been forged in an imperial context to assist the British in governing a multiethnic and multireligious territory of continental dimensions. Other large states shaped their bureaucracies and institutions over the years, but, in Pakistan, the institutions came first and have tried to shape the state.

The ethnic imbalance of these institutions was deliberate. Especially in the case of the military, Pashtuns and Punjabi Muslims were overrepresented both because of their desire for military service and because of the impunity with which they could be used in non-Muslim regions. In the case of the civil services, where selection was more by aptitude than traditional interest, some regions were underrepresented because of the disparity in educational levels among Pakistan's provinces.

It was not surprising then when the state ran into difficulty, the military would emerge as a political force, backed by the senior civilian bureaucracy. Nor was it surprising that the ethnic imbalance within these and other institutions turned out to be fatal to Pakistan in 1971 when a major ethnic group, the Bengalis, broke away.

What was surprising was that Islam failed to provide the glue to hold Pakistan together. But "Islam" often meant little more than anti-Hinduism or a longing for freedom from oppression. Bengalis weighed the balance and came to the conclusion that they could be free of both Indian and West Pakistani dominance if they had their own state. These calculations are made today in the Northwest Frontier Province, Baluchistan, Sind, and even Kashmir, and though some have opted for separatism, another breakup is less likely to recur than some observers have argued.

First, the ethnic imbalances in the services, the bureaucracies, the professions, and even in politics are not as severe now as in the "old" Pakistan. Nor are the cultural differences as great among Sindhi, Punjabi, Baluch, and Pashtun as among each of these and Bengalis. Pakistani elites have yet to find an institutional formula short of British-style parliamentary democracy and more than dictatorship by consensus. But effective institutions are possible only if the dominant ethnic group, the Punjabis, recognize the necessity for power sharing.

Second, external events have changed the context of Pakistani politics. The ethnic groups that are most discontented with Punjabi dominance do not constitute viable and distinct entities and would need considerable outside support to survive, especially from India or the Soviet Union. Although some non-Punjabi leaders have announced their break with Pakistan, many others are concerned over foreign influence to see common interest with Punjabis in reforming or reconstructing the present Pakistan.

Third, Islam, which failed to provide the path for Pakistan in the past, offers a peculiar kind of attraction today. It provides a domestic rallying point and frame of reference and defuses the orthodox right-wing parties who are still capable of generating mass protests. Externally, it is useful as part of a revivified foreign policy. Though Zia and the Islamizers run the risk of creating a Khomeini-type revolution, they regard this risk as quite low. The clergy of Pakistan are neither as powerful nor as central to the political life as those in Iran; they are divided between Sunni and Shi'a and are balanced by a more developed professional and political community (including the army) than in Iran. Islam is available for state-building purposes. The military and their civilian supporters need not follow the Shah's or Turkey's model of a secular Muslim state.

What remains troubling, however, is the military's ambivalent relationship to the political parties and constitutional government. Military rule is regarded as illegitimate in Pakistan not because it has meant the domination of a Punjabi officer corps—although that is a factor in non-Punjabi grievances—nor because the military has Islamized the country (that was initiated by Bhutto) but because there is no theoretical or practical justification for military rule beyond expediency. The illegitimacy of military rule remains even as it is thought to be occasionally necessary.

Ayub tried to deal with this tension by turning himself into a politician, only to lose the respect of the military. Yahya, a man more limited in ambition, did hold Pakistan's first free election but lacked the nerve to act on the results. Until recently Zia resisted the political path and distrusted the electoral process. He is more willing than his predecessors to undertake what he regards as the necessary Islamic and political reforms to make Pakistan unified. Zia feels that one can be a good Muslim and a good (Westernized) professional—he sees himself as a model—and asks only that Pakistan's lawyers, students, professors, journalists, doctors, bureaucrats, and politicians conform to the pattern—that they straighten out their "qibla." But the armed forces are perhaps the least qualified institution to lead a cultural revolution.

Yet there were a few important qualities of the martial law regime of 1977–85 that offered some hope. Because of the terrible ordeal undergone by the army, its senior officers, especially Zia, were more realistic than their predecessors about their external strategic and internal political situation. The present military hierarchy have no illusions about Pakistan's military might, about their capacity to rule by threat, or about the ability of Pakistani politicians to govern. They also have strong foreign support from a number of countries, which has meant a new influx of economic assistance, weapons, and political support. If a balance of Pakistan's prospects for state building were to be drawn, it would not be unfavorable for the short run—the next few months or even years. But one hesitates to speculate beyond that.

May 1986

Events in Pakistan moved with dramatic speed after this chapter was completed in August 1984. I have changed the text to the past tense, but my cautiously optimistic conclusions remain unaltered.

President Zia held a national referendum in December 1984 on two questions: the propriety of Islam as Pakistan's guiding philosophy, and his right to continue as president through 1990. The answer in both cases was yes, although the turnout for the referendum was low. Zia then held successful nonparty general elections at the national and provincial levels in February 1985, and Muhammad Khan Junejo became prime minister in March. Junejo was a relatively unknown Sindhi politician with a reputation for honesty.

After keeping his promise to restore civilian government, Zia continued the process of demilitarization. By the end of 1985 the National Assembly had passed a bill amending the 1973 Constitution. The amendments incorporated many martial law regulations that Zia had promulgated since 1977 and also indemnified from prosecution those associated with the martial law system. Martial law was completely ended in Pakistan by the end of 1985, and the country was (for the first time since the 1950s) free from any martial law or "emergency" proclamations. A fully civilian government headed by Prime Minister Junejo was sworn in on January 28, 1986. Nearly full press and political freedoms have been restored to Pakistan, as have political parties. However, Zia continued in his position as head of the Pakistan army as well as president through mid-1986.

During this transition period there was a marked decline in the political role of Islam. The Jama'at did badly at the polls, although its strength had always been in organizational, not electoral, politics. Women politicians have been prominent, most notably Bhutto's daughter, Benazir. She made a triumphal return to Pakistan in April 1986 (having boycotted the elections) and expects to challenge both Junejo and Zia. However, Benazir was cautious in her early statements about the military: it is now a constitutional violation instead of a martial law violation to criticize the armed forces. (This was also the pretext for banning at least one scholarly book on the Pakistan army.) 2016: I refer to the banning of my own book, *The Pakistan Army*, although Zia comforted me with the truth that "having been banned, it will be more widely read." He was killed in 1988 in a still-mysterious air crash that took several lives, including the U.S. Ambassador Arnold Raphel.

While post-martial law politics are fluid and unpredictable, it was evident that all concerned—Zia, the military, Benazir Bhutto and the PPP, and Junejo and his ruling Pakistan Muslim League—remember Pakistan's calamitous political history and were eager to avoid provocation. To repeat my conclusion of 1984: Pakistan's short-term prospects are encouraging: democracy has been gradually but almost fully restored to Pakistan. The long-term prospects are still uncertain. Pakistan has the requisite formal institutions, considerable material and human resources, and a deeply rooted democratic tradition. Has it, however, learned from its own past?

2003

ELEVEN

The Jihadist Threat to Pakistan

In Pakistan, radical Islamic groups seek revolutionary changes in the Pakistani political and social order, support violence to achieve those changes, and may be actively involved in violence and terrorism across Pakistan's frontiers, but their attempts to infiltrate the government of Pakistan have proven feeble and easily countered thus far. On the street, radical Islamists do not—at least not yet—have significant influence in the Punjab, Pakistan's largest and most important province. With little mass support in this deeply Islamic yet still moderate country, radical Islamists have not been able to successfully conduct an Islamic coup to seize the levers of government, and they stand little chance of doing so within the next five years. Beyond that, however, Pakistan's future is uncertain.

The political dominance and institutional integrity of the Pakistani army remains the chief reason for the marginality of radical Islamic groups. Although the army has a long history of using radical and violent Islamists for political purposes, it has little interest in supporting their larger agenda of turning Pakistan into a more comprehensively Islamic state. Pakistan's political, institutional, economic, and social decay will have to accelerate before radical groups emerge as an independent political force.

Unless steps are taken now to rebuild a moderate Pakistan, however, the rise of radical Islamists as a significant political force could be one of several unpalatable futures for this increasingly chaotic, nuclear-armed state. Pakistan's educational system must be reconstructed; its economy requires massive overhaul; and the generals' obsession with adventurist and ultimately debilitating foreign policy goals must be curbed. Otherwise, radical Islamists will see their power grow, possibly in conjunction with new separatist movements and an increase in state authoritarianism. The dangers of Islamic radicalism in Pakistan in the short run have been exaggerated, but within a decade, that country could truly become one of the world's most dangerous states.

The Scene and Scope of the Threat

Radical Islam certainly has found a home in Pakistan. Radical parties are profuse, and terrorism is an oft-employed tactic. Yet the historically complex role of Islam in the state; the diverse, specific goals of Islamic parties, as well as their limited capacities to build wider support and pose formidable threats; and the inherently disorganized nature of terrorist activity, let alone the state's interests in maintaining at least some of that activity, collectively limit the threat they actually pose to Pakistan's governing establishment.

An Islamic State or the State of Islam?

The chief objective of the Pakistan movement was to create a Muslim-majority state in South Asia—a homeland for India's Muslims. Little attention was paid to what this state would look like, exactly, or just how "Islamic" it would be; Pakistanis still debate vigorously how fully their state should reflect Islamic law, the Qur'an, and earlier models of Muslim states. Both the individual, Muhammad Ali Jinnah, and the organization, the Muslim League, that wrested Pakistan from the chaos of partition in 1947 were secular. Inclined toward electoral politics and the rule of law, they propelled Pakistan's politics in the direction of moderate constitutionalism, even in light of an inability to agree on a constitution. Of the new state's more avowedly Islamic groups and political parties, the most important was a carryover from undivided India, the Jama'at-i-Islami,[1] which had been unenthusiastic about the creation of a state that would divide India's Muslim population.

Early on, Pakistan's predominately secular leaders tried to express its Islamic nature in the form of an Objectives Resolution that the Constituent

Assembly passed in 1949. Over the years, a number of Islamic provisions—some of them of doubtful authenticity—were embedded into law. For example, the president of Pakistan must be Muslim; the Ahmadiyya sect, which claims that Muhammad was not the last prophet, was declared to be non-Muslim; there was a flirtation with a ban on interest; and, for a number of years, businesses had to close on Friday. In general, however, Pakistan has not gone very far down the Islamic road. Islamic law, or Sharia, does not yet govern the state or the personal lives of Pakistanis, although parts of the Sharia, such as a ban on alcohol, have become law, though even this ban is often privately ignored by Pakistanis.

The notion of an Islamic state is widely accepted in Pakistan, but the country cannot agree on which elements of Islam should dominate. All Pakistanis value their state's role in various international Islamic organizations and favor support for oppressed Muslims elsewhere, particularly in Palestine, Bosnia, and Kashmir. Most middle-class and urban Pakistanis, especially the Mohajirs—Urdu-speaking Pakistanis originally from what is now India—believe that Pakistan should be a modern but Islamic state, with the Islamic part confined to just a few spheres of public life.

Pakistan's Islamic Parties: Profuse but Divided

The Islamist parties have never been politically successful, and until recently, no single Islamic political party captured more than 5 percent of the national vote. In the October 2002 election, Muttahida Majlis-e-Amal (MMA), an alliance of six Islamic parties, polled 11 percent of the vote, which the electoral system translated into fifty-three seats in the National Assembly (17 percent of the total), giving the MMA control over the government in the Northwest Frontier Province (NWFP), partnership in a coalition government in Balochistan, and the status of leading opposition party at the federal level.

Pakistan's current leading Islamic organizations range from moderate to militant. Reflecting the hallowed Islamic traditions of piety and charity, there are numerous apolitical missionary, spiritual, and social groups, the most important of which is the Tablighi Jama'at.[2] Theoretically, the Tablighi could serve as a recruitment base for more radical groups or could spin off a more militant faction operating under the cover of a widely respected Tablighi member. There is some hint that this group has been infiltrated by violent sectarian groups as a way of avoiding detection by law enforcement agencies.

In organizational integrity, appeal to Pakistan's elite, and street power in the Punjab, the most influential Islamic group in Pakistan is the Jama'at-i-Islami (JI)—a powerful force in many urban areas and, reflecting its middle-class and sophisticated ideology, historically strong in Pakistan's universities, where its student wing, the Islami Jamiat-i-Tulabah, has become a formidable street force. The Jama'at-i-Islami favors a return to a strict parliamentary system with reduced presidential powers as a way of trimming the power of Pakistan's entrenched political-military establishment and, unlike most of its MMA coalition partners, favors women's education and social reform (the JI's leader's daughter was elected to the National Assembly). The party is a vocal supporter of Kashmiri militants, whom it regards as freedom fighters, but did not support the more radical Taliban. Finally, the JI is nonsectarian and stays clear of the bloody violence that has plagued Pakistan for the past twenty years.

This sectarianism, encouraged by some Ulema (Islamic clerics) is dominated by violent Sunni groups, which pose a grave threat to law and order. Armed groups supported by Pakistan's Shi'as, who constitute about 12 percent of the population, have also emerged. Today, sectarian violence rages throughout Pakistan, notably in Karachi, where professionals (especially Shi'a doctors) have been routinely targeted for assassination, leading to the mass departure of highly trained medical personnel from Karachi and, in most cases, from Pakistan itself. Numerous sectarian battles have broken out among Sunnis, with pitched battles between Barelvis and Deobandis, often for control over Karachi's mosques.[3]

The largest Islamic sects with the greatest control over religious schools are the Deobandis, who control an estimated 65 percent of Pakistan's madaris and are among the most militant in their demands for the Pakistani state to become truly Islamic—as they would define it. Deobandi groups were in the forefront of the movement to declare the Ahmadiyya to be non-Muslims and are behind much of the nation's anti-Shi'a sectarian violence. The larger Deobandi sect includes the Jamiat-e-Ulema-e-Islam (JUI),[4] which is associated with the Harkat-ul-Mujahideen (HUM), a terrorist organization operating in Kashmir and the first Pakistani group to be put on the U.S. list of terrorist organizations. HUM's chief ideologue, Maulana Masood Azhar, is also the founder of another organization,

Jaish-e-Muhammad. These, along with other Pakistani militant groups—Sipah-e-Shahaba Pakistan and Lashkar-e-Jhangvi Pakistan, both Deobandi sects—have been active in Kashmir and parts of India.

The notorious Lashkar-e-Taiba (LeT), also on the U.S. list of terrorist organizations, has been implicated in a number of terrorist acts in India and is closely linked by doctrine and possibly financial support to Saudi Arabia. LeT and related groups have had a stunning increase in membership since the 1980s, directly traceable to increased private Saudi support for their madaris, where 15 percent of the students are thought to be foreigners; recently, there has been an upsurge in new students.[5] Although LeT was and may still be active in India, informed sources indicate that it has not been involved in Pakistan's sectarian violence.

The past fifteen years reveal that, despite some overlap among them, the rapidly proliferating sectarian and religious groups have very different objectives. The Jama'at-i-Islami is focused primarily on Pakistan and seeks to restore civilian rule, although it has strong positions on Kashmir and India. Most of the violent, sectarian Sunni and Shi'a groups are Pakistan-centric, while a number of militant outfits were active in Afghanistan and/or Kashmir and retain an interest in each. The JUI, for example, has a strong Pashtun ethnic component as well as close ties to the Taliban. The Punjab-based LeT, with past operations in Afghanistan, India, and Kashmir, also has ties to the Taliban.

Although Islamist groups in Pakistan share a general identification with the Islamic world, an opposition to India's policies in Kashmir, a concern with Palestine, and a deep suspicion of the United States, none of them has a fully developed global agenda. This situation could change as anti-Americanism grows in Pakistan and in the Pakistani diaspora as a result of the U.S. war in Iraq and the Pakistani government's support for U.S. antiterrorist operations. Support for groups such as al Qaeda has thus far been limited, but recent reports indicate that JI functionaries provided several fugitive al Qaeda leaders with safe houses and, of course, the more radical Islamic parties were allied with al Qaeda in their support of the Taliban in Afghanistan. If sympathy with al Qaeda's ideas and similar ideologies should spread to Pakistan's politically moderate, educated classes, the country is likely to see new recruits for globally oriented, radical Islamic causes emerge.

The case of Omar Saeed Sheikh helps to convey how Islam has served as a unifying and mobilizing force for those with only a superficial understanding of the religion yet a deep perception of injustice. Born into a prosperous British-Pakistani family in the United Kingdom and educated at an elite college in Lahore and at the London School of Economics, Sheikh was apparently affected deeply by perceived injustices to Muslims in Bosnia and Kashmir as well as the Middle East.[6] Upon his return to South Asia, Sheikh participated in the kidnapping of foreign tourists in India and eventually the kidnapping and murder of Daniel Pearl in Pakistan. Does his career represent a trend among the Pakistani elite and the Pakistan diaspora? Great Britain, the United States, and other Western countries may not produce large numbers of radical Muslims, but they could yield a few dedicated cadres. The September 11 hijackers were drawn from the same strata of angry, professional, and Westernized Muslims. These groups are all the more worrisome for the threats they may pose to Western societies because of their ability to function within them, but thus far, these groups have had little systemic consequences for Pakistan.

Terrorism: Threatening Stability More Than the State

Pakistani terrorist groups supported or tolerated by the state operate within their own country, in Indian-administered parts of Kashmir, and in India itself. Many would like to reestablish a foothold in Afghanistan, perhaps with the assistance of the same Pakistani intelligence officers who once supported their operations on behalf of the Taliban government. The literature on terrorism frequently draws a comparison between acts of terrorism and the theater, positing that terrorists play to an audience. In South Asia, terrorism is geared toward at least three different audiences.

The immediate audience is the enemy, the target of violence. Hurting the enemy can be a cathartic act. This notion particularly applies to sectarian terrorists operating within Pakistan, who regard their mission as holy and the enemy to be worse than unbelievers: they are apostates. Although President Pervez Musharraf has made the suppression of sectarian violence a top priority, he has been unable to stem attacks on Christian churches and Western, especially U.S., facilities; there have been several reported attempts on his life. Pakistani terrorists are proving increasingly dangerous because they are using suicide squads—a new development. In the case of Kashmir, the goal is to provoke the Indian government into retaliatory measures that decrease its own legitimacy and make the terrorist/freedom fighter the defender of Kashmiris. In practice, these activities have degenerated into random acts of terrorism, often against the Kashmiris themselves.

Suicide and terrorist attacks originating in Pakistan are also prominent in India, with grave implications for regional stability. Assaults on several important Hindu temples in Gujarat and the Indian Parliament building in New Delhi as well as an attack on the families of Indian soldiers in Kashmir all contributed to a major military buildup in 2002. A dedicated, radical Islamic faction might try to use such attacks in 2003 to trigger a more serious conflict between India and Pakistan in an attempt to precipitate a harsh Indian response against Pakistan across the Line of Control, the internationally recognized boundary. From the perspective of many Islamic radicals, this outcome would, at a minimum, demonstrate the incompetence of the hated regime of General Musharraf or ultimately serve as the catalyst for an apocalyptic conflict between Islamabad and New Delhi.

The second target, the bystander, constitutes the largest audience. The goal of the terrorist is to use an extreme act to change the way in which the audience sees a new reality. As in the case of violence in literature and films, the level of horror has to increase over time to attract the attention of bystanders, who have their own mechanisms for coping with the awful. In Pakistan, the most important bystanders include the army—terrorists believe it is important not to alienate the military—the largely secular political community, and members of non-radical Islamic groups and parties. For this audience, acts of terrorism can demonstrate that violence is morally and practically superior to parliamentary methods for achieving important and shared objectives and that the groups that practice terrorism are legitimately pursuing objectives shared by a wide swath of Pakistanis. Terrorist acts may not lead to political power, but they might make the government more tolerant of these groups and less inclined to clamp down on them.

The final audience is composed of the potential pool of recruits to the cause. Suicide plays an especially important role for this audience because the act helps to undo the moral damage caused by the obvious targeting of innocents.

The death of a few martyrs who are on the side of good can compensate for the death of many innocents who happen to be on the side of evil. In addition, the message of the terrorist is that "small is beautiful" and a few dedicated cadres can take on and defeat the much larger enemy; therefore, the cause is not hopeless and is worth supporting, even with one's life. In Pakistan, the potential supporters of terrorism include the large pool of unemployed college students and graduates; the threat here lies in the fact that the numbers of such supporters will grow steadily if the economy remains stagnant and population growth continues out of control.

A Mixed Lot

In sum, Pakistan's Islamic extremists are a mixed lot. Some are criminals wrapped in the mantle of divine justice; some have modest Pakistani-related objectives; and others are seized with sectarian hatred. The radical groups' theological origins inherently divide them, and although most are Deobandis, some are not, including the extremely violent Shi'a groups. Nevertheless, all these groups tend to splinter in ways reminiscent of the extreme Right and Left in other parts of the world, and a burning sense of injustice may motivate a few foreign-born radicals to join them.

These groups expend their energy on ordinary Pakistani citizens or on one another; or they direct their efforts—usually with government assistance—toward India and, until recently, Afghanistan. Some radical Islamic groups are linked to more mainstream political movements or serve as the fighting or terrorist arm of such movements.

Moreover, Pakistan's radical groups disagree with one another in their diagnosis of the country's political, economic, and social problems. In the NWFP and northern Baluchistan, radical Islamic groups are becoming the vehicle for Pashtun dissent and anger, displacing the region's traditional Pashtun political party. Most radical Islamists hold deeply anti-U.S. sentiments, parting company with the more centrist Jama'at-i-Islami, which acknowledges that Pakistan has benefited from its ties to the United States and must maintain some links to the world's sole superpower if the country is to emerge as a state that is both modern and Islamic.

A few groups are, in fact, delusional and believe that terrorism can bring down the American empire. Even more believe that selected acts of terror will demonstrate the artificiality of India as a state and that India's Muslims are seething with discontent and must be liberated from Hindu oppression through jihad. Some radical groups prefer to direct their anger toward the Pakistani state and call for the immediate establishment of the Sharia as official, comprehensive state law, with Pakistan returning to a purer form of Islam and purging itself of corrupt Western and Hindu cultural trappings.

Where they have come to power, however, especially in the NWFP, the radical and centrist Islamists seem to have reached the understanding that, although rhetoric will continue to be inflammatory, the actual imposition of Islamic law and the more extreme parts of the MMA manifesto will continue to be held in abeyance. These groups know that the imposition of more radical measures would not only be unpopular in the NWFP but also might lead to the dismissal of the provincial government by the army-dominated government in Islamabad. Although they have grown in importance over the last year, Islamist groups do not dominate Pakistani society; they have not proven all that effective in pursuing their main goals; and they remain under the careful watch of the central government.

Radicalism's Real Effect on the State

Radical Islamist groups in Pakistan can be most accurately and collectively defined, as noted earlier, as those that seek major changes in the Pakistani political and social order and support violence to achieve those changes. Paradoxically, it has almost always been the state, especially the Pakistani army, that has allowed most radical Islamic groups to function on a wider stage—equipping and training them when necessary and providing overall political and strategic guidance for their activities. Arguably, therefore, in Pakistan, radical groups have been more of a tool of the state than a serious threat to it.

The Pakistani government's record in dealing with such radical groups is almost as mixed as the motives of the groups themselves. The government banned JeM and LeT in January 2002 under U.S. pressure, but the disbanding or banning of such radical groups usually means a name change or the temporary suspension of operations. Bans have had no impact on either the membership or the leadership of these groups, nor have they stopped the Pakistani government from using them for its own purposes. For example, the Nawaz Sharif government sought LeT's help in countering the sectarian Deobandi groups, while the Musharraf government continues to look the other way as radical groups head to Kashmir and India, where they have increased their operations since Musharraf's pledge to Washington to constrain them. Until the Pakistani government demonstrates the will and the capacity to carry out these pledges, it will not be radical Islamic groups that threaten the basic stability of Pakistan but the state organs that encourage them.

Exploited by the State

The state first exploited radical and violent Islamic groups in 1970–71 in East Pakistan, when the Pakistani army called on right-wing Islamic militants, notably the student wing of the Jama'at-i-Islami, to terrorize, torture, and murder Bengali intellectuals, politicians, and other supporters of the Bangladesh movement. Although Pakistan was confronted with an Indian-supported separatist movement, the brutal crackdown was counterproductive, and it weakened Islamabad's international position. Many of these militants were not Bengalis; they were drawn from the Bihari community of East Pakistan. Thus began a long and sordid history of the use of Islamic terror squads by the Pakistani state and its intelligence services to intimidate opponents of the regime; ethnic separatists; elements of moderate political parties; and, when necessary, other violent groups.

Pakistan's lurch toward Islamic extremism continued under Zulfikar Ali Bhutto from 1971 onward. Bhutto cynically promoted Islamization as a cover for his own autocratic tendencies, but he was deposed by the pious General Zia ul-Haq in 1977. Zia (unlike Bhutto) was an extremely devout Muslim whose views were close to the Jama'at-i-Islami. Zia was the first army chief openly to praise and support Islamic groups. He developed political ties with, and then later abandoned, the JI; in 1981 he provided massive arms and economic support for some of the most noxious and radical yet militarily effective Islamic groups in Afghanistan in the war to oust the Soviets from the country. Many of these groups had ties to counterparts in Pakistan, and most were based in the Pakistani city of Peshawar where, as in other parts of the NWFP, they developed ties to Arab and other Islamic volunteers in the jihad.[7]

In the late 1980s, Pakistan's dominant intelligence service, the Inter-Services Intelligence (ISI) directorate, began training Kashmiri dissidents, many of whom had fled to Pakistan after the rigged Kashmir election in 1989. ISI facilitated the Kashmiri operations undertaken by various Pakistani-based radical Islamic groups from 1989 onward; a few years later, under the direction of Benazir Bhutto, some of these groups were encouraged to support the Taliban, which Islamabad saw as a way to end Afghanistan's chaos and, at the same time, install a pro-Pakistani government in Kabul. The army also intervened from time to time to end sectarian disputes among radical Islamists within Pakistan, especially when they threatened to spread to the army, which has always prided itself as being above religious fanaticism. The problem persists today, as Musharraf has declared yet another crackdown on sectarianism, yet the situation remains inevitable so long as the state continues to—sporadically and to its own ends—support these groups.

Challenging the State

Within a few years of the Soviet withdrawal from Afghanistan in 1989, U.S. policy toward Pakistan hardened, and a separatist uprising broke out in the Indian-administered portions of the state of Jammu and Kashmir. These events emboldened a few radical Islamists, convinced that Pakistan was ripe for an Islamic coup, to launch one in September 1995.

The goal was to establish a strict Islamic order in Pakistan and carry the jihad more vigorously to India (and, via the Taliban, to Central Asia). The coup was a failure, even if the coup-makers actually shared some of the policy goals of the government, which implemented in the late 1980s a "forward policy" in Afghanistan and Kashmir to extend Pakistan's influence to Central Asia and weaken India's hold on the disputed province.

More typically, Pakistan army officers are guided by professional military norms, not religious ones. They wish to keep the army free of sectarianism (especially Sunni–Shi'a disputes) and do not want to see the army turned into a vehicle of religious propagation. Above all, there is a powerful incentive to follow channels and to work the system in the army because dissident and maverick officers are unlikely to reap the rewards of promotion or of plush government jobs upon retirement. The coup-makers were going against a trend, as the army was purged of ideologically motivated officers two years earlier when army chief Asif Nawaz Janjua implemented a plan to sidetrack the "bearded" ones, the more devout and blatantly pious officers. Speculatively, that purge may have sent many of these individuals into the ISI or out of the army, where they linked up with some of the radical Islamic groups that were then being cultivated for tasks in Afghanistan and Kashmir.

There is no evidence that the army is currently seething with Islamic radicalism, that an Islamic cabal is in a position to seize power in a coup, or that the lower ranks of the officer corps are any more "Islamic" than would be expected in a society that has seen the steady rise of Islamic sentiments. A recent visit to the Pakistan Military Academy, discussions with its directors and some cadets, and many conversations with active and retired Pakistani army officers all indicate little change from earlier years, which is not to say that the tenor and outlook of the officer corps remain unchanged as one generation succeeds another.

The reaction of Musharraf's generation of army officers against Zia's Islamic zealotry in no way represents a rejection of the more limited strategy of using radical Islamic groups as instruments of Pakistani foreign policy, especially against India. The dispute over Kashmir, like Pakistan's relations with Afghanistan, is viewed as a domestic matter whose resolution is vital to Pakistan's society and security.

Manipulating Islamic radicals, however, may have consequences for Pakistan's civil society—a subject that has generated considerable debate in Pakistan.

Factors to Consider

The results of the 2002 Pakistani elections and continued tension between India and Pakistan in Kashmir, especially in light of the two nations' demonstrated nuclear capabilities, have understandably attracted a great deal of attention to Pakistan's radical madaris and Islamist terrorism. Yet the reality is that most Pakistanis remain moderates while the largely nonradical army retains the preeminent political position. Longer-term trends in the nation, however, particularly those that have resulted and can continue to result from Islamic terrorist campaigns abroad and often encouraged by the state, are more troubling for their potential to give rise to stronger radical Islamism in Pakistan.

Radical Groups Do Not Make a Radical State

Although most of Pakistan's Muslims are devout, they are not particularly radical. Moreover, Pakistani politics historically have been dominated by ethnic, linguistic, and economic issues, not by religion. The power of religious parties derived from state patronage. From Zia's time onward, religious parties have been used by political leaders to balance the secular and more influential Pakistan Muslim League and Pakistan People's Party; thus, religious parties primarily derived the minimal power they currently have from state patronage. Despite their recent achievement of coming to power in one province and sharing it in another, there is reason to doubt that they will soon acquire the street power needed to threaten any military regime or democratically elected government or that they will have enough votes to win a free election at the national level.[8]

In other states, Islamic parties and radical movements often become the only outlet for anger and resentment on the part of ethnic or linguistic subgroups. In Pakistan, however, the two major centrist political parties, the Muslim League and the Pakistan People's Party, have tried to articulate a wide range of views and positions; and during the decade of democracy from 1988 to 1999, a two-party system evolved. Where these parties have failed spectacularly has been in addressing corruption, gaining the confidence of the military, and dealing with the grievances of some of Pakistan's less populous provinces, notably Sindh, Balochistan, and the NWFP. Sindhis and Baluchis have not turned to Islam, although they have at times turned to terrorism; the rise of Islamic parties in the NWFP and Balochistan may be a sign that Islam is now the vehicle for Pashtun subnationalism.

Pakistan remains ethnically, culturally, and regionally a pluralistic state, but these divisions do not correspond with the splits among its Islamic sects. In 1971, Islam was unable to keep the state together in the face of a Bengali separatist movement, and it is not likely to be a unifying factor in the future. When paired with ethnic or regional grievance, however, religion can be a potentially powerful negative force, further weakening Pakistan if the rise of religious extremism drives out its most educated and talented citizens, further isolating the country internationally. Whereas some Saudis may welcome the rise of Sunni Islamic radicalism, China, India, and the West would regard such a development in Pakistan as threatening, as would Shi'a Iran.

The Army's Preeminence

Although Pakistan still lacks a strong national identity and Islam—especially radical Islam—is not likely to provide one, the Pakistani state is nevertheless strong, and the army remains its core.[9] Unless Pakistan is defeated in a war or undergoes an internal split of unprecedented magnitude—and neither scenario is likely—the army will retain its professional and organizational integrity and will prevent any radical Islamic group's rise to power in its own right, although the army may continue to use them in its own interests.

In grasping the unique role of the army in Pakistan, the perceptions by the Pakistani security community, and by the army in particular, are of special importance. Pakistan is a paranoid state that has enemies. The strategic elite do not want to see their country become a West Bangladesh—a state denuded of its military power and politically as well as economically subordinated to a hegemonic India. Although radical groups share this assessment, Pakistan's establishment only partially shares these groups' solutions: Islamic purification of Pakistan, dependence on the Islamic world for security assistance and friendship, and a calculated use of Islamic radicalism to extend Pakistan's influence. The Pakistani establishment subscribes to the latter prescription, but not to the point where the country would provoke a war with India or allow Islamic radicals to acquire significant power within Pakistan itself.

A series of assassinations of senior army officials would only confirm the army's institutional view that it remains Pakistan's last bastion and that civilians of all stripes are not qualified to govern Pakistan effectively. This assessment applies to radical Islamists as much as to moderate Pakistanis. Nevertheless, the army's disdain for civilians—radicals and moderates alike—will not prevent the army and its intelligence services from continuing to manipulate them for domestic and foreign policy purposes. Pakistan's history shows that the army cannot run Pakistan effectively by itself but that the army is also unwilling to entrust civilians completely with the job. Although this state of affairs makes it likely that Pakistan will not progress, it also ensures that Pakistan will not soon become a radical state.

The only scenario involving the army that could bring radical Islamists to a position of influence would be the army leadership's decision to don the cloak of radical Islam, which would be unlikely in the near future because the current army leaders are openly critical of Zia's experiments in this realm. Should the quasi-secular Musharraf be disgraced and the state thus lose its capacity to govern, however, one option might be a pseudo-coalition of radical Islamists and the military. Still, at this point, such a coalition seems extremely unlikely.

Blowback

As Pakistan's ISI supported hardline Islamists in their self-proclaimed jihad against India and the war against the Soviet Union in Afghanistan—characterized as a religious struggle with U.S. support—consequences for Pakistan's domestic stability were inevitable. The blowback effect of events in Afghanistan and Kashmir is self-evident. Liberal and professional Pakistanis are deeply concerned about the rise in sectarian violence, guns, and disorder, whereas radical Islamic groups praise these operations as true jihads. Furthermore, at least one credible newspaper report indicates that foreign intelligence services have infiltrated disaffected Islamic radicals and that some of the violence directed against Christians and foreigners indicates that the Pakistani government has lost control over some sections of its carefully cultivated horde of Islamic extremists.[10]

Social, Economic, and Demographic Trends

Pakistan remains dominated by a secular establishment, presiding over the slow decay of the state and the idea of Pakistan. Formed in the 1950s in the Ayub Khan era, the establishment—an oligarchy consisting of fewer than 1,000 military, political, bureaucratic, business, and media elites—can perpetuate itself but seems unable to take the steps required to transform Pakistan into a modern state.

Pakistan's educational and demographic trends, its enfeebled institutions, and its near-flat economy could produce a situation where even the army would be unable to stem the growth of radical Islamic groups and might even be captured by them. This is a long-term prospect, however, probably more than five to eight years away. Nevertheless, the trends should be monitored closely and should shape U.S. policy, especially if the global war on terrorism moves in a direction that causes Pakistan again to lose its strategic importance for the United States, which could happen if key al Qaeda leaders who had taken refuge in Pakistan were caught or if Afghanistan were to achieve a greater degree of stability. Ironically, although it is in Pakistan's interests to deliver the occasional al Qaeda or Taliban leader to U.S. authorities, once the stock is exhausted, there will be less incentive for Washington to continue its large aid program to Pakistan.

One key warning sign of Pakistan's breakdown would be migration patterns. If Pakistan is seen as a land of no hope, more and more of its elite will send their children abroad for education and will follow them as expatriates. The number of Pakistanis emigrating to the United States provides impressive evidence for this assessment. The large number of children of the elite who have chosen to stay in Pakistan, however, even taking an active role in politics, is also impressive. If this generation becomes radicalized, who will be left to hold the center together? If not reversed, these trends pose the greatest chances for radicalization down the line; there is ample anecdotal evidence that Pakistan's young, Westernized elites are growing increasingly disenchanted with the West and more attracted to what they see as the honesty and moral clarity of the Islamists.[11]

Demonization of Pakistanis

Most revolutions are fueled by a burning sense of injustice. Some revolutions take the path to parliamentarianism, as did those led by India's Mahatma Gandhi and Pakistan's Jinnah, but others lead to dictatorship or totalitarian rule. Typically, revolutions are led by individuals who were subjected to discrimination and radicalized. Several recent incidents point to a worrisome trend that might accelerate the growth of a similar kind of movement in Pakistan.

Upper-class, educated Pakistanis, including those living abroad, are now subject to some harassment; the community's sense of beleaguerment, always present, is ballooning. Pakistan's original promise seems to have been betrayed by both the generals and the politicians; only the Islamic parties hold a pure and untainted vision of the future. Pakistan has also lost many of its foreign friends, and those that remain—China and Saudi Arabia—cannot be expected to encourage democratic solutions to Pakistan's problems. If the process continues, it will only be a matter of time before a sizable percentage of these Pakistani citizens come to share the belief held by all extremist Pakistani Muslims that there is, indeed, a conflict of civilizations between Islam and the West, or at least between Pakistani Muslims and U.S. citizens and their allies, including the Pakistani government itself.

Implications for the United States

Robert Kaplan concluded his reviews of two recent books on Pakistan by asserting that the U.S. government's best bet in Pakistan is Musharraf. Kaplan quotes General Anthony C. Zinni's claim that the U.S. interest in Musharraf is not so much his personal qualities but the likelihood that "what would come after him would be a disaster."[12] This conclusion is false: if Musharraf stepped down or was removed, he would be replaced by a colleague or peer who is unlikely to be enthusiastic about radical Islam. Musharraf's successor would be replaced in turn by still another general with a similar semisecular outlook. The army may use Islamic extremists and may not be able to reconstruct and build a normal Pakistani society, but for the foreseeable future, it is most capable of blocking anyone else from coming to power.

Though the potential for a radical leader to emerge anytime soon is not a legitimate concern and the radical Islamic threat to Pakistan generally has in fact been exaggerated, what should the United States be watching? The following list provides a summary of those developments worthy of consideration by U.S. policymakers in determining U.S. concerns in Pakistan.

1. Long-term national decay. The long-term decay of Pakistan may not unite radical Islamists, but it would provide them with a larger recruitment base and more resources by increasing the ranks of the frustrated, the angry, and the educated underemployed.

2. Popular frustration with Musharraf and the United States. A second Zia might not be attractive to the current generation of army officers, but a later generation—frustrated with Musharraf's secularism, somewhat more Islamized, and even more adamantly opposed to the United States—could move in this direction, allowing an eventual successor's successor to don the Islamic cloak.

3. Reactions to U.S. presence in Afghanistan. The war in Afghanistan was a major reason for the MMA's success in Balochistan and the NWFP; a continuing U.S. presence just next door, without tangible positive results for the Afghan people, will further intensify Pakistani grievances and fuel their discontent with any government that supports Washington.

4. Political repression. Blocking secular and ethnic channels of expression by a fresh ban on political activities would open the door wider for radical Islamists, who are capable of using informal channels for their operations, especially via the madaris.

5. Pashtun nationalism aligning with radical Islamism. If this movement were to link up with a revived radical Islamic faction in Afghanistan, such as the Taliban or Gulbuddin Hekmatyar's group, both the regime in Kabul and the integrity of Pakistan could be threatened.

6. Ongoing conflict with India. Another conflict with India could strengthen the hand of some Pakistani radical Islamists, who believe there is a civilizational war between Islam and the unholy alliance of the Christian and Jewish West and Hindu India. If Islamabad were unable to protect Pakistan from Indian pressure, the army just might move in an Islamic direction; however, a general war is a more likely outcome.

Coping Strategies for the Next Five Years

Pakistan has a long-standing, if frequently abused, tradition of parliamentary democracy. Democracy in Pakistan is feeble in comparison to that of its neighbor India and always will be problematic. The best strategy available for the United States to prevent the emergence of a radical Islamic movement in Pakistan, however, is to insist that the Pakistan government allow the moderate, secular political parties, such as Bhutto's Pakistan People's Party and Sharif's Muslim League, to function freely, as well as to be tougher on those Islamist groups, parties, and leaders that have practiced and preached violence within Pakistan and across its borders in India and Afghanistan. The United States should also seek dialogue with those Islamist parties, such as the Jama'at-i-Islami, which seek power through parliamentary means.

Ironically, the chief obstacle to the emergence of a functioning democracy in Pakistan is the army, which is also the principal barrier to Pakistan's movement toward political extremism. The generals cannot govern Pakistan, but they will not let anyone else govern it. The army is not Islamized, although its officers and men reflect the generally devout quality of Pakistanis, and under present circumstances, the army is immune to the lure of an alliance with radical Islam.

The army derives its legitimacy from its claim to be the one institution that best understands the threats to Pakistan. Officers boast that only they have the education, the discipline, and the resources to accomplish vital national objectives, including defending Pakistan against Indian aggression, ensuring domestic law and order, and establishing boundaries beyond which the political parties may not roam. The present arrangement could be overturned if the army itself were to lose its integrity through military defeat, internal professional and personal rivalries, or the meddling of politicians. Although the likelihood of the army allying with Islamic forces in the foreseeable future is slim, in the long run, Pakistan's reasonably stable system could be gradually transformed.

U.S. policy must deal not only with the tactical problem of retaining Musharraf's support but also with problems that will arise several years from now after Musharraf is gone. The global war on terrorism—a response to the direct threat from al Qaeda—is not likely to last more than a few more years in South Asia, but radical Islamic movements in Pakistan are now putting down roots. Ultimately, the residual power of radical Islamists can be further attenuated by a strategy that incorporates the following:

—Encouraging the further revival of democracy in Pakistan. Public and private support would give the moderate Islamic groups a chance to compete against the traditional, moderate political parties and give those traditional moderate parties time to develop real political organizations. In the process, support for radical Islamists will be seen to be quite limited, except in unusual cases such as the NWFP.

—Real dialogue between India and Pakistan. The United States must actively go beyond mere lip service to promote a peace process between the two countries that seeks the well-being of the Kashmiri people—not merely the legal status of Kashmir—as its primary motivation. This support would have several important consequences: (1) it would address a major cause taken up by the radical Islamists and many moderate Pakistanis; (2) it could be the basis for an effective ban on the external operations of radical Islamists; (3) it would make the army less central to Pakistan's future; and (4) it would also be in India's interest in the long run. Starting and sustaining such a process should be one of the major goals of U.S. policy in South Asia.

—Vigilance in Afghanistan. The process of nation and state building in Afghanistan must continue and must be seen as continuing with the support of the United States and the international community at large.

—Improving the benefits of U.S. aid for the Pakistani people. Pakistan must have tangible evidence that its government's tilt in favor of the United States brings significant benefits to the Pakistani people, especially in improved education. Most aid is invisible to the average Pakistani, who cares little about debt relief or balance of payment problems. A massive educational airlift that would train Pakistani educators, officials, and others, on the other hand, would demonstrate for the Pakistani people that the United States has an interest in Pakistani well-being as well as in maintaining Musharraf s support in the war on terrorism. Despite Washington's current plans for a very modest educational program, cases of maltreatment of visiting Pakistani scholars and journalists in the United States have already offset this potential benefit.

For the United States, Pakistan is both part of the problem and part of the solution. Pakistan is an ally in the war against terrorism yet, at the same time, a potential base of Islamic radicalism—if not on this administration's watch, then on the next. Washington has no option but to work with Pakistan in the short run, cajoling Islamabad to stop its support of radical Islamic groups that have operated in Afghanistan, India, and other countries. The U.S. government must also address the deeper causes of Pakistan's malaise, however, lest the country become the kind of nuclear-armed monster state that its critics already think it is.

2004

TWELVE

India and Pakistan: The Armed Forces

After decades of unfulfilled promise, India now seems to be inching ahead, with more rapid economic growth, new attention from the major powers, a more assertive foreign policy, better relations with the United States and China, and a modest nuclear arsenal. Adding these developments to India's traditional strengths—a unique and persistent democracy and an influential culture—it is no wonder that many have predicted the emergence of India as a major Asian power, or even a world-class state. However, this remains a problematic development as long as India's comprehensive and debilitating rivalry with Pakistan continues. If India cannot "solve" or better manage its relationship with Pakistan, which has become increasingly dangerous in recent years, then its wider strategic role is likely to remain circumscribed.

A Paired-Minority Conflict

The origins of the India–Pakistan conflict have been traced to many sources: the cupidity of the British in their failed management of the partition; the deeply rooted antagonisms between the Subcontinent's major religious communities, Hindus and Muslims; the struggle for control over Kashmir; that province's importance to the national identities of both states; and the greed or personal shortsightedness of leaders on both sides of the border. These and other factors all play a role, but the conflict is greater than the sum of its parts.

Like many other intractable disputes, the India–Pakistan conflict is a psychological paired-minority conflict. Such conflicts are rooted in perceptions held by important groups on both sides—even those that are not a numerical minority and may even be a majority—that they are the threatened, weaker party, under attack from the other side. Paired-minority conflicts are most often found within states, but some occur at the state level, such as that between Israel and some of its Arab neighbors. These extremely persistent conflicts seem to draw their energy from an inexhaustible supply of distrust, and are remarkably resistant to compromise or the good offices of third parties.

Indian Insecurity

In the case of India–Pakistan relations, one of the puzzles is not why the smaller Pakistan feels encircled and threatened, but why the larger India does. It would seem that India, seven times more populous than Pakistan and five times larger, would be more secure, especially since it defeated Pakistan in 1971. However, this is not the case and historical, strategic, ideological, and domestic reasons all play a role in India's obsession with Pakistan, and in Pakistan's concern with India.

Generations and Chosen Griefs

The first generation of leaders in both states were devoted to achieving independence and building new states and nations. With the exception of Gandhi, they did not believe that partition would lead to conflict between India and Pakistan. On the Indian side, some expected Pakistan to collapse, but did not see the need to hasten that collapse through war. On the Pakistani side, Jinnah hoped that the two countries would have good relations; he expected a multireligious Pakistan to be counterpoised against a predominantly Hindu India, with both possessing significant minorities whose presence would serve as hostage to good relations.

A second generation of Indian and Pakistani leaders was unprepared to solve the problems created by partition. Nothing in their experience had led them to place reconciliation ahead of their own political advantage. They reached a number of agreements that cleaned up the debris of partition, and there were trade and transit treaties, hotlines, and other confidence-building measures (CBMs) installed as early as the 1950s. At the rate they were moving, India and Pakistan seemed to be headed toward an uneasy accommodation.

For India, what set the second generation apart from its predecessors was the defeat by China in 1962; for Pakistan, it was the division of their country by India in 1971. The ten-year difference is important: Indians have had longer to reconsider their great humiliation than the Pakistanis, and even the prospect of economic competition with China was met with equanimity by an economically resurgent India.

In each case, the other side denies the seriousness of the other's grievances, and doubts the sincerity of the other's claim. In 1962 Ayub Khan stated his skepticism that there was a real India–China conflict, and Pakistanis still belittle Indian obsessions with Beijing. Indians seemed to assume that Pakistanis have more or less forgotten the events of 1971 and cannot understand why Pakistani officials remain suspicious when New Delhi professes its good intentions.

These two conflicts had profound domestic consequences, not a small matter in a democracy. No Indian politicians have admitted publicly that the Indian case against China is flawed or suggested that there should be a territorial exchange. No Pakistanis can publicly talk about a settlement of Kashmir short of a plebiscite and accession lest they be attacked for being pro-Indian and anti-Islamic.

Each trauma led directly to the consideration of nuclear weapons and the further militarization of the respective countries. In India's case, the lesson of 1962 was that only military power counts and that Nehru's faith in diplomacy without the backing of firepower was disastrously naive. The linkage between the shock of 1971 and the nuclear option is even tighter in Pakistan, and for Zulfikar Ali Bhutto a nuclear weapon had the added attraction of enabling him to reduce the power of the army. Ironically, Pakistan has wound up with both a nuclear program and a politically powerful army.

Traditions: New and Invented

While many Hindu and Islamic traditions suggest ways of reducing differences and ameliorating conflict, each also has elements that contribute to the idea of what Elias Canetti terms a war-crowd. Indians and Pakistanis draw selectively from their own traditions and point to those on the other side that seem to "prove" the other intends to conquer and dominate. For example, Pakistanis like to cite the *Arthashastra* as "proof" that the Indian/Hindu approach to statecraft emphasizes subversion, espionage, and deceit. For their part, Indian strategists, especially on the Hindu nationalist end of the spectrum, emphasize those aspects of Islamic teachings that portray a world divided between believers and unbelievers, and suggest the former are obliged to convert the latter. Additionally, while Pakistani ideologues see the spread of Islam to South Asia as having purged and reformed the unbelievers, Indians read this history as reinforcing the notion of a comprehensive civilizational and cultural threat to India.

Indians also see Pakistan as an important example of neo-imperialism, meaning that when neighbors (that is, Pakistan) are allied to powerful intruders (such as Britain, the United States, or China), their domestic politics and their foreign policies become distorted. The U.S.–Pakistan alliance is widely believed to have militarized Pakistani politics and foreign policy through the connection between the Pakistan army and the United States, making it impossible for Delhi to come to an accommodation with Islamabad over Kashmir. Most Indians also believe that Pakistan compounded the error by allowing its territory to be used for the objectives of the Cold War alliance, introducing a superpower into the region. The American tie is also seen as encouraging Pakistan to challenge the rightfully dominant regional power by providing the advanced weapons that enabled Pakistan to attack India in 1965. The preferred Indian solution to such a distortion of the natural regional power structure is for the international community to recognize regional dominant powers that are benign, accommodating, and liberal rather than allow either a global hegemon or adjacent powers to meddle in South Asia.

Pakistan is seen as an essential element in a shifting alliance against New Delhi composed of the West, Islam, China, and other hostile states. Another focus of attention in recent years has been the extremist Islamic forces led by Pakistan, with China as a silent partner. Like Samuel P. Huntington, many in the strategic community see a grand alliance between Islamic and "Confucian" civilization. The ring of states around India provides a ready-made image of encirclement, of threat from all directions. India has threats from the north, the east, the west, and over the horizon, as naval theoreticians eagerly point out the threat from the sea, from whence both the Arabs and the Europeans came, and—thirty years ago—the USS *Enterprise*.

The threat from Pakistan, Islam, China, and the West is attributed to jealousy of India: outsiders wanting to cut it down to size. India's sense of weakness, of vulnerability, is contrasted with its "proper" status as a great power, stemming from its unique civilization and history. It is India's very diversity, long regarded as a virtue, that offers a tempting target for Pakistan, the Islamic world, and others. Even its minorities (tribals, Sikhs, Christians, and Muslims) are a potential fifth column, awaiting foreign exploitation.

Pakistan as an Incomplete State

The very nature of the Pakistani state is said to pose a threat to India. According to a 1982–83 survey of India's security problems, the "Pakistan factor" looms large for reasons related to Pakistan's many shortcomings. These include Pakistan's limited cultural and civilizational inheritance, its military dictatorship, its theocratic identity, unworkable unitary system of government (as opposed to India's flexible federalism), the imposition of Urdu on an unwilling population, the alienation of Pakistan's rulers from their people, Islamabad's support of "reactionary" regimes in West Asia (India identified its interests with the "progressive" segments of Arab nationalism, such as Saddam's Iraq), its dependency on foreign aid, and the failure to develop a strong economic base. This perspective has enjoyed a renaissance in the ten years since Pakistan began to openly support the separatist and terrorist movements that emerged in Indian-administered Kashmir.

Pakistan is considered a threat also because it still claims that Partition was imperfectly carried out, it harbors some revanchist notions toward India's Muslim population, and it falsely accuses India of wanting to undo Pakistan. Thus Pakistan still wishes to claim Kashmir, and even to upset the integrity and unity of India itself. More recently, Pakistan has served as the base for Islamic "jihadists" who seek not only the liberation of Kashmir but also the liberation of all of India's Muslims.

The Pakistani Perspective

Pakistani leaders see themselves as even more threatened than their Indian counterparts but still able to withstand the challenge than the much larger and more powerful India. Its leaders have a profound distrust of New Delhi, and the latter's reassurances that India "accepts" the existence of Pakistan are not taken seriously.

The dominant explanation of regional conflict held by Pakistan's strategic community is that from the first day of Independence there has been a concerted Indian attempt to crush their state. This original trauma was refreshed and deepened by the loss of East Pakistan in 1971. Many Pakistanis now see their state as threatened by an increasingly Hindu and extremist India, motivated by a desire for religious revenge and a missionary-like zeal to extend its influence to the furthest reaches of South Asia and neighboring areas. There is also a strand of Pakistani thinking that draws on the army's tradition of geopolitics, rather than the two-nation theory or ideology to explain the conflict between India and Pakistan.

Like Israel, Pakistan was founded by a people who felt persecuted when living as a minority, and even though they possess their own states (which are based on religious identity), both remain under threat from powerful enemies. In both cases, an original partition demonstrated the hostility of neighbors, and subsequent wars showed that these neighbors remained hostile. Pakistan and Israel have also followed parallel strategic policies. Both sought an entangling alliance with various outside powers (at various times, Britain, France, China, and the United States), both ultimately concluded that outsiders could not be trusted in a moment of extreme crisis, and this led them to develop nuclear weapons.

Further complicating India–Pakistan relations is the 1971 defeat, a great blow to the Pakistan army, which has governed Pakistan for more than half of its existence. Thus to achieve a normal relationship with Pakistan, India must not only influence Pakistan's public opinion; it must also change the institutionalized distrust of India found in the army. The chances of this happening are slim.

Another source of Pakistani hostility is the Indian claim that Pakistan needs the Indian threat to maintain its own unity. This argument has an element of truth: distrust of India and the Kashmir conflict do serve as a national rallying cry for Pakistanis, and thus as a device for smoothing over differences between Pakistan's dominant province, Punjab, and the smaller provinces of Baluchistan, Sind, and the Northwest Frontier. India-as-an-enemy is also useful to distract the Pakistani public from other concerns, such as social inequality, sectarian (Sunni–Shi'a) conflict, and the distinct absence of social progress in many sectors of Pakistani society. These factors explain Pakistan's fear of India in part. A still more contentious issue between the two states is Kashmir.

Strategies in a Paired-Minority Conflict

States or groups that see themselves as threatened minorities have at least seven strategies to cope with the situation. In the abstract, these include fleeing the relationship, either physically or psychologically; demonizing the opponent; assimilation; accommodation; changing the behavior or perception of the enemy state; using outsiders to redress the balance of power; and, finally, changing the balance of power by war or other means (such as increasing one's economy or population faster than the other side). Over the past fifty years, India and Pakistan, not to mention third parties, have contemplated each of these strategies.

Flight

India and Pakistan have tried to flee their relationship several times. The first instance was literally a physical escape; the others constitute symbolic, psychological, and strategic flight. Even though its founders had no interest in creating a theocratic state, Pakistan was created as a "homeland" for Indian Muslims and most of its subsequent leaders left India to establish the new state of Pakistan. The key West Pakistani leaders were from Uttar Pradesh, Delhi, and Bombay; the key East Pakistani leaders were Bengali Muslims. Intermittently, India has pursued a policy of psychologically escaping the relationship with Pakistan by the "look East" policy, or by ignoring Pakistan, simply refusing to engage in serious negotiations with it. The late Sisir Gupta used to privately argue that India might well encourage Pakistan's ambitions to be a Middle Eastern country, if that would temper Islamabad's obsession with India.

Demonization

Demonization is another way of escaping a relationship. If the leaders of the other country are evil, misguided, or corrupt, then there is no need to talk to them. Indeed, dialogue with such a country, or its leaders, is immoral and dangerous. For many Indians, Mohammed Ali Jinnah, the founder of Pakistan, has long personified the misguided, evil leader who challenged India's civilizational unity with his two-nation theory, began the militarization of Pakistan by seeking arms from the West, and in a cold, undemocratic, and jealous spirit whipped up hatred and fear of India. His successors, largely military officers, are thought to lack even Jinnah's leadership qualities and the moral authority to place their country on a solid footing.

Pakistan's image of the Indian leadership is no less hostile. An important component of Pakistan's founding ideology was that Muslims could not trust the "crafty" Hindus, who still suffered from an inferiority complex. While Gandhi and Jinnah were once respected rivals, their successors in both states lacked even professional respect for each other.

Assimilation

Although many on both sides would like to flee the relationship, some Indians hope that Pakistan will someday rejoin India. Indeed, most of India's past leaders assumed that the Pakistan experiment would fail and that the state would come back to the fold. However, Pakistan's leaders have never contemplated assimilation.

Indians no longer talk of reintegrating Pakistan into India, but there are widespread (if generally private) discussions about how India might establish friendly relations with successor states to present-day Pakistan. Like Bangladesh today, these states might not like or love India, but they may fear and respect Indian power and would not dream of challenging New Delhi the way that Pakistan has.

Accommodation

If Pakistan did not rejoin India, many Indians expected it to accommodate Indian power. However, Pakistani strategists view the accommodation of Nepal, Sri Lanka, Bhutan, and even Bangladesh as precisely the wrong model for Islamabad. These states have lost their freedom of action, they have been penetrated by Indian culture, and New Delhi has undue influence on their domestic politics, even intervening by force where necessary. By way of example, India absorbed Sikkim, intervened in Sri Lanka, and has a military presence in Bhutan. Because Pakistan is larger and more powerful than any of these states, many of its strategists contend, it does not need to accommodate India. This resistance to accommodation or compromise with India is especially powerful in the armed forces. Pakistan, its officers argue, may be smaller but it is not weaker. It is united by religion and a more martial spirit than India and need not lower its demands of India, especially in regard to Kashmir.

Altering Perceptions

From time to time, there have been attempts to change perceptions of Indians and Pakistanis to promote better understanding between the two. Several nonregional states and organizations have tried to promote India–Pakistan cooperation or dialogue. In the 1950s and 1960s, the United States wanted to broker a détente between the two states so that they might join in a common alliance against threats from the Soviet Union and communist China. Considerable diplomatic energy was expended on these efforts but the only result was to provide each with enhanced diplomatic leverage against the other.

Within South Asia the regional organization, the South Asian Association for Regional Cooperation, has provided a venue for meetings between Indian and Pakistani leaders and sponsors some cooperative projects on regional issues. However, South Asian Association for Regional Cooperation cannot deal with bilateral issues, and the smaller members are vulnerable to Indian pressure concerning the focus of South Asian Association for Regional Cooperation initiatives. India has twice been able to force a postponement of its annual meetings when it was displeased with developments in Pakistan.

Most of the India–Pakistan dialogues, intended to promote understanding, wind up rehearsing old arguments, often for the sake of the non–South Asian participants present. History is used—and abused—to emphasize the legitimacy of one's own side, and the malign or misguided policies of the other. Meetings between Indians and Pakistanis rarely last long enough to systematically discuss the differences between the two sides and how those differences might be ameliorated or accommodated.

Proposals that emerge from the two countries rarely end up being serious, their purpose being to impress outside powers of Indian (or Pakistani) sincerity. Much the same can be said of recent proposals for the institution of CBMs (hotlines, summits, dialogues, and various technical verification proposals) between the two countries. Over the past ten years, there have also been at least one hundred programs to bring together students, journalists, politicians, strategists, artists, intellectuals, and retired generals from both countries. Much of the goodwill created by such efforts, however, was washed away by the 1999 Kargil war, an Indian Airlines hijacking, the attack on the Indian Parliament in 2001, and an extended military crisis that lasted well into 2002. A new round of agreements, reached in late 2003, will barely restore the status quo ante.

The Indian and Pakistani governments have also tried to influence deeper perceptions across the border. Several Indian governments—including those of Morarji Desai, Inder Kumar Gujral, and Atal Behari Vajpayee—have undertaken major initiatives in an attempt to win over Pakistani opinion. Recent efforts seem to have failed dramatically, with the Lahore meeting between Vajpayee and Prime Minister Nawaz Sharif in the spring of the 1999 discredited by the subsequent Kargil war, and the Nawaz linkage destroyed by the army coup of October 1999. The Indian proponents of a conciliatory line toward Pakistan came under strong attack from both the opposition parties and more hawkish elements of the BJP itself. On Pakistan's part, President Zia's "cricket diplomacy" of the late 1980s and President Musharraf's participation in the Agra Summit in July 2001 raised the prospect of a more forthcoming Pakistani policy. Nevertheless, Pakistan's two democratically elected prime ministers, Benazir Bhutto and Nawaz Sharif, both assumed a very hawkish policy toward India.

Seeking Outside Allies

The most consistent policy in both states for more than fifty years has been to seek outside allies against each other. Pakistan has enlisted several Arab states, Iran, the United States, China, and North Korea in its attempt to balance Indian power, but Washington, uncomfortable shouldering such a role, has resisted Pakistan's efforts to extend the security umbrella to cover an attack by India. The Reagan administration drew the line at calling India a communist state, which would have invoked the 1959 agreement to take measures to defend Pakistan against communist aggression.

The Chinese have been less restrained, and while no known treaty binds Pakistan and China together, Beijing has provided more military assistance to Pakistan than it has to any other state. Beijing saw its support for Pakistan as serving a dual purpose, since a stronger Pakistan could counter the Soviet Union and resist Indian pressure. Yet China has moderated its support for Pakistan's claims to Kashmir, and gradually normalized its relationship with India. After 1988 New Delhi itself saw an opportunity to weaken the Beijing–Islamabad tie by moving closer to China and lately has been circumspect in its criticism of Chinese policies in Tibet and elsewhere. This trend has continued in 2003 with the reinvigoration of border talks between China and India.

India also saw the former Soviet Union as a major ally in its competition with Pakistan. The Soviet Union provided a veto in the United Nations, massive arms supplies, and general sympathy for New Delhi. However, this support was not directed so much against Pakistan as it was against China; when the Gorbachev government began to normalize relations with Beijing, its support for India gradually declined. These and the other activities are expected to continue indefinitely, with India and Pakistan both seeking outside support against the other. This has been the dominant feature of Indian diplomacy for decades, and it is unlikely to change soon.

Changing the Balance of Power

Both India and Pakistan have also attempted to use their armed forces to change their balance of power. The closest the two have come to a decisive turning point was in 1971, when the Indian army secured the surrender of the Pakistan army in East Pakistan. However, rather than pressing on to a decisive victory in the West—which would have been very costly and might have brought other states into the contest—India settled for a negotiated peace and the Simla agreement. Both the United States and China provided verbal support for Pakistan in 1970–71, but neither seemed prepared to take any direct action that would have prevented India from defeating the Pakistanis in East Pakistan. A second opportunity came in 1987 during the Brasstacks crisis, when India had conventional superiority and Pakistan had not yet acquired a nuclear weapon.

By 1990 both India and Pakistan had covertly exercised their nuclear options and seemed to have concluded that the risk of escalation had reached a point where the fundamental balance between the two could not be achieved by force of arms. This did not prevent the discrete use of force, and Pakistan adopted a strategy of hitting at India through the support of separatist and terrorist forces and, in 1999, a low-level war in Kargil. Now this raises the prospect of escalation to nuclear war, but so far there has been no Indian or Pakistani advocacy of a *decisive* nuclear war.

Resolution or Permanent Hostility?

A paired-minority conflict does not really lend itself to the kind of sustained dialogue that leads to regional peace. But neither does it imply that war is likely. Other paired minority conflicts have been moderated or appear to be on the road to resolution, or at least manageability. On the one hand, it is possible to envision a peace process that could resolve or ameliorate the core conflicts between India and Pakistan. Drawing on the experience of other regions, as well as South Asia's own history, such a process would require major policy changes on the part of India, Pakistan, and on the part of the most likely outside "facilitator" of such a process, the United States. A regional peace now seems improbable however, given Washington's reluctance (since 1964) to become deeply engaged in South Asian conflicts and the difficulty of arriving at political acceptance in both countries at the same time.

A more likely development is that steps will be taken to encourage India and Pakistan to accommodate each other and reduce their conflict. Such measures have already been gaining support over the past fifteen years and in some quarters are seen as a prelude to a real peace agreement. The uprising in Kashmir and nuclearization of India and Pakistan have stimulated this interest, as reflected in the expansion of "Track II" diplomacy as well as increasing research on ways to stabilize the India–Pakistan relationship and various CBMs. The goal of all of these efforts is to increase regional cooperation and trust, and to moderate, if not transform, a relationship that seems to be based on fear, hatred, and distrust. These suggestions emphasize the gains and benefits that each side may reap from cooperation.

Finally, the possibility that the India–Pakistan relationship might undergo a major transformation cannot be ruled out. Several scenarios suggest themselves, and though some of these seem far-fetched at the moment, all merit at least a brief mention:

—Pakistan could collapse under the weight of its own contradictions and cease to exist in its present form, perhaps splitting into several states.

—India could cause Pakistan to change its identity or cease to exist in its present form, instead emerging as a state less able and/or willing to challenge India in any significant way.

—Some RSS and Hindu ideologues believe that India's "civilizational pull" will triumph over the idea of Pakistan, and that Pakistanis will simply succumb to India's greater cultural and social power (though not necessarily merge with India).

—India may underestimate Pakistani nationalism and power and take some action that would lead Islamabad to actually use its nuclear weapons in a Masada-like last attempt to defend Pakistan and if that fails, to bring India down with Pakistan by attacking India's cities.

—Pakistan might change its priorities, putting development ahead of Kashmir—at least for a while.

—India could accept Pakistan's identity as an Islamic state and move toward cooperating with it on a whole range of shared interests. It could declare that it disagreed with this identity and point to the accomplishments of a secular democracy, but also acknowledge that on this irreconcilable point Pakistanis have the right to continue to choose to live a different life.

None of these extreme outcomes seems likely, but together they add up to a possibility that the India–Pakistan relationship could take a dramatic and even dangerous turn. Without some fundamental changes in India and Pakistan, the most likely future of this dispute will be a continuing stalemate, one of hesitant movements toward dialogue, punctuated by attempts on both sides to unilaterally press their advantage in Kashmir and in international fora. This is a conflict that Pakistan cannot win and India cannot lose, a true "hurting stalemate."

India's Dilemma

A state of stalemate is seen to be more attractive to each side than finding solutions. From the perspective of the Pakistan military, which has an absolute veto over any policy initiative regarding Kashmir, the ability to tie Indian forces down in Kashmir is an important consequence of the dispute; cynically, it could be said that Pakistan is willing to fight India to the last Kashmiri. For India, Kashmir has so many links to India's secular political order—especially the place of Muslims—that any settlement which appeared to compromise this order is unacceptable.

Until a few years ago, the prospect of a "failed" Pakistan did not greatly disturb India. In the face of Islamic extremism, Pakistan's acquisition of nuclear weapons, and the state's economic collapse, however, the thought of a failed Pakistan is worrying India more and more. Pakistan could spew out millions of refugees, it might accelerate the spread of nuclear weapons to hostile states and terrorist groups, and it could serve as a base for radical Islamic movements that target Indian Muslims. Strategically, a failed Pakistan might draw outside powers into the Subcontinent. Conversely, a more normal India–Pakistan relationship could help India assume a place among the major Asian and even global powers. It would not be a question, as it is now, of Indian power *minus* Pakistani power, but of an India free to exercise its influence over a much wider range, without the distraction—and the cost—of a conflict with a still-powerful Pakistan.

Indians need to fully debate their relationship with Pakistan. The problem is that events may outrun India's capability to understand them. In recent years there has been a summit, a war, a coup in Pakistan, and a major crisis (in 2002). New Delhi may still seek agreement with Pakistan on Kashmir and other disputes, but the most important question one can ask of the relationship is not whether Indians or Pakistanis can be trusted to fulfill obligations incurred in agreements where they had little incentive to comply, but whether, under the influence of a pessimistic vision of the region's destiny, they can be trusted in cases where it *is* in their self-interest to comply.

THIRTEEN

Kashmir

The Roads Ahead

What standing does Pakistan have in this dispute? What is their legal standing? Pakistan is not a party to the dispute; let's get our facts right, then we can discuss it!

—*A senior Indian strategist, New Delhi, mid-March 1992*

My view is that if India continues on its present course, then consequences cannot be foreseen. I cannot say where boundaries will be drawn, but certainly the present boundaries will be changed. India must be prepared to make a reasonable agreement, then the process of partition begun in 1947 will be completed.

—*A senior Pakistani foreign policy official, Islamabad, a few days later*

Since late 1989 the Kashmir problem has become intimately linked to the larger question of war and peace in South Asia. A virtual insurrection among Kashmiri Muslims in the Valley, and in Srinagar, the largest city in the former princely state of Jammu and Kashmir—created a serious crisis between New Delhi and Islamabad. From that date onward the United States, echoing the Pakistani argument that the only point of conflict between India and Pakistan was Kashmir, has regarded the disputed state as one of the few places in the world where large-scale war could break out soon. American officials and experts have built a scenario that leads, ultimately, to the horror of nuclear weapons falling on Indian and Pakistani cities. According to this scenario a local crisis in Kashmir could trigger off a military response by either India or Pakistan; then the other side will overreact, leading to a direct clash between regular Indian and Pakistani forces; after that, the war could escalate to an exchange of nuclear weapons, since both states are thought now to be nuclear capable—even if they do not have deployed nuclear forces.[1] In a refinement of the scenario, it has been argued that even the *suspicion* of escalation might lead to a nuclear strike, presumably by the weaker or more vulnerable of the two countries (in this case, Pakistan) since it would not want to risk having its small nuclear forces destroyed in an Indian preemptive attack.

This scenario has led to a great deal of diplomatic activity, much of it by American officials, and recently (September 1994) by the secretary-general of the United Nations. There have been three strands to this diplomacy. First, the Kashmiri problem has been addressed directly by several American officials. In a series of speeches and informal addresses, the traditional American position on Kashmir was subtly altered, so that the United States now openly declares all Kashmir to be disputed territory (in the past the United States had never publicly challenged the *legitimacy* of the accession of Kashmir to India, only its *wisdom*). Second, both India and Pakistan were urged to engage in additional "confidence building measures" (CBMs) that might prevent, or slow down the escalation process described above; third, both incentives and sanctions have been wielded, in an attempt to get the two countries to talk directly about their nuclear weapons programs.[2]

It can be said that after four years none of these efforts has shown significant results. The Kashmir crisis is no closer to resolution than it was in 1990; there have been a few new CBMs introduced into South Asia, but there is some indication that the old ones have fallen into disuse or distrust; the nuclear dialogue that was to have begun a number of years ago has yet to commence; and public statements by officials and former officials on both sides seem to indicate a slow escalation of the nuclear arms race in South Asia, not any serious official dialogue on containing or managing it.

This chapter takes a somewhat different view than that of American officials and many strategists and journalists who see Kashmir as a "flashpoint" that could lead to conventional war and even a nuclear exchange.[3] Without belittling the importance of the Kashmir problem, it argues, first, that this crisis is far more complex than has been admitted by most American officials, and, therefore, that resolving the crisis—and addressing the supplementary problems of nuclear proliferation and regional distrust require a more sophisticated strategy than has hitherto been apparent. This chapter offers a *strategic* overview of the Kashmir crisis. It differs from other recent studies in that its primary focus is on a *strategy* for achieving a solution, not on the merit of individual solutions.[4]

The Several Kashmir Problems

The Kashmir problem is a mixture of terrorism, state violence, subversion, and general horror that rests on several layers of history. If the field existed, we could use the skills of a political archaeologist to entirely unearth it. There are at least *five* different components of the Kashmir problem, each with its own origins, each with its own consequences:

1. Kashmir originally came into dispute because of a British failure of will when they divided and quit India in 1947. The process by which the princely states were sorted out was inadequate. Each prince or ruler was to decide whether he would accede to India or Pakistan, presumably taking into account the makeup and interests of his population, but there was no adequate mechanism for ensuring that each ruler would make a fair or reasonable decision, or to ensure that the "third option," independence, would not be a temptation (the British, the Indians, and the Pakistanis all agreed that the further partition of the subcontinent would be wrong, and that the princes had to go to one state or the other). In the case of Kashmir, the Hindu ruler governed a largely Muslim population, he was also considering independence. While there were other failures in the partition process, none so crippled the successor states as Kashmir—and the British were no longer around to repair the damage. Indians and Pakistanis have lived with the consequences for forty-five years, but currently blame each other rather than a faulty partition process.

2. The leadership in both countries compounded the original problem when they turned Kashmir into a badge of their respective national *identities*.

For Pakistan, which defined itself as a "homeland" for Indian Muslims, the existence of a Muslim majority area under "Hindu" Indian rule was grating; the purpose of creating Pakistan was to free Muslims from the tyranny of majority rule (and, hence, of rule by the majority Hindu population). For Indians, their state had to include such predominately Muslim regions to demonstrate the secular nature of the new Indian state; since neither India nor Pakistan, so defined, would be complete without Kashmir, raising enormously the stakes for both.

3. Subsequently, Kashmir came to play a role in the respective *domestic politics* of both states—but especially Pakistan. For Pakistani leaders, both civilian and military, Kashmir was a useful rallying cry and a diversion from the daunting task of building a nation out of disparate parts. Further, there were and are powerful Kashmiri-dominated constituencies in all of the major Pakistani cities; on the Indian side, the small, but influential Kashmiri Hindu community was overrepresented in the higher reaches of the Indian government (not least in the presence of the Nehru family, a Kashmiri Pandit clan that had migrated from Kashmir to Uttar Pradesh).

4. Kashmir acquired an unexpected *military* dimension. After India crossed the cease-fire line during the course of the 1965 war, it became a strategic extension of the international border to the south. Further, China holds substantial territory (in Ladakh) claimed by India, and New Delhi itself has made claims on regions that, historically, had been subordinated to the rulers of Kashmir (Gilgit, Swat, and the Northern Territories) but that are now under Pakistani governance. More recently, advances in mountaineering techniques have turned the most inaccessible part of Kashmir—the Siachen Glacier—into a battleground, although more soldiers were cruelly killed by frostbite than bullets.[5]

5. Finally, there is a contemporary dimension to Kashmir: the stirrings of a *national self-determination movement* among Kashmiri Muslims. Encouraged by neither India nor Pakistan, it burst into full view in late 1989, and threatens the integrity of both states. There are two or three new generations of Valley Muslims, educated and trained in India, but with a window open to a wider world. Angry and resentful at their treatment by New Delhi, and not attracted to even a democratic Pakistan, they look to Afghanistan,

Iran, the Middle East, and Eastern Europe for models, and to émigrés in America, Britain, and Canada for material support. Further, in an era when the international economy is fast changing (including the advent of self-sustaining "tourist-destinations"), and the prospect of the direct linkage of Central Asia to Kashmir, the old argument that Kashmir is not economically self-sufficient unless it is attached to a major state has lost credibility.

Ironically, we can now see that Kashmir was less of a Cold War problem than some in the region had thought. Americans and Soviets certainly armed India and Pakistan (often both at the same time), they certainly supported one side or the other in various international fora, but the Kashmir issue has outlived the Cold War—indeed, the forces of democracy and nationalism that destroyed the Soviet Union and freed Eastern Europe were at work in Kashmir itself.[6] Other models were the liberation and revolutionary movements in the Islamic world—Iran, Afghanistan, and, most strikingly (since it was extensively covered on Indian and Pakistani television services) the Palestinian *Intifada*.

As a strategic issue Kashmir has waxed and waned. It was the central objective of the first two India–Pakistan wars (1948, 1965). But it was not an issue of high priority for either India or Pakistan from after the 1965 war until late 1989—and the birth of a Kashmiri separatist movement. What is striking is how little a role Kashmir played in the large-scale 1971 conflict (which was fought over the status of the separation of East Bengal from Pakistan), and even in the 1987 crisis that developed during a major Indian military exercise along the India–Pakistan border, Exercise Brasstacks. A recent study of Brasstacks indicates that the two countries were much closer to war in January 1987 than in 1990 (when Kashmir was the point of contention), yet Kashmir had little to do with the origin or evolution of the Brasstacks crisis.[7]

The Simla Summit of 1972 had seemed to offer a solution: defer a formal settlement, in the meantime improve India–Pakistan relations. In 1984, during the first major India–Pakistan conference to be held after the Soviet occupation of Afghanistan, several American participants argued that both sides had ignored Kashmir. But the conferees were told by Indians and Pakistanis alike that Kashmir was an American preoccupation, not a problem, something to be handled by another generation. Some who attended that conference disagreed—precisely because Kashmir was *not* then a subject of great controversy that it was the best time to tackle it.[8] If India and Pakistan could not solve the problems of the nineteenth century (their border dispute with each other, and with China and Afghanistan, respectively) and those growing out of partition, then how could they cope with emerging problems such as the invasion of Afghanistan by the Soviets and the incipient nuclear arms race?

Since then both regional instability and regional nuclear programs have continued on their respective paths, and are now linked to the Kashmir conflict. Many Indian policymakers believe that Pakistan intends to use its new nuclear capability, which makes escalation to conventional war risky because that in turn might become a nuclear conflict, to make a grab for Kashmir. They also point to the connections between the Afghan war and the training of Kashmiri militants, and thus the American responsibility for India's Kashmir problem.[9] Pakistanis believe that India will not negotiate over Kashmir because of Delhi's advanced nuclear capabilities—a Pakistani bomb, or at least a Pakistani bomb in the basement, is one way of getting India to the bargaining table. There is also a faction in Pakistan that does not want to negotiate Kashmir but is content to let Delhi "bleed" until India itself collapses into civil war—a view held of Pakistan by some Indian hawks.

In both countries the greatest *hawks* on Kashmir are journalists, politicians, academics, and other civilians, and some of the intelligence services, especially Pakistan's Inter-Services Intelligence (ISI). Ironically, in both countries the regular armed forces are very cautious, since both armies have calculated the risks of a large-scale war and conclude that its outcome would be very uncertain, that collateral damage would be very great, and that the possibility of escalation to a nuclear conflict is unacceptably high. This is one of the lessons that both sides drew from their retrospective studies of the 1987 crisis over Exercise Brasstacks.

What Is to Be Done?

There is a Punjabi saying: "Three things are improved by beating: women, wheat, and a Jat." The two quotations that begin this chapter are not dissimilar in spirit, and illustrate the difficulty of achieving a solution to the Kashmir dispute. The quotes are representative of wider views to the extent that many Pakistanis believe that India responds only to pressure and that many Indians deny that Pakistan has any legitimate role in Kashmir except to end its support of the militants. Kashmiris themselves—both Hindu and Muslim—have now tasted violence of a sort never experienced before as they undergo a terrible ordeal.

After 1971 Kashmir ceased to be *the* cause of bad India–Pakistan relations, but it remains a cause. It is also a symbol of their inability to compose their differences and live in peace. Kashmir is thus both cause and effect, which makes it so difficult to conceptualize as a political issue. Yet there is no shortage of solutions. Partition, plebiscite, referendum, UN trusteeship, "Trieste," "Andorra," revolutionary warfare, depopulation (and repopulation), patience, good government, a revival of "human values," and doing nothing have all had their advocates.[10]

Before we turn to a strategy for thinking about solutions, three points may somewhat clarify the matter. Physicists approach a problem by first "sizing" it. What are its parameters and contours? Here, "Kashmir" assumes an unusual shape.

First, while the Valley Muslims feel aggrieved that they are dominated by outsiders from India proper, other Kashmiri groups, especially the Valley Hindus and the largely Buddhist population of Ladakh, fear the dominance of the state by the Valley Muslims. Thus, a number of proposals have suggested the possibility of separating the Valley from other regions (Azad Kashmir, Ladakh, Jammu), and allocating parts of Jammu and Kashmir to India and Pakistan, leaving to the end the intensely disputed Valley. Here, the appropriate analogy is the Middle East peace process, where the overall strategy is to leave to the end such very contentious issues as the status of Jerusalem.

Second, there are, outside the propaganda mills of Delhi and Islamabad, remarkably diverse views on Kashmir in both India and Pakistan. Kashmir is not viewed in the same light by all Pakistanis and all Indians. Anyone who traveled throughout South Asia during the height of the 1990 Kashmir crisis quickly became aware that the farther one was from Delhi and Islamabad, the less passion there was about Kashmir. In Madras, Calcutta, Hyderabad (Deccan), and Bombay, Kashmir was and is seen as New Delhi's obsession. In Karachi, Quetta, Peshawar, and Hyderabad (Sindh), it is seen as a secondary issue; relations with Islamabad and the Punjab come first. Indeed, the size of demonstrations on behalf of the Kashmiri revolution in all Pakistani cities are in direct proportion to the presence of large Kashmiri populations. "Kashmir" is not a homogeneous issue within the states of Azad Kashmir and Jammu and Kashmir, or within India and Pakistan.[11]

Third, it is important to recognize the crucial role of time, and timing, in resolving the Kashmir problem. Ironically, one of the obstacles to reaching a solution is the belief, on all sides of the dispute, that "*time* is on our side." Since the Kashmir problem has been mismanaged by two generations of Indians and Pakistanis (and Kashmiris must accept responsibility also for their own errors of omission and commission), there is no age-group, except perhaps among the newest generation of South Asians, who believe that the time has come for a solution. And *timing* is crucial. We do not know what steps should be taken first, what should be taken second, third, and which should be reserved to the last. Like proposals to resolve the Arab–Israeli dispute, "solutions" to the Kashmir problem must operate at many levels. This suggests both caution and flexibility. But it does not suggest that doing nothing is the best course. The examples of the Middle East, South Africa, and, perhaps, Ireland indicate that seemingly intractable disputes can be resolved, or ameliorated, by patience, outside encouragement, and, above all, a strategy that will address the many dimensions of these complex disputes. Not too many years ago Indians and Pakistanis took a disparaging view of these other conflicts, and argued that they were successfully managing South Asia. Now their region stands out as conflict-ridden, nuclear-prone, and on the edge of war. The remainder of this chapter suggests the outline of such a strategy of conflict resolution.

Parallel Processing

In looking at strategies for achieving solutions (as opposed to management strategies and getting through the next month or year), we can draw on a model from the world of high-speed computers. We need a strategy that allows for parallel processing of the many issues, disputes, and tangles that make up the Kashmir problem. This approach has the virtue of honesty. We should not now pretend that we know what a suitable solution will look like. Certainly, it will protect the vital interests (including the quite conflicting identities) of India and Pakistan. Certainly, it will recognize the ambitions and legitimate interests of the Valley Muslims. But a just solution will also acknowledge the interests of other Kashmiris—not least the tens of thousands of Hindu and Muslim refugees who have fled the Valley in fear, and the ethnically quite different Muslim population in Azad Kashmir, which has its own grievances with the government of Pakistan. Indeed, a situation in which these refugees returned and again lived in harmony and under democratic norms could be defined as an acceptable solution. Sadly, some of the Hindu groups have already given up on the idea of a secular, multiethnic Kashmir, and are either seeking resettlement elsewhere in India or abroad or have begun to support the creation of a Kashmiri Hindu "homeland" within Kashmir proper.

Which of these problems do we address first? Or do we work on "building confidence" between India and Pakistan, and wait until a more opportune moment? Or do we go back in history and attempt to untangle grievances that have their origins in the tenth century or earlier? Or do we look to the law for a framework? Or do we bring an international organization (or an outside power) on to the scene, to either offer friendly persuasion or to knock heads?

The only solution that should be ruled out is doing nothing. Time will not heal the Kashmir problem. Time has made things worse in Kashmir. If a strategy for resolution of this conflict had begun in the early or mid-1980s, then we probably would have averted some of the crises that arose later in that decade, and certainly would not regard Kashmir now as one of the world's nuclear flash points. To those who would argue that the situation is not ripe for a solution (a view expressed by senior officials in the Bush administration), it should be pointed out that not only are one hundred million Indian Muslims held hostage by the fate of Kashmir (oddly, a favorite argument of those Indians who do not want to do anything) but in reality a billion people are held hostage by the dispute itself. Imagine what South Asia would be if India and Pakistan were to cooperate, not only on bilateral trade, water, and population issues but on preserving the strategic unity of South Asia? Each would, then, be truly counted among the great regional powers. It would not be a question, as it is now, of Indian power *minus* Pakistani power, but of a formidable block of states, with some differences but with even more in common.

As Lewis Carroll has suggested, if you don't know where you are going, any road will take you there. That has been the quality of many proposals to deal with Kashmir. They suggest action on one or another aspect of the Kashmir crisis. But we do not know, now, which of the Kashmir-related problems must be solved first before we can tackle a second, third, or fourth. Thus, we should begin to move down several paths at once. Some will be clear right to the end; on others there will be obstacles. Certainly, it is better to find out where the obstacles are sooner rather than later. It would be prudent, therefore, to pursue the following six paths *simultaneously*. After a few years an assessment should be made of of how far we have gone along each route, and where, if any, are the shortcuts to a settlement.

First: A Helping Hand, Not a Foreign Hand

The Kashmir issue needs an outside perspective because Indian and Pakistani strategists are locked in a mindless competition over tactical advantage and scoring diplomatic points.[12] There is little strategic thinking on Kashmir. No one is looking beyond the immediate events and short-term calculations of gain and pain. A solution cannot occur until it is supported in both states—and by Kashmiris of several varieties—but in the meantime it is important to have a place, or an institution, where ideas, possibilities, and pressures can be focused. There needs to be a helping hand, a facilitator, with no direct interest in the Kashmir conflict, yet with an interest in its resolution.[13]

Should the United States take the lead? Or should there be a joint U.S.–Russian effort, perhaps backed up by the threat of UN sanctions? Probably not, at least not soon.[14] Washington and Moscow lack expertise and interest in Kashmir and neither are likely to make it a high-priority item—although the new South Asia Bureau in the Department of State is acquiring expertise.

However, the United Nations is already engaged in Kashmir. Its role is sanctioned by numerous Security Council resolutions, and it maintains a peace keeping presence along the cease-fire line. There might be a plausible role for a UN *fact-finding* mission undertaken by a personal representative of the secretary-general. This was the pattern followed in the 1980s in the Afghanistan crisis. Such a representative could develop independent expertise, and his/her own line of communications with all of the contending parties, states, and factions. An expanded UN peacekeeping force or trusteeship is premature, and would not have the support of at least one major party, India. Nor could such a force be imposed on India. But a UN personage that coordinates and consolidates various diplomatic efforts now under way might, in three, four, or five years, bear fruit.

The possibility of an enhanced UN role in Kashmir has contributed to the government of India's interest in a permanent seat on an expanded UN Security Council, and in 1993 Indian officials put forward a number of arguments why India should be considered for such a seat. However, India could then veto any UN action on Kashmir. Obviously, the Kashmir problem must be settled *before* India is admitted to the Security Council, but such membership could be part of a larger package of incentives and assurances for India, Pakistan, and responsible Kashmiri groups.

Second: Adjust India's Federal Balance but also Pakistan's

Nowhere in the Constitution of India does the term *federal* appear. But there have been reasoned discussions in India about changing the balance between the center and the states in India—for good political and economic reasons. India already has a hierarchy of federalism, with some Union territories directly ruled from Delhi, and with some variation in the nature of the Indian states. Kashmir itself is the biggest variation; it has its own constitutional status in the form of Article 370. As many have suggested, India should now move in the direction it was headed anyway: toward greater autonomy for its component units. Within Jammu and Kashmir, there will have to be a further differentiation between those regions that want to become Union territories, and those that might arrive at a different constitutional structure.

The same process should be undertaken by Pakistan. Ideally, as some have suggested, the looser federation of the two parts of Kashmir with their respective states, along with increased flow of goods and people between them, would create a "soft" frontier where both the physical and cultural boundaries between India and Pakistan were somewhat fuzzy.

Third: Agreement on One Principle but Honest Disagreement on Another

In the past, high principle divided India and Pakistan as far as Kashmir was concerned. Pakistanis argued that India's control over most of the state violated the right of self-determination of Kashmiris. Indians argued that Pakistan, more often than not a military dictatorship, was hardly a credible advocate of democracy. Pakistan's position ignored the agreed-on basis for the division of British India (and Pakistani diplomats shamelessly try to paper over the terms by which the princely states were to go to one side or another), and Indians cannot bring themselves to recognize Pakistan as a democracy. But this change in Pakistan is important. It suggests a principle that both states should accept. They can do so without any joint statement or formal agreement. This principle is that legitimacy will only flow from the ballot box, not the gun. Both in the past have argued that "the voice of the people" should be respected—Pakistan in Kashmir, India in Hyderabad. Both have taken the opposite position where necessary, and have used force. But forty-plus years of preaching one principle and acting on another have led nowhere.

India and Pakistan should want to settle the Kashmir problem with Kashmiris who share their own commitment to democracy—a commitment that must include the protection of minority rights. Getting agreement on this principle keeps open the door to a wide range of possible future relations among India, Pakistan, and Kashmiris. It would help ensure that the future will rest on the consent of the governed, not the coercion of the gun.

As desirable as it is to help India and Pakistan move toward agreement on democratic principles as a way to solve the Kashmir problem, it should be borne in mind that another principle will continue to divide them. New Delhi is not likely to give up the belief that its secularism would be damaged and that millions of Indian Muslims would be put at risk if a settlement of Kashmir took place on the basis of religion. The argument deserves serious consideration; it cannot simply be dismissed by Pakistanis as blackmail. Pakistanis must think of ways they can reassure India that a change in the status of Kashmir (or parts of that state) would not be seen as acceptance of the two-nation theory; Indians should likewise think of a way of peacefully accommodating Pakistani sensibilities and Kashmiri demands without damaging the core principles of Indian secularism.

Fourth: Back to the Nineteenth Century?

The Kashmir crisis has deep historical roots. Particularly egregious are those elements of the crisis that stem from imperial conflicts of the nineteenth century. The British acquired Kashmir but did not make it part of British India; they established a boundary with China (and with the Afghans), but the boundaries were never fully demarcated. It seems absurd that two billion people should be entangled by conflicts generated by imperial governments that no longer exist. There are still border disputes apart from Kashmir. In Kashmir itself the line of actual control was never fully determined, which provided the opportunity for a bizarre struggle over the Siachen Glacier. Finally, China and Pakistan have come to a temporary agreement over a part of the border that is contested by India.

None of these border or territorial issues are strategically vital; all could be settled tomorrow without any loss of sovereignty or national identity. None involve significant domestic populations or ethnic rivalries. While these issues are not central to the Kashmir problem, they are related to it. Thus, prudence suggests that all of the concerned parties take more seriously the negotiations already underway to resolve the India–Pakistan and the India–China border disputes. In the long run, it would be important to associate Kashmiris themselves with such negotiations, and this might be one inducement for them to help restore order within their own state. But India, Pakistan, and China should, for their own reasons, attempt to eliminate such disputes, if only because there are more serious challenges awaiting them ahead in years to come.[15]

Fifth: Invest in Stake Building

In the most interesting debate that the U.S.–Russian study team heard while in India and Pakistan, a group of Pakistanis argued back and forth as to whether Kashmir was the cause of India–Pakistan tensions, or whether those tensions were the cause of the conflict. Both statements may be true—or we may never know what the balance of truth is. Our very ignorance about these matters suggests a heavy investment in two processes.

One is stake building: increasing the number of people in India, Pakistan, and in all parts of Kashmir that have a stake in normal relations and in a process that moves the region toward a settlement. This is one side of CBMs. Democracies that have bilateral problems need to encourage lobbies in one another. They are the bridge-builders who influence the internal debate in both countries and make it possible for governments to actually do something useful. The growth of interest in trade in the business communities of both India and Pakistan is especially encouraging.[16]

Further, a second aspect of stake building should receive immediate attention. These are the restrictions placed on the flow of information, scholars, and journalists between the two states. It is surprising that the academics in both countries (especially India) have not raised their voices to demand the same rights of travel and access that foreign scholars and journalists have. Indeed, the academic community seems least interested in finding out the truth. As of mid-1993 there were no Indian scholars of any level studying in Pakistan, and only one Pakistani graduate student studying in India. By contrast, there are thousands of Indians in the United States, and about fifty Indians and Chinese in their respective countries. No Pakistani scholar has ever written a book about Indian politics, and there is only one Indian scholar who has written a good book based on field research in Pakistan.[17] By and large there is less in the way of genuine movement of ideas and people than there was before 1965. It is in the interest of India and Pakistan to unilaterally allow the flow of journalists and academics, without demanding reciprocity—but the policy communities in both countries have a difficult time of even imagining such a step.

Sixth: End Alphabet Diplomacy

Finally, both sides should stop relying on what could be termed the alphabet diplomats and begin to constrain their self-deceiving disinformation campaigns. Alphabet diplomats are RAW, ISI, KGB, KHAD, CIA, and so forth, and the local intelligence services have created a bizarre dimension to the Kashmir problem: supposedly well-informed people in both countries make all kinds of wrong assumptions about which side is doing what to the other. Indians menacingly suggest that if Pakistani intelligence does not stop arming Kashmiris, "there will be hell to pay in Sindh." Pakistanis themselves cannot figure out whether Sindh is their Kashmir or is being stoked by the Indians. They claim that their dabbling in Kashmir is not the cause of India's problems but only the opportune exploitation of them. But then they will return the threat, and tell visitors to inform the Indians that if there is not movement of some sort in Srinagar, then India's own survival may be at risk. In a kind of reverse mirror-imaging they will then go on to compare Kashmir with East Pakistan/Bangladesh.

An outsider is at a loss to determine what is fact and what is fiction. But it is likely that the insiders do not know the truth either.[18] This has created an unstable state of affairs. Four years ago (in 1990) the risk of war between India and Pakistan over Kashmir was being exaggerated by outsiders, especially Americans.[19] Regional officials on both sides seemed to have a good grasp of the problem, and of the dangers of escalation. Neither side wanted to go to war for the sake of a few Kashmiris. That is still probably true, although there is a measure of crisis weariness, especially in India. However, while the chances of an all-out war over Kashmir remain smaller than Americans have been predicting, it is greater than South Asians think. The latter have to remember that *all* of the earlier wars between the two countries were caused in one way or another by strategic calculations that turned out to be in error. With the existing levels of misinformation and disinformation, it could happen again, even with sober, responsible leaders in charge on both sides.

Conclusion: Problems without Solutions, Solutions without Problems

While Kashmir consists of layers of problems, we cannot assume that removing the source at each layer will lead to a solution. Certainly, nothing can be done about the original British decisions. That Kashmir has strengthened the conflicting identities of the two states is a fact that will not go away, and cannot be compromised. India and Pakistan can work around this history but cannot rewrite it. However, as I have noted, Kashmir is nowhere near as important domestically in either state as it was a number of years ago, and the military/strategic issues embedded in the Kashmir conflict could be finessed by introducing various verification and inspection regimes, agreement on force levels, pullbacks, and so forth.[20] More problematic are strategies to deal with Kashmiri separatism (plebiscite or referendum—and if either, on what basis?). But here, also, there should be general agreement between India and Pakistan that accommodating Kashmiri sensibilities should not be the prelude to the breakup of either state. So, in addressing the issue of self-determination, the two sides should be able to achieve an understanding over ground rules and context.

I have suggested in this chapter that the problems of India-Pakistan-Kashmiri relations are too complex to understand with full clarity. An initial strategy of conflict amelioration, moving across a broad range of issues, is suggested as the best that can be done now. Some of these problems may not be amenable to solutions (the tension between Indian and Pakistani identity, for example). And there may be solutions in search of problems. CBMs are not solutions to any particular problem, but address the difficulty of getting both sides to meet and talk. CBMs build confidence, not solutions.

However, the biggest obstacle to movement on any of the Kashmir sub-problems seems to be their perception of time. Clearly, all sides to a dispute need to agree on the need for a solution. Yet Islamabad and Delhi seem to be on a teeter-totter—when one side is up, the other side feels that it is accelerating downward. As they briefly pass through a point of balance or equilibrium, neither wants to negotiate since both believe that time is on their side, that they are just about to, or will after some time, regain the advantage. And what is the advantage? Again, both sides seem to assume that the other will not compromise unless confronted by superior force. "Punjab rules"—a zero sum game with a club behind the back—seem to dominate India–Pakistan relations. The greater Kashmir problem is getting both sides—and now the Kashmiris themselves, whose perception of how time will bring about an acceptable solution is not clear at all—to examine their own deeper assumptions about how to bring the other to the bargaining table, and reach an agreement.

On balance, we should be optimistic that this will be done. A review of the history of the issue, and of recent crises it has helped to generate convinces me that while South Asia has had its wars and man-made disasters, it is well stocked with responsible policymakers and that India and Pakistan have increasingly well-informed publics. In the face of greater internal economic and ethnic problems, India—and now Pakistan—have built democratic institutions that are the envy of Russians and Yugoslavs, among others. They can, I believe, extend this success to their own relations. Outside powers, especially the United States, Russia, and Japan, should be willing and capable at some time in the not-too-distant future to do more than stand by and watch.

1988

FOURTEEN

The Reagan Administration and India

Right for the Right Reasons?

The Reagan administration's policy toward India was not a simplistic line encoded in some National Security Decision Directive (NSSD), but the NSDDs reflected an evolution of administration thinking as it responded to regional events, as its debated priorities, as it learned more about its own interests and those of India and Pakistan. This policy thus evolved between 1981 and 1988, with critical elements added in 1982–83 and 1985–86. Let us first look at the assumptions and background of those who made American policy, the players themselves, before turning to the evolution of the strategic principles on which that policy was based.

By the time the Reagan administration filled the various policy positions in state, defense, and the White House, some progress had already been made in rethinking American policy toward South Asia. The Carter administration had second thoughts about its erratic nuclear policy, it had already offered Pakistan a substantial aid package, and it had come to see the Soviet presence in Afghanistan as a serious threat to American interests. But it had lost credibility. Pakistan turned down the Carter offer of military and economic aid not because of the *size* of the program (which, on an annual basis was the same as that later offered by the Reagan administration), but because it wanted some assurance of long-term American support (Islamabad had concluded that the Soviets were unlikely to soon withdraw from Afghanistan—which was the Indian position at the time). The Pakistanis also wanted assurances against an Indian threat, but neither Carter nor Reagan were ever prepared to offer these.

The bureaucrats, politicians, and political appointees who filled key policy positions in 1981 were chiefly interested in containing Soviet influence. With a few exceptions, they had virtually no regional expertise and those who did were more familiar with Iran and the Gulf. Francis Fukuyama's RAND study was not a blueprint for administration policy, but did reflect this central concern with Pakistan's role in the containment of Soviet aggression and the shaky American position in the Gulf and Iran.[1]

Overall American expertise on India, and even on Pakistan, was severely depleted in the 1950s and 1960s. There was a corps of regionally qualified FSOs, military officers, and other experts; they had superb language skills and firsthand knowledge of both India and Pakistan, and the region had attracted some of the best talent in Washington. By 1980 much of this expertise had vanished and South Asia had become something of a bureaucratic backwater.

Ironically, this lack of regional expertise had an adverse impact first on Pakistan. There was no established Pakistan lobby in the bureaucracy—nor was there much concern over Pakistan in Congress, the press, or academia. When the economic and military assistance agreements were finally concluded with Islamabad, it took several years before they began to operate properly. Americans had forgotten how to deal with the Pakistani bureaucracy; the Pakistanis had not received a substantial amount of U.S. aid for twenty years. For example, in 1981–82 there were misgivings in the air force over selling F-16s to Pakistan: these were in short supply, some thought that the Pakistanis could not properly maintain or fly them, and there were fears that a renegade Pakistani pilot would deliver one to the Russians.

Later, in 1985, when the opening to India finally occurred, the U.S. bureaucracy again had to learn how to deal with a new (and considerably more recalcitrant) set of bureaucratic partners. The sale of high technology to India met with especially severe resistance from obscure corners of the Pentagon. This was not for South Asian reasons but because India was the first non-allied developing state to receive such technology and it not only had close economic ties to the Soviet Union but openly boasted that it would be a conduit to the Soviets for Western technology (American computers, for example, are matched to Indian machine tools and sold, as a package, to the Russians). This is perfectly legal and perhaps in American public and corporate interests, but it made the bureaucracy wary. It also raised a new policy issue: If we were to sell quite advanced technology to India, could we sell it to Pakistan or the People's Republic of China? In some cases, the answer was no and India has received better terms than both of its rivals on certain items (especially computers and jet engine technology).

There were also regional stylistic factors that influenced the pace of change in American policy in South Asia. The Indian and Pakistani bureaucracies treated Americans in very different ways, and Americans, especially those not familiar with the region, responded accordingly. Congressmen, bureaucrats, journalists, and politicians routinely received the red-carpet treatment in Islamabad and met with officials several grades above their own level (not infrequently, with President Zia). This contrasted sharply with the cool, indifferent, and sometimes outright hostile treatment by New Delhi of Americans who were not certified friends of India (that is, uncritical supporters of New Delhi's policies). I personally enjoy the argumentative style but have spent a number of hours trying to explain it away to infuriated American officials, who had earlier been sympathetic to Indian interests.[2]

Finally, a few additional factors should be mentioned, for they began to affect American policy toward South Asia (especially India) during this period and are likely to grow in significance. These counterbalanced, to some extent, the lack of bureaucratic and political contacts between the United States and India and Pakistan.

The first was the enormous growth of personal, educational, economic, and cultural links between the United States and both states. While the American military bureaucracies had no real contact with India, most of the corporations interested in selling advanced technology and military equipment to India had on their technical and sales staffs large numbers of South Asian expatriates, especially Indians. Northrop or Grumman could have mounted a Light Combat Aircraft program for India entirely using Indian scientists and program managers. Almost every member of every Indian delegation that came to the United States had close relatives or friends somewhere in the United States, and often in the corporations they were visiting.

The second new factor was an ideological transformation in the structure of informed American political thinking about South Asia. It is not well known or understood, especially in India, although it was fully reported on by Indian journalists, especially Bharat Karnad (*Hindustan Times*) and Dilip Mukerjee (*Deccan Herald*). It was simply that the cliché—that Republicans favored Pakistan and Democrats favored India—no longer had any basis in fact. The political consensus of the American Left on India was weakened first by the Indian nuclear explosion of 1974, by the Emergency of 1975–77, and also by the "opening" to China. American liberals came to regard India as an "ordinary" country, worthy of support but hardly worthy of special consideration or praise. While many liberals were abandoning India, some conservatives came to see it in a new light. India was, after all, a major power; it remained a democracy, and to many ideologically committed conservatives was preferable to the still-communist People's Republic of China (PRC). Further, some American conservatives had established contact with a new generation of Indians not influenced by chronic Left anti-Americanism. There were very few of these pro-Indian conservatives, but they occupied key positions in the executive and legislative branches and were critically important at certain moments. But they differed from some of their liberal predecessors in that they refused to abandon Pakistan and they refused to see American policy in South Asia as requiring a choice between Delhi and Islamabad.

Turning to our central theme, what did the Reagan administration expect from South Asia, and, particularly, what did it expect from India? There are three answers to this, because there were three major American regional objectives. The first was the containment of Soviet power (for which there were few expectations concerning India), the second the encouragement of Indian strategic autonomy (defined as a lessening of Indian dependence on the Soviet Union, a goal that was only partially met), and the third the prevention of nuclear proliferation (where India figured as a key player, albeit a somewhat disappointing one).

These three objectives were not equally pressing, nor were they all pursued at the same time. But all were discussed and adopted at the very highest levels of the U.S. government, and all, in one way or another, represented a departure from established policy. When these three goals were pursued simultaneously, they posed one of the greatest challenges to the skill and statecraft of policymakers in the Reagan administration, a challenge that has been largely—but again not entirely—met.

The Soviet presence in Afghanistan was rightly seen as the major regional problem facing the United States in 1981. America's historic policy of keeping major hostile powers out of South Asia was reactivated.[3] The Soviet occupation also had implications for the conduct of U.S.–Soviet relations elsewhere in the world and the future of the Eurasian balance power.

Pakistan

The Carter administration had made some effort to back up friendly states in the vicinity, especially Pakistan. But the Reagan administration concluded that Pakistan was important for other reasons, as well. The conservative Gulf Arab states were nervous about the Iranian revolution and the Soviet invasion of Afghanistan and Pakistan had good ties with several of these states. Iran itself was a pressing problem, but it could not be ignored; again, Pakistan had retained good ties with Iran, despite the revolution. In each case there were parallels between American and Pakistani interests (and in each case these mutual interests did not conflict with important Indian interests). Finally, in the eyes of some policymakers, Pakistan's close ties to the PRC meshed with our own strategic ties to Beijing, a case of "our friend's friend being our friend." These relationships were seen entirely in Soviet terms; the idea that the United States, Pakistan, and China might have a common interest in containing India is a fiction invented in New Delhi (or, perhaps, Moscow?). So, Pakistan had a fourfold importance for American geo-strategic interests: as a sympathetic player in the Gulf and Iran, as a friend of China, as key factor in Afghanistan, and as a possible target of further Soviet expansion.

India

India did not yet figure significantly in these calculations. If there were expectations from India at this point, they were that India would at least refrain from pressuring Pakistan (India already had a substantial military lead over Pakistan, and was determined to maintain it despite increased American, Chinese, and Saudi support for Pakistan).

While India's behavior on this issue was proper, its performance at the UN and its shrill attacks on modest American additions to Islamabad's arsenals made it seem highly unlikely to American policymakers that it could become a positive factor in persuading the Soviets to withdraw from South Asia. My own view is that the Indians had about the correct estimate of their limited influence vis-à-vis the Soviets, since they remained dependent on Moscow for advanced military hardware. Perhaps they, also, did not believe the Soviets would pull out (although Indian officials all expressed optimism that they would) and this contributed to their reluctance to pressure the Soviets.

Initially, some Pakistanis warned against a joint Soviet–India attack, but Washington has never quite accepted this argument (although Exercise Brasstacks led to some late nights at the office). The American judgment was that India would not help much on Afghanistan, but that it would not be a serious hindrance to either the effort to counter the Soviet forces or Pakistani and American diplomatic activities; this judgment was based on a correct estimate of India's own vital interest in getting the Soviets out of the region.

Operational Implications

The broader policy of containing the Soviets by supporting Pakistan had three operational implications for U.S.–Indian relations.

—The first was a continuing American effort to encourage India–Pakistan strategic, political, and economic cooperation. This hortatory policy was not at first taken seriously by India since it was based on a concern for Pakistani rather than Indian security. Supplementing this was strong support for regional cooperative initiatives, especially the South Asian Association for Regional Cooperation.

—The second operational consequence was to reassure Pakistan that the United States was committed to assisting it against direct Soviet aggression. While these assurances never fully satisfied Islamabad, they were firm enough to make credible the prospect of American assistance in case of such an attack, and thus to make the Indians think twice before acceding to Soviet suggestions for joint attack on Pakistan.

—Third, it became clear by 1982–83 that the India–Pakistan relationship could not be ignored, nor would wishful pronouncements about

India–Pakistan cooperation provide much incentive for New Delhi to undertake such cooperation. The United States had to establish a dialogue with India—if only to protect its position with Pakistan, and this could be achieved only by expanding U.S.–Indian ties. However, as American policymakers calculated the possible gains from closer relations with New Delhi, they also came to see other benefits from such a policy. Thus was born a second major regional objective, the "weaning" of India from Soviet influence.

Simultaneously, a similar calculation was probably being made in New Delhi. Indian strategists must have reached the conclusion that the U.S.–Pakistan tie could not be shaken unless India moved closer to Washington. What was called the opening to India in Washington was probably called the opening to Washington in Delhi.

Both sides saw a long-term relationship as beneficial, quite apart from short-term considerations of their respective relations with Pakistan. Some Americans (especially among the conservatives) saw India as the emergent regional great power and an ideologically palatable alternative to the PRC. No one that I know of saw India as an alternative to Pakistan as long as the latter remained a "frontline" state (a term more often heard in Washington than Pakistan). There were some Indians who saw long-term benefits from a renewed American tie, especially in matters of technology transfer and in dealing with the Soviets, when they showed signs of fading interest in Delhi.

I am sure that neither side actually intended to switch alignments even after the successful Rajiv visit in June 1985 (India trading the Americans for Russians or the United States trading Pakistanis for Indians). India was too dependent on Moscow to contemplate much strategic movement, and the United States would never have abandoned Pakistan in the face of severe Soviet pressure.

Pakistan's attitude toward these American efforts to promote better Indo-Pak relations and to move closer to India itself were interesting. Unlike any past Pakistani leader, President Zia enthusiastically supported these steps. He may have done so in the knowledge that New Delhi was likely to remain recalcitrant, but had to overcome historic Pakistani fears that the United States would once again "choose" the larger of the two South Asian states when it had the opportunity.[4] Pakistanis are legitimately concerned about long-term American support, but my judgment is that it has become an important enough state and has achieved such a degree of internal stability that it will be a major factor in regional American policy for years to come, although that may not mean an expanded military relationship.

Speculatively, the Russians may have been nervous about improved Indo-U.S. ties. The Vladivostok speech of Gorbachev, and his statements during a visit to New Delhi seemed to point to a lessened interest in India, but the Soviets have since provided significant new military technologies to India. If for no other reason than this the Indian opening to Washington seems to have paid off.

The basic American policy dilemma in attempting to wean India from Soviet influence was that advocates of this policy have not yet been able to shake loose sufficient military equipment and advanced technology to make the United States a serious alternative to the Soviets. Indeed, few had such hopes, and there were many policymakers who were perfectly aware that their efforts would only help India drive a better bargain with the Soviets. That was not seen as harmful to American interests, per se, but there was lingering sadness that India had lost considerable policy autonomy, had become chronically anti-American in various international fora, and that the Soviets had obtained a foothold in India that no Indian government could eliminate, and that one day might adversely affect American strategic interests.[5]

In the end, of course, it has been India that has benefited most significantly from the opening—whether Washington to Delhi, or Delhi to Washington. Had the opening not taken place it is doubtful whether Washington would have so uncritically backed the Indo-Sri Lankan agreement that virtually sanctions Indian regional and oceanic ambitions. In fact, one suspects that it was Sri Lanka, rather than Pakistan, that later became the chief motive on the Indian side.[6]

Nuclear Policy Changes

The Reagan administration made three significant changes in American nonproliferation policy in South Asia. The first involved India, the second Pakistan, the third a regional nuclear initiative. I think more could be done, but the policy has been successful so far in that neither state has an operational nuclear weapon and neither has conducted further nuclear tests.[7]

An earlier American refusal to provide fuel to the U.S.-supplied reactor at Tarapur had crippled U.S.–Indian relations, and certainly had no impact on the Indian or Pakistani military nuclear programs. The former had "paid the price" already; the latter had a clandestine program of significant scope that was based on the assumption that India already was a nuclear weapons state. The decision to allow the French to sell nuclear fuel to Tarapur removed significant obstacles in U.S.–Indian relations, but there were no American expectations beyond that. The decision did anger Pakistan, which could and did quite accurately claim that the United States was being tougher on a "friend," Pakistan, than on India.

The Reagan administration's second nonproliferation decision, to link military sales to Islamabad's nuclear program, did create expectations with regard to Pakistani behavior, and indirectly Indian. It was thought (and so far, correctly so) that as long as Pakistan received American military equipment it would halt or restrain its nuclear program, slowing the pace of regional proliferation. I have no doubt in my mind that had the United States pursued a tougher policy toward Pakistan, then the latter would, by now, be a nuclear military power. My own view (in 1981 testimony) was that linking the military assistance package to Pakistani nuclear restraint would defer but not terminate Pakistan's nuclear ambitions. If there was a failure in policy, it was to explore and test this linkage, to see how much leverage the United States had over the Pakistani nuclear program.

It was probably the fear of putting heavy pressure on Pakistan (and risking the entire operation in Afghanistan) that led American policy to a third initiative, that of encouraging a regional nuclear agreement.

This may have been doomed from the beginning because of the administration's narrow definition of *region*. India could—and did—claim that China was part of South Asia's nuclear system and that any regional agreement would have to include Beijing. A truly regional agreement would have to include the Soviets, and might have to involve a joint declaration of South Asia as a nuclear-free zone. A comprehensive, truly regional nuclear agreement might have stood a fifty-fifty chance of acceptance, at least for a fixed period of time, but no such proposal was ever fully articulated.

Still, the limited American regional nuclear initiative did achieve some useful results. It forced both India and Pakistan to think more carefully about their own nuclear plans and the prospect of an unrestrained nuclear arms race. It may have contributed to those regional nuclear agreements that have been reached, and it certainly encouraged further public discussion of the nuclear issue in India, and—surprisingly—in Pakistan.[8]

Other Policy Changes

There were a number of other policy objectives in the Reagan administration concerning India.[9] Two are of particular interest, but can be dealt with briefly.

For a number of years the Indian government has dismissed American concerns about terrorist acts, including hijackings. Indian leaders have conspicuously (and literally) embraced foreign political leaders who have advocated terrorism as an instrument of state policy. In turn, the United States was criticized as either not being sincere about terrorism, or was somehow responsible for terrorism against its own innocent civilians and civil aircraft (through its support for Israel, Britain, and other governments under attack). This line was followed for a while when India itself was subjected to terrorism, and while allegations were made, officially and unofficially, about American support for Khalistani secessionists and terrorists.[10]

Several years of very close government-to-government cooperation have ended such criticisms from responsible Indian authorities. From an American perspective, Indian policies toward terrorism are considerably more sensible. These are subject to slippage, however, as when Rajiv hosted the prime minister of North Korea shortly after the latter's murderous bombing of a South Korean airliner near Indian territory (the Andaman Islands). But day-to-day cooperation remains excellent in bilateral matters, where both sides have much to gain by a close working relationship.

Similarly, cooperation on combating narcotics has been effective, after a slow start. India (like Pakistan) was reluctant to work closely with American narcotics experts. Both states have discovered, however, that access to American expertise, technology, and intelligence capabilities are important in their own efforts to stem the growth and shipment of narcotics. Both states also concurred with the American proposal that narcotics (and terrorism) be added to the list of South Asian Association for Regional Cooperation subjects.

Given that few expected much concern for India in a conservative Republican administration, that the Soviet invasion of Afghanistan was the most important regional issue for the United States (and an issue on which Indian policy was notoriously unhelpful, both publicly and privately), and given that Pakistani diplomacy proved to be of extraordinary competence in pursuit of Pakistani (rather than American or Indian) interests, it is astonishing that American policy toward India turned out so well. It was not perfect—there were mistakes in judgment, timing, and implementation—but by any standard these policies advanced American interests, Pakistani ones, and at the very least, did not damage important Indian interests.

Certainly, the renewed U.S.–Pakistan tie was a political setback for those segments of the Indian leadership that had hoped to achieve hegemony over Pakistan, but a vulnerable Pakistan dominated by the Soviet Union (or the battleground between pro-Soviet, pro-Chinese, pro-Iranian, and pro-Indian factions) would have been an Indian catastrophe. And although India has had to continue an arms race with Pakistan, it has been able to extract modern weapons from the Soviets and sophisticated dual-use technology from the Americans, it has received superpower support for its operations in Sri Lanka, and it has still claimed that it is the aggrieved regional party, the victim of Chinese and superpower (especially American) machinations.[11] In short, India has been able to have it both ways. America might have preferred a different Indian response to some of its regional policies—a more serious dialogue with Pakistan on arms control issues, greater responsiveness on certain high-technology items, and as flexible and as forgiving an attitude as New Delhi apparently shows to the Soviet Union—but the absence of such Indian policies did not threaten important American regional interests.

Ending "Ups and Downs"?

I am certain that things will be more difficult in the next few years.[12] A popular metaphor of American–Indian relations is that it has been a series of "ups and downs" over the years. This is another worn-out cliché. The real variable has been the dramatic engagement and disengagement of the United States in South Asia over the years. The 1940s and 1950s saw a period of engagement, after 1965 a long spell of disengagement, and there has been a revived American regional role since 1980. During each period of American regional involvement, some important Indian interests have been advanced; a few may have been damaged. The 1981–87 period was one in which significant Indian interests were accommodated by the United States, and India took important steps to smooth out the relationship. Both states were responding to a common regional event; the agony of Afghanistan and the presence, in South Asia, of Soviet military forces.

But things are going to change. An end to the occupation of Afghanistan will not mean the end of crisis in Afghanistan, it will not mean that the advanced Indian and Pakistani nuclear programs will be shelved, and it will not diminish the impact of the Iranian revolution on India and Pakistan. The liberalization of the Chinese and Soviet systems—already responsible for serious unrest across South Asia's frontiers—will have new and still-unpredictable implications for both India and Pakistan. Finally, domestic factors will increasingly shape foreign policy decisions in both states, further complicating their own relations and their ties to the United States.

New policies and new strategies will be required to deal with these issues, but because most are primarily regional in nature we cannot expect as active an American role. We may yet look back on the past seven years as—if not a Golden Age of U.S.–Indian relations—at least an era of mostly sound policies, usually, but not always, pursued for the right reasons.

1997

FIFTEEN

The Critical Dimensions of a Possible U.S. Strategic Partnership with India

This lecture cannot begin without a few words about the man in whose memory and honor it is given. Colonel Pyara Lal epitomized the phrase, "an officer and a gentleman." He was from the old school. He pretended that the "new crop" of officers, which probably includes most of you, was not as good as those from his own era. But he did not believe that. Indeed, his professional dynamism grew out of the belief that India was capable of producing, on its own, officers of the very first quality. This marvelous building, the library that Pyara Lal built up over the years, this lecture series, and the many officers he helped and encouraged through the years to meet his own very high standards are powerful evidence of Pyara's dedication to his profession.

However, many of us encountered another human dimension of Pyara Lal. He was a friend to many scholars, Indian and foreign, including myself, who sought out his guidance and the use of the wonderful USI collection. I recall many pleasant hours in Kashmir House, where Pyara would leave me to my books and journals, but every once in a while there would appear a cup of tea and a cookie. I could not at the time do much in return, except to review books for the *Journal*, and write the occasional short article, but there was one time when I was able to reciprocate in a most unusual way.

I believe it was in 1978 when I made my first trip to Pakistan. When he heard I was going to Lahore, Pyara Lal spoke affectionately of his youth in that city and asked for a modest favor: could I take a photo of the house his family had lived in. I did track down the house, and was able to ascertain from neighbors that his family had, indeed, lived there. I am sure that his brother has the photo. What impressed me was Pyara Lal's lack of rancor toward Pakistan. Of course he deeply regretted its formation and the partition, but he had a sensible "live and let live" attitude.

Let me begin my talk with a disclaimer. Although I once served in the U.S. government, and have at times been a consultant to it, my views are my own. I left government ten years ago, and have often disagreed strongly with American policy toward South Asia. The following comments are my own, and certainly do not reflect in any way American policy.

I am reluctant to speak directly on a subject, that of a U.S.–India strategic partnership, when that remains only a very, very theoretical possibility. Therefore, this talk will dwell primarily on the constraints to such a partnership that exist on the American side.

I would begin, however, by pointing out that Washington and New Delhi at one time in the past, had a brief but close strategic tie—perhaps *partnership* is too strong a word. We actively cooperated after the India–China conflict, when the United States strongly supported India. The memory of that cooperation faded in Washington very quickly, and may be something of an embarrassment in New Delhi, but it would be worth someone reviewing so that we might better understand the misperceptions and misjudgments that guided all parties to that conflict, especially because in some quarters, both here and in the United States, there is talk again of another grand alliance against China. I have my own view on this issue, perhaps different from that held by most Americans and most Indians, and we can discuss it in the question period.

I would also refer you to a forthcoming book by Jagat Mehta, who has written with great insight into the misperception that ruled at the time.[1]

The end of the Cold War and the breakup of the Soviet Union parted a number of themes that were tied together for five decades in American strategic thinking. The struggles against Nazi Germany and the Soviet Union were characterized by a fusion of ideology, geopolitics, and terrifying military technology. Both of these countries pursued global strategic objectives, developed weapons of the most advanced (and threatening) nature, and were propelled by expansionist, totalitarian regimes. A racial/cultural element was also evident in the parallel and sequential conflicts with imperial Japan and communist China.

Woodrow Wilson's vision of a democratic world seemed to make good geopolitical sense in such circumstances. The greatest threats to democracy—implacable totalitarian states, in two cases culturally quite distant from the United States, armed with, or racing to acquire, weapons of mass destruction—were also the greatest threats to an international order compatible with vital American economic, strategic, moral, and political interests. Three generations of Americans rallied around Wilsonianism for an unprecedented global effort. We did well by doing good.

With the end of Cold War these themes have each gone their own way.

Some, such as Francis Fukuyama, argue that a democratic world would be a peaceful world because democracies by and large accepted the international status quo. A variation on this theme is the "cooperative security" school, who believe that an expanding community of like-minded states, if not all democracies, could evolve minimal security assurances toward each other, and could jointly face states that sought to upset the status quo.

Others have argued that classical geopolitics would again be important, and have looked to the nineteenth century for inspiration. The idea of "pivotal" states rests on the assumption that the world could be graded into major, minor, and intermediate powers: pivotal state being those intermediate powers whose collapse or disintegration might affect important interests of the world's great powers as well as the one remaining superpower, the United States. An updated balance of power strategy would be effective if we could identify those hard-core threats to American interests, those states that were peripheral, and those that were on the cusp—and devote our attention and resources proportionately to each.

Then there is Samuel Huntington, who has argued that older civilizational fault lines have reemerged. The new threat to America and its closest allies comes from states, or clusters of states, which reject our vision of the world, and are organized around a "civilizational" principle.

Finally, the view has grown that America is threatened by states that might have access to weapons of mass destruction—primarily nuclear weapons, but also chemical and biological devices, especially if delivered by ballistic missiles. A new category of "rogue" states has been invented to describe countries unfriendly to America that might have access to such weapons.

American post–Cold War policy has been driven largely by a combination and recombination of these threats: the totalitarian states, the culturally distant (and hostile) states, the geostrategically important states, and, finally, states that seek to acquire or spread various kinds of weapons of mass destruction. None of these can be characterized as having global geopolitical ambitions, although in some cases (Iraq, Iran) they are seen as threatening vital American economic interests, especially access to energy. These states, if they were to combine, qualify as a new threat of significant magnitude for many Americans.

The Intellectual and Policy Challenge of India

For those policymakers and scholars who developed these theories of the future of international politics, India has been an awkward fit. They have asked themselves several questions.

Is India a Liberal Power?

If there is common democratic heritage between the United States and India, can the two countries work jointly on a number of global issues? It was assumed in Washington that India, having lost its Soviet patron, and having gone through an economic crisis in 1990 would be more cooperative in dealing with global issues such as human rights, free trade, and the proliferation of weapons of mass destruction, and might even be interested in some kind of cooperative security arrangement. However, many of us were surprised by India's attempt to undercut the permanent extension of the Non-Proliferation Treaty in 1995, and the rejection of the Comprehensive Test Ban Treaty. By this action, India lost one group of allies in the United States.

Could India Be a Strategic Partner?

Those who expected India to play a cooperative geostrategic role have also been disappointed. "India"—when it was a British colony—dominated the approaches to the Persian Gulf and, with the assistance of the Royal Navy, the entire Indian Ocean. It seemed that India might welcome U.S. military cooperation, but such cooperation has been furtive and infrequent. While New Delhi may again play a larger strategic role beyond South Asia, it is bogged down in the region by its chronic conflict with Islamabad. Neither state can be expected to be other than a minor player outside the region as long as strategic arithmetic requires the subtraction of Pakistani power from available Indian power. Is India ready for a strategic partnership? Perhaps not, because it has yet to fully identify its own strategic role, nor has it had much experience in working in alliances, whereas for the United States, the alliance was, from 1941, the preferred way of dealing with international security problems. One of the most insightful books on this dilemma facing Americans is Richard Haass's new book, *The Reluctant Sheriff*.

Is India a Civilizational Power?

Huntington accords India a special "civilizational" role, as one of the few places where a religion—Hinduism—is largely coterminous with a single state. This is also the view of many Indian strategists, including Jawaharlal Nehru, who argued in the 1930s that India was one of the six or seven state-civilizations, and hence destined to play a major global role. Nehru, like the contemporary Bharatiya Janata Party (BJP), argued that there was a broad cultural sharing among Indians of all religions—Hindu, Muslim, Sikh, and Christian. Is this the basis for a strategic relationship? It is only if one assumes that these civilizational entities will act in alliance and counteralliance in the way that states have sometimes acted. I find this as unpersuasive as his evidence of a Sinic-Islamic civilizational alliance. Further India's complexity and diversity make such "civilizational" alliances unpromising, and a so-called alliance against the so-called Islamic World would be deeply divisive within India itself.

Is India a Rogue Nuclear State?

For those worried about the spread of weapons of mass destruction, India seemed to have become part of the problem, not part of the solution. India is seen by some American officials not only as a possible nuclear rogue but as a state whose actions have inspired and threatened others. This has led, they argue, to a situation in South Asia where two nuclear-armed states face each other across an armed and violent border. The contest for control over the state of Jammu and Kashmir is such a serious matter that high government officials regularly testify that Kashmir is one of the most dangerous spots on earth: the India–Pakistan conflict could slip into a conventional war that would very likely escalate into a nuclear exchange. I have not agreed with these assertions, although the region may be more dangerous than Indians and Pakistanis would admit, but in any case the possibility of a regional nuclear arms race makes an American strategic engagement with India—or Pakistan, for that matter—all the more doubtful. 2016: I would now say that formal alliance with either is unlikely, but that engagement or partnership on specific issues is happening despite each state regarding the other as a prime threat.

Reconstructing American Policy

India now falls into a unique category: nothing it can do will threaten vital American interests, yet it is important enough—because of its size, ongoing "churning" democratic revolution, its strategic and scientific potential, and its new status as a "big emerging market"—that it cannot be ignored. To me the critical questions are can the United States develop a coherent policy toward the one-fifth of the world that is not a threat to U.S. security, that does not show signs of calamitous collapse, that has not yet, and is unlikely to become, a major economic partner, and that persists in expanding a political ideology that is not hostile to American values? When a country like the United States has been engaged in a global struggle against totalitarianism for three generations, it is hard to mobilize American policymakers, let alone Congress, around a nonthreat to strategic, political, economic, and moral interests. The discipline imposed by a geopolitical framework—even a flawed one—forced earlier American policymakers to treat South Asia as a whole. This has not been apparent since 1989–90.

Perhaps the most telling fact about American policy toward India is that there was no coherent policy review after the end of the Cold War—no comprehensive survey of the several American interests embedded in India, let alone the development of a strategy indicating how pressing interests could be optimized without sacrificing less urgent, but perhaps equally important long-term interests. Instead, by default, a very few "global" issues (led by proliferation), with regional manifestations, came to dominate American policy to the exclusion of almost all other concerns.

Paradoxically, the absence today of a threat from South Asia makes it difficult to persuade the policy and legislative communities to support a policy in which real, but limited, American interests are advanced. Three criteria suggest themselves as guides for a new American policy:

1. American policy must devote *proportionate* attention to America's diverse interests in South Asia. South Asia should not be moved to the top of the U.S. foreign policy agenda, but neither should it languish as a policy backwater.

2. The policy must be presented in such a way that raises neither false hopes nor fears in India and Pakistan.

3. American policy must be achievable with available resources. There is no need for elaborate aid programs, risky military commitments, or significant American resources; this should be easy, except for the fact that the scarcest resource of all—the sustained attention of senior policymakers and Congress—has been in short supply.

With these criteria in mind, a cluster of policy goals are suggested as an initial policy framework. They have the advantage of being internally self-reinforcing—that is, movement in one area can lead to progress in another. Indeed, American policy should be seen as advancing along a wide front: pressing too hard on a single issue will be detrimental to other important interests, and in the end could be self-defeating.

A new American policy in South Asia will have to emerge from the confluence of five different interest clusters.

The first is a new, post–Cold War opportunity: the encouragement of the process of economic liberalization, which has provided (in the words of the Asia Society study group) a new "ballast" for American relations with India and Pakistan. Market reform, tariff reduction, the elimination of state subsidies for inefficient industries, and the promotion of regional free trade zones are all policies that are in American interests—and those of India and Pakistan. However, as democracies, India and Pakistan are especially vulnerable to distortions and inequalities generated by uneven economic growth. American policymakers, corporations, and investors must be sensitive to the fact that India is not China: growth without social justice will be politically unacceptable in a lively, multiparty democracy.

Second, the United States has an important ideological interest in India: the preservation and expansion of Indian democracy. A democratic India also has three important consequences:

1. A democratic India is the role model for much of the rest of South Asia. All of the South Asian states (except Bhutan) are democracies. The pro-democratic elements in each look to India for inspiration and example, even where they may disagree with particular Indian policies. Even Pakistanis envy India's democratic record, and would like to emulate it.

2. A democratic India is not only more compatible with additional movement toward market reforms, but will be sensitive to the abuses that market systems can produce. Elections are powerful ways of ensuring that economic growth will be equitable, both geographically and in terms of social class and rural and urban divisions.

3. Democratic states are less likely to go to war than nondemocracies. Over time, mature democracies develop political, cultural, and economic links that increase their interdependence and influence the gain and loss calculation regarding the use of force. No politicians in South Asia understand this better than the current Indian and Pakistani prime ministers, Inder K. Gujral and Nawaz Sharif.

Two other, closely linked, goals should be the promotion of strategic normalization between New Delhi and Islamabad and assisting the management of their de facto nuclear weapons programs. The former is an old objective of the United States, but still a worthy one. American administrations have for forty years been trying to arrange a deal on Kashmir, and for forty years have met with frustration. However, while change will not come quickly, there are signs that there may yet be an accommodation on the disputed Siachen territory and subsequently the large issue of Kashmir. For this to happen a process of internal debate and dialogue will have to proceed in both states and among Kashmiris. This debate has long been underway in India and is only just starting in Pakistan; there is a new generation of younger scholars, strategists, and politicians in both states that see these disputes as hangovers from the past, and as this generation comes to power (and assuming that Pakistan remains a democracy), there will be movement even on these intractable issues. The United States should not press for a quick solution to the Kashmir problem, but help create the conditions under which such a solution, satisfactory to a wide range of the political community in both countries, can emerge. Strategic normalization has consequences for America's concerns over the spread of nuclear weapons in South Asia. It is unlikely that Pakistan or India will soon abandon their nuclear weapons programs, but a realistic goal would be to create the conditions in which neither perceives any gain in moving their programs forward. Legislation that hampers Washington's ability to maintain the present situation needs to be reexamined—America has let the best become the enemy of the good.

A fifth major foreign policy goal should be to develop a dialogue about short-term and long-term strategic cooperation with India. No such dialogue exists at the moment. There are contingencies, immediate and distant, that need to be discussed. In the short run, India may be able to expand its peacekeeping and stabilizing role in regions adjacent to South Asia. In the long run, the emergence of China as an aggressive power could raise profound issues for all three states. Pakistan would have to decide whether its quasi-alliance with China might not drag it into conflicts for which it was ill equipped; India also must decide whether it is easier to wean a totalitarian, powerful China away from Pakistan, or whether it might attempt to wean a newly democratic Pakistan away from China. Finally, a violent or expansionist China may not pose the same kind of threat to India and the United States at the same time. Would India allow itself to be used as a "frontline state" against China, or would Washington come to New Delhi's assistance in the event of a crisis? These are still-theoretical questions—and there is a strong possibility that they will remain so, but they need to be discussed between Americans and Indians, Americans and Pakistanis, and, most important, between Pakistanis and Indians. Indeed, I have a very different future in mind for China from either aggressive expansion or imminent collapse.

American interests in South Asia are now more diverse than they were during the Cold War, but the policy process has not adapted to the management of this complexity. For almost thirty years America's South Asia policy has alternated between frenzied, episodic attention and long spells of apathy. The former overrates the importance of India and its neighbors; the latter sends exactly the wrong message to them: that the United States does not care. Balancing complex interests has always been difficult for America as it approaches the various regions of the world, now without the goad and the framework of the Cold War. But developing and implementing such a policy—in regions such as South Asia, where there are some threats to American interests, but also significant opportunities—will be an important measure of the strategic maturity of the United States as it enters the next millennium.

2011

SIXTEEN

How a Botched U.S. Alliance Fed Pakistan's Crisis

Pakistan is undergoing a prolonged crisis. Its social and political order has been in disarray for at least thirty years, a mess compounded by strained relations with neighbors, and even with allies. This much is clear. Perhaps less well understood, however, is that much of Pakistan's current crisis stems from its history of alliances, during and since the Cold War, with the West and particularly with the United States.

Pakistan's role as a U.S. ally during the Cold War exacerbated cultural, social, and economic stresses that were embedded in the country from its founding. Although it is not entirely correct to argue, as many Pakistanis do, that the U.S. relationship is the root cause of all these problems, the assertion encompasses enough truth to compel a look backward so that we might see where Pakistan is going in the future.

Indeed, Pakistan's current plight and troubled prospects can only be understood in the context of its having embraced the role of America's "most allied ally." This legacy helps explain the country's failure to establish a coherent political system, or a framework in which political justice and economic growth can flourish. It helps explain Islamabad's strained relations with Afghanistan and India. And it helps explain why Pakistan today remains vulnerable to the negative dimensions of what we call globalization.

Poorly Conceived

In 1945 "Pakistan" was an idea, not a state, and little thought was given to the strategic implications that would follow from its creation. The original idea of Pakistan was that it would be a homeland for Indian Muslims, a place where they would not be dominated by the Hindu majority in a one-man-one-vote democracy. Few who advocated the creation of Pakistan dreamed that the new nation and India would become bitter enemies, or that the Pakistani armed forces would dominate the country's politics.

By 1947, the regional security debate revolved around two questions. First, how would an independent Pakistan stand between India and the Soviet Union, on the one hand, and between India and Afghanistan, on the other? Could Pakistan maintain a viable army, and would it serve as a bulwark for India against Soviet pressure or radical Islamic movements? Muhammad Ali Jinnah, the leading figure in the Pakistan movement, argued that a new Pakistan would enhance the defense of the subcontinent precisely because of its Islamic nature. Jinnah was excessively optimistic in thinking that natural linkages between India and Pakistan, both cultural and economic, would strengthen relations between the two countries.

The second strategic calculation involved Britain's eastern territories, notably Hong Kong, Malaya, and Singapore. Some British strategists, distrusting India's Congress Party and Jawaharlal Nehru, saw Pakistan as a potential ally, one that could facilitate British contacts with these colonies, and with Australia and New Zealand. Eventually Americans, too, came to see the strategic value of West Pakistan's location, particularly as a possible bomber base on the Soviet Union's southern flank.

When Nehruvian India fled from alliances, Pakistan sought them out. In 1955, it entered into the "Middle East Defense Organization," more widely known as the "Baghdad Pact," later known as the Central Treaty Organization (CENTO). Subsequently Pakistan also became a member of the Southeast Asia Treaty Organization (SEATO). Like CENTO, SEATO was designed to be a regional NATO.

What did Pakistan receive in exchange for its alliance membership? It obtained from the United States large amounts of economic and military assistance, sometimes at bargain terms. The program of military assistance continued until the 1965 India–Pakistan War, when the United States suspended arms shipments to both Pakistan and India. (This embargo remained in place during the 1971 India–Pakistan War, and was not lifted until 1975.)

Large numbers of Pakistani officers received training in the United States, while significant numbers of Turkish, Iranian, and American officers were trained in Pakistan. American training teams visited Pakistan, making presentations on a wide range of military and strategic subjects, including nuclear warfare. Pakistan also received diplomatic support on the vexing issue of Kashmir. Both Britain and the United States supported Pakistani positions in the United Nations. However, neither would extend their NATO or CENTO commitments to include the defense of Pakistan in case of a war with India.

Pakistani officials continued unsuccessfully to seek such assurances well into the 1980s. Instead, U.S. administrations and British governments have routinely intervened in India–Pakistan crises in attempts to avert large-scale war, and even in efforts to reach an agreement on Kashmir, but with mixed results.

Pakistan's liabilities as an ally also became evident during the Cold War. Pakistan had entered into alliances with one purpose: to acquire weapons and political support so it could balance India. It made nominal gestures toward the Cold War objectives of containing the Soviet Union and the People's Republic of China, but other than providing bases for U.S. overflights and intelligence operations, Pakistan contributed little to the overall effort—with one important exception.

In July 1971, Pakistan facilitated a secret visit to Beijing by national security adviser Henry Kissinger, the first step toward a de facto U.S.–China alignment directed against the Soviet Union. In a way, this signaled the beginning of the end of the Cold War, and from this point onward, the United States made a distinction between major communist powers that were friendly (China) and those that were hostile (the Soviet Union).

Off Again, On Again

The 1971 war that resulted in Pakistan's partition brought about a major fracture in U.S.–Pakistan relations and challenged the raison d'être of the alliance as far as Pakistanis were concerned. The alliance failed to prevent the breakup of Pakistan, and after the war Pakistan's new leader, Zulfikar Ali Bhutto, expressed the view that Pakistan had been betrayed. This was the beginning of a long history of Pakistani claims of American deception and betrayal.

Bhutto moved to energize Pakistan's Islamic identity, creating new and strong ties with Saudi Arabia, Iran, and other Islamic states. This set the stage for a subsequent Islamist ideological invasion of Pakistan. Bhutto also stressed Pakistan's nonaligned credentials, calling his new policy "bilateralism," which implied neutrality in the Cold War. Pakistan withdrew from CENTO and SEATO, and subsequently became a member of the Nonaligned Movement.

Militarily, Bhutto initiated a secret nuclear weapons program that, with Chinese help, produced a nuclear warhead by the late 1980s. A device was perfected and later tested in 1998. The nuclear policy was continued by Bhutto's successor, General Muhammad Zia ul-Haq. Both Bhutto and the Pakistani army were reacting to India's 1974 "peaceful nuclear explosion," later admitted to be a weapon test.

The Pakistani bomb was not seen as merely a deterrent: by the early 1980s, Pakistani strategists had concluded that, with a bomb, they could provoke and probe India without fear of escalation to a nuclear conflict or even a large-scale war. They were correct, and once Pakistan had actually developed a weapon, subsequent regional crises were shaped by this assumption. There was a price to be paid, however, and from the late 1970s, nuclear issues became the sticking point in Pakistan's relations with its former Western allies, notably the United States.

When the Soviet Union invaded Afghanistan in December 1979, Pakistan's Cold War alliances were formally defunct—but that invasion revived the relationship between Pakistan and the United States. Pakistan accepted a 1981 offer from President Ronald Reagan of $3.2 billion in aid over six years, and a second economic and military assistance package was announced in 1986.

Pakistan's role in supporting the Mujahideen in Afghanistan led to U.S. waivers of restrictions on aid stemming from the country's unverifiable nuclear program. But with the withdrawal of the Soviets from Afghanistan in 1989 and the end of the Cold War, the United States suddenly discovered that it could no longer certify the absence of nuclear weapons in Pakistan, so assistance ended.

The September 11, 2001, terrorist attacks against America led to a third incarnation of the U.S.–Pakistan alliance. The administration of

George W. Bush moved quickly to eliminate sanctions and declared Pakistan to be a "major non-NATO ally," entitling it to buy certain military equipment at reduced prices.

Pakistan again served as a support base for an Afghanistan war, and then as a partner in tracking down al Qaeda and Taliban leaders who had fled to Pakistan. More to the point, as far as Pakistan was concerned, a massive military and economic assistance program was initiated, much along the lines of that provided under the 1950s alliances, and after the Soviet invasion of Afghanistan.

This new package amounted to more than $1 billion a year, most of it given in exchange for permission to use Pakistani facilities in support of the U.S. and NATO invasion of Afghanistan. Much of the money was unaccountable, however, and by 2008 loud criticism came from Congress that it had been misspent. More devastatingly, critics asserted that Pakistan was not pulling its weight in combating radical extremism in Afghanistan and in Pakistan itself. Indeed, Pakistan was supporting both sides of the conflict in Afghanistan.

At the same time, Islamabad never succeeded in obtaining tariff concessions from the United States that would have allowed it to increase its textile exports. This was the first and major Pakistani request to Washington after 9/11, but in this case the Carolina congressional delegation, representing the U.S. textile industry, overruled even alliance politics.

Lessons Learned and Forgotten

What are the lessons to be drawn from this history of alliance and realliance? They fall into three categories: those concerning the influence of the U.S.–Pakistan relationship on Pakistani domestic politics, notably the role of the armed forces; those concerning regional and strategic relations; and those concerning the politics of the alliance itself.

Regarding the first category, Pakistan's Cold War alliances weakened the position of the country's left and liberal forces, what would now be called civil society, and made it easy to suppress the public debate that might have checked government excess. The country's "naturally" anticommunist Islamic forces were officially favored by both the government of Pakistan and its Western allies. Thus Pakistan never developed the ideological and social diversity that might have enabled it to withstand the end of the Cold War and the onslaught of globalization, which included the spread of Islamic extremism. Indeed, Islamic extremism was at one point seen as a virtue in battling the atheistic Russians.

Pakistan is undergoing a transformation. A country with a backward political order dominated by a feudal-like elite is becoming an overwhelmingly urban state—yet one without a political system that can absorb and channel the new urban population. The country's political community remains undeveloped and is still linked to its pseudo-feudal origins.

And much of the political underdevelopment was encouraged (or at least tolerated) by Pakistan's Western allies, who desired stability above all. (Needless to say, it was also encouraged by Pakistan's other allies and close friends, notably Saudi Arabia and China. Both of these countries preferred to deal with military and establishment elites, and consequently never criticized the suppression of political dissent.)

Pakistan's failure to achieve constitutional normalcy was whitewashed on the grounds that a state under external pressure and in internal disarray had no choice but to compromise on such niceties as a Constitution and the rule of law. Further, Pakistan did not have to meet the tough test of standing on its own. It was always able to "borrow" power, but it failed to use this power to reform its social and political institutions.

Pakistan's experiments with military rule were broken only by spells of highly personalistic, sometimes autocratic, civilian governments, all of which were carefully watched—and eventually deposed—by the army. Military rule was opposed by a few Pakistani politicians, but most found a role in the system or dropped out of politics. Meanwhile, there was nary a murmur from Pakistan's democratic allies. Pakistan's army, led by Field Marshal Muhammad Ayub Khan, assumed the role of benevolent babysitter, watching over Pakistani politics and society. Later, under the ideologically driven hard-liner General Zia, the army took on the task of "correcting" or straightening out Pakistanis who had deviated in one way or another.

The army dealt with the Americans without reference to other Pakistani institutions. Like the British Raj that had governed South Asia for a century, the officers justified their rule in strategic and moral terms. Grave matters of state security were taken out of the hands of the always untrustworthy political class.

The Underdog State

Meanwhile, the idea of Pakistan underwent a transformation—changing from a homeland for Indian Muslims into a fortress where its citizens could live more or less "Islamic" lives secure from predatory India. And under Zia, the idea was transformed again—into that of a state where Pakistanis had to become "good" Muslims, as defined by the pious Zia, his Islamist supporters, and the Saudis. This amounted to an officially directed injection of sectarian poison into Pakistan's veins.

Thus, the country's embrace of military alliances with the West helped place the army at the center of power in a state under stress. Pakistan was threatened, the army was the transmission belt for Western military aid to the government, and it was easy for Pakistani politicians and Western allies to let the army assume a dominant position. This phenomenon also contributed to the myth that the army was Pakistan's most competent institution—a myth because civilian institutions never had a chance to grow, nor were they encouraged by outsiders who lavished funds on the military.

In addition to the domestic effects, the Western alliances also held paradoxical consequences for Pakistan's regional and strategic outlook. As long as India remained a mortal threat—as epitomized by the 1971 war that divided Pakistan, and by subsequent crises over Kashmir and terrorist incidents—the army could claim that it best understood the requirements of national defense and security. Its leaders, after all, were the dedicated, professional guardians of "Fortress Pakistan."

Further, it was the army's view that regional peace was possible, but only if a military balance was achieved between India and Pakistan. If Delhi refused to recognize Pakistan's legitimate existence, it would face a reality check, administered by a well-armed Pakistan. The Indians were bullies, and bullies recognize superior power. Pakistan's alliances made this a feasible strategy—until the region went nuclear around 1990, after which it was impossible to contemplate the full-scale use of military force.

Alliances with the West enabled Pakistan to hold its own vis-à-vis India for many years. Pakistanis had an intense, underdog desire to disprove Indian predictions of state failure. By merely staying afloat, Pakistanis felt they were defying India, and this psychology is still evident in the third post-Independence generation, particularly in sports rivalries with India and in public declarations of Pakistani nuclear prowess.

Pakistan's dispute with India over Kashmir was also affected by its Cold War alliances. Kashmir seemed to confirm the founding "idea" of Pakistan, that Muslims could not live peacefully or safely in a Hindu-dominated India. However, to bring Kashmir into Pakistan, or to force India to yield it, Pakistan needed to borrow even more power from its Cold War allies. It was not until the tenure of the most recent military ruler, Pervez Musharraf, that Pakistan began to engage India seriously over a settlement on Kashmir. But by this time attitudes in India toward Pakistan had hardened, and Kashmir became a treasured grievance for enough people in both countries to block any agreement.

As for Afghanistan, presently the central focus of U.S. policy in South Asia, Pakistan has always regarded it as an important strategic battleground with India. American assistance to Pakistan during the Soviet occupation of Afghanistan strengthened pro-Pakistani groups in Afghanistan. Following the Soviet withdrawal from Afghanistan—when the United States itself withdrew from engagement in the region (effectively washing its hands of Afghanistan and Pakistan)—the gates were opened for Pakistan to support its Afghan clients, first warlords and then the Taliban. A too clever strategy by far, this generated a toxic ideological blowback into Pakistan itself.

The Idea of Alliances

A final category of consequences stemming from Pakistan's alliances has to do with the politics of alliances themselves. Alliances are generally of two types: bandwagoning and balancing. A bandwagoning alliance is one of choice, with a view toward maximizing benefits. Those who enter into such an alliance will leave it when the benefits do not fulfill expectations. A balancing alliance, on the other hand, is driven by the existence of a shared enemy. One stays in such an alliance as long as the enemy remains shared and real. Indeed, under such circumstances a formal alliance may not be needed, if an understanding exists that both sides share a common threat.

During the Cold War, Pakistan's alliances with the West and with other countries were of both types. Originally, Islamabad was motivated by sheer bandwagoning, joining CENTO and SEATO in nominal opposition to communism, in exchange for substantial military and economic aid. However, this alliance was not strong enough to prevent Pakistan from edging closer to China in order to obtain Beijing's support against India, and eventually the United States itself decided that China was not quite the communist threat that the Soviets were.

The Soviets in the meantime sought a stronger alliance with India, providing military and economic support, as well as a veto in the United Nations. This completed a complex five-party relationship, with the Soviet Union and India on one side, and Pakistan, China, and the United States on the other.

The irony is that Pakistan did not play a balancing role against the Soviet Union (except regarding its limited support of U.S. intelligence operations) until after it had left CENTO and SEATO. From the American perspective, Pakistan was not an ally against China, but this nonparticipation turned into a virtue when Pakistan served as a bridge to China. Ever since, Pakistanis have claimed American support for their role (and suffering) in the Cold War. But their Cold War role was minimal until after Pakistan had left the formal alliances, and in any case was primarily directed against India.

Over the years, the American relationship with Pakistan has been one of intense engagement alternating with withdrawal. Washington turned to Pakistan in the early 1950s, and often held it up as a "model" for the Islamic world, although no other Muslim state regarded it as such. In the early 1960s, the U.S.–Pakistan alliance frayed when Pakistan turned to China for assistance while the United States backed India in its war with China. With the subsequent development of a Pakistani nuclear weapons program, the Jimmy Carter administration sanctioned Islamabad.

American policy underwent a complete about-face when Islamabad provided essential support for anti-Soviet operations in Afghanistan, and a second U.S.–Pakistan alliance took shape. At that time, U.S. ambassadors in Islamabad liked to check off the many important interests they were attempting to advance: supporting the Mujahideen, containing the Pakistani nuclear program, edging Pakistan toward a democratic political order, averting an India–Pakistan crisis, and slowing the international flow of narcotics.

But when difficult decisions had to be made, the first interest—sustaining Pakistan's cooperation in the strategic struggle against the Soviet Union—trumped all others. Washington was mild in its language regarding democratization, it underestimated the risks of an India-Pakistan war, and it averted its eyes from the Pakistani nuclear program. About the only successful policy (other than containing the Soviets) was curbing the drug trade.

Meanwhile, a second checklist could have been drawn up—of dangerous trends that the Reagan administration and some of its successors largely ignored. These included Pakistan's uneven economic development, its crumbling educational system, and the growth of Islamic radicalism. Only the nuclear program received sustained high-level U.S. attention—until links among Pakistan, the Taliban, and Osama bin Laden's al Qaeda were finally recognized in the mid-1990s.

These lists show not only how the urgent often drives out the important but also that the choice of what is "important" is often very subjective. The Reagan administration was uninterested in the consequences of supporting radical Islamists because they were thought to be the best anti-Soviet fighters, and their religious fervor appealed to some American officials and politicians. A few years later, the Bill Clinton administration was focused solely on nuclear issues and the Taliban–bin Laden nexus in Afghanistan. The subsequent Bush administration revived a formal military agreement with Pakistan.

No U.S. administration thought it important to ask why Pakistan's educational system was collapsing, and why Islamic schools were replacing it. These were considered "soft" issues. Today, they are correctly seen as critical ones. The administration of Barack Obama does seem to recognize the significance of these stark developments. The question is whether it is too late to reverse Pakistan's course.

Burdens of the Past

This history illustrates several important features of the U.S.–Pakistan relationship. First, the alliance has been episodic and discontinuous, driven on the American side entirely by larger strategic calculations during the Cold War, and later by the need for military allies in the war against terrorism. On the Pakistani side, of course, the purpose of the alliances was to acquire resources and political support for use in Pakistan's contest with India.

Second, although U.S. aid strengthened the hand of the army, the on-again, off-again quality of the relationship made the army itself wary of

Washington. Military training programs familiarized Pakistani army officers with the United States and its strategic policies, and fostered a better understanding of American society, but they did not create a cadre of "pro-American" generals. Meanwhile, anti-Americanism grew among Pakistani civilians who saw the U.S. alliances as perpetuating the army's role.

Third, the economic consequences of the U.S. relationship were equally ambiguous. Although Pakistan did receive considerable aid, and most of its economic growth took place during the periods of highest aid flows, the assistance was not conditioned on serious economic and social reform. In the end, alliance politics overruled economics, and the country was never forced to undertake economic reforms it badly needed. (Pakistan became known within the International Monetary Fund as a "one tranche" country, never qualifying for a second transfer of funds.) All the military aid that Pakistan has received has done nothing to make its economy competitive in global markets.

Finally, the most enduring and pernicious consequence of Pakistan's long association with Western-sponsored alliances has been the transformation of Pakistan's self-image from that of a staunch, reliable, moderate Muslim ally of the West to that of a victim—a country that has suffered on behalf of the West, and that has not been adequately compensated for its suffering. The sense of being used, abused, and discarded now constitutes a central theme in Pakistan's ties to America and other countries.

Victim status seems to be morally gratifying to Pakistan. It explains why so many things have gone wrong. It identifies the chief culprit (the United States). And it lays the groundwork for massive claims on U.S. and Western support. The syndrome's sturdy narrative begins with Pakistan's neglect and then abandonment when it was a formal alliance partner. It includes a claim on the resources of others, and it ends with a threat: "Help Pakistan or else it will become a radical, Islamic state."

This narrative, which also includes a concocted history of the U.S. response to Pakistan's covert nuclear program, is designed to appeal to American guilt, but it is based on a highly selective interpretation of the facts. It may be time—it may also be too late—for both Americans and Pakistanis, as well as key countries such as India, to come to a more accurate understanding of the burdens of the past. They are carrying these burdens, after all, into what will likely be an even more troubling future.

Epilogue

The chapters in this book explore the overlap between South Asia, the use of force, and policy. This epilogue offers additional comments and references to recent work. They are grouped roughly according to the subjects discussed in the individual chapters, including the relevance of history; the social role of the military; the rise, fragmentation, and nuclearization of states; and developments in Pakistan, India–Pakistan relations, and American policy.

My judgments are offered here for what they are: speculation about complex issues that usually have no clear answers, and where choices are usually between bad and worse. The hindsight of historians is marvelous but rarely captures the anguish and courage of those who have had to make quick decisions about important issues when information was bad, imprecise, or conflicting.

History and the Past

Both history and contemporary events demonstrate that in most societies the role of the warrior-soldier is critically important in shaping politics and society. To say so does not mean that "militarism" is a solution, but only that while you may be able to conquer a people from horseback, they cannot be governed from there.[1] This is a lesson the United States failed to learn in Iraq, Afghanistan, and Libya, and it is still relevant to those large areas of South Asia that are ungoverned or poorly governed.

While Indian history was made by the warrior Kshatriya, it was recorded by the Brahmin, and our understanding of history is shaped by those who wrote it—"victor's history" is as important as victor's justice. Increasingly, the views of some of India's great non-Brahmin figures such as B. R. Ambedkar are again being studied. His reading of the past and that of other great regional leaders join, but do not displace, the Nehruvian vision.

As Steven Wilkinson reminds us in his definitive book on ethnicity and the military in India, the officer corps is culturally, as well as politically, subservient to its political masters, and both are now more representative of the larger society. This is the logical end point of Indian demands after World War I that the British Raj offer greater Indian representation in the officer corps and, later, greater regional representation in the other ranks, as well as democratic politics. In India, democracy clashed head-on with the essentialist martial races theory.[2] The representativeness of the army is not perfect, but it is analogous in many ways to that of the U.S. Army, a glaring exception being Indian Muslims, who are underrepresented in both the officer corps and the other ranks.

When it comes to regional and ethnic representation in the armed forces, Pakistan is nearly a mirror image of India. Ambedkar (also the author of the Indian Constitution) wrote a book during World War II presciently arguing that an officer corps dominated by Punjabi Muslims would ultimately emerge as a powerful political force. He also supported the creation of Pakistan and was correct in that Punjabi Muslims are Pakistan's dominant political force as they comprise much of the army. Socially the two officer corps are also similar, both being drawn from their respective middle classes, not a social or caste elite.

As for the relevance of early Indian strategy, there is important new scholarship. See especially the work of Swarna Rajagopalan, who has written on the strategies embedded in ancient Indian traditions.[3] India's leading government think tank has published studies of Kautilya's influence trying to promote an India vocabulary on statecraft,[4] and there have been other recent books on Kautilya.[5] For an insightful survey of the relevance to South Asia of Islamic traditions, see a forthcoming article in *Security Studies*, "Region, System, and Order: Muslim India in Islamicate Asia."[6] Stephen Peter Rosen wrote an important book on military organization and society, and see also the writings of the late American scholar George Tanham, whose argument that India lacked a strategic tradition generated strong reactions in India, some critical, others sympathetic.[7]

At various times the Raj supported both military dominance and militarism. Pakistan inherited the Raj's military-dominant side, while India inherited the civilian-dominant pattern. This was fixed in place after independence by Nehru and Sardar Patel. I have jokingly referred to it as civilian oppression of the armed forces, but it certainly sets India apart from many ex-colonies.

The most important comparison is still with Pakistan, where one general after another was able to overwhelm civilians and ignore the premises of civilian control, many of which derive from Clausewitz's argument that strategy must guide military action. Force alone has no end. Left to itself it will always lead to total war; the strategic or political hand must direct its use.

There are parallels between Curzon and Kitchener in British India and Zulfikar Bhutto and Zia ul-Haq in Pakistan. Kitchener's strong ties to the British army and government gave him an edge over Curzon; in Pakistan strong ties to a foreign power (the United States) gave the military an edge over civilian politicians. Curzon's erratic personality may have been the deciding factor in his demise; Bhutto's personality was a mixture of modern statesman and feudal lord.

As a student I was puzzled by Subhas Chandra Bose's continuing popularity and wanted to understand his appeal in India. I learned that India had its own tradition of authoritarianism, notably Bose's melding of fascism and communism. Bose styled himself "Netaji," or leader, after Hitler and Mussolini; he had an army (made up almost entirely of captured Indian prisoners of war), plus Nazi and Japanese support.

Mohammed Ali Jinnah and Jawaharlal Nehru defended the accused at the trial of INA officers, while Mahatma Gandhi and Sardar Patel happily praised Bose after he was presumably dead. This was the last time that the two main branches of the Independence movement—Congress and the Muslim league—cooperated. Uncertainty about Bose's death has been an issue in Indian politics ever since 1947, and both British and Indian intelligence regularly intercepted mail to Bose's family to ensure that he was not somehow corresponding with them.[8]

The discussion of Bose and India's role in World War II still resonates as India officials—good diplomats but bad historians—routinely claim that India fought on the side of the Allied powers. They ignore the fact that most Indian nationalists went to jail rather than support the war, and that Bose and others sided with Germany and Japan. Only the Muslim League and the communists supported the Allies.[9] Mahatma Gandhi, for example, praised the INA's goals of Independence but not its use of violence. Pakistan followed a political model in which the army embodies the highest values of the state. For civilian control to work, civilians must demonstrate their capacity to govern, not just mouth slogans. My 1963 speculation that India could be ripe for a proto-totalitarian movement came true ten years after the INA article was published.

India avoided the trap of a man on horseback, but the lure of civilian militarism was strikingly expressed in the worship of Indira Gandhi after she organized the defeat of the Pakistan army in 1971. When faced with domestic unrest, she declared a national "Emergency" (1975–77) and ruled as a dictator for a year and a half.

In Pakistan the authoritarian streak is evident in the initial popular support for several military regimes and for Zulfikar Ali Bhutto, although in each case that support waned after the army (or Bhutto) demonstrated that they could not manage a pseudo-democracy. Ayub called his version of authoritarianism "basic" democracy, anticipating Yahya Khan, Zia ul-Haq, and Pervez Musharraf; all of them eventually turned to civilian politicians to maintain power.

Did the experience of Indira's "Emergency" inoculate India against dictatorship? The fortieth anniversary of her brief dictatorship in 2015 brought no nostalgia. The Congress Party ignored it, and the BJP stressed that Indira's Emergency was the epitome of the Nehru-Gandhi dynasty. The BJP has a very different history of Indian nationalism: to its credit it was one of the few groups that actively opposed the Emergency.

Indian democracy still pulls those on the ideological fringes to the pluralist, semisecular center; Bose combined Left–Right ideological extremes, but in the Indian context he was secular because the INA appealed to and had members from all religious communities, castes, regions, and even genders (there was a women's brigade). Bose's most important legacy was his espousal of an indigenous Indian authoritarian tradition, one that seemingly transcends caste and religion; it was as secular as it was authoritarian. While Bose is not known in Pakistan, where the army *wants* to be the (Islamic) unifying force, he is a hero in India, where militancy and authoritarianism peek out from behind a civilian facade.

While tampering with the army was used as the pretext for Indira Gandhi's dictatorship, the Indian armed forces had little to do with the

Emergency. Stanislaw Andreski's complex unpacking of the term *militarism* is still useful; not all militarists wear uniforms, and some of Nehru's writings indicate that he, too, was tempted to use violence and war to shake up Indian society. I think this is a deep undercurrent in all societies, and political, economic, and social stress will bring it to the surface. I am wary of Narendra Modi's use of military symbols and his manipulation of martial symbols, including his praise of Bose's INA. I am assured by many that India will not succumb to a second Emergency, but this was said of other states as their militaries took over, or as civilian dictatorships received popular support, and these were approved by powerful members of the international community who prized the illusion of stability over the chaos of popular (and often incompetent) democracy.

Rising and Falling States

My interest in rising and declining powers goes back many years, and it resulted in several books on India's rise as a state and one on Pakistan's wobbly future.[10] Chapter 7 was my first exploration of the proposition that India was a "great" or emerging power, and it sets out some criteria for a great state. Jonathan Pollack and Omi Marwah were editing a book on Asian great states, and this caused me to think through whether India, China, and Japan met those criteria. The chapter was written while teaching at Tokyo's Keio University, which gave me the opportunity to read widely in East Asian history and politics, and to interact with Japanese and Western experts on China.

Size and power are often linked, but I believe that India's effective control over the supreme instrument of power makes its rise less scary and more acceptable; the slow pace of military modernization may be the price India pays for civilian control, but a side benefit is that India's rise is not seen as threatening by most states.[11] The Modi administration continues the experiment: Can India have military modernization and democratic control, and not threaten its neighbors or the international community?

The chapter also started my thinking about regional systems and subsystems. I was an early adopter of the "regional" security approach to international politics pioneered by Barry Buzan and Mohammed Ayoob, and I applied it, in chapter 9, to containing the spread of nuclear weapons.[12] I would argue that overlaying regional conflicts and cultures with a grand strategic design leads to persistent bad policies, notably by setting fire to the tinder of religious or ethnic separatism. Germany did this in World War I and II, and it was recently emulated by the West in the Middle East. It was American policy when we supported the Mujahideen against the Soviets in Afghanistan, and I do not recall many U.S. officials, or members of Congress, expressing the same doubts as many of my Pakistani friends did—they warned of the flooding of their country by drugs, guns, and radical Islamists. They were right, although from an American perspective the victory over the Soviet Union was more important.

The decline of communism helped shred political orders around the world, especially in states dependent on one or the other of the superpowers, a point made in chapter 8. Simultaneously, the information revolution made it more difficult for states everywhere to govern.

The lessons of this process are not fully absorbed by the think tank and government communities, and I remain surprised that intelligent people are surprised at the turn of events in the past fifteen to twenty years. Scholars and policymakers grope for a grand theory that would lead America out of what is incorrectly perceived to be a new and widespread chaos. I leave it to others to explore the sociology of our profession, one that makes it difficult to grasp the shift from global strategy to language/region, ethnicity, and religion. The forces that deepened grievances in both the Western and non-Western worlds were well understood for many years; the end of communism and what is called "globalization" are only two of them. Ethnicity and religion were then widely understood by academics working in comparative politics to be vital. Why should they come as a surprise now?[13] Ethnic and religious passions are less constrained now but were evident to anyone working at the less-than-strategic level in Asia, Africa, and Latin America. Some of us missed the speed with which money, as well as goods, people, and ideas, could be moved around the world, but this only reinforces the point that the classic state had lost much of its authority and capability. This is evident in the shift of radical Islamist movements from seeking revenge against imagined oppressors, notably the United States, to their search for territory—the contrast between al Qaeda and the Islamic State is striking.

The world's transformation after the fall of the USSR was noted by the intelligence community, and President Carter's nominee for director of central intelligence, James Woolsey, famously testified that one large dragon (the Soviet Union) had been replaced by a world of snakes.[14] This is accurate in that as long as America does not poke its face into snake-ridden places, these new threats are of a lesser order to America than the USSR. The former editor of *Foreign Policy*, Moses Naim, recently summarized this situation, including the waning of state power.[15]

What are the policy solutions to this not-new world? The onset of a new generation of policymakers and academics—not rooted in Manichean cold war models and with experience in the non-Western world—will help, as will the development of a flexible and thinking policy process, but human nature will not change markedly. We must learn, as Robert Osgood used to teach, to realistically accept limited defeats and modestly cherish the limited victories.

Nuclear Weapons and Proliferation

The nuclear issue (chapter 9) permeates my writing because this is what separates South Asia from most other regions. Further, Pakistan's sharing of nuclear technology with other unstable states was astonishing by any standard, even if there was precedent in the actions of China and other nuclear powers. Additionally, Pakistan's instability made the conjunction of nuclear weapons and terrorism a central concern for three recent presidents. Like the Cold War there is a real-world possibility of unprecedented destruction, unpredictable technological innovations, and an element of arms racing, as well as pride and national ego. The differences are that the India–Pakistan crises have involved influential third parties, mostly the United States.[16] There are also rivalries that penetrate domestic politics.

In 1965 I wrote a brief article that reflected my training in nuclear strategy.[17] It is not included in this collection, but it argued that India might consider acquiring tactical nuclear weapons to deal with the threat from China (and Indonesia, then an expansionist state). Pakistan was not a nuclear weapons candidate state as the army opposed their acquisition. However, India is now debating a response to Pakistan's tactical nuclear program, so some of the speculation in that piece is still relevant.

As discussed in chapter 1, I left the nuclear strategic community when I went to non-nuclear South Asia, turned off by Herman Kahn and the RAND strategists, only to have the nuclear quandary catch up with me.

My early interests in nuclear strategy led me to co-found the University of Illinois Program in Arms Control, Disarmament, and International Security (ACDIS). There I encouraged work on the South Asian nuclear relationship. One of my graduate students, Rashid Naim, did the first-ever study of the consequences of a regional nuclear war, and another, Itty Abraham, wrote in a penetrating way about the Indian nuclear culture. A third probed deeply into the question of nuclear stability between India and Pakistan, and recently a fourth has made the important point that the India–Pakistan nuclear competition/crises differ from those of the superpowers because there are important outside powers (notably the United States and the West) that influence calculations during crises with a nuclear tinge.[18]

When the India test did take place, I offered my views, in a letter to *The New York Times*, that it would make India feel better but be less secure. I was wrong in assuming an India–China nuclear arms race.[19] As Munir Khan, the real father of the Pakistani bomb, once said to a group of American, Chinese, Soviet, and Indian experts, the Indians provided Pakistan with the incentive to go nuclear, the Chinese provided material assistance, the Soviets the occasion (because of the invasion of Afghanistan), and the Americans cooperated by looking the other way. In my office in the Department of State I would point to a small carving of three monkeys ("teen Bandar": see no evil, hear no evil, speak no evil) when friends asked me about the Pakistani nuclear program.[20]

I have made the case for a regional approach to nonproliferation, something that is slowly emerging as U.S. policy in North Korea, Iran, and India, and soon in Pakistan. America should have taken the Indian proposal for regional nuclear arrangements seriously, and we should have also done a "deal" with the Pakistanis; my criterion is not loyalty to the Nuclear Non-Proliferation Treaty (NPT), but to a judgment as to whether accommodating Pakistan, as India has been accommodated, might be a better way to slow or prevent proliferation and further stability among the existing nuclear weapons states.[21] There should be an "Asian Restraint Regime" that would include India, Pakistan, and China. The judgment should not be whether nonproliferation goals are better served by preserving the treaty in pristine form, but by developing an NPT outside the NPT—as has been done with Israel, the only other country to have gone nuclear without signing the NPT.

Neither view is in the nonproliferationist mainstream, but these ideas will become more acceptable. I tried to make a strong case for taking the regionalist view, but the grip of the nonproliferation purists was strong. However, a new generation of policymakers is casting about for answers to problems that were left on the table by a strict NPT-or-else approach.

I was the author of the 1987 memo noted in chapter 9. The Reagan administration and Congress were both willing to trade a Pakistani nuclear weapon for Pakistan's support in the war against the Soviet forces in Afghanistan. Washington was displeased when Pakistan did what the French, British, and Israelis had done earlier—but Islamabad had as legitimate concerns for self-defense as Israel did. I was right in predicting that the bomb would stabilize India–Pakistan relations to the degree they stabilized the U.S.–Soviet dyad. Ten years later they went nuclear and stumbled through a series of crises, all of which had nuclear overtones.[22] What was distinct in all of these, pointed out by Moeed Yusuf in his dissertation, is that each involved one or more foreign powers, a factor that was not present in the U.S.–Soviet nuclear competition. I was wrong in my speculation about biological and chemical weapons as pathways to nuclear programs (India first had a covert chemical program before they went nuclear). As Yusuf notes in his Brookings study, outsiders are usually wrong about predicting proliferation, usually guessing on the high side and not taking into account the domestic politics and self-image of potential proliferators, including India and Pakistan.[23]

Arms control is not dead, and we still need to approach a range of old problems as well as figure out technical and political answers to new ones. The question of nuclear stability is not merely a bilateral problem but now transcends regions. For example, there was always a "forensics" problem in the U.S.–Soviet competition. How would America know that detonation originated in the Soviet Union and was not an accident or that some terrorist had not gotten his or her hands on a weapon? This problem is multiplied now. Several new nuclear states may have weaker control over their own nuclear devices and possess rudimentary forensics capabilities. Similarly with many more nuclear states the possibility of a catalytic war is higher than before, a war started between two nuclear states by a third (or by a terrorist group). Admitting states into an NPT outside the NPT is useful only if they conform to the NPT and to tough norms about the transfer of nuclear technology, cooperation in defeating terrorists, and tracing the origins of unauthorized nuclear explosions.

Pakistan: Army and Politics

If one could glue together the best of the army and the best of the politicians, Pakistan would be a terrific state. The likely medium-term future is that Pakistan will muddle through; several recent and mostly critical books on the army do not change my judgment,[24] which is closer to that of two other books on Pakistan.[25] There are worse futures for Pakistan than another military takeover. Under two different chiefs, the army persuaded the civilian politicians that the radical Islamists threatened the state, and it was the army that resisted the Saudi invitation to get involved in a Sunni–Shi'a proxy war in Yemen. Yet the army cannot provide strategic and political leadership for the country.

My first contact with the Pakistan army took place in Great Britain in the 1960s, when I met a number of retired British officers who had led the Pakistan army after Independence. One of them, General Sir Frank Messervy, said that he told both Jinnah and Liaquat Ali Khan that Pakistan was "complete nonsense," although he added that he never would have told this to the troops. Other British officers were more optimistic about Pakistan's prospects and praised its fighting spirit, although several noted the "inferiority complex" of Muslims vis-à-vis Hindus, especially when it came to intellectual matters.[26] These conversations led me to take later proclamations about Pakistan's viability, as well as its critical or pivotal status, with many grains of salt. My judgment has always been that Pakistan contains enough competent people to run a really impressive and thriving state—but they are blocked from power by a khaki wall.

From the beginning of my writing on Pakistan (my first article was published in 1964[27]), I focused on several themes. One was that we had to see it in its own terms to understand why it thought and acted as it did; as a powerful bureaucracy that commanded many resources, it had the ability to replicate itself without interference from outsiders, including Pakistani politicians, the U.S. government, and India. Second, it resented *foreigners* for placing limits on Pakistan's policies. There was anger with the British for holding the army back in Kashmir, and later with the Americans for supporting a non-ally, India, and placing obstacles in the way of a Pakistani nuclear program.

Third, the army also exaggerated its role vis-à-vis India, propelled by early Indian attempts to weaken it. The largely Punjabi/Pushtun officer corps also had problems with East Pakistan and Bengalis. This had calamitous results in 1971, when India took advantage of a Bengali uprising (which included Bengali elements of the army in East Pakistan). In 1965 I also cautioned against praising Pakistan as a stable military dictatorship, predicting the oscillation between military involvement and abstention from politics.

Pakistan has a mixed British heritage—partly Curzon, partly Kitchener—and early on its diplomacy anticipated the emergence of a "nonaligned" Pakistan. While Pakistan became the "most allied" of U.S. allies, a member of both CENTO and SEATO (the latter, ironically, aimed at China), Zulfikar Ali Bhutto brought it back to nonaligned status by formalizing the China tie. After experimentation with a too-strong alliance with America, nonalignment again characterizes Pakistan's foreign policy. However, neither nonalignment nor alliance with outsiders will change the conclusion of that early article: "unless an effective basis of agreement grows up to replace the dwindling degree of trust and personal friendship, relations between Pakistan and India can head in only one irreversible direction."[28]

The original title of chapter 10 was "State Breaking in Pakistan." There was a race to the bottom between the military and civilian institutions; the military looked good because civilian institutions were so bad. None of this was preordained. Pakistan had great resources and outside support, but it could never grow out of its legacy of obsessions. After the 1971 breakup, the army was busy dismantling institutions that were vital to any normal state, and under Zia the process of de-development accelerated. Zia had America's firm support until he died, and America could never bring itself to press on Pakistan the reforms it encouraged elsewhere because of two crises: the invasion of Afghanistan, which made Pakistan a frontline state, and then the 9/11 attack, which led to a change in American valuation of Pakistan and Pakistani exploitation of its new importance—making reform unnecessary.

2016: Chapter 11 was written just before the rise of the TTP. This finally mobilized the state against the most radical and violent elements of militant Islam. The army persuaded civilian politicians that the TTP was a threat to Pakistan itself, especially after the 2014 attack on an army school in Peshawar that killed hundreds of children. The then head of the army stated that while India was the long-term threat, the TTP was the immediate threat. Blowback happens, and the army is now fighting radical Islamists in Pakistan while supporting them against Afghanistan and India. The 2014 attack was widely hailed as a "turning point" in shaping Pakistani views toward internal terrorism; that remains to be seen—this is a road with many turning points.

Pakistan has two dilemmas. The first is that the army cannot govern Pakistan, but it will not let others do it. The repeated military interventions designed to "fix" Pakistan's problems have ruined the state's feeble capacity for governance. As several have commented, Pakistan has a weak state but a strong society. This is a problem for the strongest state institution, the military, when it wants to turn pacified areas over to civilians. Pessimism is in order when it comes to long-term governance and to India–Pakistan relations. The threat is not from conservative Islamist political parties, such as the Jama'at, but from proto–al Qaeda groups and the new TTP, which did not until recently become an active force. General/President Pervez Musharraf was ineffective, which did not surprise me, but he fooled other Americans, the Indians, and many Pakistanis, and he vacillated in the face of the emergence of suicide squads. He also approved covert military operations in India, falsely believing that the Indians could be pressured into a settlement on Kashmir. Two generals later, the military leadership is still semisecular and now pursuing Islamic extremists who have attacked the state. The Pakistani paradox is that the army is a barrier to political extremism, but it cannot promote moderate institutions that would enable Pakistan to thrive. With luck, "just getting by" will be Pakistan's future.

Pakistan's second dilemma pertains to India. New Delhi would like a Pakistan that is strong enough to hold together, but not so strong that it can challenge India. Indians are unsure themselves as to how big and how weak Pakistan should be. Pakistan does not want to become West Bangladesh. Much of Indian policy consists of pretending that Pakistan will somehow go away and urging outside powers to stop "hyphenating" India and Pakistan.

Did adding nuclear weapons to Pakistan's arsenal make it stronger or weaker? They brought global attention to Pakistan but also made the army overconfident and led to the Kargil crisis.[29] Pakistan wants to be respected as a major power and seeks a nuclear agreement with the United States that would legitimate its nuclear program. For this to happen, the United States, China, and even India would have to accept Pakistan's claim, but the price would be steep. I have long argued for an NPT outside the NPT for Pakistan and India, but the terms and conditions for admitting Pakistan to this halfway house are yet to be determined, and Pakistan may not be able to meet a reasonable standard.

An Intractable Conflict and Kashmir

In earlier writings I described India–Pakistan relations as a "communal riot with armor." At first, like others, my focus was on Kashmir, but I came to understand—partly through a close association with the Indian scholar/diplomat Sisir Gupta, who wrote that a major cause of the Kashmir problem were the images of each regarding the other.[30] I later concluded that this was a manifestation of a deeper problem, not just with perception but also structural, which I called a "paired minority," the analytical core of my last book, *Shooting for a Century*.[31]

Chapter 12 set out a theory that describes the relationship between these two states, one that is relevant to the Israel Palestinian dispute. Another civil war–like conflict, that between China and Taiwan, demonstrates how paired-minority conflicts can be peacefully transformed—the two have devised ways in which each can thrive. Similarly, the East–West Germany divide was a paired-minority conflict. Indian strategists hope that Pakistan will go the way of East Germany, or at least succumb to India's greater economic power, as Taiwan has accommodated the People's Republic; neither seems likely.

The idea of paired minorities became the conceptual armature of *Shooting for a Century*, which is both pessimistic and pragmatic—a senior Indian official told me, "I hope you are wrong," and my response was that "I hope so also"—but this is where analysis led me. An unanswered question is whether the pathologies of older generations are being passed on. Put another way, is the process by which the mass media (and now social media) cover dramatic events permanently building these pathologies in the minds of new generations?[32] Work on the formation and transfer of generational attitudes has not progressed much beyond Emile Durkheim's scholarship of the 1930s, but it is still an approach worth using.

My discussion of Kashmir in chapter 13 grew out of participation in a joint U.S.–Russian project on Afghanistan and Kashmir, searching for a response to crises in Afghanistan and Kashmir; it also reflects presentations on what I called SARI—the South Asia Regional Initiative in Islamabad and New Delhi.[33]

While my 1993 policy optimism was dimmed in later writing on India–Pakistan, the Kashmir issue remains critical. Pakistan cannot foment a revolution there, and India has not delivered either democracy or effective repression. About the only thing the two states can agree on is that an independent Kashmir sets an unacceptable precedent for both. India has begun the process of dividing its megastates to provide better governance, an approach that could shape Jammu and Kashmir's future, with component parts of the state having different relations with India's center, and perhaps with Pakistan. This was the direction Pakistan was headed under Pervez Musharraf, but by 2015 the Pakistan government had retreated from his formulations of a division of the state along the Line of Control.

I have been critical of naive efforts for international activity to resolve the Kashmir issue—apparently suggested again by President Obama before his 2015 trip to India—this is the hope that does not die. I agree in spirit with Howard Schaffer's book on American policy failures in Kashmir, and I appreciate the difficulty of mounting even a subtle effort on Kashmir.[34] I turned to the Kashmir problem again in *Shooting for a Century*, arguing that Afghanistan presented a riper opportunity than Kashmir did for U.S. diplomatic and strategic intervention. However, it may be that China, not the United States, will become the strategic mover and shaker. I disagree with the urgent need to do something—anything. Given America's difficulty in focusing on the region—except intermittently and through some lens such as anticommunism or nonproliferation—an indirect strategy is best. I would like to see a U.S.-China-India-Pakistan-Iran-Russia effort to first settle Afghanistan rather than Kashmir, and, if any progress is evident, then tackle Kashmir.

U.S. Policy

America has done much good in the region, but also much damage; it still lacks a truly regional approach.[35] It is hard for the United States to focus on any region with consistency and harder still to give it proportionate attention. Crises divert attention, and the lack of expertise is evident. By and large the United States could have devised worse policies toward India, Pakistan, and the region.

As Strabo wrote 2,000 years ago, geography shapes strategic perceptions; the fabrication of a new geopolitical entity called "Af-Pak" inhibited sound American thinking for nearly a decade, and it is only now (2016) being laid to rest by Washington.

A U.S.–India "strategic relationship," discussed in chapter 15, is only a theoretical possibility, but the two countries are beginning to understand their core and different interests. After the Kargil episode, India realized that the United States would not invariably support Pakistan and learned that it could exploit the relationship to its own benefit. Similarly, the 2005 nuclear agreement has not produced any electricity, and it cleared the air regarding America's overall support for India (but not to the extent of an explicit alliance against another state). American ties to Pakistan are not the worst outcome for India and place the United States in a position where it could help India and Pakistan move down the road to normalcy.

The 2014 visit of Prime Minister Narendra Modi to the United States and the subsequent visit of President Barack Obama to India were widely hailed as a new chapter in U.S.–India relations. If so, this is a volume with dozens, perhaps hundreds, of chapters. Nevertheless, relations are changing as the two countries' social and economic relations become interpenetrated. There are still important strategic policy differences, analogous to those between America and France. I think this was best expressed by the Indian ambassador to the United States, S. Jaishankar, later India's foreign secretary.[36] India's democracy itself is a vital interest for the United States—its support of pluralism is in American interests and more than counterbalances its relations at the strategic level with some states, notably Iran, where its own domestic politics comes into play.

Compared with the mutual misunderstanding and hostility between the two states during much of the time I have traveled to and lived in India, the relationship has moved from a D to at least a B+. It will be an A when the United States and India see eye to eye on Pakistan, a country of importance to both. The United States and India can agree that this failing nuclear power somehow gets through its thirty-year crisis without triggering a new regional war and, at best, could work with India in an integrated partnership that economically reunites South Asia.

Americans, lawyer-like, want to redefine and reinterpret South Asia so that inconvenient strategic legacies can be ignored, or squeezed into an American-designed framework, often based on a moralistic approach to the conflicts of others. This does nothing to persuade South Asians themselves that the American way of looking at their region is better than their own. Creating "Af-Pak" was an attempt to ignore a basic fact of regional life—that India and Pakistan regarded each other as a prime strategic threat—and it allowed American policymakers in several administrations to reframe policy choices so that critical disagreements between India and Pakistan could be ignored until the next crisis. Indians and Pakistanis took advantage and manipulated this new view of South Asia to suit their own interests; it never changed their approach to each other.

Americans rarely take seriously writing by regional strategists and tend to ignore those that run counter to their own predilections. U.S. policymakers also tend to assume that history began last year, or in the last administration, and few are aware of or care about the deeper causes of the India–Pakistan conflict—which is not merely about Kashmir but of which Kashmir is both a cause and a consequence. Nor do Americans appreciate the very nature of an intractable conflict—whether it is in the Middle East or South Asia—yet they have poured huge amounts of money and their own time in the former, while mostly ignoring the latter.

Returning to the theme of chapter 1, America's overall relationship to South Asia could be worse. American academics are mostly disinterested in current policy issues unless their research access is threatened. The American business community has a touching faith in the impact of economic ties on strategic relations,[37] and American diplomacy is afflicted by diplospeak: the enthusiastic embrace of terms that confuse and blur policy and policy choices.[38] There is no better example than the fabricated term *natural allies*, invented in India but embraced by many Americans. It suggests the question: What is an unnatural ally? The recent Council on Foreign Relations task force struggled with terminology and chose to adopt the excellent concept of "joint venture" drawn from the business world—where two firms select areas where they will work together. (The East India Company was a joint venture with the Mughal Empire—but India can now protect itself.)

Vague discussions of strategic partnership remain the norm. There should be more explicit discussion of the sectors in which the United States and India (or the United States and Pakistan) can work together. This is the instinct of President Barack Obama, who constantly reiterates the need to work with "partners" in overseas operations, an attitude that conflicts with a tradition of American exceptionalism and the belief, generated by the Civil War but perpetuated in World War I and II, that America can lead the way to an unconditional surrender of an enemy, transform that enemy into a "friend," and then withdraw behind the safety of two oceans. This vision is defeated by the very nature of politics and the intrusions of technologies and the deterioration of coherent states around the world. In a world of increasingly shattered states, India's noisy democracy is a huge asset for the United States, and, as I have argued, rescuing a nuclear Pakistan from chaos and constructing a path to normalcy is a "strategic" interest now shared by Washington, New Delhi, and even China.

Notes

PREFACE

1. "India and Geography," in *The Oxford Handbook of Indian Foreign Policy*, ed. David M. Malone, C. Raja Mohan, and Srinath Raghavan (Oxford University Press, 2015), 341–55.

2. A definitive historical overview of South Asia is Joseph E. Schwartzberg and others, *A Historical Atlas of South Asia* (second impression with additional materials) (Oxford University Press, 1992). Online at http://dsal.uchicago.edu/reference/schwartzberg/. The term *South Asia* was used intermittently by Americans and Germans, and the first South Asia centers were established in India (New Delhi and Jaipur) in the mid-1960s. For a collection of essays on the American use of the term, see Lloyd I. Rudolph and Susanne Hoeber Rudolph, eds., *The Regional Imperative: U.S. Foreign Policy towards South Asian Studies* (Atlantic Highlands, N.J.: Humanities Press, 1980). A former student, Itty Abraham, has written a thoroughly original study of the foundations of "South Asia" and India; see Itty Abraham, *How India Became Territorial: Foreign Policy, Diaspora, Geopolitics* (Stanford University Press, 2014) and the comments by the eminent historian, Sanjay Subrahmanyam, "Afterword: On Region and Nation in South Asia," *South Asia Multidisciplinary Academic Journal* 10 (2014), http://samaj.revues.org/3826.

3. *The Andhra Cyclone of 1977: Institutional and Individual Responses to Mass Death,* with supplementary material by myself and my coauthor, Professor Chitturi Raghavulu (New Delhi: Vikas, 1979).

4. For two outstanding books on the link between past and present, see David Lowenthal, *The Past Is a Foreign Country* (Cambridge University Press, 1985), and Ernest May and Richard Neustadt, *Thinking in Time: The Uses of History*

for Decision Makers (New York: Free Press, 1986). I had been taught (by Herman Finer) that the present was the growing shoots of the past and that it made sense to explore history for ideas about the present.

5. Steven Wilkinson, *Army and Nation* (Harvard University Press, 2015).

6. Charles Tilly, "War Making and State Making as Organized Crime," in *Bringing the State Back In*, ed. Peter Evans, Dietrich Rueschemeyer, and Theda Skocpol (Cambridge University Press, 1985), pp. 169–86.

CHAPTER ONE

This chapter was originally published in *India Review* 7, no. 4 (October–December 2008), pp. 295–319.

1. See, for example, John J. Johnson, ed., *The Role of the Military in Underdeveloped Countries* (Princeton University Press, 1962); S. E. Finer, *The Man on Horseback: The Role of the Military in Politics* (New York: Frederick A. Praeger, 1962). For an excellent review of that literature, and much that has been written on the role of the military since, see Paul Staniland, "Explaining Civil-Military Relations in Complex Political Environments: India and Pakistan in Comparative Perspective," *Security Studies* 17, no. 2 (April 2008), pp. 322–62.

2. Morris Janowitz, *Military Institutions and Coercion in the Developing Nations* (University of Chicago Press, 1977); Samuel P. Huntington, *The Soldier and the State: The Theory and Politics of Civil-Military Relations* (Harvard University Press, 1957).

3. This is not the place to dwell on the visa problem, except to note that it was difficult personally and made worse by the attitude of many Indian officials. The Indian government did not say no—it just never said yes—but I gained some insights into how Indian bureaucracies operated.

4. For an overview of American historiography of India, see Benjamin B. Cohen, "The Study of Indian History in the U.S. Academy," *India Review* 5, no. 1 (2006), pp. 144–72. Fortunately, one of my Wisconsin history professors, Robert Frykenberg, had been trained as a political scientist and, along with my major adviser, Henry C. Hart, understood what I was up to.

5. Mason had earlier written several novels about India and the definitive history of the Indian civil service. For the army book, see Philip Mason, *A Matter of Honour: An Account of the Indian Army, Its Officers and Men* (New York: Holt, Rinehart, and Winston, 1974).

6. During my first and second extended trips to India (1963–65 and 1968–69), it seemed as if it was obligatory for Americans to lecture Indians on the importance of birth control. This changed, and by the 1970s we were giving lectures on economic reform, only to be followed, in the 1980s, by preaching about India's need to abandon any nuclear ambitions.

7. My Hindi became pretty good at that time. It had to be, because the purpose of the course was for me (in my case, a Jew) to teach students how to give sermons about Christ in Hindi to North Indian Hindus.

8. Sisir Gupta, *Kashmir: A Study in India–Pakistan Relations* (New Delhi: Asia Publishing House, 1966). Sisir Gupta was one of the few Indian scholars who noted that perceptions on both sides were one of the causes of the Kashmir dispute; I later used this insight in developing a theory of "Paired Minorities," discussed in chapter 12 and in *Shooting for a Century* (Brookings Institution Press, 2013).

9. Michael Brecher, *India and World Politics: Krishna Menon's View of the World* (Oxford University Press, 1968).

10. Lorne J. Kavic, *India's Quest for Security* (University of California Press, 1967).

11. Selig S. Harrison, *India: The Most Dangerous Decades* (Princeton University Press, 1960). A few years later a book by another journalist, Welles Hangen, speculated on a military takeover in India, among other outcomes after Nehru's passing, raising suspicions that the Americans were encouraging a coup. See Welles Hangen, *After Nehru, Who?* (New York: Harcourt, Brace, and World, 1963).

12. Seminarist, "The Bomb: Strategic Considerations," *Seminar* (New Delhi), January 1965.

13. Alfred Vagts, *A History of Militarism: Civilian and Military* (New York: Free Press, 1967); Hans Speier, *Social Order and the Risks of War* (New York: Stewart, 1952); Stanislav Andreski, *Military Organization and Society* (London: Routledge and Paul, 1954). Andreski is especially useful in dissecting the term *militarism*: it can mean the political dominance of the military, a foreign policy that favors the use of force, the worship of military values by civilians, and a society that reflects military culture.

14. In British and Indian military terminology, the term *class* referred to the different ethnic groups, castes, and linguistic and regional background of soldiers; thus, Punjabi Sikhs were one class, Punjabi scheduled castes another. See Stephen P. Cohen, *The Indian Army: Its Contribution to the Development of a Nation* (University of California Press, 1971).

15. Two collections provide a sampling; see Daniel P. Marston and Chander S. Sundaram, eds., *A Military History of India and South Asia: From the East India Company to the Nuclear Era* (Westport, Conn.: Praeger Security International, 2007); Kaushik Roy, ed., *War and Society in Colonial India* (Oxford University Press, 2006).

16. DeWitt C. Ellinwood Jr., *Between Two Worlds: A Rajput Officer in the Indian Army, 1905–21* (Lanham, Md.: Hamilton Books, 2005). In the pre-Internet era, Ellinwood and I began, but were unable to sustain, a network of scholars working on the social and cultural side of India's armed forces, the War and Society

in South Asia Group. This group should be revived. I know there are potential members in Singapore, Japan, India, Pakistan, the United States, Great Britain, and elsewhere. The popular website Bharat Rakshak (bharat-rakshak.com) does some of this but is often marred by polemic and nationalism.

17. It was around this time that the Indian government drew on Lyndon LaRouche, the faux politician (and subsequently, convicted felon), to do a study of American scholars working in India. My name figures in that book in a way that stops just short of libelous. I am in fine company, however, as the list of American scholars who have somehow set out to undercut India is long and distinguished. Executive Intelligence Review, *Derivative Assassination: Who Killed Indira Gandhi?* (New York: New Benjamin Franklin House, 1985), p. 35.

18. Edward Luttwak, *Coup d'État: A Practical Handbook* (Harmondsworth: Allen Lane, 1968).

19. Stephen Philip Cohen, "Indo-Pak Track II Diplomacy: Building Peace or Wasting Time," in *Security beyond Survival: Essays for K. Subrahmanyam*, ed. P. R. Kumaraswamy (New Delhi: Sage, 2004), pp. 192–217.

20. The article has been reprinted in a collection of IDSA publications. See Stephen P. Cohen, "The Indian Military and Social Change," in *India and the World: Selected Articles from IDSA Journals, Vol. I. Strategic Thought: The Formative Years*, ed. N. S. Sisodia and Sujit Datta (Delhi: IDSA/Promilla, 2005), originally published in *IDSA Journal* 2, no. 2 (July 1969), pp. 12–29.

21. My first extended work on America's South Asia policy was part of a project about this time for the U.S. Congress. See Lloyd Rudolph and Susanne Rudolph, eds., *The Coordination of Complexity* (New Delhi: Manohar Publishers, 1978); separately published as Stephen P. Cohen "U.S. Weapons and South Asia: A Policy Analysis," *Pacific Affairs* (Spring 1976), pp. 49–69.

22. A. Martin Wainwright, *Inheritance of Empire: Britain, India, and the Balance of Power in Asia, 1938–1955* (Westport, Conn.: Praeger, 1994).

23. There were some exceptional people in this group, and I learned much from the work of Americans who specialized in other South Asian states, most notably Howard Wriggins, whose work on Ceylon/Sri Lanka was unparalleled, and Wayne Wilcox, probably the most brilliant of all the younger foreign policy experts, who died a tragic death in an air crash in Europe. See Howard Wriggins, *Ceylon: Dilemmas of a New Nation* (Princeton University Press, 1960); Wayne Ayres Wilcox, *Pakistan: The Consolidation of a Nation* (Columbia University Press, 1963).

24. Gene D. Overstreet and Marshall Windmiller, *Communism in India* (University of California Press, 1959).

25. In the 1980s Leo Rose and I organized what was to be the first joint United States–Soviet study of security issues in South Asia, which morphed into

the first joint United States–Russian study of the region. It was useful to compare notes with our Soviet/Russian counterparts about what we each had been told by Indians and Pakistanis. A by-product of this effort, a paper on Kashmir, is reprinted here as chapter 13.

26. Mohammed Ayoob, *The Third World Security Predicament: State Making, Regional Conflict and the International System* (Boulder, Colo.: Lynne Rienner, 1995).

27. Kanti P. Bajpai and Harish C. Shukul, *Interpreting World Politics* (New Delhi: Sage, 1995).

28. I supported, but warned against, the consequences of India's 1971 intervention. It was not cost-free, and the use of force always has unanticipated consequences. While Indians concluded that they had established dominance over Pakistan and that India–Pakistan relations could normalize, this was not the view of the Pakistan army, and the 1971 defeat ensured that Pakistan would seek an equalizer: an atomic bomb. It also ensured that when the opportunity came (in Punjab and Kashmir), Pakistan would intervene in what was seen by the army, and most Pakistani civilians, as just retribution for India's actions.

29. It is hard to summon up much enthusiasm for AIIS, an organization that is devoted to benefiting Americans and not Indians. Contrast this with the Fulbright program, or the American Institute of Pakistan Studies (AIPS), which support a two-way flow of scholars. I think the AIPS and Fulbright models are more appropriate, and AIIS should either be folded into Fulbright or required to strengthen Indian scholarship. AIIS and the American "India establishment" are now being unfairly targeted by some on the Hindutva right as being out of touch with modern India, an absurd proposition; see Rajiv Malhotra, *Breaking India* (New Delhi: Manjul, 2011).

30. Rajni Kothari, "The Tasks Within," *Seminar* (December 1968). See also Edward Said, *Orientalism* (New York: Vintage Books, 1979).

31. There is also interest in Bose in Singapore, where I spent four months in 2008 as a visiting professor. The INA erected a monument to itself when Singapore was under Japanese occupation. This was blown up by the British when they recaptured the island. However, a small marker identifies the place where the original INA monument was erected, and the Singapore government remains characteristically noncommittal toward a movement that was pro-Japanese yet mostly Indian in nature.

32. The term used to describe Kissinger's insistence that foreign service officers not be too focused on one region, but acquire a range of regional and other expertise.

33. Stephen P. Cohen and C. V. Raghavulu, *The Andhra Cyclone of 1977: Individual and Institutional Responses to Mass Death* (New Delhi: Vikas, 1979). As a

follow-up, Raghavulu created a disaster management training center in Andhra Pradesh. The book was used as a text in a course on man-made and natural disasters taught at the Lee Kuan Yew School of Public Policy (Singapore) in 2008. Much has changed in the disaster field, notably the availability of the World Wide Web as a clearinghouse for best practices.

34. See James Manor, *Power, Poverty and Poison: Disaster and Response in an Indian City* (New Delhi: Sage, 1993).

35. See, for example, Brahma Chellaney and Nitin Pai, "Climate Change and International Security," *Pragati—the Indian National Interest Review* 3 (June 2007), pp. 7–8.

36. Stephen Philip Cohen, *The Pakistan Army* (University of California Press, 1985), and editions in India and China. The book was roundly condemned in the *Far Eastern Economic Review*—the reviewer was a serving Pakistan official who had been responsible for the ban. The *Review* never apologized.

37. Dick Park's ties to India began during World War II when he was stationed in Calcutta, as were a number of other Americans who eventually went on to form the core of America's academic specialists on India. They joined a generation of Americans whose early contacts with India were derived from the missionary experience. At Wisconsin, for example, Henry Hart, Joseph Elder, and Robert Frykenberg were all missionary children who had lived in India. These three were on my dissertation committee, and thirty years later two were on that of my son Benjamin Cohen.

38. Stephen P. Cohen and Richard L. Park, *India: Emergent Power?* (New York: Crane, Russak, and Co., 1978).

39. George Perkovich, *India's Nuclear Bomb: The Impact on Global Proliferation* (University of California Press, 1999).

40. Stephen Philip Cohen, ed., *Nuclear Proliferation in South Asia: The Prospects for Arms Control* (Boulder, Colo.: Westview, 1991). The book was a product of the Program in Arms Control, Disarmament, and International Security (which generated the acronym ACDIS, covering a variety of approaches to the subject of understanding and controlling violence). ACDIS housed the only American center for the study of Indian foreign and security policy and the training of South Asians in arms control and security matters.

41. See Regional Centre for Strategic Studies at http://rcss.org/index.php.

42. Stephen P. Cohen, *India: Emerging Power* (Brookings Institution Press, 2001).

43. See, for example, Ashley Tellis, *India's Emerging Nuclear Posture: Between Recessed Deterrent and Ready Arsenal* (Santa Monica, Calif.: RAND, 2001); Sumit Ganguly, *The Origins of War in South Asia: The Indo-Pakistani Conflicts since 1947*, 2nd ed. (Boulder, Colo.: Westview Press, 1994).

CHAPTER TWO

This chapter was originally published in *Comparative Studies in Culture and History* 6, no. 2 (January 1964), pp. 199–216.

The author is indebted to Professor A. L. Basham, University of London, and Professor Henry C. Hart, University of Wisconsin, for comments on a draft. Some references have been redacted for this reprint.

1. *Military Organization and Society* (London: Routledge and Kegan Paul, 1954).

2. Ibid., p. 429.

3. Kautilya, *Arthashastra*, trans. Dr. R. Shamasastry, 7th ed. (Mysore: Mysore Publishing House, 1961), p. 288.

4. Ibid, pp. 362–63.

5. *The Twiceborn: A Study of a Community of High-Caste Hindus* (London: Hogarth Press, 1957). See especially the first half of the book.

6. Kautilya, op. cit., pp. 319–20.

7. *Rg Veda*, X.90.

8. Bhagavad-Gita, 2.30, trans. S. Radhakrishnan, in *A Source Book in Indian Philosophy*, ed. C. A. Moore and S. Radhakrishnan (Princeton University Press, 1957), p. 109.

9. Ibid.

10. Ibid.

11. Ibid., p. 116.

12. Ibid., VII.144, p. 187.

13. "Knowledge as a sacrifice is greater than any material sacrifice . . . for all works without any exception culminate in wisdom" (Gita, 4.33, p. 119).

14. X.74–X.104, and ff.

15. Kautilya, op. cit., pp. 249, 247, 258, and ff.

16. XIII, 86.35–6, cited in A. S. Altekar, *State and Government in Ancient India* (Benares: Motilal Banarasidass, 1949), p. 101.

17. Ibid., p. 57.

18. Ibid., p. 53.

19. Ibid.

20. *A History of Indian Political Ideas* (Oxford University Press, 1959), p. 564.

21. *Edicts of Asoka*, trans. G. Srinivasa Murti and A. N. Krishna Aiyangar (Madras: Adyar Library, 1951), p. 19.

22. Ibid., pp. 19–21.

23. One punishment indicated was the wearing of white (layman's) robes.

24. Lasswell, *Psychopathology and Politics*, reprint ed. (New York: Viking Press, 1960) and Lasswell, *Power and Personality*, reprint ed. (New York: Viking Press, 1962).

25. There are exceptions to this generalization. See the Laws of Manu, VII. 8: "Even an infant king must not be despised, (from an idea) that he is a (mere) mortal; for he is a great deity in human form" (p. 186). Passages similar to this, which attribute divine origin or stature to the king, can be found throughout the Hindu literature, just as passages can be found in the Chinese literature indicating the opposite. But in practice, if not always in theory, the above was the prevalent situation.

26. Heinrich Zimmer, *Philosophies of India*, ed. Joseph Campbell (New York: Bollingen, 1951), p. 104. Quotation from *Edicts of Asoka*, introduction, p. xxxv.

27. Kautilya, op. cit., p. 32.

CHAPTER THREE

This chapter was originally published in *Comparative Studies in Society and History* 10, no. 3 (April 1968), pp. 337–55.

1. There are several accounts of the crisis from varying viewpoints. For a relatively sympathetic view of Curzon and Kitchener, respectively, see Lovat Fraser, *India under Curzon and After*, 2nd ed. (London: W. Heinemann, 1911), and Sir George Arthur, *Life of Lord Kitchener*, 3 vols. (New York: Macmillan, 1920). For recent, more critical studies, see Leonard Mosley, *The Glorious Fault* (New York: Harcourt Brace, 1960), and Philip Magnus, *Kitchener: Portrait of an Imperialist* (London: J. Murray, 1958). Dr. S. Gopal has devoted considerable attention to the dispute in *British Policy in India*, 1858–1905 (Cambridge University Press, 1965), pp. 275–91.

2. Many Indians, especially Bengalis, held this view, and regarded Curzon's removal as partial compensation to them for his action in partitioning Bengal. See the *Amrita Bazar Patrika*, August 22, 1905.

3. Curzon's most ardent supporters, such as the editor of *The Times of India*, Lovat Fraser, took this stand. Fraser wrote at the time of Curzon's resignation and Lord Minto's appointment as his successor that whether or not Lord Curzon was completely justified in his criticism, "the fact remains that unfettered militarism has won the day. The sardonic and sinister figure of Lord Kitchener bestrides India, and at his word the whole fabric of constitutional government . . . has been weakened and impaired" (editorial, August 22, 1905). Those Indian papers that did support him—they were mostly non-Congress papers in the Madras and Bombay Presidencies—did so on the grounds that Kitchener's triumph would usher in a period of increased military expenditure as well as being a victory for the military.

4. *The Times*, a powerful influence on conservative thinking, had supported Kitchener throughout the affair and was pleased to see Curzon go.

5. Balfour to St. John Brodrick, October 28, 1903. Midleton Papers, Add. MSS. 50,072. William St. John Fremantle Brodrick (1856–1942) was later the ninth Viscount Midleton and first Earl of Midleton. A conservative, he was secretary of state for India, 1903–05, and as such he was Curzon's major contact with the home government. Before this appointment he had worked closely with Kitchener as secretary of state for war.

6. In fact, Brodrick in 1905 argues against giving Curzon a high honor upon his enforced retirement after the dispute with Kitchener on the grounds that there were several cases of Curzon acting against the wishes of the government, or acting provocatively, besides those of Tibet and Afghanistan. Brodrick to Francis Knollys, September 4, 1905. Midleton Papers, Add. MSS. 50,072. Knollys was private secretary to Edward VII.

7. John Arthur Godley (1847–1932), first Baron Kilbracken, was permanent undersecretary of state for India from 1883 to 1909: he was influential throughout this period in the management of Indian affairs.

8. Godley to Curzon (copy), January 1, 1904. Kilbracken Coll., /60a.

9. Godley to Curzon (copy), January 8, 1904. Kilbracken Coll., /60.

10. Ibid.

11. Curzon to Godley, January 27, 1904. Kilbracken Coll., /60.

12. Ibid.

13. Ibid.

14. The development of an "articulate" and "powerful" public opinion did not, however, deter Curzon from offending certainly its most advanced Indian component when he partitioned Bengal to great protest. In this connection Lord Ronaldshay's comment is appropriate: "it was wholly in keeping with his almost Patriarchal conception of the relations between himself and the India of his vision, that he should have come to believe that his own judgments of what was in her interests were the judgments of the Indian people. This was the public opinion—opinion which had passed through the sieve of his own approval—which he bade the authorities in England not to ignore" (*The Life of Lord Curzon*, 3 vols. [London: Ernest Benn, Ltd, 1928], 2:420).

15. Ibid. Brodrick also argued for a consideration of "public opinion," but he meant British not Indian opinion. Brodrick to Curzon, January 20, 1905. Midleton Papers Add. MSS. 50,077.

16. Also, each argued that the other man was cowing his own dissident subordinates.

17. "A Note on the Military Policy of India" (July 19, 1905). See Magnus, op. cit., p. 223. Kitchener never really cared for the Indian army, according to Lord Roberts. Roberts to Curzon, November 2, 1913. Curzon Coll., /408.

18. Even frontier conflict was seen by Kitchener as requiring more than just Indian direction. The potential war with Afghanistan or Russia was one of vital

importance to the empire at large, he wrote, for they would require the resources of the empire but, under the existing division of labor, it would be managed by the Indian military administration. To counteract this Kitchener had advocated the removal of military policy from India and its centralization in Britain. See Kitchener's "Minute of Dissent" in the *Gazette of India Extraordinary*, June 23, 1905.

19. For a study of the patterns of action of several viceroys over one continuing crisis, the relations with Afghanistan, see D. P. Singhal, *India and Afghanistan 1876–1907* (Queensland: University of Queensland Press, 1963).

20. "Minute of Lord Curzon," *Gazette of India Extraordinary*, June 23, 1905, p. 21.

21. Ampthill to Brodrick, July 7, 1904, in "Extracts from Private Letters from Lord Ampthill to the Secretary of State for India." Curzon Coll., /400. Arthur O. V. Russell, second Baron Ampthill (1869–1935), was governor of Madras, 1900–06, and served as acting viceroy during Curzon's absence in England between his viceregal terms of office.

22. Roberts to Kitchener, June 18, 1903. Kitchener Papers, /28/GG 14. Fredrick Sleigh Roberts (1832–1914), first Earl Roberts of Kandahar, had been commander in chief, Indian army, 1885–93, and commander in chief British army, 1901–04.

23. Kitchener to Stedman (copy), March 8, 1905, 18. Curzon Coll., /400. Stedman was military secretary at the India Office; through him Brodrick and others saw the letter, written "behind my back" according to Curzon's annotation of his copy.

24. Ibid., 23.

25. Ibid., 34.

26. Kitchener to Lord Minto, January 3, 1906. Morley Papers, /39w. Morley was Brodrick's successor as secretary of state for India under the Liberals.

27. Baron Sydenham of Combe. Clarke was a strong advocate of a centralized imperial defense system and was serving at this time on the newly formed Committee of Imperial Defence.

28. Clarke to Kitchener, December 12, 1905. Kitchener Papers, /32/CC 12.

29. Dual Control (January 1906). Kitchener Papers, /32/CC 13.

30. Ibid.

31. Kitchener to Roberts (copy), November 27, 1904. Kitchener Papers, /29/Q33.

32. Kitchener to Roberts (copy), March 22, 1906. Kitchener Papers, /29/Q42.

33. Kitchener to Roberts (copy), January 26, 1905 and Kitchener to Brodrick (copy), July 15, 1904. Kitchener Papers, 29/Q40 and 32/CC 2, respectively.

34. Kitchener to Sir George Arthur, December 13, 1906. Kitchener Papers, /31/BB 38. Kitchener favored a military man for this position, and in fact held it himself—ineffectively—during World War I.

35. Summary of the Administration of Lord Curzon . . . in the Military Department (Simla, Government Central Branch Press, 1906), copy in Curzon Coll., /414.

36. "I wonder if you feel as I do that from the business point of view soldiers with rare exceptions are the most impossible men. They seem to me to be congenitally stupid. Their writing is atrocious. . . . I have a few good men. But the majority fill me with despair: and as for a Military Committee—I would as soon remit a question of State to a meeting of Eton Masters." Curzon to Brodrick, March 16, 1902. Midleton Papers, Add. MSS. 50,074. Both Curzon and Brodrick had been to Eton.

37. Curzon to Brodrick, October 2, 1903, and Curzon to Brodrick, March 3, 1904. Midleton Papers, Add. MSS. 50,074 and 50,075, respectively.

38. Speech on the Budget, Viceroy's Council, March 29, 1909. Also printed in *The Times*, April 13, 1909.

39. Kitchener to Lady Salisbury, January 25, 1903 (partial typescript copy). Kitchener Papers, /31/BB 8. This letter is quoted fully in Blanch E. C. Dugdale, *Arthur James Balfour*, 2 vols. (London: Hutchinson and Company. 1936).

40. Dugdale, op. cit.

41. Ibid.

42. Curzon to Brodrick, January 19, 1905, and Curzon to Brodrick, June 8, 1905. Midleton Papers, Add, MSS. 50,077.

43. Brodrick to Curzon (copy), June 30, 1905. Midleton Papers, Add. MSS. 50,077.

44. Godley to Curzon (copy), March 24, 1905. Kilbracken Coll., /60.

45. Ibid.

46. Ibid. See also Godley to Curzon (copy), May 11, 1905. Kilbracken Coll., /60.

47. Curzon to Godley, April 20, 1905. Kilbracken Coll., /60.

48. See Alexander L. and Juliett L. George, *Woodrow Wilson and Colonel House* (New York: J. Day, Company, 1956), and the review by Bernard Brodie, "A Psychoanalytic Interpretation of Woodrow Wilson," in *Psychoanalysis and History*, ed. Bruce Mazlish (Englewood Cliffs, N.J., Prentice-Hall, 1963), 15–23.

49. Besides his conflict with Brodrick, and through Brodrick, the home government, Curzon had several clashes with Indian politicians and with informed Indian opinion. Two acts of his were particularly self-defeating: the reform of the universities and the partition of Bengal. When Curzon was forced to resign, most Indians regretted the triumph of the military but on balance rejoiced at Curzon's downfall.

50. These spells of depression occurred in the Sudan, in South Africa, in India, and during World War I in Britain. They were severe enough to nearly incapacitate him as a decisionmaker and may have contributed to his ineffectiveness as a secretary of state for war.

51. Kitchener's public image reflected his morose personality. The public saw him as a man of gravity, seriousness, and depth, beset by enemies whom he surely overcame by his masterful ability that never verged on overt egoism.

52. Especially *Psychopathology and Politics* (New York: Viking, 1960) and *Power and Personality* (New York: Viking, 1948). Lasswell's paradigm, $p > d > r$, summarizes the development of the political type in terms of motives; private motives are displaced on public objects and then rationalized in terms of the public interest (*Power and Personality*, p. 38).

53. They are closely related to his "administrator" and "agitator" types (*Power and Personality*, pp. 62–63).

54. Ibid.

55. It should be made clear that Curzon paid little attention—especially in his second term as viceroy—to the "public opinion" of vocal, educated Indians, although he had done so in his first term. Rather, he sought to appeal to the true public of India as he saw it, the huge masses of silent villagers; in Ronaldshay's words, Curzon thought himself a "modern Joshua leading the peoples committed to his charge along their divinely appointed way" (*Life of Lord Curzon*, 2:328).

56. For discussions of this problem, see Lasswell, *Power and Personality*, 148ff., and Arnold A. Rogow, *James Forrestal: A Study of Personality, Politics and Policy* (New York: Macmillan Press, 1963), 344ff.

57. This statement is based on the observations of several senior retired British Indian army generals, including the last British commander in chief, Field-Marshall Sir Claude Auchinleck, who were interviewed in 1963. Auchinleck indicated to the author that in his judgment the "Kitchener tradition" vanished with Kitchener. He and his predecessors yielded to tight budgetary and political limitations, and even in wartime had little operational control.

58. Ray Strachey and Oliver Strachey, *Keigwin's Rebellion* (Oxford: Clarendon Press, 1916).

59. A. Mervyn Davies, *Clive of Plassey* (London: Charles Scribner's Sons, 1939).

60. Alexander Cardew, *The White Mutiny* (London: Constable, 1929).

61. Court of Proprietors of the East India Company, *Discussions between the Marquis of Dalhousie and Lieut.-Gen. Sir C. J. Napier, G.C.B.* (London: India Office Records, 1854).

CHAPTER FOUR

This chapter was originally published in *Public Affairs* 36, no. 4 (Winter 1963–64), pp. 411–29.

1. A full-length—if one-sided—treatment of the European INA has been presented in N. G. Ganpuley, *Netaji in Germany* (Bombay: Bharatiya Vidya Bha-

van, 1959). For a generally balanced history of the INA movement, see Hugh Toye, *The Springing Tiger* (London: Cassell, 1959).

2. These are British figures, apparently official. See Winston S. Churchill, *The Hinge of Fate*, vol. 4, *The Second World War* (Boston: Houghton Mifflin, 1950), p. 69; also see Lieut.-Gen. Sir Francis Tuker, *While Memory Serves* (London: Cassell, 1950), p. 69.

3. Sri Nandan Prasad, *Expansion of the Armed Forces and Defence Organisation, 1939–1949. Official History of the Indian Armed Forces in the Second World War*, gen. ed. Bisheshwar Prasad (New Delhi: Ministry of Defence, Combined Inter-Services Historical Section, 1956), p. 182ff.

4. Ibid. See also Major-Gen. Shah Nawaz [Khan], Col. Prem K. Sahgal, and Col. Gurbax Singh, *The INA Heroes* (Lahore: Hero Publications, 1946), pp. 80–81.

5. Ibid., p. 106.

6. Ibid.

7. Ibid., p. 7.

8. S. A. Ayer, *Unto Him a Witness* (Bombay: Thacker, 1951).

9. Tuker, op. cit., p. 59.

10. Ibid., pp. 53, 120.

11. Maulana Abul Kalam Azad, *India Wins Freedom* (Bombay: Longmans, 1959), p. 132.

12. Tuker, op. cit., p. 59, pp. 81 ff. See the communications addressed to Auchinleck from other senior British commanders in India urging, as did Tuker, no leniency in punishment. Auchinleck notified Wavell (and later Mountbatten) of these pressures, but apparently did not fully support this viewpoint; the political decision to opt for relative moderation in this case overrode the "purely" military course of severe punishment, especially after the INA trials had been converted into a nationalist issue. John Connell (pseudonym for John Henry Robertson), *Auchinleck* (London: Cassell, 1959), esp. pp. 803–09 and appendix 2.

13. Alan Campbell-Johnson, *Mission with Mountbatten* (New York: Dutton, 1953), pp. 52–53.

14. Humphrey Evans, *Thimayya of India* (New York: Harcourt Brace, 1960), pp. 110ff.

15. See the note of Field-Marshal Auchinleck to Defense Member Sardar Baldev Singh, January 6, 1947: "The Indian officers of the Army, already uneasy and apprehensive lest the officers of the 'INA' should be reinstated, would, I fear, regard this action [release of INA prisoners] as the thin edge of the wedge and would become increasingly nervous of their future prospects" (Connell, op. cit., p. 857).

16. Sita Ram Goel, *Netaji and the CPI* (Calcutta: Society for Defence of Freedom in Asia, 1955).

17. R. Palme Dutt, *India Today* (Bombay: Peoples Publishing House, 1947), p. 5.

18. Jayaprakash Narayan, *Toward Struggle* (Bombay: Padma Publications, 1946), pp. 44–46.

19. Ibid.

20. Major-Gen. Shahnawaz Khan, *My Memories of INA and Its Netaji* (Delhi: Rajkamal Publications, 1946).

21. Ibid. Also see Azad, op. cit., p. 133, and D. G. Tendulkar, *Mahatma* (Bombay: Times of India Press, 1953), 7:17–18. For useful information, see Bhulabhai J. Desai's address at the trials printed in his *INA Defence* (Delhi: Rajkamal Publications, 1947).

22. Azad, op cit., p. 41.

23. Ibid.

24. Mohandas K. Gandhi, *Non-Violence in Peace and War* (Ahmedabad: Navajivan Publishing House, 1942, 1949), vol. 2 (1949), p. 30.

25. Ibid.

26. Ibid, pp. 37–39.

27. Tendulkar, op cit., p. 23.

28. Kavalam Madhava Panikkar, *Problems of Indian Defence* (Bombay: Asia Publishing House, 1960), p. 27.

29. This is the conception of a pro-British, professionally officered army, led at the top by British officers (with the help of carefully selected and indoctrinated Indians). While derivative from the colonial experience, some features of this model were thought applicable to the postwar situation: most notably the maintenance of close ties between the Indian and British officer cadres, through professional and personal contacts, and the subsequent retention of British influences in Indian policymaking.

30. For a work typical of the period, dedicated to Subhas Bose and the future of a "peoples' army," see Lanka Sundaram, *India's Armies and Their Costs* (Bombay: Avanti Prakashan, 1946).

31. Even the neo-communist Blitz (Bombay) hailed the army that was the former ally of Nazi Germany and militarist Japan in a series of articles on the INA trials in late 1962.

32. See Myron Weiner, *Party Politics in India* (Princeton University Press, 1957), pp. 124–27.

33. A more optimistic interpretation of "what might have been" has been suggested by one of Bose's biographers. S. A. Ayer saw Bose's role in a free India as head of the Ministry of Defense, invigorating and encouraging the services and the nation toward greater military preparedness (Ayer, op. cit., pp. 282ff).

34. See J. A. Curran Jr., *Militant Hinduism in Indian Politics—a Study of the RSS* (New York: Institute of Pacific Relations, 1951).

35. See the provocative discussion of Menon in Welles Hangen, *After Nehru, Who?* (New York: Harcourt, Brace & World, 1963), pp. 61–105. A relative newcomer to politics, Patnaik has yet to be made the subject of detailed scrutiny, but see ibid., pp. 178, 279, and the interview with Patnaik in *The Sun* (Baltimore), March 20, 1963, held when he was in Washington, D.C., on a military mission for Nehru.

CHAPTER FIVE

This chapter was originally published in *Journal of Asian Studies* 28, no. 3 (May 1969), pp. 453–68.

1. For recent contributions to the literature, see Morris Janowitz, *The Military in the Political Development of New Nations* (University of Chicago Press, 1964); John J. Johnson, ed., *The Role of the Military in Underdeveloped Countries* (Princeton University Press, 1962); and Wilson C. McWilliams, ed., *Garrisons and Government* (San Francisco: Chandler Publishing Co., 1967).

2. For a discussion of the terminological problem, see Harold L. Isaacs, *India's Ex-Untouchables* (New York: John Day, 1964). Useful reports and monographs include the annual Report of the Commissioner for Scheduled Castes and Scheduled Tribes (forthcoming), and Andre Beteille, "The Future of the Backward Classes," in *Perspectives*, supplement to the *Indian Journal of Public Administration* 11, no. 1 (January–March 1965), pp. 1–39. For a recent study indicating academic interest in caste and untouchability in the military, see M. S. A. Rao, "Caste and the Indian Army," *Economic Weekly*, August 29, 1964.

3. I use the term *class* in the same sense as it was employed by the British. It was synonymous with clan, caste, race, or religion, and comprised the unit of recruitment. Thus a particular Hindu caste (*jati*) may have comprised a discrete military "class," but so did various categories of Muslims. Thus, Punjabi Muslims, Pathans, Deccan Muslims, and so on, were all separate "classes." The term carried with it no sense of "social" class as understood in contemporary usage, although some classes were regarded as relatively high and others relatively low.

4. For general surveys of this period, see Jadunath Sarkar, *The Military History of India* (Calcutta: M. C. Sarkar, 1960), and Maj. G. Sharma, *Indian Army through the Ages* (New Delhi: Allied, 1966).

5. The sepoy system of recruitment—originally devised by the French—represented a major accommodation to traditional society in that it meant that Indian manpower was substituted for foreign manpower, but it was modern in the sense that recruitment was relatively systematic and the officer corps was relatively professional. Sepoy armies had many of the characteristics of modern rational

hierarchies; Indian attempts to emulate the sepoy system were generally unsuccessful, the crucial factor being a unified officer corps.

6. The opinion of Sir J. Hope Grant, recorded in the *Précis of Replies Connected with the Re-Organization of the Armies of India*, Library of the Ministry of Defence, New Delhi. Grant's comments were recorded in connection with the work of the Eden Commission of 1879, which was examining the structure of the Indian military. Only Grant and two other officers specifically urged the recruitment of low-caste soldiers out of several dozen officers whose opinion was solicited. For a study of the recruitment patterns of the Bengal army, see Amiya Barat, *The Bengal Native Infantry, 1796–1852* (Calcutta: Firma K. L. Mukhopadhyay, 1962), pp. 119ff.

7. See Henry Dodwell, *Sepoy Recruitment in the Old Madras Army* (Calcutta: Indian Historical Records Commission, 1922).

8. For an informed and suitably scathing attack on this policy, see the series of articles by one of India's most remarkable students of military policy, Nirad C. Chaudhuri, "The 'Martial Races' of India," *Modern Review* (Calcutta), July–September 1930, January–February 1931.

9. Sir Patrick Cadell, *History of the Bombay Army* (London: Longmans, Green and Co., 1938), appendix 2. The British also recruited at various times Bhils, Santals, Mhairs, Moplahs, Ahirs, Minas, Christians, Kolis, and other scheduled tribes and castes.

10. The ninth Guru, Tegh Bahadur, had been slaughtered by Aurangzeb in 1675. His quartered body was snatched from a Muslim crowd in Delhi's Chandni Chowk by three Chuhras and carried back to Tegh Bahadur's son, the great Guru Govind Singh. As a reward for their effort the sweepers were admitted to the Khalsa and bestowed with the title "Mazbhi": faithful. They thus became a special sub-caste of outcastes in the Sikh community, and in fact distinguish among themselves between recent and historic converts to the faith. See A. Rose, ed., *A Glossary of the Tribes and Castes of the Punjab and North-West Frontier Province* (Lahore: Punjab Government, 1914), vol. 3.

11. Major A. E. Barstow, *Sikhs* (Government of India Central Publications Branch, 1928), pp. 74–75. This volume is one of the series of handbooks on each class recruited to the Indian army that were published periodically over several decades beginning in the late nineteenth century. At the same time a few Mazbhis were enlisted by the British for service in Pioneer regiments.

12. Lt.-Gen. Sir George MacMunn, *The History of the Sikh Pioneers* (London: Sampson Low, Marston Co., 1936), pp. 20–22. See also Lt.-Col. H. R. Brander, *32nd Sikh Pioneers: A Regimental History*, 2 vols. (Calcutta: SGP, 1906).

13. The unit histories of several untouchable regiments (all written by British officers) indicate a generally high standard of performance. So did official inspections of such units, conducted on an annual basis. See, for example, *Report of 1874*

by Maj.-Gen. A. MacDonnell (a military inspector) reprinted in Gt. Britain, HMSO, *Copy of Recent Correspondence on the Subject of the Organization of the Native Army,* 1877.

14. Lord Roberts of Kandahar, *Forty-One Years in India*, 2 vols. (London: Bentley and Son, 1897), 2:383, 441.

15. Madras was notorious as a backwater. One British officer posted to an obscure and desolate post in the Madras command made good use of his time by reading and studying before he wangled his way out: he was Winston Churchill, whose later disparaging opinion of the Indian army may have been formed at that time.

16. Anon., *Organization of the Native Army* (n.d., n.p.). This volume is a reprint of a series of articles in the *Pioneer* that originally appeared in June 1879. The copy used is in the Ministry of Defense Library, New Delhi.

17. Gen. Sir O'Moore Creagh, *Indian Studies* (London: Hutchinson & Co., n.d.), p. 233. An identical theory was propounded by Field Marshal Ayub Khan on the occasion of the signing of the new Pakistan Constitution. He noted that for the successful operation of a parliamentary system, "above all, you need a really cool and phlegmatic temperament, which only people living in cold climates seem to have" (radio broadcast, March 1, 1962, *New York Times*, March 2, 1962).

18. For World War I, see *Recruiting in India before and during the War of 1914–1918* (October 1919)—an unclassified and unpublished printed volume on file in the Archives of the Ministry of Defence Historical Section, New Delhi; also see Government of India, *The Army in India and Its Evolution* (Supt. of Government Printing, 1924). For World War II, see Sri Nandan Prasad, *Expansion of the Armed Forces and Defence Organization, 1939–45* (New Delhi: Orient Longmans, 1956), pp. 84ff.

19. Cadell, op. cit., pp. 297–98.

20. MacMunn, op. cit., p. 518.

21. Total figures by class, region, and service for the 1939–45 period are in various appendices of Prasad. Exact annual recruitment figures by absolute number and percentage are on file in the Ministry of Defence Historical Section, New Delhi.

22. For an exploration of the entire question, see Stanislaw Andrzejewski, *Military Organization and Society* (London: Routledge and Kegan Paul, 1954); specifically, see Marion J. Levy Jr., *Modernization and the Structure of Societies* (Princeton University Press, 1966), 2:600–601.

23. There are obvious parallels between the place of the untouchable and the role of the African American in American society. See Gerald D. Berreman, "Caste in India and the United States," *American Journal of Sociology* 67 (September 1960), pp. 120–27; John Dollard, *Caste and Class in a Southern Town* (Garden

City, N.J.: Doubleday, 1957). For the military parallels, see David G. Mandelbaum, *Soldier Groups and Negro Soldiers* (University of California Press, 1952); and, more recently, Charles C. Moskos Jr., "Racial Integration in the Armed Forces," *American Journal of Sociology* 75, no. 2 (September 1966), pp. 132–48. One study indicates certain parallels between Japanese Burakumin and untouchables, even in their recruitment to the military. See George De Vos and Hiroshi Wagatsuma, *Japan's Invisible Race* (University of California Press, 1966), pp. 41, 51.

24. Beteille, op. cit., p. 27.

25. At one time B. R. Ambedkar seriously considered conversion to Sikhism. The Sikh belief in meeting oppression with a "love for the cause" of martial Sikhism, and fighting back to defend one's interests held great attraction for him and other scheduled caste leaders. After negotiations with Sikh leadership, Ambedkar rejected Sikhism, fearing a second-rate status within the community. See Dhananjay Keer, *Dr. Ambedkar: Life and Mission*, 2nd ed. (Bombay: Popular Prakashan, 1962), pp. 275ff.

26. "All Sikh traditions whether national or religious are martial in times of political excitement—and to the Sikhs politics and religion are closely allied—the military spirit re-asserts itself" (Barstow, op. cit., p. 40).

27. "A Sikh Village," in *Traditional India: Structure and Change*, ed. Milton Singer (Philadelphia: American Folklore Society, 1959), p. 280.

28. Ibid.

29. Gandhi's own position was a typical blend of principle tempered by compassion. After a Harijan worker (who believed in military training) stated that "those who join the army are rid of fear and untouchability and learn of self-respect," Gandhi replied: "You have gone to the wrong man with this question. You know that I do not believe in military training. Nor do I believe with you that Harijans who join the army are so suddenly transformed. But I should not make an attempt to dissuade those Harijans who voluntarily want to enlist as recruits. If sons of the well-to-do go in for military training and if Harijans would like to follow their example, how can I prevent them? It is a difficult thing any day to teach the lesson of Ahimsa. How can one inculcate Ahimsa to those who are doubly suppressed? The wonder to me is that even among the suppressed there are some Harijans who have truly learnt the lesson of Ahimsa." See Mohandas K. Gandhi, *The Removal of Untouchability* (Ahmedabad: Navajivan Press, 1954), p. 257.

30. The government and the military are careful to praise particular classes for unusual military accomplishments or on festive occasions. See, for example, Dharm Pal, *Traditions of the Indian Army* (Delhi: Publications Division, 1961), and the military weekly *Sainik Samachar*.

31. My use of the term is somewhat different from that of William T. R. Fox in his "Representativeness and Efficiency: Dual Problems of Civil-Military Relations," *Political Science Quarterly* 76 (September 1961), pp. 354–66.

32. This is obviously the case with sweepers, menials, porters, and caretakers of animals, but is at least partly true of military bands.

33. The British took great care to separate Hindus, Sikhs, and Muslims, and saw to it that the latter group never had their own "pure" regiment. It was the classic expression of the "divide and rule" doctrine, and it also caused great difficulty for Pakistan, which received no large intact military formations.

34. Interview with a Mazbhi Sikh MP, New Delhi, 1964. My translation from Hindi.

35. Keer, op. cit., p. 8.

36. See the reply of the defense minister (Y. B. Chavan) in the Lok Sabha to charges of discrimination made by scheduled caste politicians, including a Congress Chamar. They urged the creation of a Bhil unit and the reraising of the Chamar Regiment. Chavan reiterated government policy: no new caste-based units were to be raised, and indicated that the British bore the responsibility for the disbanding of the Chamar unit. *The Hindu* (Madras), September 23, 1964.

37. This was carried to great lengths in India as British officers came to identify with relatively high-caste soldiers. This identification was carried to the extreme case of some officers who refused to permit their high-caste troops to play hockey with troops from a lower caste. This kind of ritualistic caste consciousness has practically vanished from the Indian army. For an account of the incident, see Edmund Candler, *The Sepoy* (London: John Murray, 1919), p. 47.

38. Before World War I there were situations in which high-caste soldiers were reluctant to obey orders from low-caste NCOs. The British used this fact to argue against the recruitment of all Mahars, but the latter countered by pleading for separate regiments of Mahars, or for separate companies of Mahars attached to Muslim regiments. They expected fairer treatment from the Muslims than from their Hindu coreligionists. See N. Navalkar, *The Life of Shivaram Janba Kamble* (Poona: S. J. Kamble, 1930), pp. 143–57. According to Professor Eleanor Zelliot, Mahar leadership was at one time drawn in large part from retired noncommissioned officers.

39. See David Mandelbaum, *Soldier Groups and Negro Soldiers* (University of California Press, 1952); Charles Moskos, "The Negro Soldier," in Eli Ginsberg, *The Negro Potential* (Columbia University Press, 1956).

40. The Bihar Regiment is half-Adivasi. See "Proud Record of the Bihar Regiment," *Sainik Samachar*, February 16, 1964.

41. The Sikh Light Infantry, composed of untouchable Sikhs, was formerly called the Mazbhi and Ramdasias Sikhs (M & R Sikhs), but under pressure from scheduled caste politicians the name was altered to remove what was thought to be a disparaging caste title.

42. Major R. D. Paloskar, MC, "Man-Management in Guards Battalions," *United Service Institution of India Journal* 91 (April–June 1962), pp. 107–09. A

critical rejoinder by Maj. Gulcharan Singh was printed in the *United Service Institution of India Journal* 92 (October–December 1962) letter to the editor.

43. Correctly or incorrectly, the attitude of many untouchable politicians is reflected in the statement of a young Chamar MP in an interview in 1965: "I know I could do as well as anyone else, but what about my people? Would most of them be treated fairly? Imagine a Chamar and a Brahmin applying for the same job, and being judged by Brahmin or high-caste employers. Who do you think would get the job? Don't try to tell me what would happen!" 2016: the MP was the late B. P. Maurya.

44. Absolute figures of the numbers of individuals from scheduled castes and tribes are not released by the Ministry of Defense. Percentage of increase/decrease in the number of persons of these categories are made available through the Commissioner for Scheduled Castes and Scheduled Tribes, but lacking a comparative base or starting point the figures are virtually worthless. From 1961 to 1962 the army reported a 6.82 percent gain in scheduled caste officers and a 17.83 percent gain in junior commissioned officers, warrant officers, and other ranks. Report of the Commissioner for Scheduled Castes and Scheduled Tribes, 1962–63, p. 161.

45. Levy, op. cit., 2:600–601; M. N. Srinivas, *Social Change in Modern India* (University of California Press, 1966), pp. 48, 66. Levy notes the great impact of military service on individual soldiers but also argues that this is minimized by the isolation of the military.

46. This statement is based on interviews with several dozen Indian officers of various ranks. Most acknowledge the inequalitarian implications of caste-based units but argue that India has still not reached a point where patriotism can be substituted for regional, caste, or martial traditions. As one very high-ranking "left-wing" officer of international fame put it: "for morale purposes and fighting spirit men have to be in one class; otherwise it is like having Americans, Frenchmen, Germans, Swedes in one unit, it will not work. Instead you can tell a Sikh and he will fight like a tiger, or tell a Mahratta of Shivaji, and so forth." 2016: the officer was Lieut. Gen. B. M. Kaul, interviewed in 1965.

CHAPTER SIX

This chapter was originally published as "The Military," in *Indira Gandhi's India. A Political System Reappraised*, Henry C. Hart, ed. (Boulder, Colo.: Westview Press, 1976).

1. *The Times of India* (Bombay), June 21, 1975.

2. *Hindustan Times* (New Delhi), June 25, 1975.

3. Both quotes are from the *Hindu* (Madras), June 27, 1975. The latter statement comes from Mrs. Gandhi's broadcast to the nation on June 26. After this date press censorship was imposed throughout the country.

4. *Statesman* (New Delhi), January 15, 1967.

5. For discussions of the theoretical context, see Morris Janowitz, *Sociology and the Military Establishment*, rev. ed. (New York: Sage, 1965); Samuel P. Huntington, *The Soldier and the State* (Harvard University Press, 1957).

6. For an elaboration of this, see Alfred Vagts, *A History of Militarism: Civilian and Military*, rev. ed. (New York: Meridian, 1959).

7. For the most comprehensive analysis of the meaning of militarism, see Stanislav Andreski, *Military Organization and Society* (University of California Press, 1968), pp. 184ff.

8. Jawaharlal Nehru, *Toward Freedom: The Autobiography of Jawaharlal Nehru* (New York: John Day, 1941), p. 284.

9. Jawaharlal Nehru, *The Discovery of India* (London: Meridian Books, 1969), pp. 478–79.

10. For a collection of Mahatma Gandhi's thoughts on the subject, including conversations he had with Indian officers, see Mohandas K. Gandhi, *My Non-Violence* (Ahmedabad: Navajivan Publishing House, 1960).

11. Bose left behind a large body of writings and speeches. For collections, see *Crossroads* (Bombay: Asia Publishing House, 1962) or *The Indian Struggle* (Bombay: Asia Publishing House, 1974), both published under the auspices of the Netaji Research Bureau of Calcutta.

12. Seymour M. Lipset, *Political Man* (New York: Doubleday, 1960), pp. 131ff.

13. Coined by the president of her party in a speech applauding her decision not to resign upon her initial conviction for corrupt election practices. *The Hindu*, June 19, 1975.

14. "Subhas Chandra Bose and the Indian National Army," *Pacific Affairs* 36 (Winter 1963–64), p. 429.

15. Indian Institute of Public Opinion, *Monthly Public Opinion Surveys* 19, no. 11 (August 1974), pp. 5–6. The phrase *peace bomb* was used by one of the chief scientists in the nuclear explosive program. See N. Seshagiri, *The Bomb!* (New Delhi: Vikas, 1975).

16. A number of retired Indian generals and bureaucrats have published their memoirs. For a review of some of the literature, see Stephen P. Cohen, "India's China War and After: A Review Article," *Journal of Asian Studies* 30 (August 1971), pp. 847–57.

17. The most important of the many Indian military professional journals, published by the United Services Institution of India (USI), has an article on the subject in almost every quarterly issue. These have examined such issues as cantonments, the junior commissioned officer (a unique South Asian military rank), politics in the military, and the need to reconcile military practices with ideological and social developments in India.

18. For an explicit comparison, see Stephen P. Cohen, *Arms and Politics in Bangladesh, India, and Pakistan, Special Study no. 49* (Buffalo, N.Y.: SUNY Council on International Studies, 1973).

19. For a contemporary Indian study by a senior Indian Civil Service official, see Nagendra Singh, *The Theory of Force and Organization of Defense in Indian Constitutional History* (Bombay: Asia Publishing House, 1969).

20. Stephen P. Cohen, *The Indian Army* (University of California, 1971), chap. 5.

21. Ibid., pp. 117–18.

22. This is a judgment of a number of British and Indian officers who had a chance to observe the products of both Sandhurst and the IMA, and is supported by internal studies of battle performance in World War II.

23. Cohen, *The Indian Army*, pp. 152ff.

24. A number of retired Indian generals have discussed the moral dilemmas of serving a foreign master, most notably B. M. Kaul, *The Untold Story* (Bombay: Allied Publishers, 1967), part 1, and K. S. Thimayya. For the latter, see Humphrey Evans, *Thimayya of India* (New York: Harcourt Brace, 1960), pp. 180–81.

25. The most recent head of the Indian Army (T. N. Raina) received an emergency commission in 1942 after attending college. Despite his rudimentary military training he performed with distinction in World War II and several subsequent wars.

26. The best guide to the organizational and legal frameworks in which the military function in India is A. L. Venkateshwaran, *Defense Organization in India* (New Delhi: India, Publications Division, 1967). Although ostensibly a popular history of defense issues, it is clearly designed to serve as a handbook for civilian bureaucrats who must deal with the military.

27. Ibid. See also Maharaj K. Chopra, *India: The Search for Power* (Bombay: Lalvani, 1969).

28. Exact figures for officer recruitment are unavailable. This judgment is based on an examination of casualty figures in various wars, government statements, and visits to various Indian military establishments.

29. For a critical discussion of the incongruity of some of the Indian army's British and authoritarian traditions, including the swagger stick, see Group Captain K. D. Singh, "Coercion to Coaction," *USI Journal* 102 (July–September 1972), pp. 236–53.

30. Of the Indian army chiefs since Independence there have been two Coorgis (Cariappa, 1949–53, and Thimayya, 1957–61), two Tamils (Shrinagesh, 1955–57, and Kumaramangalam, 1966–69), a Rajput from Gujarat (Maharaj Rajendra Sinhji, 1953–55), a Punjabi Hindu (Thapar, 1961–62), a Bengali (Chaudhuri, 1962–66), a Parsi (Maneckshaw, 1969–73), a Maharashtrian (Bewoor, 1973–75), and a Kashmiri (Raina, 1975–present). Thus, only Thapar came from the region

that supplies the most soldiers and has a historic connection with the Indian army. There has never been a Sikh COAS.

31. For a summary of Raina's career, see the article by "M. S." in *Illustrated Weekly of India* (Bombay), June 8, 1975. For details about the earlier controversies, see Lorne Kavic, *India's Quest for Security* (University of California Press, 1967), pp. 154ff.

32. A recent government press release boasts that India now has the world's fourth-largest army, fifth- or sixth-largest air force, and eighth- or ninth-largest navy. *Hindustan Times*, October 31, 1975.

33. The latter has usually been for the purpose of training in advanced or new equipment acquired from abroad—most recently from the Soviet Union. The Indian armed forces also routinely train a large number of foreign officers and technicians, particularly from Nepal, Bangladesh, and various Middle Eastern countries.

34. Figures on foreign military assistance to India can be found in U.S. Arms Control and Disarmament Agency, *World Military Expenditures and Arms Trade, 1963–73* (U.S. Government Printing Office, 1974).

35. For a partial description, see Venkateshwaran, op. cit., and some of the annual reports of the Ministry of Defense. A more comprehensive and technical handbook is Brig. Rajendra Singh, *Organization and Administration in the Indian Army* (New Delhi: Army Educational Stores, various editions).

36. For example, Col. R. Rama Rao (ret.), "Defense Planning and Preparations—New Imperatives," *USI Journal* 102 (January–March 1972), pp. 3–12.

37. The book that best conveys the frustration and anger of those Indian officers involved in the 1962 war is Brig. John P. Dalvi, *Himalayan Blunder* (Bombay: Thacker, 1969). Dalvi's account is based on his own experiences. More recently, see Brig. J. Nazareth, "If We Rest We Rust," *USI Journal* 102 (July–September 1972), pp. 231ff.

38. This works well when, as in 1971, there is sufficient time for the military to digest what is expected of them and for political leaders to learn what is within the realm of military feasibility. It does not work well when war arises suddenly or no decisive outcome can be expected.

39. K. Subrahmanyam, until recently the director of the Institute of Defense Studies and Analyses, has written perceptively of the problem from an Indian point of view. See his *Perspectives in Defense Planning* (New Delhi: Abhinav, 1972).

40. For a recent evaluation of the militarization of Indian and Pakistan foreign policy, see Stephen P. Cohen, "Security Issues in South Asia," *Asian Survey* 15 (March 1975), pp. 203–15.

41. India has yet to produce an adequate high-performance fighter-bomber, a reliable air transport, or tanks in adequate numbers. But even some imported

systems, such as the Sukhoi 7, seem to be very bad bargains. For a recent critical evaluation of the entire arms procurement problem by a former senior official in the Ministry of Defense, see V. Shankar, "Defense Needs of India," *USI Journal* 104 (January–March 1974), pp. 1–6.

42. See Dalvi, op. cit., and Lt. Gen. B. M. Kaul, *The Untold Story* (New Delhi: Allied, 1967). Kaul, one of those generals most responsible for the debacle, once admitted to this writer (in 1965) that he still could not figure out why the Chinese had attacked.

43. "The manner in which the army was emasculated by furthering the cause of careers of political generals and breaking competent ones, in the years which culminated in our humiliating defeat in 1962, is a striking example" of the interference of politicians, and "is a weakness . . . apt to reoccur in a democracy such as ours" (Nazareth, op. cit., p. 231).

44. Neville Maxwell may have had access to the Henderson-Brooks report, and it might be that document he quoted in *India's China War* (London: Jonathan Cape, 1970). For a full discussion, see Cohen, "India's China War and After."

45. This separation of civil and military authority has been vigorously criticized by a former secretary in the Ministry of Defense, P. V. R. Rao. See his *Defense without Drift* (Bombay: Popular Prakashan, 1970).

46. Exemplified by Maj. Gen. D. K, Palit (ret.), *The Lightning Campaign: The Indo-Pakistan War, 1971* (New Delhi: Thomson Press, 1972).

47. There are, of course, only oblique references to this in the Indian literature, but Pakistani authors claim that the Indian-supported guerrilla struggle was proving ineffective. For an authoritative Pakistani perspective, see Maj. Gen. Fazal Muqeem Khan (ret.), *Pakistan's Crisis in Leadership* (Islamabad: National Book Foundation, 1973). Khan is now secretary in the Pakistan Ministry of Defense. The mainstream of Indian military thought has always given guerrilla warfare a low priority, and it would not be surprising to discover that their guerrilla campaign was ineffective.

48. Every year the Ministry of Defense lists such activities. They are also extensively covered in the Indian press and the military's own popular weekly magazine, *Sainik Samachar*, published in a dozen languages.

49. For a thoughtful discussion, see Brig. N. B. Grant, "London Cantonment, Dear," *USI Journal* 192 (January–March 1972), pp. 40–45.

50. Maj. Gen. S. K. Sinha, "In Aid of the Civil Power," *USI Journal* 104 (April–June 1974), p. 117. This article is a typical example of discussions on aid to the civil that have appeared in Indian professional military journals for almost fifty years, as each generation passes on its knowledge and interpretation of the problem to the next.

51. Ibid., p. 115.

52. As any tourist can see, Srinagar resembles an armed camp. Nagaland and Mizoram are off-limits to virtually all outsiders, and the struggle still continues

in the region. A recently announced "truce" in Nagaland is one of many that have been concluded in the past fifteen years.

53. As reported in *The New York Times*, October 24, 1974.

54. The point was made quite bluntly by G. G. Bewoor, shortly before he became COAS. Bewoor linked Pakistan's defeat in 1971 directly to the Pakistan army's extensive involvement in "civil works" and "civil administration," warning that the same thing could happen in India if the military were diverted from its primary defense role. *The Times of India*, September 10, 1972.

55. Sinha claims that the Indian army chose to retain olive green after World War II so that it would not be mistaken for the police, who wore khaki (op. cit., p. 116).

56. For one brief study of the event, see A. D. Pandit, "Uttar Pradesh: The Roots of the P. A. C. Mutiny," *Monthly Public Opinion Survey* 18, no. 8 (May 1973), pp. 6–8.

57. The Garhwali Mutiny of 1930 (largely the fault of poor British leadership) was the other incident.

58. Sinha, op. cit., p. 120.

59. Generally, the military is content with present levels of manpower and technology; it might well be, considering the resources lavished on it in comparison with other Indian bureaucracies and services. Indeed, much of the poor performance of lethargic sectors of India could be improved simply by an increase in resources unaccompanied by an increase in responsibility.

60. For example, Karl von Clausewitz, *On War* (New York: Modern Library, 1943), p. 9; and a recent discussion in Bernard Brodie, *War and Politics* (New York: Macmillan, 1973), pp. 1–28.

61. Bansi Lai, appointed minister of defense in late 1975, is a man with no apparent qualifications for the post other than his very close ties to Mrs. Gandhi and her son Sanjay. However, he does come from a state with strong military interests (Haryana), where he was chief minister.

62. In the recent Bangladesh coup, for example, personal considerations interacted in the minds of the professional military with perceptions of threat. For discussion of the intervention problem, see S. E. Finer, *The Man on Horseback* (London: Pall Mall Press, 1962); Edward Luttwak, *Coup d'état* (London: Penguin Press, 1968); Claude E. Welch Jr. and Arthur K. Smith, eds., *Military Role and Rule* (Belmont, Calif.: Wadsworth, 1974); and Wilson C. McWilliams, ed., *Garrisons and Government* (San Francisco: Chandler, 1967).

63. In a discussion that exactly anticipates the caution exercised by the Indian military in response to Narayan's call for disobedience of illegal orders, Huntington writes that the professional soldier, when confronted with this situation, is advised to wait until a decision is reached by the judiciary, "whose function it is to decide such issues" (op. cit., pp. 77–78). He describes other situations in which the military must consider disobedience: urgent crises when the judiciary cannot

be consulted, immoral orders, and militarily impossible orders by ignorant or incompetent civilians.

64. Cohen, *The Indian Army*, pp. 124ff. The officer corps may not be convinced that *it* is a fully integrated national military. This is the same view that was held by the officer corps in Pakistan, Indonesia, Egypt, and other states that have experienced military takeovers.

65. As far as the military are concerned the politically most sensitive region encompasses the Punjab, Haryana, western Uttar Pradesh, and Delhi, which together supply a disproportionate number of jawans and officers. However, these regions are well represented among Indira Gandhi's supporters, are among the most prosperous regions in India, and would have little incentive to dream of autonomy or independence even were India to suffer massive dislocations or disruptions.

66. The first full-scale study of the Pakistan army is Hasan Askari Rizvi, *The Military and Politics in Pakistan* (Lahore: Progressive Publishers, 1974).

67. The coup of August 15, 1975, was led by professional officers who feared that they would be balanced by the Rakhi Bahini and eventually displaced. Their image of the defense requirements of Bangladesh were largely derived from their Pakistani and American training.

68. The "National Discipline Scheme" was run by an ex-INA general for several years, but was disbanded. Plans to introduce a compulsory National Cadet Corps have not been implemented. If India were to veer toward an authoritarian or totalitarian direction, one would expect the revival of such programs. The military might view them with great skepticism.

69. A new truce with the Nagas has been announced (December 1975), but this may be a temporary respite, due to the worsening situation in Bangladesh.

70. Cohen, *Arms and Politics*, p. 47.

71. Since the Indian media are entirely censored by the government of India itself, such pressure would clearly be part of an orchestrated public relations campaign, and would mean that the government had already decided to intervene.

72. In recent years the defense budget has crept to more than $2 billion, although on a per capita basis India ranks near the bottom of the scale of all nations. There are few serious analyses of the defense budget in the Indian literature, but see *Vikrant's Defense Diary* (New Delhi), March 1975. A major study of the defense burden of India, in comparison with other states, is Emile Benoit, *Defense and Economic Growth in Developing Countries* (Lexington, Mass.: Lexington Books, 1973).

73. For a blunt assessment see Shankar, op. cit., pp. 5ff.; and Rao, "Defense Planning and Preparations," pp. 3–12.

74. In fact, the inclusion of nuclear weapons in India's arsenal will require a substantial improvement in conventional forces to increase their mobility and communications facilities, both expensive items. Pressure for the development of

nuclear weapons did not come from the military. For an extremely hawkish evaluation of the Indian nuclear program by a retired naval officer, see Ravi Kaul, *India's Nuclear Spinoff* (Allahabad: Chanakya, 1974).

75. Shankar, op. cit.

76. Speculation about Indian politics has already become closer to Kremlinology or Peking-watching than anything else. Indian politics have become a variety of "palace" politics, dominated by rumor, uncertainty, surprise, and secretiveness. I have some degree of confidence in these conclusions with respect to the military as an institution, but as Gandhi's political opponents have discovered, predicting her political behavior is infinitely more difficult.

CHAPTER SEVEN

This chapter was originally published in Onkar Marwah and Jonathan D. Pollack, eds., *Military Power and Policy in Asian States: China, India, Japan* (Boulder, Colo.: Westview Press, 1980). Referred to as Marwah/Pollack in the text below. All tables are omitted.

1. Heinrich von Treitschke, *Politik* (Leipzig: Max Cornelius, 1897), 1:38. For a careful discussion of the power politics school, see Raymond Aron, *Peace and War* (New York: Praeger, 1968), pp. 585ff.

2. An inventory of these limits is contained in Ellen P. Stern, ed., *The Limits of Military Intervention: Contemporary Dimensions* (Beverly Hills: Sage, 1977). See especially chapter 7, "Epilogue," by Morris Janowitz.

3. This viewpoint is expressed in a number of books and publications, but most consistently by those of the Stockholm International Peace Research Institute. See, for example, SIPRI, *Armaments and Disarmament in the Nuclear Age: A Handbook* (Stockholm: Almqvist and Wiksell, 1976).

4. Morton A. Kaplan, "Current Issues in European Security" (paper presented to the Chicago Council on Foreign Relations, May 1977); Ray S. Cline, *World Power Assessment: A Calculus of Strategic Drift* (Washington, D.C.: Center for Strategic and International Studies, 1975). Kaplan writes: "The geopolitical world of which Sir Halford Mackinder once wrote has now become a reality. John Nicholas Spykman's intra–World War II recommendation that only by controlling the peripheral areas could the U.S. contain the central power has become the critical reality of the new international geopolitical system" (p. 1). Also see his contributions in Morton A. Kaplan, ed., *Isolation or Interdependence?* (New York: Free Press, 1975), especially pp. 15, 31.

5. Cline, op. cit., pp. 133ff.

6. There is now a substantial literature on the determination of hierarchy and relative status among nations. For an introduction, see Michael D. Wallace, *War*

and Rank among Nations (Lexington, Mass.: D.C. Heath, 1973); Steven L. Spiegel, *Dominance and Diversity: The International Hierarchy* (Boston: Little, Brown, 1972); and George Modelski, *World Power Concentrations: Typology, Data, Explanatory Framework* (Morristown, N.J.: General Learning Press, 1974).

7. *Politics and Culture in International History* (Princeton University Press, 1960), p. 389.

8. Denis Sinor, quoted in ibid., p. 398. See also Carlo M. Cipolla, *Guns, Sails, and Empires: Technological Innovation and the Early Phases of European Expansion, 1400–1700* (New York: Pantheon, 1965).

9. For the most thorough treatment of the subject, see the work of Klaus Knorr, especially *The Power of Nations* (New York: Basic Books, 1975).

10. Emile Benoit, *Defense and Economic Growth in Developing Countries* (Lexington, Mass.: D.C. Heath, 1973), pp. 162ff. See also Henry J. Barbera, *Rich Nations and Poor in Peace and War* (Lexington, Mass.: D.C. Heath, 1973), p. 126. Barbera concludes that the two total wars of this century "have neither helped nor hindered development or noticeably affected the inequalities between rich nations and poor," although poorer nations may benefit from the integrative effects of war more than richer ones.

11. Military and paramilitary groups take up a wide variety of productive and "nation-building" tasks in China.

12. A useful corrective to the "superstate" syndrome, which has exaggerated this base, is in John K. Emmerson, *Arms, Yen and Power* (Tokyo: Tuttle, 1972).

13. For full-length studies, see Robert A. Scalapino, *Asia and the Road Ahead* (University of California Press, 1975); Wayne Wilcox, Leo Rose, and Gavin Boyd, eds., *Asia and the International System* (Cambridge, Mass.: Winthrop Publishers, 1972).

14. Pakistan's dilemma is acute and growing worse with each passing year. Several years ago a united Pakistan would have been a candidate for inclusion in this volume as a "near great" state. Today, truncated, it is unable to order its domestic affairs and is at the mercy of India. Recent (June 1977) reports of the withdrawal of French support for a major nuclear program make Pakistan's position even more precarious. (2016: Pakistan eventually received support for its nuclear program from China, as well as stealing critical plans from Europe; it obtained political cover for the program when it became a vital front after the Soviet invasion of Afghanistan in December 1979.)

15. For example, the implicit hope in the ACDA project title, "India and Japan: The Emerging Balance of Power in Asia and Opportunities for Arms Control, 1970–75," prepared by Columbia University, 1970. The final project conclusion was that, indeed, there was little if any opportunity for cooperation between India and Japan in terms of the Asian balance of power. (2016: The idea of U.S.-India-Japan strategic cooperation was revived after the 2005 U.S.-India civilian nuclear agreement.)

16. The Indian navy's inventory now includes almost thirty destroyers and frigates, plus a number of patrol boats, many of which are armed with sophisticated ship-to-ship missiles; without its full protective screen such a major ship as the *Enterprise* would run a substantial risk if it were facing a hostile Indian navy.

17. For an overview of the subject of perception and image, see two excellent studies by Robert Jervis, *The Logic of Images in International Relations* (Princeton University Press, 1970) and *Perception and Misperception in International Politics* (Princeton University Press, 1976).

18. John Steadman, *The Myth of Asia* (New York: Simon and Schuster, 1969), p. 25; Harold Isaacs, *Scratches on Our Minds* (New York: Harper, 1958). See also Ignacy Sachs, *The Discovery of the Third World* (MIT Press, 1976).

19. This was a favorite theme of many colonial powers even as they recruited their imperial armies from the more warlike and militant groups in several Asian societies. In India, for example, the British often proclaimed their reluctance to depart on the grounds that the Punjab would come to dominate the rest of the subcontinent; this has come to pass in Pakistan, although not in India.

20. "Quarterback Nixon's Asian Game Plan," *The New Republic*, February 19, 1972.

21. This is one of the assumptions of much of the so-called nation building literature. For an excellent study of the politics of predevelopment or underdevelopment versus the politics of development, see Gerald A. Heeger, *The Politics of Underdevelopment* (New York: St. Martin's, 1974); and for the role of foreign policy in such systems see Howard Wriggins, *The Ruler's Imperative* (Columbia University Press, 1969), pp. 221–38.

22. I omit any discussion of such events as crises in political succession, major calamities, floods, famine, and so forth, because these states—even India and China—are capable of managing such crises. However, perceptions of such events by outsiders are important, and will be considered below. Of particular interest is the different ways in which India and China have permitted outsiders to observe the effects of natural calamities.

23. In the words of Rep. Clarence Long, testifying before the Nuclear Regulatory Commission hearing on the supply of enriched uranium to India, "I wouldn't trust any commitment that the Indian government as presently constituted made . . . India has demonstrated its bad faith . . . India is becoming a police state . . . [it] is practically moving towards a totalitarian police state. For us to be encouraging this sort of development, to be helping it in any way, I think is a reflection on our good faith as a country which claims to be the chief sponsor of democratic regimes in the world" (NRC, Hearing in the Matter of Edlow International Company, Docket No. 70-2131, Tuesday, July 20, 1976, pp. 21, 22, 26 of transcript). In fact, a decision to ship the uranium was not reached until after Gandhi was defeated in 1977, despite the State Department's advice that there was a long-standing commitment to do so (p. 127).

24. There seems to be an emerging consensus on the rationality of democratic systems that is opposite (but not all that different) from former president Nixon's belief in the relative stabilizing influence of right-wing as opposed to left-wing dictatorships.

25. Pakistan is particularly vulnerable. The United States has effectively ceased supplying major weapons since 1966, although the slack was taken up by China. Now, with an emerging China-India rapprochement and a U.S. refusal to sell even subsonic attack aircraft to Pakistan (the A-7D), Pakistan must attempt to meet its requirements from a European seller (France or Great Britain) or the Soviet Union. The disadvantage of the former is that there are no broader political gains attached to sales, while the disadvantage of the latter is that unacceptable terms (such as agreement to the Indian position in Kashmir) may be imposed. According to G. Choudhury, this was in fact the condition for earlier Soviet arms supplies. See *India, Pakistan, Bangladesh, and the Major Powers* (New York: Free Press, 1975), p. 68. (2016: As noted, Pakistan's position was transformed when it became a "frontline" state in the effort to oust the Soviet Union from Afghanistan after 1980. The effort succeeded, but one unforeseen consequence was Pakistan's transformation because of an influx of drugs, guns, and radical Islamic ideologies.)

26. A useful pairing of the two approaches is in Ted Greenwood, Harold A. Feiveson, and Theodore B. Taylor, *Nuclear Proliferation* (New York: McGraw-Hill, 1977). See also Ted Greenwood, George Rathjens, and Jack Ruina, "Nuclear Power and Weapons Proliferation," in *Adelphi Paper no. 130* (London: International Institute for Strategic Studies, 1976).

27. Stephen P. Cohen, "U.S. Weapons and South Asia: A Policy Analysis," *Pacific Affairs* 49 (Spring 1976), pp. 49–69.

28. For two surveys, see James Digby, "Precision-Guided Weapons," in *Adelphi Paper no. 118* (London: International Institute for Strategic Studies, 1975); and Richard Burt, *New Weapons Technologies, Adelphi Paper no. 126* (London: International Institute for Strategic Studies, 1976). An earlier, broader survey of a future system is contained in several chapters of Nigel Calder, ed., *Unless Peace Comes: A Scientific Forecast of New Weapons* (New York: Viking, 1968).

29. Burt, op. cit., p. 4.

30. We cannot do justice to the argument in a short space, but George Quester has written an excellent guide to the problem, with a sound historic framework, in *Offense and Defense in the International System* (New York: John Wiley, 1977), pp. 183ff. See also Robert Jervis, "Cooperation under the Security Dilemma" (Center for Arms Control and International Security, UCLA, Working Paper no. 4, April 1977).

31. For a critique of our "arms controller" approach by a fervent advocate of "disarmament," see Alva Myrdal, *The Game of Disarmament: How the U.S. and Russia Run the Arms Race* (New York: Pantheon, 1976).

32. Laid out in full by Ashok Kapur in *India's Nuclear Option* (New York: Praeger, 1976).

33. Lewis A. Dunn has explored the latter issue in "Nuclear 'Gray Marketeering," *International Security* 1 (Winter 1977), pp. 107–18.

34. Spiegel, op. cit., p. 252.

35. See his *Footsteps into the Future* (New York: Free Press, 1975), pp. 135ff. and appendix.

36. Michael Wallace's study seems to indicate an order of magnitude of ten to fifteen years between enhancement of capability and status recognition (op. cit., pp. 52–53).

CHAPTER EIGHT

Abbreviated version published as "U.S. Security in a Separatist Season," *Bulletin of the Atomic Scientists* 48, no. 6 (July 1992), pp. 28–32.

CHAPTER NINE

This chapter was originally published in Joseph S. Nye, ed., *New Threats: Responding to the Proliferation of Nuclear, Chemical and Delivery Capabilities in the Third World* (originally presented to the Aspen Strategy Group Aspen, Colo., August 1989), pp. 163–95.

1. For an analysis of the spread of advanced missile technologies, particularly improvements in accuracy, see Janne Nolan and Albert Wheelon, "Ballistic Missiles in the Third World," in Nye, op. cit., appendix 3.

2. The Soviets have had to defend the Yalta agreement during Indo-Soviet discussions on nuclear arms control. See K. Subrahmanyam and Jasjit Singh, eds., *Security without Nuclear Weapons: Indo-Soviet Dialogue* (Delhi: Lancer International, 1986), p. 212.

3. The response of a generation of regional scientists and engineers is exemplified in the remark of a Pakistani nuclear scientist to his former teacher at my university. Upon returning to Urbana for a short visit in the late 1970s, he boasted: "Ah! You thought that you were the only ones who could do this—but we can also. You'll see what we are capable of—we'll show you how good we are."

4. House of Representatives, Committee on Foreign Affairs, Hearings, April 27, 1981, pp. 118ff.

5. This also had a strategic dimension. At the same moment, American policymakers saw the regional approach as a chance to reduce Indian dependence on

the Soviet Union while Indians claim credit for their "opening to Washington." Both views are correct; both sides were driven by the logic of a complex, five-sided strategic game and might have moved in this direction even if the nuclear factor had not existed.

6. One senior American official (the late Arnold Raphel, who was a key architect of the Pakistan policy and who died in an air crash in Pakistan while ambassador to Islamabad) told me that the difficulty of keeping any long-term plans secret was also a factor in the absence of long-term planning.

7. There were actually several other opponents to the regional approach; I circulated a memo to other officials in 1987 likening the opposition of various government bureaus to the story of the five blind men trying to describe the "elephant" of regional proliferation: each saw a different and partial view of the problem; none could agree on a common strategy that combined nonproliferation interests and their own special concerns.

8. Inder Malhotra writes that the language of the joint communiqué invalidates Soviet obligations to aid India against China, since it commits the Soviet Union and China not to use force or the threat of force against each other in any manner including through the use of the "territory, territorial waters and air space of any third country adjacent to the other" (*India Abroad*, June 16, 1989).

9. For discussions of Pakistani nuclear objectives, see the two books by Akhtar Ali, *Pakistan's Nuclear Dilemma* (Karachi: Pakistan Economist Research Unit, 1984) and *South Asia: Nuclear Stalemate or Conflagration* (Karachi: Research on Armament and Poverty, 1987); see also Stephen P. Cohen, *The Pakistan Army* (University of California Press, 1984).

10. The similarity between the Pakistani and the Israeli programs is by design. Whereas India defended its program and its option, on principles of self-reliance and national sovereignty, Pakistani officials closely studied the Israeli–U.S. connection and utilized the loopholes created for Israel to shield their own program.

11. Even Nehru left the option open by approving an experimental reprocessing facility; this facility produced the plutonium used in the 1974 Pokhran test.

12. For a discussion of alternatives subsumed under the option strategy—ranging from genuine uncertainty about the future to a specific end point, after which weaponization would occur—see Stephen P. Cohen, *Perception, Influence, and Weapons Proliferation in South Asia* (Department of State, Office of External Research, Bureau of Intelligence and Research, 1979).

13. This position has been most fully articulated by Pierre Gallois, Kenneth Waltz, and, in South Asia, K. Subrahmanyam.

14. Several pieces by Michael Intriligator and Dagobert Brito examine this issue. For example Intriligator and Brito, "Nuclear Proliferation and Stability," *Journal of Peace Science* 3, no. 2 (Fall 1978), pp. 173–83.

15. For one estimate, widely discussed in India and Pakistan, see Rashid Naim, "Asia's Day After," appendix 2, *The Security of South Asia: Asian and American Perspectives*, ed. Stephen P. Cohen (University of Illinois Press, 1987), pp. 251–82.

16. Of course, consistency is important in dealing with foreign governments, as well. Our shifting policies toward Pakistan have made that state distrustful of American motives and have confused other important states such as India: Washington ignored Pakistan's regional strategic role because of its opposition to Islamabad's bomb; after the Soviet invasion, this was reversed, and we began to tolerate the bomb because of Pakistan's regional importance. Now, in 1989, because Pakistan's bomb program is so delicately poised (and a nuclear Pakistan would create many problems in and out of the region) Washington seems to be willing to tolerate and support Pakistan's regional policies to retain some leverage over its nuclear decisions.

17. These mileposts include the impending certification of the Pakistan nuclear program (October 1989), which will require the president to assure Congress that Pakistan does not possess a nuclear weapon; the next NPT review conference (1990); and the expiration of the U.S.–Indian agreement on Tarapur (1992), which places restraints on India's use of the vast stocks of plutonium contained in Tarapur's unreprocessed spent fuel.

18. There are conditions that would make a Pakistani nuclear force highly vulnerable. Dispersing Pakistani nuclear weapons will create real problems of command and control, as Zia acknowledged to me in mid-1988. Under conditions of internal disorder, dispersed nuclear weapons may become the target of factions in one or more of the armed services. This scenario may be intolerable for Islamabad's neighbors, and Pakistan's lack of depth means that its nuclear facilities, airfields, and missile fields will be vulnerable to accurate conventional attacks (India may have, or will soon have, target location through use of satellite imaging).

19. There are other elements of this policy. American support must also be conditional on India continuing to pursue a generally nonconfrontational policy toward Asia's other nuclear and near-nuclear states.

20. *Washington Post*, October 29, 1985.

21. It might begin with talks about containing or preventing the proliferation of chemical and biological weapons. Indian firms have sold chemical precursors to Iran, and the Indian government has reacted strongly and negatively. *The New York Times*, July 1, 1989.

22. There should be no surprise at the reported statement of a U.S. official who did not know where the 5 percent restriction on Pakistani enrichment had come from. Because of the fragmented nature of the U.S. record-keeping system, no single bureau or office has a complete record of regional nonproliferation policy. *Washington Post*, June 15, 1989.

23. It might begin with talks about containing or preventing the proliferation of chemical and biological weapons. Indian firms have sold chemical precursors to Iran, and the Indian government has reacted strongly and negatively. *New York Times*, July 1, 1989.

24. This ambivalence—being alternatively fascinated and terrorized by these devices—communicates itself to the strategists of India and Pakistan. They skillfully exploit our qualms about our nuclear programs to justify their own.

CHAPTER TEN

This chapter was originally published in *The State, Religion, and Ethnic Politics: Afghanistan, Iran, and Pakistan*, ed. Ali Banuazizi and Myron Weiner (Syracuse University Press, 1986), pp. 299–332.

1. "The state" is not a mythical entity, but achieves concrete expression in the various institutions that purport to act on behalf of the state and its interests. See Ernst Cassirer, *The Myth of the State* (New York: Anchor, 1955).

2. Samuel P. Huntington, *Political Order in Changing Societies* (Yale University Press, 1968).

3. Katherine Chorley, *Armies and the Art of Revolution* (Boston: Beacon Press, 1973), p. 243. For a similar view, see Stanislav Andreski, *Military Organization and Society* (University of California Press, 1968).

4. See Arend Lijphart, *Democracy in Plural Societies: A Comparative Exploration* (Yale University Press, 1977).

5. A recent rediscovery of this integrated into a broader theoretical and historical framework is presented by Theda Skocpol, *States and Social Revolutions: A Comparative Analysis of France, Russia, and China* (Cambridge University Press, 1979), p. 30. See also Eric A. Nordlinger, *On the Autonomy of the Democratic State* (Harvard University Press, 1981).

6. Elias Canetti, *Crowds and Power*, trans. Carol Stewart (New York: Seabury Press, 1978), p. 141.

7. See William L. Richter, "The Political Dynamics of Islamic Resurgence in Pakistan," *Asian Survey* 19, no. 6 (June 1979), pp. 547–57.

8. There are many studies of this process and of the breakup of Pakistan in 1971. For a Bangladeshi perspective, see Rounaq Jahan, *Pakistan: Failure in National Integration* (Columbia University Press, 1972); for an informed military analysis, see Fazal Muqeem Khan, *Pakistan's Crisis in Leadership* (Islamabad: National Book Foundation, 1972).

9. Selig S. Harrison has discussed this at length; see *In Afghanistan's Shadow: Baluch Nationalism and Soviet Temptations* (New York: Carnegie Endowment for International Peace, 1981).

10. The states that might be most concerned include two of Pakistan's neighbors, Iran and India. The latter is currently witnessing in the Punjab and Assam two major ethnic/linguistic disputes.

11. There has not, however, been the kind of agreement found in Lebanon and several European democracies and other states, which Lijphart would term *consociational.*

12. There are a number of excellent recent books about Pakistani political and administrative institutions. See Lawrence Ziring, *Pakistan: The Enigma of Political Development* (Boulder, Colo.: Westview Press, 1980); Henry F. Goodnow, *The Civil Service of Pakistan* (Yale University Press, 1969).

13. Karl von Vorys, *Political Development in Pakistan* (Princeton University Press, 1965), p. 124.

14. Ibid., p. 125.

15. Bhutto's own writings demonstrate some of this ambition; for the best biography and political analysis, see Salmaan Taseer, *Bhutto: A Political Biography* (London: Ithaca Press, 1979); Shahid Javed Burki, *Pakistan under Bhutto, 1971–1977* (New York: St. Martin's Press, 1980).

16. About 100 of the 288 named members of the Majlis came from legally defunct political parties, including as many as sixty members of Bhutto's People's Party. For a discussion, see Marvin G. Weinbaum and Stephen P. Cohen, "Pakistan in 1982: Holding On," *Asian Survey* 23, no. 2 (February 1983), pp. 123–32.

17. 2016: This comment and some others have been overtaken by events, but the overall analysis stands. For good updates on Pakistani politics, see several books cited in the epilogue, especially those by Haqqani, Jaffrelot, Lieven, and my own *Idea of Pakistan.*

18. Karachi Domestic Radio, Foreign Broadcast Information Service, January 22, 1983.

19. The laws of evidence draft was summarized in *Overseas Dawn*, March 10, 1983, which also carried the text of the telegram and the names of the signatories on April 14, 1983.

20. See Agence France-Press reports of March 26 and 29, 1983, in Foreign Broadcast Information Service, March 28 and April 1, 1983.

21. *Overseas Dawn*, May 19, 1983.

22. Some of the following is based on Stephen P. Cohen, *The Pakistan Army* (University of California Press, 1984).

23. An exception and an important ethnic halfway house in the security forces are the various scout and ranger units operated by the Pakistan army. These are commanded by regular commissioned officers on deputation from their "home" regiment, but are manned entirely by soldiers drawn from the local region in which the unit (such as the Khyber Rifles or Pishin Scouts) serves. While the scout units are well trained and adapted to local conditions, they are not required

to master complex military technologies or operate as part of larger standard military formations.

24. Hamoodur Rahman, "Ideology of Pakistan: The Raison d'Être of Our Country," *Pakistan Army Journal*, June 1978, p. 9. Also see the writings of former chief justice Muhammad Munir, *From Jinnah to Zia* (Lahore: Vanguard Books, 1980).

25. Interview with the author, 1980.

26. Interview with the author, 1980.

27. For contrasting views, see Gerald Heeger, "Politics in the Post-Military State," *World Politics* 29, no. 2 (January 1977), pp. 242–62; Hasan Askari Rizvi, *The Military and Politics in Pakistan 1947–1986* (Lahore: Progressive Publishers, 1986); Eqbal Ahmad, "Pakistan: Signposts to What?" *Viewpoint* (Lahore), May 18, 1974; and "Zia Is No Spokesman," *The New York Times*, October 1, 1980.

28. For the best discussions of the political role of paramilitary forces in developing countries, see Morris Janowitz, *Military Institutions and Coercion in the Developing Nations* (University of Chicago Press, 1977).

CHAPTER ELEVEN

This chapter was originally published in *Washington Quarterly* 26, no. 3 (Summer 2003), pp. 7–25.

1. For an authoritative account of the Jama'at-i-Islami, see Seyyed Vali Reza Nasr, *The Vanguard of the Islamic Revolution: The Jama'at-i-Islami of Pakistan* (London: I. B. Taurus, 1994).

2. For a history of this group, see Yoginder Sikand, *The Origins and Development of the Tablighi-Jama'at (1920—2000): A Cross-Country Comparative Study* (Hyderabad: Orient Longman, 2002). See also Khaled Ahmed, "The Grand Tableeghi Congregation," *Friday Times*, November 7, 2002.

3. For a reasonably accurate Indian account of these groups, see "Pakistan Terrorist Groups," satp.org/satporgtp/countries/Pakistan/terroristoutfits/index.html (accessed April 15, 2003). The site is maintained by the Institute of Conflict Management, whose leading member, K. P. S. Gill, was responsible for the strategy that eventually defeated the Khalistan movement in India's Punjabi state.

4. Mandavi Mehta and Teresita C. Schaffer, "Islam in Pakistan: Unity and Contradictions," Project on Pakistan's Future and U.S. Policy Options, Center for Strategic and International Studies, Washington, D.C., October 7, 2002.

5. Peter Singer, "Pakistan's Madrassahs: Ensuring a System of Education, Not Jihad," Analysis Paper #14 (Brookings Institution, November 2001).

6. For a revealing account of Omar's transformation by a former school friend, see Mohamed Ahmed Khan, "A Pakistani Gora in Lahore," *Herald* (Karachi), August 2002.

7. See Stephen Philip Cohen, *The Pakistan Army*, 2nd ed. (Oxford University Press, 1998), postscript; see also Hasan Askari Rizvi, *Military, State and Society in Pakistan* (London: Macmillan, 2000), p. 245, for a discussion of the army and religion.

8. See International Crisis Group, "Pakistan: The Dangers of Conventional Wisdom" (intl-crisis-group.org/projects/showreport.cfm?reportid=578).

9. For a discussion of Pakistan as a state versus its identity as a nation, see Stephen Philip Cohen, "The Nation and the State of Pakistan," *Washington Quarterly* 25, no. 3 (Summer 2002), pp. 109–22.

10. Wajahat Sajjad [pseud.], "RAW Penetrates Disgruntled Jihadi Groups," *Friday Times*, October 11–17, 2002.

11. John Lancaster, "Secular Pakistanis, Upset by War, Turn to Religious Parties," *Washington Post*, April 4, 2003.

12. Robert Kaplan, "A Nuclear Yugoslavia," reviews of *Pakistan: In the Shadow of Jihad and Afghanistan*, by Mary Anne Weaver, and *Pakistan: Eye of the Storm*, by Owen Bennett Jones, *New York Times Book Review*, November 3, 2002, p. 13.

CHAPTER TWELVE

This chapter was originally published in "The Militaries of South Asia," in *Encyclopedia of India*, vol. 3, ed. Stanley Wolpert (Farmington, Mich.: Thompson-Gale, 2004), pp. 262–70.

CHAPTER THIRTEEN

This chapter was originally published as "India and Pakistan" entry in "The Militaries of South Asia," in Marvin G. Weinbaum and Chetan Kumar, eds., *South Asia Approaches the Millennium: Reexamining National Security* (Boulder, Colo.: Westview Press, 1995), chap. 7, pp. 127–44.

This chapter was first presented to a MCISS–South Asia seminar in 1992, and revised as a note prepared for the Center for the Study of Foreign Affairs of the Foreign Service Institute, U.S. Department of State. Both were based on research conducted during the course of a joint U.S.–Russian study of Kashmir and Afghanistan in Nepal, India, and Pakistan in March–April 1992. See Stephen P. Cohen, Sergei Kamenev, Vladimir Moskalenko, and Leo Rose, *Afghanistan and Kashmir* (New York: Asia Society, 1993). I made some minor additions in view of a year in residence with the Ford Foundation, New Delhi, 1992–93.

1. The exact status of Indian and Pakistani nuclear capabilities remains uncertain. For recent overviews, see George Perkovich, "A Nuclear Third Way in

South Asia," *Foreign Policy* (Summer 1993), pp. 85–104; Devin Hagerty, "The Powers of Suggestion: Opaque Proliferation, Existential Deterrence, and the South Asian Nuclear Arms Competition," *Security Studies* 2, nos. 3–4 (Spring–Summer 1993), pp. 256–83.

2. The most notorious of these was offering Pakistan some forty F-16 aircraft in exchange for the "capping" of its nuclear program; no equivalent offer was made to India, and both Islamabad and Delhi publicly and vehemently rejected this strategy of arms for peace.

3. For examples of this scenario building, see the testimony of the director of the Central Intelligence Agency, R. James Woolsey, before the Senate Select Committee on Intelligence, "Nomination of R. James Woolsey, Hearing," 103rd Congress, First Session (Government Printing Office, 1993), and the exaggerated analysis by William E. Burrows and Robert Windrem in their *Critical Mass: The Dangerous Race for a Superweapon in a Fragmented World* (New York: Simon and Schuster, 1994).

4. For a fine collection of essays on different aspects of the Kashmir crisis, see Raju Thomas, ed., *Perspectives on Kashmir: The Roots of Conflict in South Asia* (Boulder, Colo.: Westview Press, 1992); for a balanced summary of the Indian perspective on Kashmir, see Sumit Ganguly and Kanti Bajpai, "India and the Crisis in Kashmir," *Asian Survey* 34, no. 5 (May 1994), pp. 401–16.

5. For a vivid overview see P. S. Sidhu, "Siachen: The Forgotten War," *India Today*, May 31, 1992.

6. This point is made by several Indian and Pakistani authors in Kanti P. Bajpai and Stephen P. Cohen, eds., *South Asia after the Cold War* (Boulder, Colo.: Westview Press, 1993). See especially the chapters by Pervaiz I. Cheema and M. L. Chibber.

7. For a study of the origins and resolution of the Brasstacks crisis, see Kanti Bajpai, P. R. Chari, Pervez Cheema, and Stephen Cohen, *Brasstacks and Beyond: Crisis Perception and Management in South Asia* (New Delhi: Manohar, 1995). For a discussion of the subsequent 1990 crisis by a number of the policymakers in government at the time, see Michael Krepon and Mishi Farugues, eds., *Conflict Prevention and Confidence-Building Measures in South Asia: The 1990 Crisis* (Henry L. Stimson Center, Occasional Paper No. 17, April 1994). For an overview of these crises, see Pervaiz Iqbal Cheema, P. R. Chari, and Stephen P. Cohen, *Four Crises and a Peace Process: American Engagement in South Asia* (Brookings Institution Press, 2007).

8. See Stephen P. Cohen, "Conclusion," in *The Security of South Asia: Asian and American Perspectives*, ed. Stephen P. Cohen (University of Illinois Press, 1987), p. 240.

9. The Indian logic is that if the United States had not supported extremist Muslim elements in Afghanistan with lavish supplies of arms, then Kashmir would not have been radicalized. This conveniently ignores the large-scale supplies of weapons by both Iran and China, and, above all, India's own mismanage-

ment of Kashmiri politics, especially the imposition of corrupt governments and the absence of free elections.

10. Some elements of the Bharatiya Janata Party have recommended that Kashmir be repopulated with Hindus, once its special constitutional status (Article 370) was eliminated; the Andorra precedent of the thirteenth century—a treaty between Spain and France guaranteeing Andorra's internal autonomy—has been discussed by Jean Alphonse Bernard of Paris; Jagmohan, one of the key principles in the most recent crises in Kashmir, has written that the long-term solution rests in a revival of the Indian spirit. See his own record of the crises of Kashmir—and his pivotal role—in *My Frozen Turbulence in Kashmir* (New Delhi: Allied, 1991).

11. These impressions are, of course, based on personal experiences; however, in the absence of accurate poll data, serious academic studies, or other objective measures of Indian and Pakistani public opinion, this remains the only way to judge public opinion on Kashmir in the two countries. What is astonishing is the absence of serious academic or even journalistic studies of the shape and intensity of regional public opinion.

12. Not only has bilateral diplomacy collapsed between India and Pakistan; there has been, over the past year, a number of incidents in which the diplomats of both sides have been harassed, and even beaten, by security forces, and the intelligence services of both countries have harassed ordinary scholars and journalists attending functions in each other's country. Recent reports indicate that some in Pakistan now see some value in perpetuating the crisis over Siachen, while being "soft" on offers to open up nuclear facilities for inspection, as part of a complex game of getting outsiders, especially the United States, to come down harder still on Delhi. These verbal games are brilliantly played by both sides, but they also reveal a lack of interest in achieving a settlement. For a fuller description of these diplomatic stratagems, see the editorial in *The Frontier Post* (Peshawar), December 17, 1993.

13. For an informative discussion of private third-party involvement, see Gennady I. Chufrin and Harold Saunders, "A Public Peace Process," *Negotiation Journal*, April 1993, pp. 155–77.

14. I have outlined a strategy based on the possibility that the United States and other outside powers play a larger role on both the Kashmir and the proliferation issues—which are inextricably linked in many ways. For a presentation of this strategy to an Indian audience, see Stephen P. Cohen, "Is there a Road to Peace in South Asia? An American Perspective," *Journal of the United Services Institution of India*, April–June 1993, pp. 146–53.

15. These include the successful transition to more open, competitive economies; the management of their own nuclear arms race (which is linked directly to the amelioration or resolution of the Kashmir problem); and simply coping with the increased demands placed on the struggling Indian and Pakistani states by new regional, economic, ethnic, class, and caste groups.

16. For a discussion of the recent history of private, or Track II diplomacy, including efforts by the business communities of India and Pakistan to foster dialogue, see Sundeep Waslekar, *Track-Two Diplomacy in South Asia*, Occasional Paper, Program in Arms Control, Disarmament, and International Security, University of Illinois, 1994, especially the appendix. This includes a list of more than thirty recent Track II and confidence-building activities conducted in South Asia.

17. See D. D. Khanna and Kishore Kumar, *Dialogue of the Deaf: The India–Pakistan Divide* (Delhi: Konarak Publishers, 1992). Khanna and Kumar have one chapter devoted to Kashmir, based largely on interviews in India and Pakistan.

18. In 1993 the Indian prime minister, P. V. Narasimha Rao, told a visiting American group that there was no need to worry about incidents on the border leading to a larger conflict between India and Pakistan, since the Pakistanis, at least, were aware of what *they* were doing and knew what the consequences would be if they went too far. He described the situation as analogous to the "magic circle" that surrounded Sita: she could not break out, but no one could break in.

19. A view put into print by Seymour Hersh, in a useful, if not always accurate, article on the 1990 crisis. See Seymour Hersh, "On the Nuclear Edge," *The New Yorker*, March 29, 1993.

20. For an overview of regional verification and CBM possibilities, see Moonis Ahmar, "Indo-Pakistan Normalization Process: The Role of CBMs in the Post–Cold War Era," Research Series, Program in Arms Control, Disarmament, and International Security, University of Illinois, October 1993.

CHAPTER FOURTEEN

This chapter was originally published in *India International Centre Quarterly* 1988 (revised version of a paper presented at the Association for Asian Studies, March 1988).

1. Frank Fukuyama, *The Security of Pakistan: A Trip Report*, RAND Corporation N-1584-RC, September 1980.

2. I know of one case where on a mere courtesy call, a senior Indian official casually mentioned to a Cabinet-level American official that the Afghan problem would end if the United States were to cease support for the Mujahedin and Pakistan. I am sure that there were similar horror stories on the Indian side. A great deal of effort must have been spent putting out brush fires caused by ignorant or careless remarks.

3. This was a policy that had historically led the United States to align with the British against the Japanese, with Pakistan against a perceived Soviet threat (from 1954), and with India against China (from 1962).

4. I think he was sincere. Zia once proposed to Indira Gandhi that India sell advanced military equipment to Pakistan. Gandhi, probably astonished, did not

respond. India's failure to take seriously most of Zia's gambits—even if he was bluffing—may have been a tactical error.

5. India has been used as a base for Soviet propaganda and disinformation with several worldwide anti-American campaigns originating there.

6. And China may have been a factor, as well. The brief India–China border crisis of 1986–87 was certainly anticipated by India, which may have been testing the degree of support it would receive from both superpowers in case of a confrontation with China—or trying to demonstrate India's importance to the Soviets by threatening a crisis with China—we may never know.

7. I have discussed alternative arrangements in "South Asia's Nuclear Arms Race: How the U.S. Can Help Freeze It," *Chicago Tribune*, March 4, 1988.

8. Until the issue was raised in a series of visits by Michael Armacost and others, almost all Pakistanis uncritically supported a military nuclear program. Three years later (and in a much freer atmosphere) there is a range of debate and discussion in Pakistan that is bound to contribute to more sensible policymaking.

9. Our focus here is on India, and regional policies affecting India, but the major American effort to encourage the democratization of Pakistan must be noted. American officials repeatedly and forcefully argued with President Zia, Prime Minister Junejo, and other senior Pakistan officials that democratization was an important factor in the U.S.–Pakistan relationship. I think the military would have moved to a more open system (and a less fundamentalist one) on its own, but American pressure certainly helped.

10. Although the Indians had reason to be concerned about statements from Senator Helms and others, these were never taken seriously in the executive branch, and soon ceased from Capitol Hill, once pro-Khalistani terrorism became widely known and understood.

11. For the curious combination of bellicosity and fearfulness, see Rajiv Gandhi's speech of February 3, 1988, and for a set of essays on Rajiv's foreign policy, see Mani Shanker Aiyer and M. K. Rasgotra, eds., *Rajiv Gandhi's India*, vol. 3: *Foreign Policy* (New Delhi: South Asia Books, 1998).

12. For a discussion of post-Afghanistan American policies, see my "Balancing Interests in South Asia," *The National Interest*, October 1987.

CHAPTER FIFTEEN

This chapter was originally published in "Inaugural Colonel Pyara Lai Memorial Lecture," *USI Journal* 127, no. 530 (October–December 1997), United Service Institution of India, pp. 491–501.

1. Jagat S. Mehta, *Rescuing the Future: Bequeathed Misperceptions in International Relations* (New Delhi: Manohar, 2008).

CHAPTER SIXTEEN

This chapter was originally published in *Current History*, April 2011, pp. 138–43.

EPILOGUE

1. The phrase has been attributed to an adviser to the Mongol emperor Kublai Khan, the argument being that China (just conquered by the Mongols) had to be governed in a way that matched up with China's complex society. See *Kublai Khan*, entry in Encyclopedia Britannica Online, www.brittanica.com/biography/Kublai-Khan.

2. For a general discussion of essentialist view of non-Western armies, see Patrick Porter, *Military Orientalism: Eastern War through Western Eyes* (Columbia University Press, 2009); for recent scholarship on recruiting and the "martial races," see Anirudh Deshpande, *British Military Policy in India, 1900–1945: Colonial Constraints and Declining Power* (New Delhi: Manohar Books, 2005).

3. "Grand Strategic Thought in the Ramayana and Mahabharata," in *India's Grand Strategy: History, Theory, Cases*, ed. Kanti Bajpai, Saira Basit, and V. Krishnappa (New Delhi: Routledge, 2014), pp. 31–62, and "Security Ideas in the *Valmiki Ramayana*," in *Security and South Asia: Ideas, Institutions and Initiatives*, ed. Swarna Rajagopalan (New Delhi: Routledge, 2006), pp. 24–53. Some classic older scholarship should not be forgotten, especially because it appeared in the professional journal of the American Political Science Association—usually given over to other kinds of methodology. George Modelski, "Kautilya: Foreign Policy and International System in the Ancient Hindu World," *American Political Science Review* 58, no. 3 (1965), pp. 549–60.

4. Especially the collection Pradeep Kumar Gautam, Saurabh Mishra, and Arvind Gupta, eds., *Indigenous Historical Knowledge: Kautilya and His Vocabulary* (New Delhi: IDSA and Pentagon Press, 2015).

5. L. N. Rangarajan, ed. and trans., *Kautilya: The Arthashastra* (New Delhi: Penguin Books, 1987); Jairam Ramesh, *Kautilya Today* (New Delhi: India Research Press 2002); and Amrita Narlikar and Aruna Narlikar, *Bargaining with a Rising India: Lessons from the Mahabharata* (Oxford University Press, 2014).

6. Also see David Gilmartin and Bruce B. Lawrence, eds., *Beyond Turk and Hindu: Rethinking Religious Identities in Islamicate South Asia* (New Delhi: India Research Press, 2002).

7. Stephen Peter Rosen, *Societies and Military Power: India and Its Armies* (Cornell University Press, 1996); Kanti Bajpai and Amitabh Mattoo, eds., *Securing India, Strategic Thought and Practice: Essays by George K. Tanham, with Commentaries* (New Delhi: Manohar, 1996) (includes a reprint of Tanham's 1991 RAND study).

8. See the story in *India Today* alleging a cover-up by various Indian governments regarding Bose's death, Sandeep Unnithan, "When Nehru Spied on Netaji," *India Today* (New Delhi), April 10, 2015 (http://indiatoday.intoday.in/story/jawaharlal-nehru-spied-netaji-subhas-chandra-bose-exclusive/1/429392.html).

9. Authoritative biographies of Subhas Bose include Sugata Bose, *His Majesty's Opponent: Subhas Chandra Bose and India's Struggle against Empire* (Harvard University Press, 2011); Leonard A. Gordon, *Brothers against the Raj: A Biography of Indian Nationalists Sarat and Subhas Chandra Bose* (Columbia University Press, 1990).

10. Stephen P. Cohen and Richard L. Park, *India: Emergent Power?* (New York: Crane Russak, 1979); Stephen P. Cohen, *India: Emerging Power* (Brookings Institution Press, 2002); Stephen P. Cohen and others, *The Future of Pakistan* (Brookings Institution Press, 2011).

11. Stephen P. Cohen and Sunil Dasgupta, *Arming without Aiming* (Brookings Institution Press, 2008).

12. Closely related are theories of Subaltern realism and the Copenhagen school. For the regionalist perspective, see Barry Buzan, *People, States, and Fear* (London: Harvester Wheatsheaf, 1991); Mohammed Ayoob, *The Third World Security Predicament* (Boulder, Colo.: Lynn Reinner, 1995). See Mohammed Ayoob, "Inequality and Theorizing in International Relations: The Case for Subaltern Realism," *International Studies Review* 4, no. 3 (Autumn 2002), pp. 27–48.

13. For one text of the time, see Ted Robert Gurr and Barbara Harf, eds., *Ethnic Conflict in World Politics* (Boulder, Colo.: Westview Press, 1994).

14. Precisely: "We have slain a large dragon. But we live now in a jungle filled with a bewildering variety of poisonous snakes. And in many ways, the dragon was easier to keep track of" (https://www.cia.gov/library/center-for-the-study-of-intelligence/csi-publications/books-and-monographs/directors-of-central-intelligence-as-leaders-of-the-u-s-intelligence-community/chapter_12.htm).

15. Moises Naim, *The End of Power* (New York: Basic Books, 2013).

16. For comparisons with the Cold War, see the essays in Stephen Philip Cohen, ed., *Nuclear Proliferation in South Asia: The Prospects for Arms Control* (Boulder, Colo.: Westview Press, 1991). For the critical difference, see Moeed Wasim Yusuf, "Brokered Bargaining: Nuclear Crises between Middle Powers," Ph.D. dissertation, Boston University, 2014.

17. Discussed above, page 9. See Seminarist, "The Bomb: Strategic Considerations," *Seminar* (New Delhi), January 1965.

18. See, respectively, S. Rashid Naim, "Aadhi Raat ke Baad [After Midnight]," *Nuclear Proliferation in South Asia: The Prospects for Arms Control*, ed. Stephen P. Cohen (Boulder, Colo.: Westview Press, 1991), appendix 2, pp. 278–90; Itty Abraham, *The Making of the Indian Atomic Bomb: Science, Secrecy and the Postcolonial*

State (New York: Zed, 1998); Sumit Ganguly and Devin Hagerty, *Fearful Symmetry: India–Pakistan Crises in the Shadow of Nuclear Weapons* (Oxford University Press, 2005); and Yusuf, "Brokered Bargaining."

19. "India's Strategic Misstep," June 3, 1998. I did not fully appreciate the Indian assumption, developed by K. Subrahmanyam, that India's bomb would be "political," not military, and that an open-ended arms race would not take place. I also miscalculated the rapid shift in Pakistani military attitudes toward nuclear weapons. It was facilitated by its global theft of sensitive technology and by Chinese assistance. A competition—or a race—with both China and Pakistan moves the Indian program forward, but the critical moment will come if India feels it has to test new warheads and delivery systems for their reliability and effectiveness.

20. For authoritative accounts of the Pakistan and Indian bombs, respectively, see Feroze Hassan Khan, *Eating Grass: The Making of the Pakistani Bomb* (Stanford University Press, 2012); George Perkovich, *India's Nuclear Bomb: The Impact on Global Proliferation* (University of California Press, 1999).

21. For a careful discussion of such an arrangement for Pakistan, see Toby Dalton and Michael Krepon, *A Normal Nuclear Pakistan* (Washington, D.C.: Carnegie Endowment and Stimson Center, 2015). This contains references to others, including Mark Fitzpatrick, who have written on the problem of accommodating Islamabad in nuclear matters.

22. See P. R. Chari, Pervaiz Iqbal Cheema, and Stephen P. Cohen, *Four Crises and a Peace Process: American Engagement in South Asia* (Brookings Institution Press, 2008).

23. See Moeed Yusuf, "Predicting Proliferation: The History of the Future of Nuclear Proliferation," Brookings paper, 2009 (www.brookings.edu/~/media/research/files/papers/2009/1/nuclear-proliferation-yusuf/01_nuclear_proliferation_yusuf.pdf).

24. C. Christine Fair, *Fighting to the End, the Pakistan Army's Way of War* (Oxford University Press, 2014); T. V. Paul, *The Warrior State* (Oxford University Press, 2014); and Aqil Shah, *The Army and Democracy: Military Politics in Pakistan* (Harvard University Press, 2014). For the best overview of Pakistan available today, see Christophe Jaffrelot, *The Pakistan Paradox: Instability and Resilience*, trans. Cynthia Schoch (London: Hurst, 2015).

25. Anatol Lieven, *Pakistan: A Hard Country* (New York: Public Affairs Press, 2011); Christophe Jaffrelot, *The Pakistan Paradox: Instability and Resilience*, trans. Cynthia Schoch (London: Hurst, 2015). Both argue that Pakistani society is very strong, even if the state is weak and failing, and that for the short run at least, Pakistan will get through its crises.

26. From a series of interviews conducted in the United Kingdom in 1962 and 1963, to be deposited in an archive.

27. Stephen P. Cohen, "Arms and Politics in Pakistan: A Review Article," *India Quarterly* 20, no. 4 (October 1964), pp. 403–20.

28. Cohen, "Arms and Politics in Pakistan: A Review Article," 420.

29. For an overview of the Kargil crisis by several scholars and practitioners, see Peter R. Lavoy, ed., *Asymmetric Warfare in South Asia: The Causes and Consequences of the Kargil Conflict* (Cambridge University Press, 2009).

30. Sisir Gupta, *Kashmir: A Study in India–Pakistan Relations* (Bombay: Asia Publishing House, 1966).

31. Stephen P. Cohen, *Shooting for a Century: The India–Pakistan Conundrum* (Brookings Institution Press, 2013).

32. I am more realistic now about the coming of a "new" generation in India and Pakistan, and retrospectively accept the warning of the late Emily MacFarquhar, who suggested that "Steve Cohen is optimistic about a more dovish generation to come. I fear the hawks who are still in control" ("Capitol and Rasina Hills," *Seminar*, October 1994). I would now say that while they are not in control, they have a veto over normalization between India and Pakistan and on such hot-button issues as Kashmir and nuclear weapons.

33. See Stephen Philip Cohen, "Is There a Road to Peace in South Asia? An American Perspective," *Journal of the United Services Institution of India* (April June 1993), pp. 146–53. The talk was delivered in India's South Block, but I learned that the Indian government already had the text, and my informant agreed that I had said the same thing in both countries. What became known briefly as the Cohen Plan was leaked to the press by an unidentified official—probably Pakistani. It was also thoroughly trashed by a leading Pakistani leftist, Eqbal Ahmed, who thought that the roots of the Kashmir problem were to be found in India's policies. On this point he did not differ from the Pakistani army. For an overview of my off-line approach, see Shaheen Sehbai, "U.S. Plan to Broker Peace in S. Asia," *Dawn*, July 1, 1996. Also see Carollee Bengelsdorf, Margaret Cerullo, and Yogesh Chandrani, eds., S*elected Writings of Eqbal Ahmed* (Columbia University Press, 2006).

34. Howard B. Schaffer, *The Limits of American Influence* (Brookings Institution Press, 2009).

35. A recent Council on Foreign Relations task force addresses this problem, proposing a new center in the government that could coordinate India policy, but only in the context of improving U.S.–Indian relations. See "Working with a Rising India," November 2015 (www.cfr.org/india/working-rising-india/p37233).

36. S. Jaishankar, "India–U.S. Ties: The Long View," address to the Belfer Center, Harvard University, April 17, 2014 (http://belfercenter.hks.harvard.edu/publication/24173/ambassador_s_jaishankar.html?breadcrumb=%2Fproject%2F66%2Findia_and_south_asia_program).

37. One reason these problems are hard is that there is no known objective way to measure the closeness between states and governments, rather than simplifications about "ups and downs," and no agreed-on criteria or methodology, whether in government or academia.

38. George Orwell's 1946 guide to the ways in which the English language obfuscates and blurs ideas is still potent. George Orwell, "Politics and the English Language," first published in *Horizon (UK)* and widely reprinted (www.orwell.ru/library/essays/politics/english/e_polit/).

Index

COPYRIGHT ACKNOWLEDGEMENTS

'Approaching India's Military and Security Policy, with a Detour through Disaster Studies' first appeared in *India Review*, Vol. 7, No. 4, October–December 2008, pp. 295–319, www.tandfonline.com;

'Rulers and Priests: A Study of Cultural Control' first appeared in *Comparative Studies in Culture and History*, Vol. VI, No. 2, January 1964, Cambridge University Press;

'Issue, Role, and Personality: The Kitchener–Curzon Dispute' first appeared in *Comparative Studies in Society and History*, Vol. X, No. 3, April 1968, pp. 337–355, http://dx.doi.org/doi:10.1017/S0010417500004953;

'Subhas Chandra Bose and the Indian National Army' first appeared in *Pacific Affairs*, Vol. XXXVI, No. 4, Winter 1963–64, pp. 411–429;

'The Untouchable Soldier: Caste, Politics, and the Indian Army' first appeared in *Journal of Asian Studies*, Vol. XXVIII, No. 3, May 1969, pp. 453–468; www.aasianst.org;

'The Military in Indira Gandhi's India' first appeared in *A Political System Reappraised*, Henry C. Hart, ed., Westview Press, Boulder, Colorado, 1976;

'Toward a Great State in Asia?' first appeared in *Military Power and Policy in Asian States: China, India, Japan*, Onkar Marwah and Jonathan D. Pollack, ed., Westview Press, Boulder, Colorado, 1980;

'The State Is Dead: Long Live the Armed Ethnic Group' first appeared as an abbreviated version as 'U.S. Security in a Separatist Season' in *Bulletin of the Atomic Scientists*, Vol. XLVIII, No. 6, July 1992, pp. 28–32, www.tandfonline.com;

'Solving Proliferation Problems in a Regional Context: South Asia' first appeared in *New Threats: Responding to the Proliferation of Nuclear,*

Chemical and Delivery Capabilities in the Third World (edited by Joseph S. Nye), originally presented to the Aspen Strategy Group, Aspen, Colorado, August, 1989;

'State Building in Pakistan' first appeared in *The State, Religion, and Ethnic Politics: Afghanistan, Iran, and Pakistan*, Ali Banuazizi and Myron Weiner, eds, Syracuse, Syracuse University Press, 1986;

'The Jihadist Threat to Pakistan' first appeared in *The Washington Quarterly*, summer 2003, pp. 7–25;

'India and Pakistan: The Armed Forces' first appeared in *Encyclopedia of India*, 1E. © 2006 Gale, a part of Cengage Learning, Inc. Reproduced by permission; www.cengage.com/permissions;

'Kashmir: The Roads Ahead' first appeared in Chapter 10 in Marvin G. Weinbaum and Chetan Kumar, eds, *South Asia Approaches the Millennium: Reexamining National Security*, Westview Press, Boulder, Colorado, 1995;

'The Reagan Administration and India: Right for the Right Reasons?' first appeared in *India International Centre Quarterly, 1988*, a revised version of a paper presented at the Association for Asian Studies, March 1988, www.aasianst.org;

'The Critical Dimensions of a Possible U.S. Strategic Partnership with India' first appeared in *Journal of the United Service Institution of India*, Vol. CXXVII, No. 530, Oct–Dec 1997 at The Inaugural Colonel Pyaralal Memorial Lecture; and

'How a Botched U.S. Alliance Fed Pakistan's Crisis' by Stephen Philip Cohen appeared in *Current History*, April 2011, pp. 138–43.